HOSPITALITY MANAGEMENT

SAGE LIBRARY OF TOURISM, HOSPITALITY AND LEISURE

HOSPITALITY MANAGEMENT

VOLUME II
The Hospitality Industry – Structures, Strategies and Markets

Edited by

Tom Baum

Los Angeles | London | New Delhi
Singapore | Washington DC

© Introduction and editorial arrangement by Tom Baum, 2011

First published 2011
Reprinted 2012

Apart from any fair dealing for the purposes of research or private study, or criticism or review, as permitted under the Copyright, Designs and Patents Act, 1988, this publication may be reproduced, stored or transmitted in any form, or by any means, only with the prior permission in writing of the publishers, or in the case of reprographic reproduction, in accordance with the terms of licences issued by the Copyright Licensing Agency. Enquiries concerning reproduction outside those terms should be sent to the publishers.

Every effort has been made to trace and acknowledge all the copyright owners of the material reprinted herein. However, if any copyright owners have not been located and contacted at the time of publication, the publishers will be pleased to make the necessary arrangements at the first opportunity.

SAGE Publications Ltd
1 Oliver's Yard
55 City Road
London EC1Y 1SP

SAGE Publications Inc.
2455 Teller Road
Thousand Oaks, California 91320

SAGE Publications India Pvt Ltd
B 1/I 1, Mohan Cooperative Industrial Area
Mathura Road
New Delhi 110 044

SAGE Publications Asia-Pacific Pte Ltd
3 Church Street
#10-04 Samsung Hub
Singapore 048763

British Library Cataloguing in Publication Data

A catalogue record for this book is available from the British Library

ISBN: 978-0-85702-776-4 (set of four volumes)

Library of Congress Control Number: 2010942924

Typeset by R.S. Prints, New Delhi
Printed on paper from sustainable resources
Printed and bound in Great Britain by the MPG Books Group

Contents

Volume II: The Hospitality Industry – Structures, Strategies and Markets

Editor's Introduction: Hospitality Management *Tom Baum*	vii
17. International Hotel Development *Robert E. Smith*	1
18. Multinational Corporations in the International Hotel Industry *John H. Dunning and Matthew McQueen*	11
19. From Globalisation to Internationalisation to Americanisation: The Example of 'Little Americas' in the Hotel Sector *Dennis Nickson and Chris Warhurst*	31
20. Internationalization of US Multinational Hotel Companies: Expansion to Asia versus Europe *Seoki Lee*	55
21. Research in Strategic Management in the Hospitality Industry *Michael D. Olsen and Angela Roper*	71
22. Choice between Non-Equity Entry Modes: An Organizational Capability Perspective *M. Krishna Erramilli, Sanjeev Agarwal and Chekitan S. Dev*	87
23. Stock Market Reactions to Entry Mode Choices of Multinational Hotel Firms *Nicolas S. Graf*	109
24. Hotel Management Contracts – Past and Present *Jan A. deRoos*	133
25. Real Estate Investment Trusts: Performance, Recent Findings, and Future Directions *Peng (Peter) Liu*	149
26. Hotel Brand Strategy *John W. O'Neill and Anna S. Mattila*	167
27. Post-merger Stock Performance of Acquiring Hospitality Firms *Jing Yang, Woo Gon Kim and Hailin Qu*	179
28. Hotel Reform in China: A SWOT Analysis *Larry Yu and Gu Huimin*	191
29. China's Hotel Industry: Serving a Massive Market *Ray Pine*	209
30. The Future of Small Firms in the Hospitality Industry *Alison Morrison and Rhodri Thomas*	223

31. Economic Impact and Institutional Dynamics of Small
    Hotels in Tanzania 237
    Amit Sharma
32. A Descriptive Examination of Corporate Governance in the
    Hospitality Industry 259
    Basak Denizci Guillet and Anna S. Mattila
33. Going Green: Decisional Factors in Small Hospitality Operations 279
    Nadia A. Tzschentke, David Kirk and Paul A. Lynch
34. Customer Loyalty: The Future of Hospitality Marketing 295
    Stowe Shoemaker and Robert C. Lewis
35. Tourism and Hospitality Marketing: Fantasy, Feeling and Fun 323
    Alistair Williams
36. Exploring Chinese Cultural Influences and Hospitality
    Marketing Relationships 339
    David Gilbert and Jenny Tsao
37. E-Mail Marketing by International Hotel Chains:
    An Industry-Practices Update 355
    Peter O'Connor

Editor's Introduction: Hospitality Management
Tom Baum

The management of hospitality in a business context is not a new phenomenon. Far from it. Hospitality businesses have existed, in various forms, for as long as *homeo sapiens* have lived in organised communities. O'Gorman, in his work, reports on evidence of the business of hospitality in both Ancient Greece and Ancient Rome, and the existence of such enterprises may lead one to the reasonable conclusion that some element of management was present within their organisation. Firebaugh (1928) also addresses hospitality businesses (in his case, inns) in the context of Ancient Greece and Rome, but extends his discussion to include reference to their Egyptian and Hebrew counterparts. Likewise, Zhang, Pine and Lam (2005), in tracing the origins of tourism in China back some 5,000 years, point to the existence of service providers to facilitate the travel of key groups, the emperor and his cortege, officials, scholars and the religious.

However, scholarly interest in hospitality management and how it is executed is much more recent. Reference to the hospitality industry in the mainstream management literature is scarce in the formative years of major journals in this field. The *Academy of Management Journal*, as one of the earliest contributors to the development of a business/ management literature from the 1930s onwards, does not appear to have included any article reporting studies located in the hospitality industry, over the full duration of its existence. Similar analysis of a range of 'leading' business, economics and sociological journals – all founded in the early years of the 20th century – highlights an absence of research studies which investigate themes and issues relating to the sector. There is evidence of a nascent research literature on hotel and hospitality-related themes (for example, Demolis, 1936; Yamamura, 1936), but these articles were largely published in what can be called the peripheral literature of the time. By contrast, the range of research studies undertaken within the context of public sector administration, public utilities, automobile manufacturing, finance and insurance and, more recently, information technology are extensive and wide-ranging.

This neglect undoubtedly is directly related to historical prejudice against the sector and those who worked in hotels and other hospitality enterprises. Nailon, in this work, notes this through reference to Victorian literature.

> *Typical of the status accorded to the early hotelier is that given by Strindberg (1888) describing a count's valet, 'He was the son of a poor peasant, and has now educated himself to the point where he is a potential gentleman. . . . He is, as he himself says, an aristocrat; he has learned the secrets of good society, is polished, but coarse underneath; he knows how to wear a tail-coat, but can offer us no guarantee that his body is clean beneath it . . . and will quite possibly end as a hotelier.*

While undoubtedly a caricature, this depiction of the hotelier (and, by inference, the status of the sector as a whole), has by no means disappeared in the intervening 120 years, and remains a factor in public perception of the industry in many countries, impacting upon political, investment and career choice decisions, among others. It is also arguable that this perception impacts upon the status of the academy in hospitality. With some notable exceptions, hospitality management exists as a Cinderella discipline within universities that are not in the top tier of their national rankings. As a field, hospitality management struggles to compete with other fields in accessing public research funds. There is little doubt that these factors impact on the overall quality of published research in hospitality management and this is, in some measure, reflected in the collection of articles included here.

It is probably true to say that serious and scholarly interest in the hospitality sector and its management began with the publication of bespoke journals in the field, including

- The *Cornell Hospitality Quarterly*, established as the *Cornell Hotel and Restaurant Administration Quarterly* in 1960;
- The *International Journal of Hospitality Management*, first published in 1982;
- The *FIU Hospitality Review* (now the *FIU Hospitality and Tourism Review*), dates from 1983; and
- The *International Journal of Contemporary Hospitality Management*, of which the first number appeared in 1989.

Alongside these specifically hospitality journals, allied publications in tourism did accommodate the emerging hospitality literature, notably the *Journal of Travel Research* (1968), *Annals of Tourism Research* (1973), *Tourism Recreation*

Research (1975) and *Tourism Management* (1982), although in recent years they have increasingly eschewed contributions located within hospitality.

The challenge with any discussion of hospitality and hospitality management is the diversity which underpins the industry sector. The hospitality industry (and, therefore, its management) is, literally, located within every community so that geographical, economic and cultural context plays a major role in determining the nature of the products and services that are delivered and how these and managed. This diversity further extends to encompasses varied product and service types including hotels and other accommodation providers; and food and beverage service outlets across restaurants, fast-food, transport and institutional contexts. These businesses, in turn, serve the needs of customers with diverse motivations for their travel and consumption – family, religion, sport, leisure and business, to name some of the most significant. Diversity extends to business size, structure and ownership, ranging from micro operations, frequently sole-trader operated, through to mammoth outlets (7,372 room hotels in the MGM Grand, Las Vegas; 95,000 meals per day flight kitchens throughput by the Emirates Flight Kitchen in Dubai) and global businesses with up to 657,954 hotel rooms, in 4,507 properties (IHG). Finally, hospitality businesses themselves can be complex, and offer a range of products and services under one roof, notably accommodation and sustenance (food and beverages) but frequently also business and convention services, gaming, entertainment, retail and sports, health and wellness facilities. Each of these demands a differing focus within management. The research literature on hospitality management does not wholly reflect the diversity which exists within the industry – certainly, there has been bespoke coverage of small businesses in hospitality as well as a specialist literature on aspects of food and beverage and gaming – but the majority of published work relates to the mainstream hotel sector.

The structure of this major work recognises the evolution of hospitality and hospitality management as a theme for academic study and research. While the focus is predominantly contemporary, in recognition of the fast-changing environment within which the hospitality industry operates, there is also due recognition of its historical antecedents, both in terms of the origins of modern hospitality and in recognition of key pioneering research work in the area. Without a sense of historical benchmarking, it is difficult to appreciate exactly why and how hospitality and its attendant management issues have evolved to their current position internationally. While source material is drawn from the English-language literature, these volumes also seek to pay due recognition to the internationalism of the industry and to reflect how hospitality and its management varies across time and place.

The organisation of the four volumes presented a challenge. There is, arguably, a wide range of themes that merit comprehensive representation, including

- the nature of hospitality and hospitality management
- strategic management of hospitality businesses
- management of international businesses and culture
- the management of hospitality markets and marketing
- the management of service
- the management of people
- the management of hospitality operations
- the management of assets and facilities
- the management of investment and finance.

In addition, there are interdisciplinary themes which link these areas within one study.

These themes have been consolidated into four volumes here, viz.

1. The idea of hospitality: past and present perspectives The main body of this volume brings together articles that address two key themes, interpretations of the meaning of hospitality from a multi-cultural perspective and illustration of how our understanding of hospitality has changed through time and place. Key to this section is Lashley and Morrison's collection of articles in *In Search of Hospitality* (2001) and the companion volume, *Hospitality: a social lens* (2007) edited by Lashley, Morrison and Lynch. Between them, these books provide a strong and multi-disciplinary backcloth to hospitality and hospitality management. At the same time, there are both antecedental and contemporary sources which complement these volumes and which will provide alternative historical and current perspectives on hospitality.

2. The hospitality industry – structures, strategies and markets This volume combines key themes that contribute to our understanding of hospitality management – how the industry is structured, the strategies that are employed in response to varying structural dimensions of the industry and how the industry relates to its consumers from a marketing perspective. A number of contextual and historical sources are addressed – notably Dunning and McQueen (in this collection) – but the main focus will be on contemporary consideration of themes such as internationalisation, business structures (ownership, size), stakeholder relations including CSR, and key marketing themes such as branding and customer loyalty.

3. The management of people and service in hospitality This is a key and differentiating area within hospitality. Service and service quality has implications that straddle both the guest and those who work in the industry. This volume considers a range of themes relating to the measurement and implementation of service quality in hospitality. It also looks at the nature of work and skills in the industry, providing both historical (for example, Orwell, in this collection) and contemporary perspectives in a cross-cultural context.

4. Management of hospitality's tangible resources – operations, assets and finance The final volume addresses key operational and tangible resource management themes, including the key department/sub-sector considerations relating to hospitality (restaurants, hotels, food service, rooms division), asset management, financial and revenue management, security, quality management and environmental management. While these are disparate themes, coherence will be maintained through recognition of the reality that, for the average hotel manager, all these considerations require attention during a normal working week.

The process of defining both external boundaries (what is/ what is not hospitality) and internal dividers (service - operations - marketing - finance - human resource management - etc.) was a challenge which required both hard-nosed pragmatism and delicate subjectivity in compiling this work. Studies which are of direct pertinence to hospitality management but where the research is not directly located within the sector have been specifically excluded. Therefore, this collection represents a perspective on hospitality management, based on research that is specifically located within the sector. It is one perspective and there is no doubt that there can be sustained debate about what has been included here and what has been excluded. Such debate is healthy and must help to stimulate critical consideration of research in hospitality management. Certainly, others would have approached this task with different philosophical glasses and would have viewed the published resources in the field in a very different way. As a consequence, others would have made different selections and organised material in a different way. However, there can be no apologies for what has been included here.

Acknowledgements

I was, naturally, flattered when Sage approached me to undertake the task of putting together the best of hospitality management, as represented in the published literature. After all, there are many others who would be equal to, if not better suited, for the task. It was only after a rash 'Yes, sure' that I started to give serious consideration to the implications of my agreement. In the event, the process was illuminating, educational and enjoyable!

My contribution to what the reader finds in these volumes is peripheral. The true contributors are the authors of the articles in this collection and I want to acknowledge their status within the leadership of hospitality research. The oddities of copyright mean that some of them may be surprised to find their work reproduced here, but I trust that this surprise will turn to pleasure, given the academic company they are keeping. Some of the authors have a posthumous presence here and it is testimony to the durability of their work that they have been included.

I am indebted to colleagues in the hospitality academy, too many to name, for helping to hone my understanding of the field. Although the choices in these volumes are mine, there is no doubt that their influence has helped to shape my selections.

I want to thank Alana Clogan of Sage for keeping me on track with this Work. She showed the virtues of patience and persistence in ensuring that I met my commitments to this project.

Finally, my thanks and love to Brelda for her enduring encouragement and support.

References

Demolis, E. (1936) 'How our hotel industry might escape the crisis' from *Journal Financier Suisse* and published in *Annals of Public and Cooperative Economics*, 12(1), 253–256.
Firebaugh, W.C. (1928) *Inns of Greece and Rome*, New York: Benjamin Blom.
Lashley, C. and Morrison, A. (eds) (2001) *In Search of Hospitality*, Oxford: Butterworth-Heinemann.
Lashley, C., Morrison, A. and Lynch, P. (eds) (2007) *Hospitality: a social lens*, Oxford: Butterworth-Heinemann.
Yamamura, Douglas. (1936). 'Attitudes of Hotel Workers.' *Social Process in Hawai'i*, 2,15–19.
Zhang, H.Q., Pine, R. and Lam, T. (2005) *Tourism and Hotel Development in China. From Political to Economic Success*, New York: Haworth.

17

International Hotel Development
Robert E. Smith

Tourism is the largest single item in world trade, accounting for about $11.4 billion in 1965. General awareness of this simple fact has led to full advocacy of tourist and hotel development by the United Nations Economic and Social Council and by the Organization of American States in the last four years.

What are the economic and social benefits of tourism? The late Professor Krapf, a United Nations consultant from the University of Berne, Switzerland, presented an important paper on this subject to the United Nations Conference on International Travel and Tourism in Rome in 1963. It would be useful to summarize and expand on some of his observations.

1. The Contribution of Tourism to the Balance of Payments. Tourism has long been associated with international trade and payments settlements. There are a limited number of countries in the world with a positive balance of trade, i.e., more exports than imports. If it were not for the invisible export of services, particularly through tourism, the balance of payments world-wide would be a more critical factor than it is. Tourism has therefore made up the deficit of the balance of payments, or has reduced the deficit of the balance of payments, in a great number of developing countries. Notable examples are Spain, Greece, Austria, Yugoslavia, Mexico, Lebanon, Egypt and Thailand.

Receipts from tourism alone in Mexico in 1963 amounted to about $850,000,000. In 1962, for the first time since 1955, Mexico had a surplus in its balance of payments current account. The record net tourist income of $442 million in 1962 more than offset the trade deficit of $200 million in the same year, plus all of the service payments such as interest and dividends on foreign investments in Mexico amounting to $209 million. Tourism can become the largest single factor in the production of hard currency for the developing countries.

2. The Geographic Dispersion of Tourist Benefits. Tourism tends to distribute its economic benefits away from industrialized centers towards the economically under-developed regions. Tourist areas are usually characterized by the absence of large-scale industry. The development of hotels in principal cities around the world has the effect of spreading tourism out from industrialized centers and encouraging the development of tourist facilities in peripheral regions. This is true on both an international and a national basis. It counteracts the concentration of population in cities and the exodus from rural areas.

3. The Stimulating Effect of Tourism on All Sectors of the Economy. Economists have recognized the multiplier effect of tourism or the phenomenon that tourist expenditures turn over 3.2 to 5.5 times before "disappearing."[1] The impact of the multiplier effect of tourist spending depends on how fast it is passed into the first, second, third, and other levels of the country's economy. Thus one unit of hard currency – received largely from the sale of services which are replaceable and non-extractive of natural resources – generates further demand for services within a country and also for productive industries such as agriculture, mining, manufacturing. This process of generating fresh income continues until "leaks" occur in the economic cycle: imports, foreign investment, hoarding, and the slowing down of transfer spending.

4. The Increase of Economic Opportunities Through Tourism. Tourism belongs in the tertiary sector of production after the primary sector of agriculture and forestry and the secondary sector of productive industry; it is a service industry. For this reason, tourism has a significant effect in countries with surplus labor, since human labor will always be the dominant element of tourism as a service industry.

There is no foreseeable saturation point for service industries as compared with the primary and secondary sectors of production. This argues well for the future of tourism since public demand for tourist goods and services is steadily increasing and it is doubtful that the saturation point will ever be reached. The spectacular rise in world tourism will particularly benefit the developing countries through the increase of employment opportunities and the development of consumer goods.

5. Tourism's Role in Creating Balanced Economic Growth. The development of the emerging countries was long regarded as relying on forced industrialization, based mainly on the production of capital goods. It is now widely recognized that this is not the only touchstone to economic development and that there is a need for balanced growth. Since most developing countries have definite tourist potential, tourism can play an important role in efforts toward balanced growth. It means new or additional business production for food and beverage and other expendables suppliers, printers, public utilities, banks, entertainers, insurance companies, advertising tourist agencies, retail trade, liberal professions, transports, etc.

6. Social Progress Through Tourism. International tourism has a deep influence on the social progress of the visitors and the visited. The dramatic expansion of tourism in the past decade has been accompanied by a broadening of the economic and social base of the tourists involved. We are witnessing a revolutionary democratization of international travel. Higher wages, paid holidays, longer vacations, incentive tours, international congresses and conventions, the growth of automobile ownership, economy travel clubs, pay later plans, reductions in air fares, excursion plans, etc., have all had the effect of extending the travel market. Whereas travel was once the privilege of a few persons at humanity's apex, it now has a broader base: salaried employees, wage earners, teachers and students, small entrepreneurs, civil servants, and others. This broadened base of tourism in turn has stimulated a new demand for language training, a new interest in world affairs, geography, foreign mores and customs, a new understanding and appreciation for the "foreigner" and the "foreign:" It is pleasant to speculate on the affect this burgeoning force might have on the elimination of war and the development of peaceful cooperation of all peoples of the world in seeking to raise global standards of living.

7. Encouragement of International Investment Through Tourism. We are witnessing another fundamental change in world affairs: the upsurge of international investment in geometric proportions. Capital is flowing into developing areas. It is offsetting the endemic lack of national savings in marginal economies. This dramatic increase in international investment is paralleling the growth of international tourism and demonstrates a degree of interdependence of the two forces. A mobile society is one exposed to new ideas and new investment opportunities. The large commercial enterprises of the world know they must serve and sell and invest in the global market place. One large bank advertises with the familiar figure of the New York executive set in far off countries – he's their "Man on the Spot," ready to extend the bank's services to the business community.

The international businessman is looking for a new concept in hotelry. He seeks hotels where he can obtain such amenities as direct dial telephones, a guest room which is a pleasant working area by day, business meeting rooms, secretarial and duplicating services in a businessmen's lounge, private and public dining rooms, entertainment, travel services, garages and rental automobiles, air conditioning where necessary, shops for travelers' necessities, etc. All of these items increase his efficiency and invite his patronage. He will travel more often to such places and stay longer. Such increased travel will set the stage for increased investment.

Problems of International Hotel Development

Well-developed tourist countries of Western Europe have recognized the significance of hotel development to their economics. France, Switzerland, Austria, Italy, Ireland, Spain, Greece and Western Germany have all sponsored the construction of new hotels in the past five years by such measures as long-term, low interest credits; providing low cost, central building sites; loan guarantees; cash grants; exemptions, reductions or rebates on real estate and income taxes waivers on customs duties; favorable public utilities charges, etc. It is important to note that these concessions are given by advanced countries in recognition of the difficulties inherent in hotel financing as well as in recognition of the direct economic benefits hotels bring to communities. (See pages 29–32).

Hotel investment is characterized by heavy capital costs in fixed property assets and moderate return on capital. A modern international hotel with adequate public and service areas may have a ratio of only 55 to 60% of its costs and areas in guest room units, and the total cost of the hotel measured in guest room units alone may exceed $20,000 per guest room. The hotel may take three years to plan and build and another two or three years to become established in the trade. Therefore, it is desirable and even necessary to obtain at least two-thirds of hotel capital costs in long-term, low interest credits.

It is difficult to attract equity capital for hotel investments, particularly in developing countries where venture capital is looking for an immediate return of 15% to 25% per year rather than a 6% to 15% return such as might be afforded four to six years after the initial hotel financing takes place. Therefore, equity capital in hotel projects must often come from persons or entities with other collateral interests such as government, transportation companies, land developers, banks or other community-minded institutions. The shortage of risk capital is also a major factor in establishing a high debt-equity ratio on hotel projects in developing areas. This applies in the practical matter of raising the equity required and also in providing such capital with the leverage obtained from long-term, low interest credits for the major part of the fixed property investment.

The major problem in most countries is the total absence of long-term, low interest debt capital for heavy fixed-asset projects such as hotels. Coupled with this problem is the requirement that international credits must be serviced in hard currency. It has been demonstrated, however, that such hard-currency hotel investments in a country's principal cities generate hard-currency earnings equal to the long term loans during every eighteen to twenty-four months of operation. Since such earnings can hardly be matched by any other capital investment, this is reason enough to justify the government's venturing hotel loans with a twenty-year repayment period. Hotels should rank with basic, infrastructure investments in the primary priorities established by developing countries for international credit applications. Moreover, hotel credits warrant host government guarantees since the foremost beneficiary of hotel development is the host government.

Recommendations to Host Governments

What can and should a host government do to encourage hotel development in its country?

As we have seen, hotels are difficult to develop and finance. Hotels are also difficult to operate at a profit in certain areas. Hotels merit government assistance as they produce substantial returns to the community in hard currency earnings and in broad scale economic and social benefits. And these benefits more than equal the contribution a government makes toward the realization of the hotel. It is recommended that each host government consider the following measures (listed in order of importance) necessary parts of its program for self-help and development.

1. Sites. Hotels in principal cities should be centrally located. The sites should be close to commercial and shopping areas, near transportation centers and agencies, points of tourist interest, government offices, city parks, and lakes or rivers. The size of the site should be a minimum of about 5,000 square meters (53,800 square feet). It would be even better to have 15,000 to 20,000 square meters or more in order to develop an international shopping and commercial center related to the hotel in a gracious setting. It is obvious that such sites would be commercially very expensive even in emerging countries. Yet the more one invests in land costs, the less feasible is the financing possibility.

One rule of thumb is that the hotel site should not cost more than 10% of the value of the hotel on it. When land is more expensive, consideration must be given to a long-term land lease. Therefore, governments can contribute to the successful financing of a hotel by donating the site, or by selling it at a moderate cost; or by leasing the site under favorable conditions with purchase options, etc. If the site is not owned by the government, then the government can acquire it and transfer it to the hotel under even more favorable conditions than the government acquired it.

2. Hotel Credits. Commercial mortgages under long-term, low interest conditions are not available for hotel projects in most countries. Wherever possible, government credits for part or all of the loan capital (65% to 75% of total costs) should be made available to hotel enterprises under preferential rates of interest and twenty to thirty-year terms of repayment. Often such loans may have to be subordinated to commercial credits and particularly to international credits for the import of goods and services. This may mean only a second mortgage or no security for the government loan.

3. Loan Guarantees. Governments should provide full financial guarantees without fee for domestic or international hotel credits. Consideration should be given to "no recourse" on the hotel owning company, or to accepting repayment of any government advances for defaults under the guarantee from future, excess earnings of the hotel company.

4. Income Debentures. Government institutions can assist hotel financing by purchasing long-term income debentures (non-cumulative) issued by hotel owning companies in place of junior loan capital. This would mean that the interest on the debentures would be paid only if earned. This would be particularly helpful to the hotel owning company during the initial years of operation, or the period of becoming established in the travel market. It would obviously add to the attraction of equity investment.

5. Cash Grants. Some governments have adopted the policy of cash grants to hotel enterprises. This can take the form of a cash contribution toward building costs measured by number of guest rooms and public facilities created. Or it may take the form of interest payment on the long-term credits during the first five or more years of operations, or of paying for blocked guest room space whether or not occupied by government guests or others.

6. Share or Stock Underwriting. In communities where venture capital for hotel equity investments is scarce – or where there is no developed capital market for shares – it may be necessary for the government or development banks to underwrite part or all of the equity financing for a public issue at an appropriate time. This would lend confidence and provide official support and recognition of the project, with the probability in most cases that the public issue would be completely sold to an interested public.

7. Custom Duties. It is usual for countries not producing hotel equipment and materials to waive customs duties on each imports. This is essential to maintaining completion costs at a level consonant with financing possibilities and to keeping hotel rates and charges competitive with international prices.

8. Income and Real Estate Taxes. Exemptions, reductions or rebates on income and real estate taxes are often necessary to economic feasibility. This is a usual incentive for new industries but is particularly necessary to new hotel projects with high costs in fixed assets operating at competitive prices with older, depreciated hotels.

9. Foreign Exchange Guarantees. As primary foreign exchange producers, hotels require assurances to obtain foreign exchange for payment of international operating costs, commissions, management's earnings, interest and dividends, salaries of foreign personnel, etc.

10. Immigration Privileges for Foreign Personnel. Hotels should not be hampered by unduly restrictive immigration regulations for personnel during the restrictive immigration regulations for personnel during the construction and operation of the hotels.

11. Favorable Public Utilities Charges. When light, power, heating and telephone charges of government-owned systems are higher than the level of competitive rates in developed economies, these charges become a most significant added cost of operations, particularly in fully air-conditioned, highly automated modern hotels. Special or maximum rates should be established in accordance with the needs.

12. Advertising and Sales Promotion. Governments, particularly city governments and official tourist agencies, should coordinate advertising and sales promotion with similar programs of the leading hotels in their area. Combined efforts and budgets could contribute much to a hotel's campaigns to attract group and convention business.

13. Freedom from Rent and Price Controls. It is obvious that hotels not owned by the State must adjust charges to meet local and foreign competition and still operate at a profit consonant with those limitations.

All of the foregoing forms of assistance are simply measures of enlightened self-interest by the host government, which is the chief beneficiary of hotel development. It is unlikely that any assistance will "cost" the government anything which will not be returned to the government many fold.

National and International Sources of Hotel Finance

National sources of credit for hotel development within a country are limited and largely restricted to industrialized areas such as Europe and Japan. There is, however, a new and potential source of finance being created – and growing rapidly in many countries throughout the world – which can become important to hotel finance. This is the national development banks and institutions. The Agency for International Development (AID) of the Government of the United States has participated in or made credits available to 54 such organizations in 37 countries.[2]

National development banks are a potential source of direct, subordinated or junior credits, to hotels. Even more important, they may become a source for the sale of income debentures as described heretofore, either with own funds or as the vehicle through which international credit agencies can make credits available for the purchase of income debenture securities. Thus hotel companies are enabled to service such securities in the national currency through arrangements made between the host government and the international source for repayment of the foreign currency concerned. Finally, the development banks might be sources for underwriting public issues of share capital, or of loaning local currency equity to qualified and creditworthy foreign investors.

Foreign financing of hotel projects, particularly for imports of goods and services, is the only source for hard currency credits for projects in many of the emerging countries. Foreign financing of hotel projects is almost exclusively the province of government-owned credit institutions. The Export-Import Bank of Washington has been the leader in this field.

A number of Intercontinental Hotel Corporation[3] hotels have been financed in part by the Export-Import Bank, notably in Lebanon, Jordan, Pakistan, India, Thailand and Australia. Project loans of this type have been for the export from the United States of goods and services up to 50% of the total cost of the project, repayable in 36 semi-annual installments beginning one year after the opening of the hotel at a current annual interest rate of 5½%, with a suitable financial guaranty from a host country source.

The Agency for International Development (AID) of Washington has also made available Cooley Fund credits for hotel projects where there is a substantial minority equity investment, usually at least 20% of the total equity, from U.S. sources. IHC hotels in Pakistan and Colombia have been financed in part by AID.

The Extended Risk Guaranty Program of AID is available for hotel projects in certain countries. AID has established procedures enabling a repayment guaranty for use with U.S. banks and institutional investors, for loans up to 75% of the total U.S. private investment. AID participates in numerous national development banks and has provided them credits which in theory may be re-loaned to hotel projects. The newly formed Asian Development Bank, sponsored by U.S., Japan and about twenty other countries, no doubt will consider travel projects when it gets under way in 1967.

Japan has provided war reparations payments for hotel projects, particularly in Indonesia. The Colonial Development Corporation of Great Britain provided hotel credits for projects in Africa. The West German Development Fund is in theory available for hotel credits or guarantees covering the export of West German materials and services for hotel projects in certain emerging countries. Soviet Russia has financed two hotels in Burma and Guinea.

In general, the hotel credits from EXIM and AID are for a longer term and at a lower rate of interest than other foreign credits, a factor often offsetting the somewhat higher costs of U.S. materials and equipment.

The International Finance Corporation and the Inter-American Development Bank have not as yet had any direct participation in hotel projects. But this does not rule out the possibility of future participation.

International Hotel Companies

Hotels of the classic tradition built in the first half of the twentieth century or earlier, particularly those located outside of the United States and four or five major world capitals, were usually owned or operated by a family or by small enterprise. Often these were and are fine service institutions, sometimes preferred by the experienced international traveler today. However, they were not designed to meet the needs of the jet age, either in size or capacity, or in the character of the public and service facilities. A new concept for hotels and hotel organization was needed to meet the requirements of modern travel.

Large, institutional type hotels were first developed in the United States during the 19th-century. It follows that the latest hotel design practices and standards and the latest hotel operating methods were also first developed in the United States. These standards and methods have come to characterize modern, international hotels and this explains why the leading international hotel companies are often American in origin. Such hotels do not fit easily or logically into the usual hotel classifications of "luxury" or "first class," but are referred to as "modern international type" hotels. (Important hotel groups, national and international, of Belgium, West Germany, Great Britain and others are in another category not discussed here.)

Within the limitations of economy and efficiency of design and operations, the objective of each international hotel company is to create hotels and hotel operations that are in the cultural tradition of the respective host countries and that avoid the characterization of "just another American hotel overseas." The style and decor of hotels of the same hotel management group in Latin America, Europe, the Middle and Far East and acific areas are – and should be – different. Key personnel are recruited from all nations.

The chief contributions international companies can bring to a host country are:

1. Experience in the development and design of the hotels.
2. In at least one case, special experience in the financing and complete supervision of the design, construction, decoration and equipment of the hotel on a turn-key basis.
3. Uniform systems of operating techniques, efficiencies and economies.
4. World-wide sales, reservations and advertising organizations.
5. In at least one case, the availability of a world-wide, private network of telecommunications.
6. In at least one case, equity investment.

Notes

1. *The Future of Tourism in the Pacific and Far East*, published in 1961 by the Bureau of Foreign Commerce of the U.S. Department of Commerce, reports on page 18: "Available evidence indicates, however, that it takes 13 to 14 transactions before the money 'disappears,' and that probably no more than 5 or 6 transactions actually take place in the first 12 months after the tourist spends his money."–Ed.
2. The International Finance Corporation, the Inter-American Development Bank and the World Bank have also participated in the same or additional national development finance institutions. More such banks are being created and the capitalization of existing banks is being increased. New on the scene is the Asian Development Bank.
3. Intercontinental Hotels Corporation was the pioneer in constructing overseas hotels. During the 1930's, President Roosevelt asked Juan Trippe (Pan-American World Airways' president at that time and also a Presidential adviser on economic development) to develop plans through which the U.S. Government could help South American economy. Pan-America's first hotel, constructed in Belem, Brazil, thus helped formulate the pattern for international hotel development and financing, and IHC was formed as the hotel operating division of Pan-American. –Ed.

18

Multinational Corporations in the International Hotel Industry

John H. Dunning and Matthew McQueen

Introduction

This article arises out of research recently completed by the authors (Dunning and McQueen 1981) which, *inter alia*, collected a considerable amount of new data on the growing internationalization of the hotel industry. As well as presenting new information on the structure of the international hotel industry the data also suggests that some of the traditional ideas about the nature of international production need to be re-examined. In particular, the structure of the international hotel industry strongly suggests that the criteria for identifying and defining ownership and control of assets needs to be re-examined. Thus 100 per cent equity participation in a hotel may be combined with little control over the hotel's operations, and conversely a multinational enterprise (MNE) may exert almost complete control without any equity participation. This paper explains the reasons for and distribution of multinational involvement in the international hotel industry and, in particular, the reasons for alternative forms of involvement in the industry. In this paper international involvement is taken to mean any form of transaction by an enterprise outside its national boundaries in which assets, rights or goods are transferred and there is come continuing *de facto* control over the use of these and/or complementary indigenous resources.

Source: *Annals of Tourism Research*, 9 (1982): 69–90.

The Geographical Origin of MNEs in the Hotel Industry

The analysis of the transnational characteristics of the hotel business is limited to enterprises which had associations with two or more foreign hotels at the end of 1978. Table 1 sets out the picture for some 81 MNEs from 22 countries. At that date, these MNEs were associated with 1,025 foreign hotels and 270,646 rooms. It is believed that these account for at least 95 percent of all the rooms in all foreign associated hotels and that no important MNE with hotel interests is omitted. They exclude the activities of referral chains which are solely reservation and marketing agencies.

As shown in Table 1, hotels associated with United States-based transnational corporations account for about 50 percent of all transnational-associated hotels studied and for 56 percent of the rooms, while hotels associated with transnational corporations based in the United Kingdom and in France accounted for another 30 percent of all transnational-associated hotels studied and for 25 percent of the rooms. The remaining hotels and rooms are associated with transnationals from 17 other countries; nine hotels, with 10,548 rooms, are affiliated to transnational from developing countries, but three of the four Hong Kong chains are managed by nationals from developed countries. There are seven transnational from Japan with two or more hotels outside Japan.

The 26 leading transnational corporations which, among them, accounted for 78 percent of the estimated total number of foreign hotels at the end of 1978 are listed in Table 2. Of these, eight are based in the United States, five in France, and six in the United Kingdom. There is one transnational corporation from a developing country, namely India. The foreign propensity ratio (defined as foreign located hotels as a proportion of total hotels controlled by the MNE) of the 26 leading corporations varies from nearly 100 percent in the case of three United States chains that specialize in foreign hotels, and some of the European tour operators, to below 10 percent in the case of more domestically oriented hotel chains.

The distribution of transnational-associated hotels abroad by the main activity of their parent groups is shown in Table 3. In 1978 there were 16 hotel chains linked with international airlines; they accounted for only 5 percent of the domestic and foreign hotels of all leading hotel or tour operating companies, but for 27 percent of all foreign hotels and for 34 percent of those in developing countries. On average, nearly three quarters of the airline-associated hotels were foreign based, and of these, three fifths were in developing countries (see Table 4). They exclude the purely portfolio investment stake in hotels of some airlines, for example, British Airways, Lufthansa, Alitalia, Cathay Pacific, and Korean Airlines, and also the involvement by these and other airlines, for example, KLM, in hotel referral or reservation systems. It should be noted that the airlines have very different

Table 1: Number of units and rooms in transnational-associated hotels abroad by country of origin, and market/area share of leading chains of total foreign operations, 1978

All countries	Trans-national corporations	Trans-national associated hotels abroad	Rooms in trans-national associated hotels abroad	Leading countries or groups of countries	Parent group	Trans-national associated hotels abroad	%	Rooms in trans-national associated hotels abroad	Percentage of all rooms of leading chains[a]
United States	22	508	152,118	United States	22	508	49.6	152,118	56.2
France	8	156	35,374	France	8	156	15.2	35,374	13.1
U.K.[a]	13	149	31,765	U.K.[a]	13	147	14.5	31,765	11.7
Japan	7	23	9,093	Other Europe	14	87	8.5	21,190	7.8
Ireland	1	24	6,995	Japan	7	23	2.2	9,093	3.4
Canada	3	25	6,212	Other developed					
Hong Kong	4	14	5,480	market economies	8	65	3.9	10,557	3.9
Sweden/Denmark	3	21	4,638	Developing					
Germany, F.R.	2	19	4,435	countries	9	37	3.6	10,549	3.9
Australasia	3	32	3,149						
India	1	10	2,582						
Netherlands	3	9	1,420						
Italy	2	5	1,281						
South Africa	2	8	1,196						
Spain	2	5	1,171						
Switzerland	1	4	1,250						
Colombia	1	4	901						
Mexico	1	3	814						
Guatemala	1	4	471						
Saudi Arabia		2	301						
Total Above	81	1,025	270,646		81	1,025	100.0	270,646	100.0

Source: Hotel directories and field data.
[a] Excluding the Travelodges in the United States owned by Trust House Forte.

Table 2: Number of hotels abroad associated with leading transnational corporations, 1978

Transnational-corporation	Country of origin	Number of transnational-associated hotels abroad			Foreign propensity
		Developed countries	Developing countries	Total	
Holiday Inn[a]	United States	67	47	114	7.8[d]
Inter-Continental	United States	28	46	74	97.4
Hilton International	United States	33	39	72	98.6
Sheraton Hotels	United States	34	30	64	15.9
Club Mediterranee	France	30	26	56	57.1
Trust Houses Forte	United Kingdom	37	16	53	20.1
Novotel	France	27	18	45	27.8
Travelodge (International)[b]	United States	31	3	34	7.2
Ramada Inns	United States	25	8	33	5.1
Hyatt International	United States	6	20	26	100.0
Western International	United States	13	13	26	55.3
Southern Pacific Hotel Corporation	Australia	15	10	25	41.0
PLM Hotels	France	2	22	24	54.6
Dunfey Hotels	Ireland	24	–	24	100.0
Crest Hotels Europe	United Kingdom	18	–	18	23.7
UTH	France	–	13	13	100.0
Thomson Travel	United Kingdom	13	–	13	n.a.
Commonwealth Holiday Inn	Canada	7	4	11	18.6
Meridien	France	1	10	11	73.3
Grand Metropolitan Hotels	United Kingdom	11	–	11	18.6
Penta Hotels	United Kingdom	7	3	10	76.9
Canadian Pacific	Canada	2	8	10	34.5
Caledonian Hotel Management	United Kingdom	9	1	10	100.0
Oberoi Hotels	India	–	10	10	50.0
Steigenberger Hotels[c]	Germany, Fed. Rep. of	8	2	10	30.3
Neckerman + Riesen	Germany, Fed. Rep. of	6	3	9	n.a.
Total		454	352	806	17.7
Percentage of all transnational-associated hotels abroad:		84.2	72.4	78.6	

Source: Hotel directories and field data.
[a] Excluding investment in Canadian hotels of Commonwealth Holiday Inn, but including Holiday Inns, South Africa.
[b] Owned by Trust Houses Forte (UK).
[c] Including their involvement in Robinson Hotels, but excluding hotels attached only to their reservation system.
[d] This percentage rises to 12.8 per cent if the hotels of the Canadian and South African Holiday Inn are included.

attitudes towards such involvement. Some, such as TWA, which owns Hilton International, and Pan American, which until 1981 owned Inter-Continental Hotels, are professional and specialist hoteliers. Although there was, at first, a close synergy between airlines' routes and the location of hotels, today this is no longer the case. At the other end of the scale, some airlines are now entering the hotel business (though not necessarily through the ownership route) in a bid to exploit new routes or markets. Japan Airlines, for example, owns or manages seven hotels outside Japan and has marketing or referral agreements with 48 others.

Table 3: Distribution of transnational corporation-associated hotels abroad by main activity of parent group, 1978

	Number of transnational corporations	Transnational-associated hotels abroad		In developed market economies		In developing economies	
		Number	%	Number	%	Number	%
Hotel chains associated with airlines	16	227	27.1	113	21.0	164	33.7
Hotel chains independent of airlines	56	687	67.0	384	71.2	303	62.4
Hotel development and management consultants	3	15	1.5		0.2	14	2.9
Tour operators and travel agents	6	46	004.5	41	7.6	5	1.0
Total	81	1,025	100.0	539	100.0	486	100.0

Source: Survey Data

The Hospitality Industry – Structures, Strategies and Markets

Table 4: Airline linked transnational-associated hotels classified by country of origin, 1978

Country or region	Number of hotel chains	Number of hotels	Number of transnational-associated hotels abroad	Percentage of transnational-associated hotels abroad	Number of transnational-associated hotels in developing countries	Percentage of transnational-associated hotels in developing countries
United States	6	223	186	83.4	112	60.2
France	2	39	24	61.5	23	95.8
United Kingdom	1	10	10	100.0	1	10.0
Other Europe	2	35	34	97.1	10	29.4
Japan	2	30	9	30.0	6	66.7
Other developed economies	2	36	12	33.3	10	83.3
Developing economies	1	3	2	66.7	2	100.0
All countries	16	376	277	73.7	164	59.2

Source: Survey Data

The other three groups shown are the hotel chains independent of airlines (except possibly through minority equity investment, loan capital, or referral system), the small number of specialist hotel development and management companies, and the large European tour operators (wholesalers).

Geographical Distribution by Home and Host Countries

In 1978, some 53 percent of transnational corporation-associated hotels were located in developed market economies and the balance in developing countries, as shown in Table 5. Europe accounted for more than one third of the rooms in these hotels, while Asia – mainly South East Asia – was the dominant host region for developing countries. Africa, the Caribbean and Latin America each attracted about the same number of hotels.

Canada ranks first among host countries with transnational corporation-associated hotels, as shown in Table 6, reflecting primarily the extension of United States hotel and motel chains across the border. Spain, the most favored summer destination for European sun-seeking tourists, because of its relatively low cost of living, comes second. In the western hemisphere, Mexico plays a similar role to Spain. In Asia, which dominates all developing country regions, the foreign-associated hotels are mainly concentrated in capital cities and are frequented as much by the business traveller as the holiday tourist. Countries experiencing high rates of expansion include the countries of the Middle East, Zambia and Senegal in West Africa.

The distribution by country of origin of transnational corporation-associated hotels and rooms in main host regions is shown in Table 7. Hotels associated with transnational corporations based in the United Kingdom are strongly concentrated in Europe, have about an average involvement in Africa and the Caribbean, and are almost completely absent elsewhere in the world although such companies are now becoming involved in the Middle East and North Africa. France has slightly more than an average share of hotels in Europe, and is strongly represented in French-speaking African countries. The comparative strength of United States companies appears to be in Asia and Latin America; that of Japan is in North America (largely Hawaii and the West coast of the United States) and Asia, particularly South East Asia; and that of other developed economies (reflecting significant Australasian interests) is in Oceania. Transnational corporations from developing countries operate hotels abroad exclusively in other developing countries. Here again, however, geography plays an important role, with transnational corporation-association hotels initially tending to involve themselves in the same continent (the participation of India in hotels in the Middle East being one exception).

Table 5: Geographical distribution of transnational corporation-associated hotels abroad, 1978

Region	Developed market economies			Developing countries			All countries		
	Countries	Hotels	Rooms	Countries	Hotels	Rooms	Countries	Hotels	Rooms
North America	2	137	35,095	–	–	–	2	137	35,095
Europe	28	365	95,658	–	–	–	28	365	95,658
Middle East	–	–	–	13	63	16,292	13	63	16,292
Africa	2	4	1,040	26	104	22,235	28	108	23,275
Asia	1	9	5,835	14	86	33,323	15	95	39,158
Oceania	2	24	4,344	8	33	5,055	10	57	9,399
Latin America	–	–	–	16	101	27,444	16	101	27,444
Caribbean and W.A.I.[a]	–	–	–	16	99	24,325	16	99	24,325
Total	35	539	141,972	93	486	128,674	128	1,025	270,646
Percentage of All Countries		52.6	52.5		47.4	47.5		100.0	100.0

Source: Hotel directories and field data.
[a] Western Atlantic Islands including the Bahamas and Bermuda.

Table 6: Number of transnational corporation-associated hotels and rooms in selected host countries, 1978

All countries	Hotels	Hotel bedrooms	Average number of rooms
Developed Market Economies			
Canada	99	23,318	235
Spain	58	14,883	257
Germany, Fed. Rep. of	51	13,691	268
United States	38	11,777	310
France	30	8,968	298
United Kingdom	28	8,631	308
Italy	29	8,439	291
Japan	9	5,835	648
Switzerland	24	5,314	221
Netherlands	27	5,271	195
Greece	15	4,630	309
Belgium	25	4,592	184
Top 3 of 35 Developed Market Economies	38.6	36.6	
Top 12 of 35 Developed Market Economies	80.3	81.3	
Developing Country or Territory:			
Mexico	39	11,173	286
Philippines	14	5,708	408
Indonesia	14	5,299	379
Hong Kong	6	4,655	776
Venezuela	16	4,538	284
Bahamas	13	4,448	342
Puerto Rico	14	4,127	295
Morocco	20	3,989	199
Singapore	9	3,985	482
Israel	12	3,757	313
Brazil	13	3,647	280
Top 3 of 93 Developing Countries	13.8	17.2	
Top 12 of 93 Developing Countries	35.0	43.0	

Source: Hotel directories and field data.

Form of Involvement

Eighty-one transnational corporations were studied and each was asked to classify its foreign-associated hotels into four main categories:

- Those in which it had an equity interest sufficient to ensure that it had some *de facto* if not *de jure* management control;
- Those in which it operated some kind of leasing arrangement;

Table 7: Distribution by country of origin of transnational corporation-associated hotels and rooms in main host regions, 1978 (percentages)

	Home countries													
	United States		France		United Kingdom		Other Europe		Japan		Other developed market economies		Developing countries		All countries	
Host Regions	H	R	H	R	H	R	H	R	H	R	H	R	H	R	H	R
North America	19.1	14.7	0.6	1.7	4.7	7.4	26.1	29.0	26.1	28.3	3.1	6.6	2.7	3.8	13.4	13.0
Europe	26.6	26.2	40.4	45.6	70.5	73.5	56.8	57.4	8.7	11.9	13.9	27.0	2.7	2.9	35.6	35.3
Middle East	8.5	8.0	6.4	6.7	2.0	1.0	–	–	–	–	6.2	9.5	8.1	4.6	6.2	6.0
Africa	5.5	5.3	30.1	26.8	11.4	8.7	5.7	5.5	–	–	12.3	11.3	8.1	6.7	10.5	8.6
Asia	13.4	19.1	–	–	0.7	0.5	–	–	47.8	48.5	1.5	1.9	37.8	50.3	9.3	14.5
Oceania	3.2	2.7	2.6	2.5	–	–	–	–	–	–	47.7	27.9	5.4	3.3	5.6	3.5
Latin America Caribbean and W.A.I.	13.2	13.8	8.3	7.2	1.3	1.0	8.0	7.2	17.4	11.3	3.1	2.1	27.0	17.6	9.9	10.1
	10.6	10.3	11.6	9.5	9.4	8.0	2.3	1.0	–	–	12.3	13.6	8.1	10.8	9.7	9.0
	100.0	100.0	100.0	100.0	100.0	100.0	100.0	100.0	100.0	100.0	100.0	100.0	100.0	100.0	100.0	100.0
Developed Market Economies	49.4	47.0	41.0	47.3	76.5	81.0	83.0	86.4	43.5	40.0	41.5	48.2	5.4	6.7	52.6	52.5
Developing Countries	50.6	53.0	59.0	52.7	23.5	18.2	17.0	13.6	56.5	60.0	58.5	51.8	94.6	93.3	47.4	47.5

Source: Hotel directories and field data:
Note: H = Hotels.
R = Hotel Rooms.

- Those in which the main form of association was a management contract; and
- Those in which the main form of arrangement was a franchise or some form of marketing agreement, over and above that which might normally be involved in a referral or reservation system.

The task proved quite difficult, mainly because, in several instances, a particular transnational corporation had more than one type of association with the same foreign hotel. For example, a number of corporations had a small equity interest in a foreign hotel and at the same time operated a management contract or a franchise; others had a majority equity interest but shared a managerial responsibility with other transnational corporations. Some leasing arrangements also involved either equity capital or a marketing or managerial agreement. In such cases, a hotel was assigned to the category which best reflected the nature of the association between it and the transnational corporation concerned.

Not all the transnational corporations approached supplied all the information requested, but coverage, which varied slightly according to the degree of detail of the data asked for, was between 75 and 80 percent of the hotel rooms of the 1,025 hotels presented in the earlier tables. Including hotels which at the end of 1978 were under construction, about one third of the foreign hotels studied were associated with transnational corporations through equity participation by the latter in the former. Two-thirds had some form of contractual arrangement with the transnational corporation concerned, with management contracts accounting for at least two-fifths of all cases of such involvement. Management contracts may embrace both the development, design and construction of a hotel and its day-to-day operations.

There are noticeable differences between developed and developing countries in the mode of transnational corporation involvement. According to Table 8, about 48 percent of the rooms in hotels in developed countries are in hotels which are owned or partially owned by transnational corporations, as compared with only 18 percent in the case of hotels in developing countries. In no less than 63 percent of developing country hotels, the form of association is the management contract; the franchise agreement is also less prevalent in the developing countries. Since the 1960s, the predominant form of transnational corporation involvement has been through management contracts and technical service agreements. Of the 174 hotels in which transnational corporations have been involved since 1975 on which information has been collected, in no less than 107, or 61.5 percent, the form of involvement was a management contract. Over the period as a whole, the late 1960s and early 1970s saw a resurgence of interest in equity participation, mainly owing to the fact that the European hotel chains chose to enter the international hotel arena by acquiring existing hotels rather than becoming

22 The Hospitality Industry – Structures, Strategies and Markets

Table 8: Percentage of rooms of transnational corporation-associated hotels abroad by type and date of involvement, 1978

	Ownership (or part-ownership)[a]	Leasing arrangements	Management contract[b]	Franchising
Developed Market Economies				
Before 1964	41.0	28.1	30.9	
1965–1974	60.1	10.5	29.5	
1975 + after	25.7	8.8	65.4	
All periods	47.8	11.9	23.5	16.8
Developing Countries				
Before 1964	21.8	45.0	33.2	
1965–1974	22.2	22.2	56.8	
1975 + after	6.7	2.7	90.6	
All periods	17.6	10.3	63.1	9.0
All Countries				
Before 1960	19.0	38.0	33.8	9.3
1960–1964	31.7	21.1	47.2	–
1965–1969	42.2	21.8	29.0	6.9
	38.0	14.9	36.8	10.3
1975–1978	21.4	10.3	52.2	16.0
1979 + after	3.3	1.2	87.1	8.3
All Periods	31.4	12.2	44.7	11.7

Source: Hotel directories and field data in respect of 491 foreign hotels with a total number of 156,869 rooms.
[a] Where accompanied by some operating participation.
[b] Including technical assistance agreements.

involved in new hotels; this was certainly the strategy both of Trust Houses Forte and of Grand Metropolitan Hotels. Later on, the tour operators also chose to penetrate the foreign market (in this case, for clients in search of "sun lust" holidays) by acquiring hotels. Club Méditerranée, on the other hand, has chosen to expand mainly through the management contract route.

Some variation in the patterns of involvement among countries can be observed in Table 9. The United States, French, Japanese, and developing country chains appear to favor non-equity forms of participation. They see their role primarily as suppliers of technology, management, and marketing expertise to foreign hotels. In contrast, the other European chains, including those of the United Kingdom, seem to prefer at least some ownership participation. In Europe, transnational corporations have equity participations in about half of all affiliated hotels, while in most developing countries the corresponding proportion is under one fifth and in the Middle East less than 5 percent. Management contracts in European hotels account for 2 percent of rooms, compared with 75 percent in the Middle East, 72 percent in Africa, 60 percent in Asia and 47 percent in Latin America. Leasing of hotel properties is also more widely practised in developed countries, but it is popular in some developing countries as well, notably in the Caribbean region.

Table 9: Percentage of rooms of transnational corporation-associated hotels abroad by form of involvement of the corporations, 1978. (Regions and main countries)

	Ownership (or part-ownership)	Leasing arrangements	Management contract	Franchising
North America	24.1	15.5	41.0	19.5
United States	16.3	20.0	44.2	19.7
Europe	53.7	13.3	20.5	12.6
United Kingdom	62.0	3.0	20.3	14.8
France	21.6	0.5	73.1	4.8
Middle East	4.5	11.6	74.5	9.7
Africa	18.4	8.1	72.2	16.0
Asia	14.9	1.9	59.9	23.2
Japan	36.2	7.9	55.9	–
Oceania	31.4	21.0	32.7	15.0
Latin America[a]	17.8	19.4	49.1	13.6
Caribbean + W.A.I.	21.1	21.9	49.1	8.0
All regions	30.5	11.9	44.2	13.4
developing countries	21.1	4.9	74.2	–

Source: United Nations Center on Transnational Corporations, based on hotel directories and field data in respect of 619 foreign hotels with a total number of 182,925 rooms. The slight difference in the total proportions in each category between the figures in this and table 8 is due mainly to the inclusion of some Holiday Inn hotels in this table which were excluded from the other.
[a] Excluding Holiday Inn hotels.

The Explanation of Foreign Involvement in the Hotel Sector

An explanation of the growth, distribution, and form of involvement of multinational enterprises (MNE's) in the international hotel industry can best be conducted within the framework of the eclectic theory of international production (Dunning 1977, 1979). According to the theory, an enterprise with headquarters in one country will have some form of involvement with firms outside their national boundaries whenever they have a competitive or *ownership* advantage over other firms (whether domestic or foreign) and can combine their advantage with resources *located* in foreign countries and which are attractive to the MNE. In the process of producing goods and services, firms carry out many other activities, including marketing, training of labor, design and development of products, all of which are interdependent and linked through flows of intermediate products, which mostly take the form of knowledge and expertise. For various reasons it is difficult to organize efficient intermediate product markets and thus there is a strong incentive for firms to *internalize* these markets, by acquiring control over resources either through ownership of equity capital or through contracts. Internalization of markets across national boundaries in turn gives rise to MNE's. It is this which gives rise to the dual aspect of MNE's, since on the one hand the ability to internalize markets increases their power, while on the other hand internalization increases efficiency in the allocation of resources.

To evaluate the *ownership advantage* of MNE's, the characteristics of the product need to be examined. Fundamentally international class hotels provide a high quality service to customers who are not able to inspect the "product" before purchase and where knowledge of the product is only obtained after the product is purchased. They are, therefore, "experience goods" rather than "search goods" (whose attributes can be examined and compared with the advertised claims of the supplier). In these circumstances a trademark of guaranteed quality provides a powerful competitive advantage on a firm, particularly where customers are purchasing the service in an unfamiliar environment. Thus in developed industrialized economies, with a lively domestic market for luxury hotels, a well developed local tourist industry, and where indigenous hotels may have established a brand image in other parts of the world, one would not expect to find – and, in fact, does not find – such a strong presence of foreign associated hotels. In most developing countries, where these characteristics are less likely to be present, such hotels play a much more significant role.

The research also indicates that hotels associated with foreign firms often operate on a superior production function to indigenous firms. In particular, to the extent that international hotel chains are larger, more diversified and experienced than their domestic rivals (or potential rivals), they are able to enter new markets more easily. There may be various reasons for this. First, and most important, where the MNE is already involved in the hotel business, it has built up a set of intangible assets and logistical skills which it can make available to any newly associated hotel at a much smaller transaction cost than a *de novo* entry into the hotel business (Johnson 1970). In general, the larger and more luxurious a new hotel, particularly if it is designed to serve business traffic, the greater is the advantage of the kind of capacity possessed by MNEs. Indeed as Magee (1976) has pointed out, because sophisticated technologies are less easy to imitate than simple technologies, MNE's may seek to create and protect their appropriable economic rents by creating the former type of technologies and information. Second, according to their degree of multinationality, their sourcing of management and professional staff, foodstuffs, beverages, furnishings, and fitments, linen and china, etc., are likely to be wider (which add to the advantages of size, e.g., via quantity discounts, centralised purchasing procedures etc.) can be supplied at lower marginal costs and may be of superior quality and design. Third, their managerial and organizational expertise, their ability to invest substantial sums in training hotel staff, plus their detailed instruction manuals often enables them to have superior expertise in the overall planning and design of hotel complexes and to employ technically superior methods of production in the day-to-day operation, control and maintenance of hotels, etc., and to recruit and retain better staff by offering good promotional prospects.

As research and development are often essential elements in the maintenance of the ownership advantages of MNEs in the manufacturing sector, so investment in training may be regarded as essential to MNE hotels. It is not possible to give a precise estimate of investment in training by international hotel chains. But certainly for the larger chains, substantial sums are involved in direct staffing and resource costs (including the opportunity cost of staff receiving training), in maintaining training facilities at each hotel, regional centers and at the flagship hotel in preparing training literature and manuals, organizing seminars, and in the constant dissemination of information on new designs, procedures, techniques, equipment etc. Admittedly, part of the training costs arise from the size and geographical spread of the hotel chain and from its internalization of the markets (as opposed to arm-length market contracts) for intermediate products (including skilled labor). Additional accounting and control information is required, compared to that needed by an individual hotel enterprise, while additional problems may arise from the need to ensure that the information collected is relevant, accurate, and flows to all relevant parts of the organization, while at the same time remaining confidential to the MNE. However, the benefits outweigh the costs. Fundamentally, investment in training enables the MNE to maintain the quality of its distinctive brand image and hence market share of this experience good. The competitive advantage of the MNE is also enhanced by internalizing training, because it can more accurately assess employees' abilities and prospects, while maintaining a ready pool of skilled and mobile labor for expansion.

These knowledge advantages may extend to off-premise activities, which may be particularly important for first time visitors traveling to an unfamiliar environment and again relates to an appreciation of what is perceived tourists want, and their ability to supply or persuade indigenous firms to supply. The final advantage an MNE associated hotel may have is links through a reservations or referral system (another economy of size) for hotels on the itinerary of guests (most important in the case of business travelers) and, occasionally, links with particular airlines, railways, or coach operators to assist in travel arrangements. For clients unfamiliar with the international environment, such services greatly reduce the costs and risks associated with international communication.

The eclectic theory of international production suggests that ownership advantages may be evenly distributed according to the country of origin and destination. In the case of the hotel industry, the importance of knowledge of the requirements and tastes, particularly of business visitors, from the tourist generating countries should be emphasized. One would therefore expect, as Table 1 indicates, that the countries most likely to be involved in foreign hotel operations would also be those which tend to generate the most foreign direct investment. However, there do appear to be other factors. In particular, it is suggested that the size and structure of the hotel industry of the home country of the MNE may be important in generating management expertise, knowledge of markets, and a pool of trained labor. The contrast between the USA (with 50 percent of foreign associated hotels), France and the United Kingdom (with 15 percent each), with West Germany (with only 2 percent of foreign associated hotels), is instructive. Clearly the 2 percent share does not reflect West Germany's importance in international trade and investment (and hence business travel). The explanation would appear to be that, unlike the other three countries, the West German domestic hotel industry is not characterized by chains of hotels and it is experience in the management of domestic hotel chains, (i.e., multi-plant operations), which is a necessary condition for the establishment of international hotel chains. Another factor may be differences in the relative status of hotel management as a career in the countries concerned, affecting the ability of hotel groups to attract the most able staff.

Size and investment in training are firm specific variables determining ownership advantages, but within these categories variations occur. Some hotels emphasize their advantages in marketing and concentrate on referral systems (e.g. Best Western) and franchising (e.g. Holiday Inns). Others regard themselves as providing a package of professional managerial and organizational services which cover every stage of hotel operations (e.g. Hilton International, which explicitly rejects involvement solely through franchise agreements). Airline associated MNE chains clearly have a marketing advantage in being able to arrange advertising and reservations in conjunction with that of the parent company airline. Economies of joint supply may also be attained through using the central purchasing facilities in furnishings, food, catering equipment etc. of the airline. Similarly, hotels associated with tour operators (wholesalers) will also presumably be able to plan for and maintain higher occupancy rates because the parent company is in a control position in channelling tourists towards its own hotel.

With few exceptions the *location* is clearly specific to the tourist destination. A fundamental set of determinants of foreign involvement in the hotel industry will therefore comprise all the factors determining the size and rate of growth of tourism, particularly business tourism, to a particular country. Government policy towards foreign direct investment and involvement in production in general will also be important. In view of this it is hardly surprising that the geographical pattern of foreign involvement in the hotel sector shown in Tables 5 to 7 bears a close relationship to the geographical distribution of foreign direct investment. Variation from the pattern will occur depending on the quality of general infrastructure for tourism, the availability and quality of hotel staff, and the adequacy of supply of inputs which cannot be imported. *Firm specific* variations will also occur. For example, there is some reason to suppose that the airline associated MNE's chains favor countries, and locations within countries, served by the parent company airline. Indeed the airline's international hotel operations may be regarded at least in the initial stage of development as an important part of the "development arm" of the airline, consolidating market shares on particular routes or indicating commitment to a particular country, thereby increasing the chance of being offered traffic rights on new and potentially lucrative routes. This was certainly the case in the early years of Inter-Continental Hotels (at that time owned by Pan-Am) and Hilton International Inc. (owned by TWA) and appears to be currently so for Japan Airlines, Continental Airlines and, to a lesser extent, British Caledonian and Air France (Meridian Hotels).

Determinants of Forms of Involvement

The literature on the multinational enterprise (MNE) has tended to assume that the degree of control over resources transferred by the MNE to an affiliate together with the complementary resources owned by the transferee, is directly reflected in the extent of equity ownership of the affiliate by the MNE. However, it is quite clear that in the case of the international hotel industry much of the equity investment in hotels has the characteristics of portfolio investment carried out solely for reasons of income and capital appreciation.

It is equally apparent that some MNE involvement in foreign hotels through the non-equity route has the characteristics usually associated with direct investment in the sense of providing *de facto* control. A great deal of influence is exerted on the day to day operation of some hotels and on their long term production and marketing strategy, through the management contract (which usually authorizes the MNE to "supervise, direct and control the management and operation of the hotel"). While these contracts are time limited, they initially run for up to 20 years, with an option for renewal. Within this period, the contractee (usually the owner of the hotel) assigns to the contractor the right to exercise control over resources normally undertaken by the owner, as specified in the contract.

It would appear that the principal reason why the hotel industry is characterized by a relatively high degree of non-equity control by MNEs is that, in general, there is no conflict of interest between the objectives of the parent company seeking to maximize worldwide profits or growth and the objectives of the individual hotels in the group. Unlike many other activities of MNEs, international hotel chains cater for customers physically present at the point of production. They earn foreign currencies from foreign visitors but they do not export, or practice market allocation. Nor is there any product specialization. Although the hotels within a chain do differentiate their products, there is no intra-group trade (not, at least, as far as the final product is concerned), neither is there any process specialization, although the extent to which individual hotels import equipment, and current inputs (e.g., food and furnishings) may differ. Moreover, even where they are owned by foreign capitalists, most hotels are geared towards self-contained goals and are operated as independent entities. Control is exerted primarily to ensure these goals are met, rather than because of any difference in objectives between affiliates and parent companies, although such differences may occur between host governments and the companies, for example, with respect to the employment of local personnel and sourcing of Inputs.

Reliance on contract-based control of course carries its own risks to the MNE. In particular, long term contracts may well require adaptions to changing market conditions and although this risk is usually reduced by specifying certain provisions in the contract, for example, compulsory arbitration, compensation for *force majeure* (defined in the contract), such safeguards can only be used *in extremis*. A more important safeguard, however, is that opportunistic behavior by a hotel owner will be inhibited by the knowledge that the MNE will probably react in a way which will reduce the profitability of the hotel, for example, by reducing the transfer of know-how and the marketing of the hotel. A further potential disadvantage of contract-based control is that it may, over time, lead to a greater diffusion of knowledge than a wholly owned affiliate, and hence loss of competitive advantage to the host country's hotel sector. Field studies seem to show that the process has been of some significance in developing countries and in a number of cases (for example, in Brazil, Hong Kong, India, Singapore, South Korea, Thailand) has assisted the development of an indigenous international hotel sector. One would expect, however, that an important element of the intangible assets transferred, particularly in operating hotel chains, would remain within the organization as a whole and thus for the MNE to continue to retain its ownership advantage. This arises partly from the economies of scale associated with size, for example, in purchasing, and in enabling the functional specialization and division of labor; and partly from the international operation of the MNE which increases the collective knowledge and experience of the group. The nature of the ownership advantages of the MNE also enables the economic rent to be appropriated through contracts (without the need to rely on equity investment), for example, for the use of the hotel's name, the marketing and reservation system, physical inputs supplied by the central purchasing unit of the chain, and fees charged for supplying specialist personnel.

As Table 9 shows, the form of contract-based control varies, but closer inspection reveals that this depends upon certain country and firm specific variables. For example, the lack of indigenous hotel trained staff and the very fast rate of growth of hotel construction (with the attendant risk of excess capacity) in the Middle East, coupled with the plentiful supply of local finance capital, explains why foreign based companies of all nationalities prefer to be involved in hotels in these countries via the management contract rather than the equity investment or franchising route. On the other hand, in

India, Government regulations coupled with a strong indigenous hotel sector and the need to gain and maintain an entry into the main tourist generating markets, explains why few hotels are either owned or managed by foreign companies, although links to international chains via the franchising or reservation/referral route are still important. In the more advanced developing countries, like Mexico and South Korea, general management contracts are gradually giving way to marketing oriented and/or specific technical assistance agreements, as indigenous hotel skills and experience increase. Franchising is mainly the preserve of MNEs which are well established, from countries which generate a great deal of tourist traffic and are hosted by countries with a strong indigenous hotel sector.

From the point of view of firm specific factors it should be noted that hotels associated with MNEs with interests in related tourist activities are more likely to wish to have some equity participation so that they can capture the full benefits of integration of these activities. On the other hand, specialized hotel companies which regard their expertise as extending to property development and speculation may seek an ownership stake. This might be done by reading the market correctly and taking advantage of differences in capitalization ratios and exchange rate expectations; this is Aliber's (1970) explanation for movements in direct investment between different currency areas and would seem borne out by the marked rise in net inward investment into the US hotel industry in the late 1970s. Others, which regard their main ownership advantage as lying in marketing, may be content with a franchise agreement.

Conclusions

The rapid post-1960 growth, distribution and form of involvement of the multinational enterprise (MNE) in the international hotel industry has been analyzed in terms of ownership, locational, and internalization advantages as modified by home and host country and firm specific characteristics of the MNEs. Ownership advantages have been found to derive from the characteristics of foreign hotel accommodation as an "experience good" often purchased in an unfamiliar environment where the trademark of the MNE hotel chain guarantees a standard of service with the characteristics demanded by tourists (principally business tourists) from the principal tourist generating countries. An important element in maintaining the ownership advantage of the MNE hotel chain is investment in training (which has been likened to the importance of research and development to MNEs in certain areas of manufacturing). A further advantage is that the human and physical resources of the MNE can be supplied to a newly associated hotel at a lower incremental cost than that incurred by a new entrant into the market.

A particularly interesting aspect of the international hotel industry is the often sharp division between ownership and control. Ownership often has the characteristics of portfolio investment and control is exercised by a professional management company which may be unwilling to invest in the ownership of the hotel because it regards itself as having little expertise in property development, because it regards ownership as a high risk venture, or because expansion would be reduced by the need to borrow large sums of capital.

This paper is not intended to explore the policy implications of the analysis, but host Governments should be aware that, to a much greater extent than in manufacturing industry, alternative forms of involvement by different groups of MNEs are possible. Governments should evaluate the costs and benefits of each in relation to the country's social and economic objectives and be conscious of the possibility that existing laws controlling foreign involvement may be based on the assumption that foreign direct investment is required and may therefore be inadequate to monitor contract-based control by MNEs.

References

Aliber, R. 1970 A Theory of Direct Foreign Investments. *In* The International Corporation, C. P. Kindleberger, ed. Cambridge, MA: MIT Press.

Dunning, J. H. 1970 Trade, Location of Economic Activity and the Multinational Enterprise: A Search for an Eclectic Approach. *In* The International Allocation of Economic Activity, B. Ohlin, P. O. Hesselborn, and P. J. Wiskman, eds. London: Macmillan.

—— 1979 Explaining Changing Patterns of International Production: In Defence of the Eclectic Theory. Oxford Economic Papers, Volume 41.

—— 1981 Explaining the International Direct Investment Position of Countries: Towards a Dynamic or Developmental Approach. Weltwirtschaftliches Archiv, Band 117, Heft. 3.

Dunning, J. H. and M. McQueen 1981 Transnational Corporations in International Tourism. New York: UNCTC.

Johnson, H. G. 1970 The Efficiency and Welfare Implications of the International Corporation. *In* The International Corporation. C. P. Kindleberger, ed. Cambridge, MA: MIT Press.

Magee, S. P. 1976 Technology and the Appropriability Theory and the Multinational Corporation. *In* The New International Economic Order, J. Bhagwati, ed. Cambridge, MA: MIT Press.

19

From Globalisation to Internationalisation to Americanisation: The Example of 'Little Americas' in the Hotel Sector

Dennis Nickson and Chris Warhurst

Introduction

There is currently much debate and discussion about the globalisation of the world's economy. Much of this rhetoric, however, has little empirical purchase. A range of studies have questioned both the ontology and epistemology of globalisation (for a review of this literature, see Warhurst *et al.*, 1998). These authors conclude that the epistemology of globalisation is erroneously applied to the ontology of an international economy. At the same time, despite claims for its demise, some commentators are suggesting that Americanisation best characterises the world's economy (see for example, Friedman, 1999; Hutton, in Giddens and Hutton, 2000). This chapter enjoins these debates by critiquing the globalisation thesis and asserting the internationalness of the world's economy, providing an empirical illustration of Americanisation with the development of the international hotel sector.

The chapter thus examines Americanisation by reference to the American model of production within the international organisation of economy activity

Source: J. Taggart, M. McDermott and M. Berry (eds), *Multinationals in a New Era: International Strategy and Management* (Basingstoke: Palgrave, 2001), pp. 207–225.

coupled with a sectoral analysis. Specifically, with a review and critique of secondary literature concerning the globalisation, internationalisation and Americanisation of economic activity, the chapter firstly examines the diffusion of ideology, ideas and techniques associated with the American model. The chapter then develops these themes with an examination of the role of American organisations in the genesis, development and consolidation of the international hotel sector. This section draws on original empirical material from three multinational hotel companies, and in doing so is doubly important because analysis of the American model to date has tended to focus on the manu-facturing sector. This material clearly indicates the continuing influence of the American model of hotel internationalisation in terms of both the 'hardware' and 'software', that is for the former, the physical product, for example the rooms and operating systems; and with the latter, the utilisation of human resources and style of service delivery. Through this analysis we aim to reiterate the residual importance of Americanisation and the American model within the international economy.

Lest We Forget . . . Bringing Back America/NA into the Analysis

In this section we provide a critique of the globalisation thesis, presenting and augmenting some of the arguments made by Warhurst *et al.* (1998). As these authors point out, from the 1970s, it is argued that a number of 'global shifts' have occurred in the organisation of the world's economy with regard to transport and telecommunications technology; increased and increasingly diffused flows of foreign direct investment (FDI); and the emergence of stateless, footloose transnational corporations (TNCs), supranational institutions and regional proto-states (Dicken, 1992) and a single world market (Levitt, 1983). The global economy then is more than an *inter*national economy in which trade and investment flows across national borders directed by essentially national companies engaging national markets. Together, it is argued that these developments have rendered the national state dead and national state economic management ineffective at best and superfluous at worst (Ohmae, 1995). Three dimensions of globalisation – economic, political and cultural – have been identified by Sklair (1991) which encapsulate these shifts, manifest firstly in TNCs; secondly in the emergence of a transnational capitalist class (TCC); and, finally, in the diffusion of a cultural ideology of consumerism.

The Importance of the (US) Firm

Any critique of globalisation must begin with an analysis of TNCs for it is these organisations that are 'the single most important force creating global shifts' according to Dicken (1992, p. 47) and, as the putative 'stateless' company, have become the exemplar and leitmotiv of the newly 'globalised' world economy. Despite the rhetoric, however, many remain sceptical of the extent to which such companies have emerged. Using four key measures – geographical spread and scope, ownership and control, people in the organisation and legal nationality and taxation – Hu (1992) has been at the forefront of those refuting the notion of the 'stateless' TNC, arguing that there are no global enterprises, but rather national firms with international operations. Consequently, it comes as no surprise to learn that genuinely 'stateless', global organisations are rare, perhaps 4–5 per cent of all ascribed TNCs (Dicken, 1992, p. 49).

Moreover, the geographical origin and diversity of these TNCs can be exaggerated. Ninety per cent of all TNCs are registered lo just ten developed countries and most of these are from the US, Germany, Japan and Britain (Waters, 1995). Moreover, the largest of these TNCs are from the US. The *FT 500 Annual Review* (1999) demonstrates that nine out of ten of the world's top firms are American. Outside the top ten, US firms comprise 15 of the top 20 and 18 of the top 25 in the ranking. This ranking is based on market capitalisation and is not without limitations (Dickson, 1999). However, it does highlight two points: first, the pre-eminence of US companies and, secondly, the sharp decline of Japanese and emerging market country companies. In the top 500 as a whole, 244 companies are now from the US, up from 222 in 1998. Japan's number declined from 71 to 46, Hong Kong's from eleven to seven, Singapore four to one, Taiwan eight to two, while Malaysia has lost all representation. From South America, Brazil's contingent has dropped from five to two. A third point worth noting is that investors believe that US companies are at the technological 'leading edge' rather than the 'trailing edge' in comparison with companies from other countries – especially Japan.

It is more than presence that contributes to Americanisation. The hegemonic national economy will often provide 'methods of organising production and work organisation which establish standards of "best practice" argues Ferner (1994, p. 94). The 'American model' was once regarded as one such best practice. By the early twentieth century US firms were becoming more important players in the international economy, beginning to eclipse their established European competitors. As early as 1902, *The American Invaders* was signalling the US challenge with increased and increasingly successful FDI in Europe (cited in Dicken, 1986). By 1913 the US contributed 36 per cent of world industrial output compared to the UK's 14 per cent

(Dicken, 1998). This rise to dominance can be attributed to US firms use of (then) leading edge manufacturing techniques or Fordism. This system involved the extensive use of machinery, the interchangablity of manufacturing machinery and parts, and the standardisation of products. The critical addition was the moving assembly line which facilitated mass production and a drastic lowering of labour costs. This American model emerged when it did as a consequence of social and institutional considerations (the public education system, less rigid craft manufacture and labour mobility) and economic factors in the US (huge national resources, and labour shortages requiring labour saving production techniques). General Motors further enhanced this system with more stringent cost accounting methods in which US accountants became 'partners in production', not merely noting outcomes but part-determining inputs – with an emphasis on 'higher output for less costs' (Williams, n.d., p. 16). During the Second World War and into the postwar period, US firms were thus in a position to exploit, by trade and with foreign direct investment, firstly the inadequacies and then the decline in European manufacturing capacity, aided of course by Marshall Aid and US government desires to create bulwarks against communism in Europe and Asia – *Pax Americana*. During this time American management methods were vigorously exported through FDI, and education and training institutions in Europe (Locke, 1996). The outcomes were European economic subordination to the US and exposure of Europe to the American model of production as best practice. In the words of Dunning (1993, pp. 10–11):

> The argument in the 1950s and early 1960s seemed to run something like this. US industry in the US is efficient; its technology, management and marketing skills are the best in the world. Therefore when a US industry goes abroad, US products, skills and production methods should follow . . . From the perspective of a hegemonic power any reaction of other firms or governments to what US firms or the US government did or did not do was assumed to be of negligible significance.

US economic hegemony began to slip in the postwar period due to a number of factors, both macro and micro-economic and political: the ending of the convertibility of gold into dollars, so dismantling the 'gold standard'; the financial burden of the war in Vietnam; the 1973 oil crisis; the increased competitiveness of European firms utilising cheaper labour with relocated production in Asia; and, finally the rise of corporate Japan (Ruigrok and van Tulder, 1995). The latter has been prominent because of Japanese FDI in Europe and the US underpinned by a supposedly superior technique of production – the Japanese model of lean production or Toyotism. The American model's weaknesses were now exposed: the over-emphasis on both the financial costs of production which was subject to manipulation by organisational politics and short-term financial considerations at the expense of long-term investment (Williams, n.d). With its just-in-time rather than just-in-case stock inventory system and emphasis on flexibility and quality, for example, suddenly all countries and firms were exhorted to 'learn from Japan' and 'Japanisation' became the management buzzword of the 1980s and 1990s (see, in this respect, Womack et al., 1990). The end of US economic hegemony seemed imminent. With the 'shock' of Japan, even Locke (1996) announced the death of American management as best practice.

Nevertheless, as the FT 500 indicates, US firms have bounced back and continue to dominate. Part of the reason is that US firms such as Ford have learnt from Japan and partly reconfigured their organisational structures and practices (see, for example, Starkey and McKinlay, 1994). Part of the reason is that Japanese superiority vis-à-vis US firms has been exaggerated by the proponents of lean production, as Williams et al. (1994) point out. Those proponents also failed to appreciate that the Japanese model of production incorporated and developed rather than simply obviated elements of the American model (see, for example, Warner, 1994). Another reason is that US firms appear to have rediscovered the importance of production techniques, as Fernandez with Barr (1993), demonstrate. The most obvious new such technique is business process re-engineering (BPR). Significantly, BPR is 'Made in the USA' exploiting 'the same characteristics that made Americans such great business innovators: individualism, self-reliance, a willingness to accept risk and a propensity for change.' (Hammer and Champey, 1993, p. 2) BPR seems to be the latest best practice for adoption around the world, as Peppard and Fitzgerald (1997) demonstrate with the case of Germany (and for a more general discussion of the Americanisation of German management see also, Schlie and Warner, 2000).

World and US Economic Governance

The unfettered mobility of capital, in the form of footloose TNCs integrated by technology, leads many writers to also assert that national states are usurped by a 'borderless economy' (Omhae, 1994). Dicken (1992) has also suggested that the national state is further eroded by the development of supranational governance institutions such as the European Union (EU), United Nations, World Bank and International Monetary Fund (IMF). The TCC claimed by Sklair (1993) to now govern the world's economy comprises senior TNC management, globalising politicians and state bureaucrats as well as consumerist elites, for example individuals working in the media. With its 'global capitalist project' (ibid., p. 9) this class intends to transform the world and 'is growing stronger and is more united.' (Sklair, 1991, p. 62) Owning and controlling the means of production and ideas through its TNCs, economic governance is now no longer national or even international but a transnational process.

And yet national economic management is still both existent and desired, as Henderson (1993), Tomlinson (1993), Hutton (1995) and Porter (1990) respectively illustrate. Barnevik, the CEO of ABB, one of the oft-cited global companies, has noted the role that national governments play in his company's production location decisions: production in Germany or Italy for example, depends on the direct and indirect support received by the company from Bonn and Rome (Taylor, 1991). By noting that 'there are very few countries anywhere in the world that do not have some incentives to attract FDI', Sklair (1991, p. 62) too acknowledges residual state economic management. This management even occurs in the US and UK – the champions of the 'free market'. 'It is far from the case,' Hirst and Thompson (1995, p. 408) thus rightly conclude, 'that national economies are being subsumed in and dominated by a global economy driven by volatile and ungovernable market forces.'

If the governments of national states both desire and engage economic management, then the extent and capacity of such management by supra-national institutions must be questioned. Indeed, the usurping of national sovereignty by supra-national institutions seems more apparent than real. In reality, the national state remains a 'pivotal institution of governance within the international economy' (ibid., p. 409). Supranational institutions are not detached from national states but, instead, heavily reliant upon them. With political and financial support as well as personnel deployment, national states create, maintain and offer legitimacy for these supra-national institutions. Moreover, it is not unusual for the attitudes and actions of these institutions to be extensions of particular national government attitudes and actions.

Importantly, it is the US particularly and to a lesser extent the industrialised countries of the EU which drive the operations and policies of institutions such as the World Bank, IMF and the World Trade Organisation (WTO), as even Jeffrey Sachs (1998) acknowledges. Historically, this situation arose with the post-war desire for US internationalisation and the 'One World' concept which in reality was an attempt to create a 'US-led liberal world economic order.' (Ruigrok and van Tulder, 1995, p. 123.) This new order was formalised at Bretton Woods with the creation of the IMF and what would become the World Bank, both of which were and continue to he bank-rolled by the US. As Hoekman and Kostecki (1995) note, world trade is characterised by horse trading between national governments. Each government has its own agenda and constituents, and each differs in its level of economic power. This latter point is important because the countries of the EU, and the US more particularly, shape the policies and rules of the WTO. Japan is often regarded by these others as a country with which they must contend. It is in this light that the drive for the liberalisation of world trade should be seen:

an ideology that creates a particular form of economic organisation which serves particular interests. A good example is the changes impressed upon the patent system in the Indian pharmaceutical industry by the US. Even the loopholes in multinational agreements are best exploited and even created by the more powerful Members. The recently failed Multilateral Agreement on Investment would have bound all national states to accept investment indiscriminately but which contained exception clauses for US states. Such clauses exist, we would argue because an ambiguous agenda exists on the part of the US government to promote the free market idea with its necessary deregulation for other countries but which is to be implemented by regulation by the US government through these three pillars of world economic governance. In other words, the World Bank, WTO and IMF operate to the benefit of the US whilst claiming to be beneficial to all. As Wade (1998–99, p. 47) states:

> It is the US interest to have the rest of the world play by American rules for both international finance and multinational corporations. The goal is to make the rest of the world adopt the same arrangement of shareholder control, free labor markets, low taxes, and minimal welfare state that US corporations enjoy at home. US firms could then move more easily from place to place and compete against national of regional firms on a more equal basis.

This situation exists for a number of reasons; the need for the US to access the rest of the world's savings (which are larger than domestic US savings) and emerging markets (which are growing faster than the domestic US market). A very good example of the way in which the US government is prepared to flout international agreements occurred with the 'banana war' between the US and the EU, despite majority support within the WTO for the EU position (Watson, 1999). This war was effectively about the US government leveraging US firms' competitive advantage against European firms in the same sectors, and being willing and able to circumvent international agreements to do so. This incident is not isolated. The US has broken a myriad of internationally brokered trade policies (see for example the Japanese claims reported by Thompson, 1992). Although not specifically referring to the 'banana war' or any other particular incident, Ruigrok and van Tulder (1995, p. 124) seem right to argue then that even the European states are integrated into the 'game of international competition according to US rules' – as are the newer emerging national markets, such as China. As that country attempts to join the WTO and normalises its trade relations with the US to do so, the deal agreed between the two countries is 'so one-sided in favour of the US you have to pinch yourself', Hutton (2000, p. 18) wryly commented.

Undoubtedly, those people identified by Sklair (1991, 1993) as comprising a TCC do have formal and informal occasion to meet, but to suggest that they have a specified collective project is to exaggerate their coherence. National economic interests still prevail. Moreover, it must be recognised that a particular national state – the US – dominates world economic governance. As Hutton (2000, p. 18) commented succinctly recently, 'The US runs the world for its own advantage, just as any other hegemonic power would do.'

Culture, Consumerism and Americana

Sklair (1991, 1993) claims that an ideology or culture of consumerism now exists across the world's economy. Necessarily, therefore, that economy is governed by market transactions. This culture has emerged as one consequence of TNCs' ownership and control of worldwide media vehicles.

There does seem to be some evidence to support Sklair's basic premise, as consumerism becomes more pervasive. It is no secret that the General Agreement on Tariffs and Trade (GATT) and its recent transmutation, the WTO, along with the World Bank and IMF are intended to promote and implement the market system. These supra-national organisations are thus the instruments through which one ideology – capitalism and its expression in the market – is imposed on all by the more economically powerful countries. Indeed, starting at Bretton Woods, the task of the GATT and now the WTO appears to be the opening up the world's national economies to trade from the US and, to a lesser extent, industrialised Europe. It is for this reason that the management of trade between the US and EU on the one hand and the emergent economies of South East Asia on the other is likely to be the future central issue for the WTO as identified by Hoekman and Kostecki (1995).

Through trade liberalisation, privatisation and deregulation the market now pervades the economic organisation of countries in Europe, the Americas, most of Asia and increasingly Africa and the Middle East. However, the market is not abstract. Instead, 'the market' is an institution. Comprising social rules that provide for an organised pattern of action for economic actors, the market is the mechanism of co-ordination and allocation within capitalism. To date, the rules which affirm these social relations are determined by national states, either directly or indirectly through their client supra-national organisations. China's acceptance and assuming of this task has been a key condition of its membership application to the WTO.

This last point also serves to illustrate the weakness of those who move from accepting the existence of a global culture of consumerism – which has some validity – to asserting that a homogenised global market has emerged for goods and services. Even within a global culture of consumerism, consumer needs, wants and demands across the globe may continue to vary by country. In short, it is one thing to argue that the world's economic activity is becoming dominated by consumerism and market transactions and quite another to then insist that this market and its consumers are homogenised. The two phenomena should not be conflated: a domineering ideology of consumerism does not equate with a single world market. Even Ford has failed so far to produce an acceptable 'world car' and its latest attempt will still be 'tailored to local tastes' (Flint, 1994, p. 41).

Nevertheless, there are some products which are undoubtedly consumed around the world. Disney and McDonald's for example, are available to consumers in most countries and, likewise, demand for IBM laptops and Microsoft software is shared by industrial markets across the globe. However even these products, while ubiquitous, are, as with the companies which produce them, often reflective of their country of origin, either by design or default. Two points are worth raising here in relation to country of origin. Firstly, companies often draw upon the identity of their country of origin to create brand identity; Nestle and Switzerland, and Marlboro and the US offer good examples. Secondly, although there are such products from firms of countries other than the US, the most iconic are from the US. The roll-call of putatively global products, such as Coca-Cola, Pepsi-Cola, McDonald's, Levi's and GM, is dominated by the US as country-of-origin. With retail outlets sited in almost every continent, McDonald's is instructive here. Although Ritzer (1993, p. 1) maintains that McDonaldisation is 'an inexorable process . . . coming to dominate more and more sectors of American society as well as the rest of the world', he has also more recently acknowledged that this global reach cannot be equated with 'globalisation'; for McDonald's, in terms of product and production process, is distinctly American. In this respect, although it is ubiquitous, McDonald's offers an example not of globalisation but *Americanisation*. 'There appears to be a growing passion around the world for things American and few things reflect American culture better than McDonald's' Ritzer (1996, p. 299) suggests, citing others' statements that the company is 'a piece of America'. This argument is not new, being first aired in 1901 in Blunt's *The Americanisation of the World* (cited in Spybey, 1996) but its force is more convincing in the postwar period of US hegemony.

The domination of US products in so-called 'global markets' should surprise no-one. The *Pax Americana* of the postwar period was, and continues to be underpinned by US military and economic hegemony, as argued by Hirst and Thompson (1995). Of course there is a more nuanced argument here and one which is articulated by Waters (1995). He suggests that the so-called 'global' markets that are being created are merely those responding primarily to European culture (with its subsequent, derivative manufactured artefacts) as it expands across the world 'via settlement, colonisation and cultural mimesis' (ibid., p. 3). Thus the culture of consumerism with its emphasis on individual choice is the particular masquerading as the universal or, in marketing jargon, the local repackaged as the global. The hegemony of European culture, transmuted in North America is now being promoted by TNCs as a global culture. The storylines of Disney movies are an obvious illustration. The classic *Snow White*, adapted from the fairytales of the brothers Grimm, is one example.

These products, therefore, cannot properly or accurately be described as 'global products'. It is more fitting to describe them as 'universalised products' to indicate that they have particular locales of origin – typically Western products at least filtered through the US, if not US in origin – that are then marketed on a huge scale. As Friedman states (1999, p. 309):

> the distinction between what is globalisation and what is Americanisation may be clear to most Americans, it is not to many others around the world. In most societies people cannot distinguish anymore between American power, American exports, American cultural assaults, American cultural exports and plain vanilla globalisation. They are now all wrapped into one.

Despite pronouncements to the contrary, the US is still hegemonic in the world's economy. It is in this context that the influence of the American model in the hotel industry, to be now presented, should be perceived. Discussions of Americanisation have tended to focus on the cultural imperialism outlined above or, with reference to the diffusion and the adoption of American best practice, the manufacturing sector. The following section offers a brief history of hotel internationalisation and the emergence of the American model before going on to examine evidence of the continuing dominance of American-type practices current in the industry.

Setting the Standards: The International Hotel Sector

Conrad Hilton is often talked of in venerable terms as the 'founder' of internationalisation in the hotel industry. Strand (1996, p. 83) suggests that Hilton 'had the vision of what we now call globalisation back in 1947, but he did not have the means to achieve such a vision because the board of directors wanted no part of it'. Nonetheless due to Hilton's pioneering spirit and his ability to persuade the board of the company to give him greater latitude (see Comfort, 1964; Hilton, 1957), the company did internationalise and Strand (1996, p. 84) further argues that 'The genesis of Hilton's – and the industry's – globalisation was a confluence of three factors, almost historic accident.' These factors being: demand and particularly the fact that the only tourists travelling in any numbers in the immediate post war period were

American; the entrepreneurial spirit of Hilton; and, the availability of financing through relationships established between Hilton and host governments. Allied to these factors Nickson (1997) notes a further reason for Hilton's internationalisation, the role of his hotels as a bulwark against communism. Indeed, such an overt political rationale for internationalisation is not unusual given the contemporary prevailing political circumstances engendered by the Cold War and the need for American business to be seen as championing free enterprise against the perceived evils of communism (for a general review of this issue see Mills and Hatfield, 1999).

Hilton is, then, perhaps the best example of the American model of hotel internationalisation which Nickson (1998, 1999) argues continues to dominate the sector and provide notions of best practice. What, then, was the American model exported by Hilton, and others such as Holiday Inn, Intercontinental and Sheraton? Nickson (1998, p. 56) believes that 'companies like Hilton, Holiday Inn, Intercontinental and Sheraton were concerned with creating a, usually upmarket, home-away-from-home for American travellers, particularly business travellers'. Thus they sought to offer, in Hilton's own words, 'little Americas' which drew heavily on the certainties offered by the chains in the US (Hilton, 1957). Consequently Hilton and his fellow entrepreneurs, such as Kemmons Wilson (the founder of Holiday Inn) sought to develop for export a product based on concept standardisation to ensure operational control and guest consistency, allowing chains to make their reputation on the basis of universality, quality and consistency. This seemingly, though, was what the majority of American travellers were comfortable with in their search for the 'pseudo-event', where they could disregard the 'real' world outside (Boorstin, 1963). Urry (1990, p. 7) describes this in terms of the familiar American-style hotels providing an 'environmental bubble' which 'insulates the tourist from the strangeness of the host environment', or more prosaically *'instant America'* (Comfort, 1964, p. 231, emphasis in original).

As Nickson (1998) notes this model was one that endured in the international hotel sector for the period from the late 1940s until the mid-1980s. However changes in ownership – most obviously and iconically the acquisition of Hilton International and Holiday Inn by, respectively, the British-owned companies Ladbrokes and Bass – and a recognition of the potential limitations of standardisation as a source of competitive advantage led to much speculation on the decline of the American model. Nevertheless as Nickson (1999) argues standardisation and the creation of a home-away-from-home remains an integral part of the competitive strategies of major international hotel companies, whatever their country of origin. Thus this aspect of the American model remains alive and well. Furthermore in a more concrete sense, despite the aforementioned acquisition of several well known American companies the dominance of American chains is still apparent. Again, nine of the top ten hotel chains in the world are American (*Hotels*, 1999). (See Table 1.)

Table 1: Top 10 hotel chains in the world

Rank	Firm	Country
1.	Cendant Corporation	US
2.	Bass Hotels	UK
3.	Best Western	US
4.	Choice Hotels International	US
5.	Marriott International	US
6.	Accor	France
7.	Starwood Hotels and Resorts	US
8.	Promus Hotel Corporation	US
9.	Hilton Hotels Corporation	US
10.	Carlson Hospitality	US

Source: HOTELS *Magazine* Corporate 300 ranking (1999). HOTELS is a Cahners Business Information Publication, a division of Reed Elsevier. (Reprinted with permission.)

Moreover the shift from a concentration on the hardware of the physical product to the software and the role of people as a source of competitive advantage could equally be seen to be still indirectly dominated by an American influence. There is still much support for the notion that the US continues to be the predominant supplier of what is considered good practice approaches to both general business practices and particularly human resource management (HRM). For example, Brewster (1995, p. 207) asserts that, 'the analyses and prescriptions laid out in the standard management textbooks are, fundamentally, drawn from one particular culture: that of the USA'. The contention is that American dominance of the international hotel sector is well established and this view is now discussed in relation to empirical material drawn from three case study organisations. It should be noted here that all of the companies are represented pseudonymously to allow for anonymity amongst interviewees.

Case Study Evidence

This section develops an analysis based on over 80 semi-structured interviews undertaken in three international hotel groups with managerial personnel, including representatives from corporate headquarters and unit-level managers throughout the world (for further details of this research, see Nickson, 1999). The first case study company is Americo which is regarded as exemplifying the established organisational form in the international hotel sector. Their approach, although more recently overlaid with a recognition of the need to customise the service encounter in response to the demands of local markets, continues to be characterised by high levels of standardisation, certainty and consistency, particularly for the American business traveller abroad. Second, evidence is drawn from interviews within the hotel operation of the French travel and tourism group Frenco, a major player across the globe with a presence in over 70 countries. The final case study organisation is Swedco, a relatively small regional player whose major strength lies within the Nordic region, with only limited coverage in other parts of Europe.

Given that Americo's interest in internationalisation is relatively recent their overall approach could be characterised as ethnocentric or even Amerocentric, reflecting the fact that a large part of their overseas hotels customer base was Americans travelling abroad. In the Americo export product the importance of brand identity continued to be significant, and consistency and certainty in the hardware, in terms of catering for the American customer, were perceived to override local considerations: 'obviously in places like Jedda there are separate rules there, but the product itself, the rooms, the size of the rooms, they are designed here because our customers, 50 per cent of them are Americans, so we want them to feel at home' (general manager, American). Americo managers saw little problem with attempting to disseminate the archetypal home away from home which characterised the American model of hotel internationalisation: 'respective of whether you are in Warsaw, London or downtown Washington, or whatever, it is very American, Holiday Inn were, but [Americo] are more so' (front of house manager, British). Although the company were seeking to move away from a prescriptive approach, based solely on the application of standard operating procedures (SOPs), in individual units Americo still insisted that each hotel contained the 'core deliverables', which included a copy of *USA Today* and an American flag.

While Frenco managers were keen to differentiate the Frenco product and approach from the model established by the pioneering American chains it is clear that, in fact, the benefits of standardisation and standard operating systems were well understood within, and were a central organising principle for, Frenco. This underpinning is perhaps most apparent within the company's budget and mid-market brands:

> The fundamental characteristic of [Frenco's mid-market brand] is of international standardization of the offering. What is therefore required is consistency of the offering in every location in which it is available . . . Standardization of the offering means putting into place a service delivery system that is robust enough to survive transferability across borders and generate consistent service standards to satisfy customer expectations, irrespective of local conditions or infrastructure. (Segal-Horn, 1995, p. 16)

Certainly this was a point recognised by a British front of house manager who, in response to the question of what attracted people to the mid-market brand, replied, 'standardisation, yes the concept is simplicity, the bedroom is very basic but it has got in there everything that you need' consequently 'whichever hotel you go to, people expect the same, that is the attraction.'

Any minor concessions to local markets tended to be in terms of things such as regional variations in the menu in the hotel restaurant.

As with Frenco, within Swedco there was strong evidence to suggest that the physical product developed by the company drew heavily upon an approach established by the American chains, particularly in the use of concept manuals and SOPs. Thus although some managers (reflecting a similar view as Frenco managers) liked to see the company as qualitatively different from the American model-type approach, evidence suggested that this manuals driven approach was still very apparent in Swedco. Manuals had been produced to cover operational aspects of front of house, food and beverage and conference facilities. The manuals were supposed to be operative both as an overall approach and specifically applicable in departmental areas, with checklists being used for ensuring adherence to correct standards:

> Of course there are concepts for how the rooms are to look, the number of opening hours, the marketing programmes that we have to follow, there are a number of facilities in the room of course, what kind of bar, restaurant, brasserie, you should have, the lay out of the conference room, all these things. (General manager, Swedish)

In summary, in relation to the hardware, it is clear that many aspects of the standardisation, certainty and consistency which characterise the American model are still apparent within the case study organisations. Equally interesting is the extent to which a number of managers in the non-American case study organisations sought to deny the debt owed to the American model. In many respects this ambiguity illustrates the janus nature of Americanisation, as noted by authors such as McKay (1997) and Ritzer (1998, p. 71), the latter citing Kuisel's (1993, p. 3) view that 'America appeared [to the French and Europeans in general] as both a model and a menace.' Thus Americanisation becomes something to either be decried or embraced, or in the case of the case study companies, seemingly both. Indeed, this ambiguity was also apparent in terms of the software of the management style.

In relation to management style Americo were still concerned with exporting an 'American way of life' (head of the works council, Austrian) and managers had some awareness of the likelihood of this being seen as imperialistic or in pejorative terms by host countries. More recent debates about the character of the successful global company have arguably intensified the belief that the most successful companies are those who are able to, in the oft-repeated prescription, 'think globally and act locally'. This is most clearly expressed in the notion of the transnational as a company with the ability to manage across national boundaries, whilst retaining local flexibility (see, for example, Scullion, 1993). Within Americo though it is interesting to note that the espousal of transnationalism was tempered by the view that the

US was perceived to be the benchmark for other countries in terms of providing an internationally acceptable management and operating style:

> What is right? What are the standards? What are the systems that are appropriate internationally and in the United States? When you are a US company you make an assumption that expectations are fairly uniform . . . Now the interesting thing is, and we're still studying this, is that if a person travels to an [Americo] in Munich, are they expecting a German hotel or a [Americo] American hotel. We still do have quite a few US travellers going abroad, because they're the ones who know the name. Now what happens when an Arab or a Chinaman or an American goes there, do they have different expectations and perceptions? Right now we seem to think that our standards are pretty good, they're fairly uniform, there are some challenges, with it, but there doesn't seem to be an overriding issue right now with other people accepting the US standard in a foreign country. (Director of service development, American)

The ethnocentrism implicit in this statement was further exemplified by the recognition by the same interviewee that in the early phase of internationalisation, host country managers were likely to be sent to the US as 'it's in their best interests, they can come over and learn our standards and take them back'. The company also used specialist 'task forces' to train within the country of operation, although the underlying rationale was still to train 'the local people in our way of doing things'. This highlights the assumption that American companies perceive their practices and systems to be 'natural' rather than constructed in or contingent upon a particular institutional framework – that of the US.

There was also evidence of Frenco utilising several HRM techniques in a similar way to Americo, and in many respects these could be considered anathema to traditional conceptions of a French management style, as described by Barsoux and Lawrence (1997) and Poirson (1993). Most obviously this was in relation to the ideas of autonomy, openness and responsibility which were held to characterise the Frenco management style and the Frenco concept of intrapreneur or in-house entrepreneur in which managers were expected to identify improvements themselves. In relation to autonomy it was though noteworthy that managers within Frenco again liked to consider the company as qualitatively different from the American chains who exemplified the American model:

> It's two worlds, it's completely different. American chains are structured, fully centralised, everything comes from the top and this makes a whole difference. If you take Sheraton, Hilton, Marriott we have nothing in

common, nothing. We are fully de-centralised, maximum power at the lowest level, we don't have books, they have books and they have a lot of things, if you don't know something open page 250 and find the answer. This is the American way. (Managing director of hospitality studies and training, Swiss)

An American chief concierge also suggested that Frenco's approach could be compared favourably to the more rigid American approach, which was concerned with creating 'robots' who were supposed to do as they were told. In contrast, in Frenco, 'you are completely free . . . and that is one of the main ingredients that make employees loyal and productive . . . they don't change your personality like some other companies.' Although this was somewhat contradictory with his later recognition that at times employees were told to say things in specific ways in interacting with the customer. Thus Frenco were perceived to have 'standards and philosophies' which provided 'guidelines' as opposed to 'rules'.

With the shift in emphasis towards the softer aspects of the product, it is noteworthy that, initially, Frenco continued to base some aspects of their operations around established business systems. An example of the continuing use of American-type practices was seen within their mid-market brand where attempts to base quality in both the hardware and the software were on the basis of what were known as the 'Frenco Bolts'. This system to monitor standard procedures was introduced into the company in 1987 and was centrally designed and centrally driven and emphasised structural elements of service. As the then managing director of the brand wrote in the introduction to the booklet outlining the 'bolts':

In our language a 'bolt' signifies a quality requirement which contributes towards our client's loyalty to the brand. There are some 'bolts' that define your attitude to the different clients and to the service you provide, while others are more technical and concern investment. By respecting all the 'bolts' mentioned in this booklet, we will obtain the total satisfaction of our clientele.

The 'bolts' covered thirteen areas within the hotel, including elements of staff-customer interaction, these areas being: reservation, arrival/access, parking, check-in, the lobby area, bedrooms, bathroom and WC, restaurant evening, breakfast, boutique, bar, playground/swimming pool and check-out. In effect, the 'bolts' were a series of compulsory directives to staff in terms of how to set out a bedroom, lay a plate setting, welcome a guest and so on. Moreover the 'bolts' became an integral part of the induction and socialisation of all new recruits as they received the booklet as part of their orientation procedure.

Despite the view of the managing director of the company of the efficacy of this approach, within interviews, there was some disquiet amongst some managers at the attempt to codify a 'zero defects' quality approach via the 'bolts', as, in reality, it was very much like the old SOPs, as developed by the Americans, a point not lost on one French general manager:

> Yes, I don't give a damn about 'bolts', why are they there? The company has them, you just make sure you do it, but I don't think they make a big issue out of it. There is also an inspection when people come twice a year, and when I lose a point because we didn't say 'thank you for choosing [Frenco]', I don't give a damn . . . that is very American, and the American way of doing things.

Discussion and Implications for Practice

The earlier discussion of the importance of, in particular, the American firm and the contention for the inextricable link between culture, consumerism and Americana would seem to be supported by the sectoral overview and case study evidence.

In relation to the sector context generally, Mather and Todd (1995) recognise that a consequence of American hegemony of the early years of the international hotel industry is that even though there may have been a shift in ownership, there is, it seems, a residual and somewhat amorphous notion of American influence within such hotels:

> While some of the larger chains are no longer American in ownership – to take Holiday Inn and Intercontinental as two significant examples – many nevertheless have their roots and culture based in North America and can be regarded as American in spirit if not in fact. (Ibid., p. 54)

Indeed, they go on to suggest that, in the general public's eyes, it is unlikely there is any real awareness of who owns what, and as an example, most people would still perceive Holiday Inn and Hilton International as American. Moreover the lack of awareness of ownership of these famous names extends to academia, as Kumar (1995) exemplifies. Discussing globalisation, and particularly how it is synonymous with standardisation and homogeneity and the 'global product', he suggests we should look to the 'global marketing of McDonald's, Mickey Mouse, Dallas and Disneyland, Hilton and Holiday Inn' and just to make his point clear adds in parenthesis, 'the American provenance is of course significant' (ibid., p. 189).

More specifically the case study evidence supports the contention that much of what is considered to be good practice in the international business arena would seem to stem from American influences, as Brewster (1995), cited earlier, noted in his comments on the contents of standard management textbooks. In the 1950s, British and Scottish manufacturing were exhorted to learn from America and US FDI was encouraged to the UK in that respect. The same exhortations are still being made today. In 1999 the Institute of Directors Scotland launched a programme to 'enable Scottish firms to learn from the best American practice' (Fraser, 1999, p. 16). Now, however, the service sector and not just the manufacturing sector can learn from America. The Scottish tourist industry, for example, might learn from Disney it is suggested. The durability of the American model is certainly apparent within the international hotel sector, both in relation to the hardware and software. Therefore, despite claims as to a lessening of the competitive advantage to be derived from high levels of standardisation, it is clear from the evidence that standardisation, for example, remains an integral part of the competitive strategies of major international hotel companies, whatever their country of origin.

The interesting aspect of this finding is not so much that standardisation remains a major part of the companies' approach, rather, it lies in the perception of managers as to its desirability. In those terms the evidence did produce something of a dichotomy between Americo, and Frenco and Swedco managers. For example, Americo managers saw little problem with attempting to disseminate the archetypal home away from home that characterised the American model of hotel internationalisation. Likewise within Frenco and Swedco there was strong evidence to suggest that the physical product developed by these companies drew heavily upon an approach established by the American chains. They continued to rely to a great degree upon the business and financial systems developed by chains in the US, particularly in the use of concept manuals and SOPs. Nonetheless some managers within Frenco and Swedco liked to see their companies as qualitatively different from the American model-type approach. In a limited sense this may of course be true in the way that Frenco and Swedco also utilised obvious national signifiers to infuse their products with elements of 'Frenchness' and 'Swedishness', reflecting Mathe and Perass' (1994) view of international service organisations seeking to strive for 'exotic' or 'foreign' appeal in their product. Overall though it is clear that the underpinning approach of standardisation remains unchanging.

As was noted in the review of the importance of the US firm a key theme which would offer some explanation for the durability of American hegemony is the ability of American business to develop new techniques, such as BPR. Reflecting Schuler et al.'s (1993) view that the 'competitive strategy imperative' is likely to depend on the existence of a common set of needed employee role characteristics for quality improvement and a common set of human resource practices for those characteristics, the case study organisations evidenced a high degree of similarity in their approaches. Most obviously this convergence can be seen in relation to empowerment-type mechanisms, which were an integral part of the competitive strategies of all of the companies. Thus it could be suggested that the organisations exemplify Waters (1995) view that increasingly there is a recognition of a burgeoning idealisation of organisational behaviour premised on a strong corporate culture which, in turn, envisions a key role for the new cultural paradigm's symbols and tools, such as BPR, total quality management, empowerment, functional flexibility/multi-skilling, and high levels of staff training and development. In short, much of what is considered best practice traces its lineage to America.

The recognition of prevailing American dominance in business life is also likely to have significant implications for the likes of headquarters managers, subsidiary managers, policy makers and academics. As prime minister of the UK, Tony Blair has repeatedly exhorted other European political leaders to adopt American business culture arguing that its free market emphasis is superior to the of the European 'social model'. This superiority arises because, as Madeleine Albright, US Secretary of State, put it, 'Americans "see farther" because they "stand taller" (Pfaff, 2000, p. 8). Some worry however, that the Wilsonian 'benevolent hegemony' that would be said to result from American ideology, ideas and techniques dominating the world's economy is a mask for a more self-serving purpose. As Hutton (2000, p. 18) states boldly in reference to the US leverage of other countries' economies:

> it gives the lie to those who would argue that globalisation is somehow driven by the invisible hands of markets and technology. This is a self-conscious political programme with one major author who is a self-declared beneficiary – the US. We have all become pawns in the great game of designing the world so that it befits Wall Street and Main Street . . .

While Hutton is sceptical, even cynical, he is accepting of US hegemony for its Schumpterian creative and destructive tendencies, and because alternatives to it are 'retreating as globalisation spreads' (in Giddens and Hutton, 2000, p. 12). His plea however is for non-US policy makers to be able to conceptually distinguish the practical conflation of Americanisation and globalisation so that European states do not passively accept or eulogise the latter but instead make conscious choices about the appropriateness of their own models of economic organisation.

Paradoxically, this point is likely to be particularly true for American TNCs, especially those seeking to become more 'global' in their outlook. A certain reflexivity on the part of both headquarters and subsidiary managers is likely to be crucial in any attempts by TNCs to become 'global' and less tied to a national outlook. Continuing belief in the synonymity of American and 'global' standards may in reality sustain a world view which remains Amerocentric. A further issue which has been implicit throughout this analysis is the extent to which organisations' business practices, and particularly their human resource practices are becoming similar or remain distinctive. The recent collections by *The International Journal of Human Resource Management* (vol. 9, no. 4) and Rowley (1998) illustrate that the issue of convergence and divergence remains a source of interest and debate to both academics and practitioners. Generally a case for convergence can be made on the basis of several trends which are likely to drive converging tendencies, most notably: patterns of globalisation; economic integration; opening of markets; and the transference by TNCs of what is considered best practice. To date, much of this analysis has been dominated by debates within the manufacturing sector and the re-emergence of what Martin and Beaumont (1998) term 'one-best-wayism' – perhaps best illustrated by the lean production literature. However, within the service sector this literature remains relatively sparse. Consequently, there is scope for further research to consider two key questions. First, to what extent can converging tendencies still be considered American? Secondly, is the American dominance of the hotel sector described in this chapter apparent in other industries within the service sector and, indeed, more generally across the whole range of the manufacturing sector?

Conclusion

This chapter had two aims; firstly, through critique of the global economy, to affirm the residual importance of the US and Americanisation within the international economy and, secondly, to illustrate this residual importance by reference to the hotel sector. We have examined claims that a global economy has now emerged and sought to evaluate such claims by reference to the empirical evidence, drawn from secondary and then primary sources. Such evidence strongly indicates that an international, rather than a global economy still exists. National states continue to matter, as does the relationship between states and firms. US firms still dominate this international economy, as do their products and practices. Likewise, US national economic management is central to the governance of the world's economy. Of course, presence alone does not establish dominance. The American model and US government influence is underpinned by a pervasive ideology, diffused by the US through the main institutions of world economic governance. Similarly, the ideas and techniques of the American model are again dominating the organisational structures and practices of other firms. Those who prosecute the globalisation thesis therefore lack both an understanding of the developments and an appreciation of the empirical data. The international economy remains strongly shaped by America – firms and government – and Americanness in terms of ideology, ideas and techniques, so that it is still premature to talk of the end of US economic hegemony.

Despite its dominance, that American ideology, ideas and techniques are diffused and adopted elsewhere within the international economy is an issue to be tested empirically. We have gone some way to address this issue with the research presented here on the international hotel sector which, it was argued, exemplifies continuing American dominance in terms, again, of ideas and techniques. The high level of standardisation of the physical product has long been recognised as an essential part of the success of the American-driven internationalisation process in the hotel sector in the period to the early 1980s and it is clear from the evidence that international hotel companies will continue to see standardisation of the physical product as a central feature of their internationalisation strategies. Thus, in relation to the hardware, the American model of internationalisation established by the early international chains continues to provide many of the key organising principles and the decline and demise of the model is exaggerated. In relation to the software, the key finding is that the self-perception of Americo managers of the company becoming more transnational is within the framework of American standards being seen as synonymous with global standards. Equally, claims as to the distinctiveness of management style in Frenco and Swedco seem spurious when much of their approach could be considered as drawing on notions of good practice HRM, which in turn traces its origins to the US (see for example, Guest, 1990). As with BPR, this latter author suggests that HRM arose in the US as a response to the changing political and economic climate of the 1980s, and became popular because it reinforced existing American managerial values.

The description of American hegemony should not be surprising given the economic strength, and political and cultural influence of America. No doubt there will be continuing debate as to whether the influence represents a menace or a model, but to deny American dominance of the international economy, and business ideology, ideas and techniques is premature.

Bibliography

J. Barsoux and P. Lawrence, *French Management: Elitism in Action* (London: Cassell, 1997).
D. Boorstin, The Image or What Happened to the American Dream (London: Penguin, 1963). J. Urry, *The Tourist Gaze* (London: Sage, 1990), 7.
C. Brewster, "National Culture and International Management" in S. Tyson (ed.) *Strategic Prospects for Human Resource Management* (London: IPD, 1995), 207.
M. Comfort, *Conrad N. Hilton – Hotelier* (Minneapolis: T.S. Dennison and Company, 1964) and C. Hilton, *Be My Guest* (Englewood Cliffs New Jersey: Prentice-Hall, 1957).
P. Dicken, *Global Shift* (London: Paul Chapman, 1992, 2nd edition).
M. Dickson "How to Find Your Way Around the Tables", *FT 500 Annual Review Financial Times*, 28 January 1999.

J. Dunning, *The Globalization of Business* (London: Routledge, 1993), 10–11.
J. P. Fernandez with M. Barr, *The Diversity Challenge* (New York: Lexington, 1993).
A. Ferner, "Multinational Companies and Human Resource Management: An Overview of Research Issues," *Human Resource Management Journal*, 4:2 (1994), 94.
T. Friedman, *The Lexus and the Olive Tree*, (London: Harper Collins, 1999).
FT 500 Annual Review Financial Times, 28 January 1999.
D. Guest, "Human Resource management and the American Dream," *Journal of Management Studies*, 27:4 (1990).
M. Hammer and J. Champey, *Re-engineering the Corporation* (London: Brearly, 1993), 2.
J. Henderson, "Industrial Policy for Britain: Lessons from the East," *Renewal*, 1:2 (1993).
P. Hirst and G. Thompson, "Globalization and the Future of the Nation State," *Economy and Society*, 24:3 (1995).
B. Hoekman and M. Kostecki, *The Political Economy of the World Trading System* (Oxford: Oxford University, 1995).
Y. Hu, "Global or Stateless Corporations are National Firms with International Operations." *California Management Review*, Winter (1992).
W. Hutton, *The State We're In* (London: Vintage, 1995).
R. Kuisel, *Seducing the French: The Dilemma of Americanization* (Berleley, CA: University of California Press, 1993), 3.
T. Levitt, "The Globalization of Markets," *Harvard Business Review*, May–June (1983).
R. R. Locke, *The Collapse of the American Management Mystique* (Oxford, Oxford University Press, 1996).
G. McKay, "Introduction: Americanization and Popular Culture" in G. McKay (ed.) *Yankee Go Home (& Take Me With U)* (Sheffield: Sheffield Academic Press, 1997).
A. Mills and J. Hatfield, "From Imperialism to Globalization: Internationalization and the Management Text" in S. Clegg, E. Ibarra-Colado and L. Bueno-Rodriquez (eds) *Global Management: Universal Theories and Local Realities* (London: Sage, 1999).
D. Nickson, "'Colorful Stories' or Historical Insight? A Review of the Auto/biographies of Charles Forte, Conrad Hilton, J. W. Marriott and Kemmons Wilson," *Journal of Hospitality and Tourism Research*, 21:1 (1997).
D. Nickson, "A Review of Hotel Internationalization With a Particular Focus on the Key Role Played by American Organizations," *Progress in Tourism and Hospitality Research*, 4:1 (1998).
K. Ohmae, *The Borderless World* (London: Collins, 1994).
K. Ohmae, *The End of the Nation State* (London: Harper Collins, 1995).
J. Peppard and D. Fitzgerald, "The Transfer of Culturally-grounded Management Techniques: the Case of Business Re-engineering in Germany," *European Management Journal*, 15:4 (1997).
P. Poirson, "Human Resource Management in France" in S. Tyson et al (eds) *Human Resource Management in Europe* (London: Kogan Page, 1993).
M. E. Porter, *The Competitive Advantage of Nations* (London: Macmillan, 1990).
G. Ritzer, *The McDonaldization of Society* (London: Sage, 1993), 1.
G. Ritzer, "The McDonaldization Thesis: Is Expansion Inevitable?" *International Sociology*, 11:3 (1996), 299.
G. Ritzer, *The McDonaldization Thesis: Explorations and Extensions* (London: Sage, 1998), 71.
W. Ruigrok and R. van Tulder, *The Logic of International Restructuring* (London: Routledge, 1995).
J. Sachs, "Out of the Frying Pan into the IMF Fire," *Observer (Business section)*, 8 February, 1998.
H. Scullion, "Strategic Recruitment and the Development of the 'International Manager': Some European Considerations," *Human Resource Management Journal*, 3:1 (1993).

S. Segal-Horn, "Core Competence and International Strategy in Service Multinationals" in R. Teare and C. Armistead, (eds) *Service Management: New Directions, New Perspectives* (London: Cassell, 1995), 16.

T. Spybey, *Globalization and World Society* (Cambridge: Polity Press, 1996).

L. Sklair, *Sociology of the Global System* (London: Harvester Wheatsheaf, 1991).

L. Sklair, "Going Global – Competing Models of Globalization," *Sociology Review*, November (1993), 9.

K. Starkey and A. McKinlay, "Managing For Ford," *Sociology*, 28:4 (1994).

C. Strand, "Lessons of a Lifetime," Cornell Hotel and Restaurant Administration Quarterly, 37:3 (1996).

R. Thompson "Japan Accuses US and Europe of Widespread Trade Violations", *Financial Times*, 8 June 1992.

J. Tomlinson, "Full Employment and National Economic Management in the 1990s," *Renewal* 1:2 (1993).

R. Wade, "The Coming Fight over Capital Flows," *Foreign Policy*, Winter (1998–99), 47.

C. Warhurst, D. Nickson and E. Shaw, "A Future for Globalization? International Business Organization in the Next Century", in T. Scandura & M. Serapio (eds) *International Business and International Relations*, 7 (Conneticut: JAI Press, 1998).

M. Waters, *Globalization* (London: Routledge, 1995).

K. Williams et al, "Deconstructing Car Assembly Productivity," *International Journal of Production Economics*, 34 (1994).

K. Williams, *The Organisation of American Production*, mimeo, (Department of History, University of Wales at Cardiff, n.d).

J. P. Womack, D. T. Jones and D. Roos, *The Machine That Changed The World* (New York: Macmillan, 1990).

20

Internationalization of US Multinational Hotel Companies: Expansion to Asia versus Europe

Seoki Lee

1. Introduction

Internationalization has been a major expansion strategy for many US corporations including hotel companies. Some researchers argue that internationalization adds value to firms while others hold an opposite perspective. Financial economists have attempted to explain the phenomenon of internationalization for multinational companies (MNCs) using three main theories: internalization, imperfect capital market, and agency costs theory (Saudagaran, 2002). Mixed results appear in extant literature, and moreover, while financial literature on this particular issue acknowledges differing impacts from internationalization across industries (Mishra and Gobeli, 1998), mainstream financial literature fails to explore specific aspects of multinational hotel companies (MNHCs).

Therefore, this study explores and investigates internationalization issues of US MNHCs. More specifically, the study, first, investigates impacts of general internationalization of US MNHCs on firm value estimated by Tobin's Q. Second, the study compares two regions, that is, Asia and Europe to examine if internationalization of US MNHCs to Asian countries has different impacts on firm value than to European countries because the two markets exhibit

Source: *International Journal of Hospitality Management*, 27(4) (2008): 657–664.

different characteristics. Third, the study tests a curvilinear relationship of internationalization with firm value as proposed by Gomes and Ramaswamy (1999).

The study presents a literature review, followed by the variables and model specification sections. Hypothesis and data sections precede the results of the analysis. The final two sections provide implications and discussions of the results, and limitations and suggestions for future research.

2. Literature Review

Financial economists investigated and explored various internationalization issues regarding firm value by adopting and examining three main theories: internalization, imperfect capital market, and agency costs theory. In general, mixed results are still present in the literature. Moreover, full attention to the hotel industry with regard to this issue has been lacking.

The internalization theory argues that internationalization will add value to a firm if the firm has a competitive advantage with its intangible assets, such as patents, unique know-how or managerial skills (Caves, 1974; Dunning, 1980; Horst, 1972; Mishra and Gobeli, 1998; Morck and Yeung, 1991; Wolf, 1977). According to the theory, a firm can create value only when its competitive advantage from intangible assets exceeds costs of operating a foreign subsidiary. The literature has often used research and development (R&D) expenditure as a proxy for an intangible asset; however such expenditure does not frequently occur in the hotel industry. Further, perhaps, firm size is somewhat representative of intangible assets in broad terms, even though firm size may include more than just intangible assets. Therefore, while the internalization theory is not explicitly hypothesized and examined in this study, the implicit finding of the theory is further discussed in Section 9.

According to the imperfect capital market theory, a firm can enhance its value by offering a more diversified portfolio to its shareholders, created by expanding its operation abroad (Doukas and Travlos, 1988; Errunza and Senbet, 1981; Mikhail and Shawky, 1979). However, several studies argued against the theory by showing no difference in firm value when comparing domestic and MNCs (Brewer, 1981; Fatemi, 1984; Jacquillat and Solnik, 1978; Michel and Shaked, 1986; Morck and Yeung, 1991; Senchack and Beedles, 1980). The theory may not hold because investors might place an investment directly in an international portfolio, not in an internationally diversified multinational firm (Adler and Dumas, 1983). Findings of the current study may provide implicit evidence to (not to) support the theory by showing (not showing) positive impacts of internationalization on firm value.

Agency costs occur when a discrepancy in interest exists between shareholders and managers. In such situations, managers do not attempt to maximize shareholders' value by maximizing firm value, but seek benefits for themselves (Brealey and Myers, 2003). The theory applies to the internationalization issue. MNCs normally have more complex systems and hierarchies. Therefore, shareholders' monitoring of their managers becomes more difficult, thus, expectedly, incurring more agency costs in such a situation. If this argument holds, internationalization will reduce firm value by increasing the monitoring costs (Saudagaran, 2002). Eun et al. (1996) implicitly argued for the agency costs theory by showing that managers of UK companies often acquired US companies even when such projects had negative net present value. Findings of the current study may provide implicit evidence to support (not support) the agency costs theory by showing (not showing) negative impacts of internationalization on firm value.

In addition to the three main theories, the literature also discussed some interesting issues. Doukas and Travlos (1988) found that shareholders benefit more from firms' expansions to less developed countries than to more developed ones. This can occur, possibly, because shareholders only view expansion into a less developed country than the US as a value added strategy. In detail, Doukas and Travlos (1988) performed an event study by examining standardized cumulative abnormal returns (SCARs) of US bidding firms' stocks at the time of their acquisitions of foreign companies. The study divided the acquired foreign companies into two categories: companies in more developed or less developed countries, and used a dummy variable to investigate different impacts on SCARs.

The hotel industry has a long history in European countries compared to that of Asian countries. According to Doukas and Travlos (1988), this implies that a more established and developed system for the hotel industry is the expectation for European countries, and shareholders may expect more benefits from investing in MNHCs expanding more into Asian countries than into European countries. The setting for the hotel industry is different from that which Doukas and Travlos (1988) investigated. The current study does not perform an event study by examining SCARs, nor does it use a dummy variable to investigate such an issue. However, this particular issue undergoes examination by introduction of two separate independent variables into the current study's model. Further description appears in later sections.

Gomes and Ramaswamy (1999) argued for a curvilinear relationship between internationalization and firm value. They examined a curvilinear model and found that after the benefits of internationalization reached its optimum point, the effect became negative as the costs exceeded the benefits. However, a different curvilinear relationship is also possible. Before a certain point, internationalization may not create more benefits than the costs because initial costs of internationalization may be huge compared to its immediate benefits. However, after that certain point, the benefit may increase more than the costs, thus exceeding the costs. However, this is an empirical question, and the curvilinear relationship, regarding US MNHCs, is an examined component in this study.

Last, several multinational studies examined the industry effect on internationalization and found differences across industries. Therefore, several studies included the industry variable in the model to control for such an effect on firm value (Gomes and Ramaswamy, 1999; Buckley et al., 1977, 1984; Haar, 1989; Kumar, 1984; Mishra and Gobeli, 1998). The current study, however, does not include the industry variable in the model because the focus of the study is only on the hotel industry; and thus, the entire sample observation consists of hotel companies. No need exists to control for the industry effect in this situation.

3. Variables

This section presents and discusses dependent, main, and control variables included and examined in the study's model.

3.1. Dependent Variable

This study estimates and examines firm value as a dependent variable. Firm value is estimated by using Tobin's Q. Tobin's Q is the ratio of the market value of a firm to the replacement cost of its assets (Chung and Pruitt, 1994). Several multinational studies have used Tobin's Q as a proxy for firm value (Christophe, 1997; Christophe and Pfeiffer, 2002; Mishra and Gobeli, 1998; Morck and Yeung, 1991), and the current study follows the literature in estimating firm value. Tobin's Q (Q) is defined as

$$Q = \frac{(MVE + PS + DEBT)}{TA},$$

where Q is the Tobin's Q; MVE the market value of the firm's equity; PS the firm's preferred stock liquidating value; $DEBT$ the value of the firm's short-term liabilities net of short-term assets, plus the book value of the long-term debt; and TA is the book value of the firm's total assets.

3.2. Main Variables

Of four main, explanatory variables, the first two main variables are the internationalization variable ($MNHC\%$) and its squared form ($MNHC\%^2$). $MNHC\%$ is proportionate levels of international operations of a firm compared to its total operations, representing the level of internationalization. $MNHC\%^2$

is the square of MNHC% for an examination of a curvilinear relationship between internationalization and firm value. The variable is defined as

$$MNHC\% = \frac{MNHC_F}{MNHC_T},$$

where $MNHC_T$ is the number of total properties and $MNHC_F$ is the number of properties operated in foreign countries.

The other two main variables are EP% and AP%. EP% (AP%) is a proxy for the proportionate amount of the firm's levels of international operations in European (Asian) countries. These variables are included and analyzed to examine different impacts of internationalization to two regions, Asian and European countries. The variable is defined as

$$EP\%(AP\%) = \frac{MNHC_{E(A)}}{MNHC_F},$$

where $MNHC_{E(A)}$ is the number of properties operated in European (Asian) countries and $MNHC_F$ is the number of properties operated in foreign countries.

The number of total properties and properties operated in foreign countries are used to estimate the four main variables due to data availability. The main challenge of this study is data limitation. The study originally searched for the number of properties and rooms through annual reports filed with the Securities and Exchange Commission (SEC), and foreign and domestic sales data through *Compustat* database to estimate internationalization. Most of the data the study could collect is the number of properties, thus its use for the current study.

3.3. Control Variables

The model includes two control variables in this study: size and leverage. Market capitalization (*SIZE*) measures firm size, and its inclusion in the model controls for any systematic size-related impacts on firm value. The size variable estimate arises from multiplying stock price by the number of outstanding shares on the last day of each year. The other control variable is leverage (*LEVERAGE*), measured by debt-to-equity ratio, to control for any variation in the firm's capital structure (Mishra and Gobeli, 1998). While multinational studies normally include an industry variable in the model to control for possible industry effects on firm value (Gomes and Ramaswamy, 1999; Buckley et al., 1977, 1984; Haar, 1989; Kumar, 1984; Mishra and Gobeli, 1998), as discussed in Section 2, the current study focuses only on the hotel industry, thus does not include such a variable in the model.

4. Model Specification

The study develops and tests five models for investigating various internationalization issues for US MHNCs. The five models regress firm value *(Q)* for various combinations of four main and two control variables. Accordingly:

Model 1:
$$Q = \alpha_0 + \alpha_1 MNHC\% + \alpha_2 SIZE + \alpha_3 LEVERAGE + \varepsilon,$$
Model 2:
$$Q = \beta_0 + \beta_1 MNHC\% + \beta_2 MNHC\%^2 + \beta_3 SIZE + \beta_4 LEVERAGE + \varepsilon,$$
Model 3:
$$Q = \chi_0 + \chi_1 MNHC\% + \chi_2 EP\% + \chi_3 AP\% + \chi_4 SIZE + \chi_5 LEVERAGE + \varepsilon,$$
Model 4:
$$Q = \omega_0 + \omega_1 MNHC\% + \omega_2 MNHC\%^2 + \omega_3 EP\% + \omega_4 AP\% + \omega_5 SIZE + \omega_6 LEVERAGE + \varepsilon,$$
Model 5:
$$Q = \lambda_0 + \lambda_1 EP\% + \lambda_2 AP\% + \lambda_3 SIZE + \lambda_4 LEVERAGE + \varepsilon,$$

where *Q* is the firm value estimated by Tobin's *Q* as defined in the variable section; *MNHC%* the proportional level of international operation of a firm compared to its total operation; *EP%* the proportional level of operation in European countries of a firm compared to its total international operations; *AP%* the proportional level of operation in Asian countries of a firm compared to its total international operations; *SIZE* the market capitalization estimated by number of outstanding shares multiplied by stock price; and *LEVERAGE* is the debt-to-equity ratio.

Model 1 is to examine the impact of general internationalization on firm value by using *MNHC%* as a main variable and controlling for firm size and capital structure. Model 2, additionally, includes $MNHC\%^2$ to investigate a quadratic relationship between internationalization and firm value. Models 3 and 4 analyze incremental impacts of internationalization expansion into each of the European (*EP%*) or Asian regions (*AP%*) after considering impacts of *MNHC%* and/or $MNHC\%^2$. Model 5 only includes *EP%* and *AP%* without *MNHC%* and $MNHC\%^2$. When the model includes $MNHC\%^2$, the difference between the average of *MNHC%* and *MNHC%* was calculated and squared so that multicollinearity can be controlled better (Chatterjee et al., 2000).

5. Hypothesis

This study proposes three general hypotheses:

H1. Internationalization of US MNHCs has a significant impact on firm value.

The study does not explicitly test the internationalization theory because hotel companies normally do not possess large intangible assets. If the imperfect capital market theory holds for MNHCs, internationalization will present a positive impact on firm value. If the agency costs theory holds, on the other hand, a negative impact will appear. The current study is exploratory in the sense that it does not support a particular theory and tests a non-directional hypothesis (H1).

H2. Internationalization has a significant curvilinear relationship with firm value.

The impact of internationalization may diminish after the level of internationalization passes a certain point, implying a curvilinear relationship with firm value as proposed by Gomes and Ramaswamy (1999). However, a reversed curvilinear relationship is also possible because the impact of internationalization may initially reduce firm value due to the potential costliness of initial expansion into foreign countries. After a certain point, however, internationalization may increase firm value because incremental costs, after the initial expansion stage, can be reduced substantially.

H3. Internationalization of US MNHCs into Asian regions will have a greater impact on firm value than internationalization into European regions.

According to Doukas and Travlos (1988), shareholders would benefit more when MNCs expand their operations to less developed countries compared to more developed ones. Many European countries are more developed than Asian countries. Also, because the hotel industry has a longer history in European countries than in Asian countries, a more established and developed system is expected in European countries, and thus, shareholders may expect more benefits from investing in MNHCs expanding into Asian countries than expanding into European countries.

6. Data

Data collection is from two sources: (1) primary financial databases (CRSP and *Compustat*) and (2) first-hand from companies' annual reports (10Ks). The 10Ks provide the number of properties operated in US, foreign, European, and Asian countries. CRSP (center for research in security prices) is the source for all stock prices, and collection of the majority of other annual financial data is from the *Compustat* database. However, for the year 2006, hand-collection from 10Ks was necessary because *Compustat* was not yet updated. The sample period is from 1997 to 2006.

7. Empirical Results

The most significant limitation of this study is its small sample size. The reason for this is that US MNHCs began to provide the information required for this study, in relatively recent years. The initial total sample size is 45 after thoroughly evaluating all annual reports of all publicly traded US hotel companies. Six observations were eliminated because of negative book equity values used to calculate book-to-equity ratio. Therefore, the final sample size for Models 1 and 2 is 39 as presented in Table 1. However, for Models 3, 4, and 5, the final sample size is 25 because 14 observations did not disclose the number of properties operated in European and Asian countries. The total number of hotel companies included in the sample is five as shown in Table 1. Hilton is not included in the sample because Hilton Corporation had operated only domestic properties until it completed acquisition of Hilton International early in 2006. On February 23, 2006, Hilton acquired Hilton Group, PLC including its subsidiary of Hilton International Corp. Sample observations of 39 and 25 are subsequently used for main statistical analyses.

Table 2 presents descriptive statistics of variables used in the study. Total number of properties operated by a firm (TP) ranges from 39 (Four Seasons)

Table 1: Sample companies[a]

Company	Sample size	
	Models 1 and 2	Model 3, 4, and 5
Starwood	8	8
Intercontinental	4	4
Choice	4	0
Marriott	14	4
Four Seasons	9	9
Total	39	25

[a]Starwood, Intercontinental, and Four Seasons provide aggregate information for Europe and Asia-Pacific, not for individual countries. For Choice, Asian countries consist of Japan, China, Australia, Indonesia, Malaysia, Singapore, India, and New Zealand. For Marriott, Asian countries consist of Japan, China, Guam, Indonesia, Malaysia, Singapore, India, Pakistan, Philippines, South Korea, Thailand, and Vietnam.

Table 2: Descriptive statistics[a]

Variable	N	Mean	S.D.	Minimum	Maximum
TP	39	1626	1 383	39	4392
FP	39	363	342	15	1148
USP	39	1263	1091	20	3244
EP	25	154	131	4	441
AP	25	77	54	11	162
PERF	39	$471.62	$371.72	$10.07	$1421
Q	39	1.8262	0.8280	0.6946	3.6350
MNHC%	39	31.11	18.17	5.12	64.38
SIZE	39	$6245.49	$4595.96	$594.86	$18,586.94
LEVERAGE	39	1.6467	1.4733	0.2102	6.6155

[a]All data is at a firm level; TP, total number of properties operated; FP, number of properties operated in foreign countries; USP, number of properties operated in US; EP, number of properties operated in European countries; AP, number of properties operated in Asian countries; PERF, firm performance estimated by operating income before extraordinary items, depreciation and amortization; Q, firm value estimated by Tobin's Q; MNHC%, internationalization estimated by dividing FP by TP; SIZE, firm size estimated by market capitalization (= stock price x number of shares outstanding); and LEVERAGE, capital structure estimated by debt-to-equity ratio.

to 4392 (Choice) with a mean value of 1626. The number of properties operated in foreign countries by a firm (FP) ranges from 15 (Four Seasons) to 1148 (Choice) with a mean value of 363 while the number of US properties (USP) ranges from 20 (Four Seasons) to 3244 (Choice) with a mean value of 1626. The number of European properties (EP) ranges from 4 (Four Seasons) to 441 (Marriott) while the number of Asian properties (AP) ranges from 11 (Four Seasons) to 162 (Choice), out of total sample size of 25. Firm value (Q), estimated by Tobin's Q as defined in Section 3.1, has a minimum of 0.6946 and maximum of 3.6350. Percentage of internationalization (MNHC%) ranges from 5.12% (Marriott) to 64.38% (Four Seasons) with a mean value of 31.11%. Firm size (SIZE), estimated by market capitalization, ranges from $594.86 to $18,586.94 (in millions of USD), while capital structure (LEVERAGE), proxied by debt-to-equity ratio has a maximum (minimum) of 6.62 (0.21).

Before performing the main analysis, three plots were drawn (see Figs. 1–3). Fig. 1 shows plots of internationalization and Tobin's Q of the total sample. The plot is quite clearly U-shaped with a turning point around 0.40 of internationalization. This plot generally suggests that internationalization has a U-shaped relationship with firm value proxied by Tobin's Q. This means that internationalization from the lowest point to approximately 40% shows a negative relationship with firm value while internationalization from 40% and higher positively impacts firm value. Fig. 2 presents plots of internationalization and Tobin's Q for the European sample. The plot does not show a particular trend, thus suggesting that internationalization to European countries does not have an impact on firm value. Fig. 3 shows plots of internationalization and Tobin's Q with the Asian sample. The plot appears linear, suggesting that internationalization to Asian countries positively impacts firm

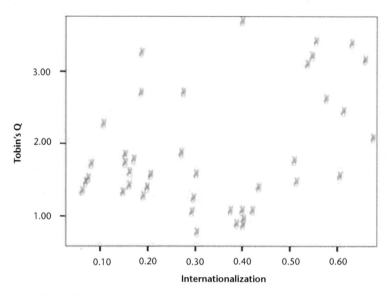

Figure 1: Plots of internationalization and Tobin's Q from the total sample

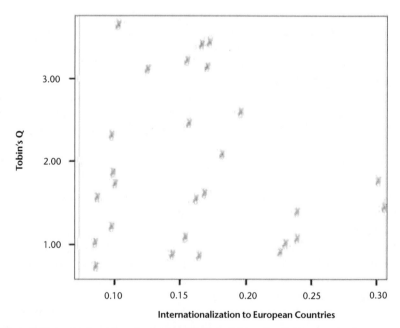

Figure 2: Plots of internationalization and Tobin's Q from the European sample

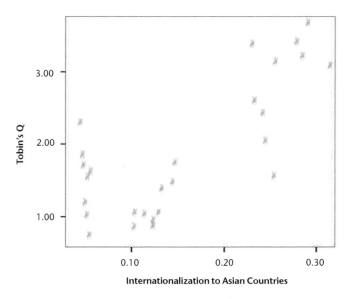

Figure 3: Plots of internationalization and Tobin's Q from the Asian sample

value. Even though the plots provide insightful information, all these suggestions are based on graphical plots, not statistical analysis. Performing a multiple regression analysis statistically tests the three main hypotheses, including the issues discussed above.

The results of the multiple regression analysis appear in Table 3. Model 1 investigates impacts of internationalization (*MNHC%*) on firm value (*Q*) controlling for firm size (*SIZE*) and capital structure (*LEVERAGE*), and suggests that the internationalization (*MNHC%*) does not have an impact on firm value (*Q*) with a t-value of 1.11. Only firm size shows a negative and significant impact on firm value (t-value = –2.98) at the 0.01 significance level. The results of Model 1 reject H1.

Model 2 adds $MNHC\%^2$ to Model 1 to investigate a curvilinear relationship between internationalization and firm value. *MNHC%* still does not show any significance, but $MNHC\%^2$ shows a positive and significant impact on firm value with a t-value of 2.30 at the 0.05 significance level. The findings suggest that a curvilinear relationship exists (i.e., U-shape) between internationalization and firm value, and accept H2. This confirms what Fig. 1 shows and suggests. Firm size consistently shows a negative and significant relationship with firm value while capital structure presents an insignificant impact on firm value in both Models 1 and 2.

Models 3, 4, and 5 examine internationalization issues regarding expansion to European (*EP%*) and Asian countries (*AP%*). Model 3 analyzes impacts of *EP%* and *AP%* with consideration of *MNHC%*, but without $MNHC\%^2$.

Table 3: Regression analysis with Tobin's Q
$$Q = \alpha_0 + \alpha_1 MNHC\% + \alpha_2 MNHC\%^2 + \alpha_3 EP\% + \alpha_4 AP\% + \alpha_5 SIZE + \alpha_6 LEVERAGE + \varepsilon$$

	Variable	Intercept	MNHC%	MNHC%²	EP%	AP%	SIZE	LEVERAGE
Model 1	Coeff.	5.36	0.93				−0.46	0.01
	t-value	3.39**	1.11				−2.98**	0.01
	VIF	0	1.96				1.82	2.04
	N				39			
	Adj. R² (%)				34.04			
Model 2	Coeff.	3.98	1.75	8.90			−0.37	0.07
	t-value	2.47*	2.01	2.30*			−2.49*	0.63
	VIF	0	2.35	1.20			1.93	2.21
	N				39			
	Adj. R² (%)				41.24			
Model 3	Coeff.	−4.85	0.64		−1.37	6.60	0.65	−0.64
	t-value	−2.05	0.79		−1.51	5.84***	2.44*	−3.24**
	VIF	0	1.96		3.62	2.95	6.94	1.46
	N				25			
	Adj. R² (%)				76.64			
Model 4	Coeff.	−4.45	0.20	11.18	−1.93	6.30	0.59	−0.31
	t-value	−2.15*	0.27	2.67*	−2.37*	6.38***	2.54*	−1.44
	VIF	0	2.07	1.74	3.88	2.99	7.01	2.24
	N				25			
	Adj. R²				82.34			
Model 5	Coeff.	−4.13			−1.49	6.62	0.60	−0.65
	t-value	−1.91			−1.69	5.93***	2.34*	−3.34**
	VIF	0			3.51	2.99	6.57	1.45
	N				25			
	Adj. R² (%)				77.08			

All data is at a firm level; Q, firm value estimated by Tobin's Q; MNHC%, internationalization estimated by dividing FP by TP where TP represents total number of properties operated and FP represents number of properties operated in foreign countries; EP%, internationalization to European countries, estimated by dividing number of properties operated in European countries by TP; AP%, internationalization to Asian countries, estimated by dividing number of properties operated in Asian countries by TP; SIZE, firm size estimated by market capitalization (= stock price × number of shares outstanding); and LEVERAGE, capital structure estimated by debt-to-equity ratio.
* Significance level of 5%.
** Significance level of 1%.
*** Significance level of less than 0.1%.

EP% shows a negative, but not significant impact while AP% shows a positive and significant impact on firm value (t-value = 5.84) at less than 0.0001 significance level. This supports the argument of Doukas and Travlos (1988) that shareholders benefit more when the internationalization involves a less developed region, and thus, supports H3. This also confirms what Figs. 2 and 3 show and suggest. Firm size shows a positive and significant impact (t-value = 2.44) while capital structure shows a negative and significant impact on firm value (t-value = −3.24). However, general internationalization (MNHC%) does not show any significant impact.

Model 4 inspects a curvilinear relationship (MNHC%²) between internationalization and firm value while simultaneously examining regional differences between European and Asian countries. The coefficient of EP%

becomes significant in Model 4 showing a negative impact on firm value (t-value = −2.37) while *AP%* consistently presents a positive and significant impact on firm value (t-value = 6.38). The results show that *MNHC%*^{2} has a positive and significant impact on firm value, suggesting a curvilinear relationship, while *MNHC%* does not show any significance (t-value = 0.27). The results still support H3. Other results show that firm size positively correlates with firm value while capital structure does not.

Fig. 2 alone suggests a non-relationship between internationalization and firm value. However, when the curvilinear relationship of general internationalization is controlled in Model 4, the statistical analysis suggests a negative relationship for European samples. Perhaps, Fig. 2 cannot show such a negative impact suggested by the regression analysis when the curvilinear relationship of general internationalization is controlled. This may be a limitation of a graphical presentation.

The last model, Model 5, excludes *MNHC%* and *MNHC%*^{2} from Model 4 to examine impacts of *EP%* and *AP%* without consideration for general internationalization impact. This analysis is conducted because a possibility exists that *EP%* and *AP%* already consider some aspect of general internationalization impact. The results suggest that *EP%* does not impact firm value, but *AP%*, again, positively impacts firm value at a less than significant level of 0.0001 (t-value = 5.93).

The models with *EP%* and *AP%* variables (Models 3, 4, and 5) explain more variations of firm value compared to the models with only *MNHC%* and *MNHC%* (Models 1 and 2), suggesting that Models 3, 4, and 5 are better specified than Models 1 and 2. The model that explains variations of firm value the most is Model 4, with all six explanatory variables, after consideration of different numbers of explanatory variables (adjusted R^2 = 82.34%). The model that explains the least is Model 1, with only *MNHC%* and two control variables (adjusted R^2 = 34.04%). The results also suggest no severe multicollinearity problem as none of variance inflation factors (VIF) exceed 10.

8. Implications and Discussion

According to the results from the main analysis, internationalization does not seem to have a significant impact on firm value for US MNHCs when examined alone. However, when using a curvilinear relationship for the examination, *MNHC%* still does not present a significant impact, but *MNHC%*^{2} shows a positive and significant impact on firm value. The findings suggest a curvilinear relationship between internationalization and firm value. This curvilinear relationship seems to suggest that until reaching a certain level of internationalization, expanding abroad does not enhance firm value (i.e., insignificant impact of $MNHC\%$), but after that level, internationalization begins to increase firm value (i.e., significant impact of $MNHC\%^2$), which is exactly opposite to what Gomes and Ramaswamy (1999) found. For a hotel business, initial cost may be greater than for other industries because hospitality is a capital-intensive industry and this difference could require more time for MNHCs to begin to realize benefits.

Further analysis on differences between expansion into European and Asian countries reveals that, first, inclusion of such variables ($EP\%$ and $AP\%$) increases the explanatory power of the model. For example, Model 4 with all six explanatory variables shows the highest adjusted R^2 of 82.34%. The analysis also finds that expansion into Asian countries benefits MNHCs in terms of firm value while expansion into European countries does not benefit or negatively impacts firm value of MNHCs. With consideration of expansion into European and Asian countries, a curvilinear relationship persists between general internationalization and firm value (i.e., significant impact of $MNHC\%^2$), suggesting that after a certain level of internationalization, general internationalization enhances firm value of MNHCs.

The findings of a curvilinear relationship between general internationalization and firm value support the recommendation that US MNHCs not rush to a conclusion immediately after expanding operations to foreign countries, but rather, take time to realize benefits because the findings show that the benefits will be realized after the internationalization level passes a certain point, not before that point.

Another important finding of this study is that expanding into Asian countries benefits US MNHCs while expanding into European countries does not benefit or negatively impacts firm value of US MNHCs. Strategically, US MNHCs may want to seek more opportunities to expand their foreign operations into Asian countries, or to even less developed countries, to enhance their firm value, but may want to remain cautious when considering expansion into European countries.

9. Limitations and Suggestions for Future Research

A major limitation of this study is its small sample size. As discussed previously in Section 8, the small sample size occurred because US MNHCs began to provide the required information for this study, only recently. However, this study did its best to collect as many sample observations as possible by thorough examination of all major US publicly traded hotel companies' annual reports (10Ks). A strong recommendation is to perform a follow-up study at a future date when more data becomes available.

For future research, a more rigorous analysis including data of regional areas other than Europe and Asia is recommended. However, data availability will be a major issue for conducting such a study because not many publicly traded hotel companies provide such data. Another interesting research topic will be to include franchising or branding issues in an internationalization study. Such a study will reveal more interesting and comprehensive findings of internationalization when considering other significant factors.

An additional thought regards the firm size variable. Perhaps firm size may represent intangible assets in a broad term even if it may include more than just intangible assets. If the size variable, in fact, represents intangible assets, by including the variable, the analysis controls for intangible assets. After controlling for intangible assets, the analysis still shows statistically significant curvilinear impacts of internationalization on firm value. Such findings may implicitly argue against the internalization theory. The internalization theory suggests that internationalization positively impacts firm value only if the firm possesses intangible assets. If after controlling for intangible assets, internationalization still impacts firm value, the theory does not hold. However, further research, such as considering the role of intangible assets in different markets with different levels of competition, is certainly necessary to shed more light on this issue.

Lastly, the two plots of internationalization and firm value with total and Asian samples do not show any high points. The two plots present a U-shaped, not a mound-shaped, relationship between internationalization and firm value. An empirical analysis provides the same result by consistently presenting positive and statistically significant coefficients of $MNHC\%^2$ and $AP\%$. However, that the positive impacts will remain indefinitely is difficult to believe, but examining such an issue is not feasible using the currently limited sample. Further investigation on this issue in the future with more sample observations is strongly recommended.

Acknowledgments

I thank the Center for International Business Education and Research (CIBER) at Temple University for their generous financial support. I also thank Jianan Chen who provided excellent research assistance.

References

Adler, M., Dumas, B., 1983. International portfolio choice and corporation finance: a synthesis. Journal of Finance 38 (3), 925–984.
Brealey, R.A., Myers, S., 2003. Principles of Corporate Finance, seventh ed. McGraw-Hill, New York.
Brewer, H., 1981. Investors benefits from corporate international diversification. Journal of Financial and Quantitative Analysis 16, 113–126.
Buckley, P.J., Dunning, J.H., Pearce, R.D., 1977. The influence of firm size, industry, nationality and degree of multinationality on the growth and profitability of the world's largest firms. Weltwirtschaftliches Archiv 114 (2), 243–257.

Buckley, P.J., Dunning, J.H., Pearce, R.D., 1984. An analysis of the growth and profitability of the world's largest firms 1972 to 1977. Kyklos 37 (1), 3–26.

Caves, R.E., 1974. Causes of direct investment: foreign firms' shares in Canadian and United Kingdom manufacturing industries. Review of Economics and Statistics 56, 279–293.

Chatterjee, S., Hadi, A.S., Price, B., 2000. Regression Analysis by Example, third ed. Wiley, New York.

Christophe, S.E., 1997. Hysteresis and the value of the US multinational corporation. Journal of Business 70, 435–462.

Christophe, S.E., Pfeiffer, R.J., 2002. The valuation of MNC international operations during the 1990s. Review of Quantitative Finance and Accounting 18 (2), 119–138.

Chung, K.H., Pruitt, S.W., 1994. A simple approximation of Tobin's Q. Financial Management 23 (3), 70–74.

Doukas, J., Travlos, N., 1988. The effect of corporate multinationalism on shareholders wealth: evidence from international acquisitions. Journal of Finance 43, 1161–1175.

Dunning, J.H., 1980. Toward an eclectic theory of international production: some empirical tests. Journal of International Business Studies 11, 9–31.

Errunza, V., Senbet, L., 1981. The effects of international operations on the market value of the firm: theory and Evidence. Journal of Finance 36, 401–417.

Eun, C., Kolodny, R., Scherega, C., 1996. Cross-border acquisitions and shareholder wealth: tests of the synergy and internationalization hypotheses. Journal of Banking and Finance 20, 1559–1582.

Fatemi, A., 1984. Shareholder benefits from corporate international diversification. Journal of Finance 39, 1325–1344.

Gomes, L., Ramaswamy, K., 1999. An empirical examination of the form of relationship between multinationality and performance. Journal of International Business Studies 30 (1), 173–188.

Haar, J., 1989. A comparative analysis of the profitability performance of the largest US, European and Japanese multinational enterprises. Management International Review 29, 5–18.

Horst, T., 1972. Firm and industry determinants of the decision to invest abroad: an empirical study. Review of Economics and Statistics 54, 258–266.

Jacquillat, B., Solnik, B., 1978. Multinationals and poor tools for diversification. Journal of Portfolio Management 4, 8–12.

Kumar, M.S., 1984. Growth, Acquisition and Investment. Cambridge University Press, Cambridge, UK.

Michel, A., Shaked, I., 1986. Multinational corporations versus domestic corporations: financial performance and characteristics. Journal of International Business Studies 17, 89–100.

Mikhail, A., Shawky, H., 1979. Investment performance of US-based multinational corporations. Journal of International Business Studies 10 (1), 54–66.

Mishra, C., Gobeli, D., 1998. Managerial incentives, internationalization, and market valuation of multinational firms. Journal of International Business Studies 29 (3), 583–598.

Morck, R., Yeung, B., 1991. Why investors value multinationality. Journal of Business 64, 165–187.

Saudagaran, S.M., 2002. A review of the literature on the market valuation of multinational firms. Managerial Finance 28 (3), 5–18.

Senchack, A., Beedles, W., 1980. Is indirect international diversification desirable? Journal of Portfolio Management 6, 49–57.

Wolf, B.M., 1977. Industrial diversification and internationalization: some empirical evidence. Journal of Industrial Economics 26, 177–191.

21

Research in Strategic Management in the Hospitality Industry

Michael D. Olsen and Angela Roper

The concept of strategy suggests that organizations seek alignment with the forces in their environment in order to achieve sustained performance. This effort is often referred to as the *co-alignment principle*. In abiding by this principle organizations scan the relevant environment of their business domain, develop competitive methods and grand strategies to take advantage of threats and opportunities in that domain and, allocate resources to the most appropriate competitive methods. If the organization is successful in this endeavor, it usually achieves its desired level of success.

As the definition of this activity implies, strategy making is a way of thinking that is contingent upon the forces driving change in a complex and dynamic industry. As such, the extensive number of variables to be studied and, the interdependencies among them, makes conducting research in this field extremely challenging. This challenge is further complicated by the industry setting in which this work is done. The industry is very fragmented, made up of hundreds of thousands of business units, and distributed across many countries. These units can be individually owned and/or parts of chains and management companies. This international fragmentation, coupled with a wide variety of brands and segments makes it very difficult to conduct large-scale studies that are designed to contribute important theoretical frameworks to enhance our understanding of this industry.

Source: *International Journal of Hospitality Management*, 17(2) (1998): 111–124.

1. Strategy: Conceptualisation and Empirical Evidence

The bulk of research to date in strategy in the hospitality industry has been of two types. Early work for the most part has been conceptual (Canas, 1982; Reichel, 1982, 1986; DeNoble and Olsen, 1982; Olsen and Bellas, 1980; Reid and Olsen, 1981; Olsen and DeNoble, 1981) as has some more contemporary work (Zhao and Merna, 1992; Nebel and Schaffer, 1992; Tse and West, 1992; Webster and Hudson, 1991; Slattery and Boer, 1991). This can best be described as strategy-related models, developed in other sectors, being applied to the hospitality industry without the actual conduct of empirical investigation. Anecdotal work is also present that focuses upon the analysis of specific companies (Langton et al., 1992; Hazard et al., 1992; Webster, 1994).

The second line of research activity has attempted to apply more empirical approaches to theory building. Utilizing the underpinnings of the work of Chandler (1962), Miles and Snow (1978) and Porter (1980) researchers such as Tse and Olsen (1988), West and Olsen (1989, 1990) and Dev and Olsen (1989), Crawford-Welch (1990) and Schaffer (1987) tested various hypotheses designed to investigate the relationships among strategy, environmental scanning and firm structure. Elwood-Williams and Tse (1995) demonstrated a further use of empirical methods in their investigation of the relationship between strategy and entrepreneurship in the US restaurant sector. Olsen et al. (1994) looked at the environmental scanning practices of chief executive officers of multinational hotel chains. These latter studies relied primarily upon survey research methods and while they represented rather rigorous attempts, unfortunately only achieved marginal success in contributing to the body of knowledge.

Recognizing that strategy is such a contingent process and the challenges of trying to define strategic typologies with large sample sizes, researchers most recently have begun to rely more frequently upon the use of case study methodology to assess strategy. These case studies have addressed such issues as: international development and modes of entry into new foreign markets (Zhao, 1992), strategy implementation (Schmelzer, 1992; Schmelzer and Olsen, 1994), and strategic alliances (Monga, 1996; Dev and Klein, 1993). These case study investigations have permitted in-depth analysis of several national and multinational hospitality firms. The bulk of these investigations was exploratory in nature and resulted in the formulation of propositions encouraging further research and theory building.

2. Competition and Competitive Advantage

Most recently strategy research has focused upon the types of competitive methods that firms use. A typology of competitive methods in the hotel industry has been developed by Murthy (1994) and, for the restaurant industry by Jogaratnam (1996). These studies have focused upon identifying a wide range of competitive methods and some have employed factor analysis to bring about a more parsimonious classification of methods to be used in further research. In these cases the investigations further explored the relationship between these typologies and firm performance. Significant results were obtained between the choice of competitive methods and firm performance.

In another study by Olsen (1995), the competitive methods of major multinational firms over a 10-year period were identified. Using content analysis methodology, attempts were made to demonstrate the relationships among broad environmental forces driving change, the choice and number of competitive methods chosen by each organization and, firm performance over the ten-year period from 1984 to 1994. The results of this research suggested that a relationship did exist but no rigorous testing of the proposed relationships was conducted. This study was also complemented by another study completed by Olsen (1995) who focused upon the business environment of the multinational hotel industry. This study utilized a series of nominal group sessions employing a modified Delphi technique. The sessions were conducted with senior level executives from all elements of the hospitality industry and were designed to identify the major forces driving change. The sessions took place at various locations in Europe, Asia and North America. Burgess, Hampton, Price and Roper (1995) have also looked at the factors underlying the success of international hotel groups.

The latest additions to the literature have focused upon the core competencies that firms have used to seek to obtain competitive advantage. Cho (1996) considered the role of information technology as a core competency in multinational hotel companies while De Chabert (1997) has looked at core competencies in three casual theme restaurant concepts in the US. In this case study, an attempt was made to see if firms are able to match what senior level managers consider as core competencies with what unit managers believe them to be. Brotherton and Shaw (1996) completed work towards the identification and classification of critical success factors in UK Hotels Plc., while Griffin (1994) attempted to ascertain the identity of critical success factors of yield management systems in lodging firms. Rispoli (1997) looked at competitive analysis and competence-based strategies in the hotel industry. Roberts and Shea (1996) characterized core capabilities in the hotel industry. Overall, the focus here has been to seek to identify what abilities within firms or industry sectors offer competitive advantage. While the work has been primarily case study and/or descriptive, little has been done to assess the relationships between these competencies and other constructs of the strategy paradigm.

3. Internationalization

There has been sustained industry and academic interest in the process of internationalization of business, as such it is an area of general strategic management research which is predicted to need further research development. To date the bulk of hospitality empirical work has been focused upon a national or regional domain, as illustrated in Table 1.

Less theoretical and empirical research has undoubtedly been undertaken into the internationalization of hospitality businesses, however, knowledge of the internationalization of the hospitality industry is slowing developing through increased academic inquiry into this vast area. Interestingly research is mainly concentrated in the internationalization of hotel groups. This may not be surprising since these types of hospitality firms were the first to develop significantly overseas. Numerous studies have aided in the general understanding of particularly the international hotel market, examples of these are illustrated in Table 2. However, although these analyses are mostly based on a numerical framework and the importance of growth in international travel, they have added little theoretical knowledge about internationalization. In addition, they are only partial, they often cover only one geographical area or international firms originating from one nation state or are limited to studying only publicly quoted corporations.

A number of authors have attempted to establish more hypothetical bases for the internationalization of hotel groups. The seminal work of Dunning and McQueen (1981, 1982), carried out in the late 1970s on behalf of the United Nations, explained the growth, distribution and forms of involvement of international hotel groups through the framework of the eclectic theory. More recently, Beattie (1991) and Litteljohn and Beattie (1992) have identified

Table 1: Examples of research into national or regional hospitality firms

Geographical focus	Types of hospitality firms	Authors (in date order)
United States of America	Lodging Firms:	Ingram and Baum (1997)
		Baum and Haveman (1997)
		Murthy (1994)
		Chon and Singh (1993)
		Schaffer (1987)
		Dev and Olsen (1989)
	Restaurant Firms:	Bradach (1997)
		Schmelzer (1992)
		West and Anthony (1990)
		West and Olsen (1988)
		Tse and Olsen (1988)
United Kingdom	Hotel Groups:	Phillips (1997, 1996)
		Roper (1995, 1992)
		Webster (1994)
		Clark (1987)
Portugal	Hotel Sector:	Costa and Teare (1994)
Italy	Hotel Sector:	Rispoli and Tamma (1995)

Table 2: Examples of articles on hospitality internationalization

Authors (in date order)	Focus
Go and Pine (1997)	Globalization in the hotel industry
Slattery (1997)	International expansion of quoted hotel chains in the USA, Europe and Asia
Olsen (1996)	Multinational firms in the lodging industry
Go and Pine (1995)	Globalization in the hotel industry
Moutinho et al. (1995)	International comparison of the development of the hotel industry
Gannon and Johnson (1995)	Emergence of Continental companies in the global hotel industry
Todd and Mather (1995)	International hotel industry and analysis of the leading industry players
Olsen et al. (1994)	Strategic planning in the multinational lodging industry
Clifton and Johnson (1994)	Structural analysis of the European hotel sector
Wise (1993)	Hotel chains originating from and developing in the Asia Pacific Rim
Slattery and Johnson (1993)	Development of quoted hotel companies in European Union countries
Litteljohn and Slattery (1993)	Evaluation of growth opportunities for quoted hotel companies in France, Germany, Italy, Spain and UK
Olsen (1993)	Globalization of North American hotel chains
Tse and West (1992)	Developmental methods employed by hospitality firms entering international hospitality markets
Litteljohn and Roper (1991)	Comparative assessment of internationalization strategies of hotel chains from late 1970s to early 1990s
Olsen et al. (1991)	Global hospitality industry of the 1990s
Slattery and Boer (1991)	Implications of structural demand trends on development of hotel companies internationally
Crawford-Welch and Tse (1990)	Mergers, acquisitions and strategic alliances in European hospitality industry

competitive groups of hotel companies in Europe, whilst Kim (1992) and Turnbull (1996) have explored political and financial risk factors affecting foreign investments by multinational lodging firms. The contextual focus of Kim's work was multinational firms from newly industrialized countries in Asia whilst Turnbull investigated multinational hotel companies developing in the Caribbean. John Dunning, this time with Sumit Kundu (1995), has re-examined some of the reasons for the increase in multinational activity in the hotel sector. Their empirical research is based upon the answer to a questionnaire completed in 1992 by 34 of the leading multinational hotel chains. Dunning and Kundu (1995, p. 104) evaluate this data utilizing the previously formulated 'eclectic paradigm' which answers the questions '*what, where* and *how*' do MNE hotels develop internationally.

There has also been significant research inquiry into the forms of expansion of international hospitality firms. Dunning and McQueen (1981) and Dave (1984), in particular, seemed pre-occupied with entry modes such as franchise, management contract and technical agreements and the doctoral work of Zhao (1992) focuses on the entry mode choices of multinational lodging firms in more contemporary times. Articles by Khan, Barge, Byrne in the same 1993 publication explain issues to do with international restaurant franchises, international management contracts and international hotel consortia, respectively.

There are clear directions for future internationalization research in the literature. Olsen and Merna (1993), for example, advocate that the hospitality firm is unique in that it must do business on a very local level even though it may be multi-national. Thus, it must address two sets of managerial challenges: those that exist from a multi-national perspective and those that exist at the local level. The particular character of the multinational hospitality firm implies that future research should investigate more closely unit- or operational-level strategies and structure. Another perspective on hospitality internationalization is forwarded by Alexander and Lockwood (1996), who advocate that joint research into the internationalization of the hotel and retail sectors will prove a rewarding and constructive means by which to develop understanding in the development of these two service sectors. The research being undertaken by Roper et al. (1997), which utilizes the concept of centricity or management orientation, will enable the examination of the internal decision-making process and the dynamics of this process within a sample of culturally diverse international hotel groups. Such qualitative and internal, in-depth analysis of the intended and implemented strategy of hospitality multinationals has for too long been avoided by strategic researchers and it is hoped that more research is carried out in this area in the future. Finally, one cannot assume that the research findings of studies into Anglo-Saxon firms, using Anglo-Saxon strategic frameworks are relevant to other regions of the world and to other firms with different operating backgrounds. As Whittington (1993, p. 9) states, "now more than ever, history and society matter to competitive strategy". The implications for strategic management research are therefore clear, because strategies reflect the social systems in which they are enacted, firms from different countries will vary in their characteristic approaches to strategy. Future hospitality strategic management research needs to investigate firms from other cultural foundations, whose objectives and context might be more complex than the simplicities of profit maximization and perfect markets. In addition, the use of alternative strategic management frameworks will be a necessity.

4. Research into Strategy Implementation

Strategic management textbooks related to the hospitality industry such as those written by Olsen, Tse and West (1992) and Knowles (1995) include chapters on strategy implementation and in the case of international hotel management literature the conceptual text by Go and Pine (1995) forwards implications for implementation in international firms. Eliza Tse (1988) also pragmatically assessed whether defining strengths and weaknesses is an essential part of strategy implementation. However, there has been very little research into strategy implementation as related to firms in the hospitality industry. Although there has been some work related to implementation, it has focused mainly on the impact of different entry methods (Zhao, 1992; Turnbull, 1996). Findings from these efforts related more to an investigation of growth strategies rather than tending to be developed into a fuller strategy implementation picture. However, more substantial research is beginning to appear in the implementation fields, for example, Okumus (1997) aims to investigate strategy implementation in international hotel groups, utilizing a qualitative methodology. Schmelzer's (1992) qualitative research is probably the only empirical research on strategy implementation as applied to the hospitality industry. For her primary research, a case study approach was taken incorporating a sample of different types of US multi-unit restaurant firms.

While many mainstream strategic implementation authors (e.g. Mintzberg, 1994; Heller et al., 1988) do not support the separation of strategy formulation and implementation, many authors in hospitality still continue to see the two as separate stages. While it may be argued that it is important to focus upon a narrowly defined unit of analysis, this approach contradicts the argument given earlier that strategy cannot be understood from such a narrow perspective.

Studying strategy implementation in the context of the co-alignment model is one area where hospitality researchers could really contribute to mainstream strategic management literature. It is also an area where it may be more realistic regarding research opportunities. For it is at the regional/divisional or unit level where strategy is most often operationalized (see Johns and Lee-Ross, 1996; Eccles et al., 1997; Olsen, 1991 for their different perspectives on the decentralization of strategic decisions). It is arguably easier for researchers to gain industry collaboration at these levels and because the context of investigation may be more manageable and controllable, the issues of implementation may be more simple to both detect and investigate. More challenging however, would be studying implementation at the unit level, in international firms, where the plural environment must be considered and sensitivity is needed to the diverse textures of different business systems.

5. Reflections and Thoughts for Future Research

Much of the research reported here has followed the patterns which were developed in the so-called 'classical approach'. It has focused upon the traditional constructs of the strategy paradigm such as environmental analysis (Brotherton and Leslie, 1991; Olsen et al., 1994; Costa and Teare, 1997a, b);

strategy formulation (Gannon and Johnson, 1995; Elwood-Williams and Tse, 1995; Murthy, 1994; Schaffer, 1987); strategic planning (Philips, 1996; Webster, 1994; Nebel and Schaffer, 1992) and the strategy–structure–performance relationship (Roper, 1995; Tse, 1991; Tse and Olsen, 1988; West and Olsen, 1989; Schaffer, 1986).

These mostly uni-dimensional views and research in strategy do reinforce the conventional wisdom found in the strategy literature throughout the West but are perhaps, a little naïve in the context of how strategy really functions in the competitive marketplace. While the classical view supports the belief that organizations succeed when they operate in states of stability and harmony and adapt intentionally to their environments (Stacey, 1996), contemporary strategic management literature attempts to offer a more dynamic viewpoint. It takes into account the fact that organizations tend to prosper in highly changeable environments when they sustain states of instability, contradiction, contention and creative tension in order to provoke new perspectives and continual learning (Hamel and Prahalad, 1994). Authors such as Stacey (1996, p. 19) advocate the applicability of extraordinary strategic management, defined as ". . . the use of intuitive, political, group learning modes of decision-making and self-organizing forms of control in open-ended change situations. It is the form of management that managers must use if they are to change strategic direction and innovate".

Hospitality researchers such as Edgar and Nisbet (1996) propose the use of the concept of chaos theory rather than long-term strategic planning as more pertinent to understanding the increasing complexities which surround hospitality organizations, especially small firms. Peng and Litteljohn (1997) suggest that the complexity of hotel organizations should be examined from a wider or different set of dimensions.

We believe that it is in this more contemporary and portentous direction that future research into strategy in the hospitality industry should proceed. This is more a reflection of the true state of nature and the dynamics and complexities surrounding the industry today. In contrasting this present scenario with the more naive approaches present in the literature today, the challenges ahead for researchers are many and exciting. Pursuing this direction is more complex requiring less prescriptive fine-grained research and favours more qualitative methods designed to reach deep into the internal workings of organizations. This will yield a more authentic, real-world view of strategy in the contemporary marketplace.

Even though one could argue that strategic management is one of the more pluralist disciplines researchers in hospitality management have been criticized for adopting research methods that revolve around a multi-disciplinary, rather than interdisciplinary framework (Edgar and Taylor, 1996). The illustration below perhaps highlights the difficulty in approaching research from the latter perspective.

In a research project investigating what makes a successful international hotel group (Roper et al., 1997) a team of four (representing two UK Universities) are drawn from the managerial disciplines of marketing, financial, human resource and strategic management. They firstly approached the study in a multi-disciplinary way; each member of the team reviewed the factors that were reported to lead to success in each of their respective disciplines. It was only upon discovering that a recurring theme in the literature was the concept of management orientation and its causal impact upon the success of international firms that the research objectives were then realigned in order that 'centricity' could become a conceptual unifying dimension. After almost three years, the resulting research framework is now more representative of an interdisciplinary approach and comprehensive primary research is being presently conducted worldwide.

The point that this illustration makes is that research in the strategic management field can reflect a more holistic and interdisciplinary perspective if researchers have the time and the colleagues to research with. However, there are often structural as well as socially embedded reasons why research collaboration may not be possible. If conceivable to accomplish however, there is far more to be gained in strategic management research if viewed holistically and an interdisciplinary approach can provide strategy researchers in hospitality with a real opportunity to contribute more universally. Further, the cross-cultural collaboration of researchers will allow for an evaluation of the transferability of strategic management and organizational practices.

6. Concluding Thoughts

Although we began by suggesting that strategy means alignment between firms and their contextual environment, we finish with the notion that the strategic concept is substantially more than just this. Rumelt et al. (1995) state that the subject matter of strategic management is 'the purposeful direction and natural evolution of enterprises' and is therefore central 'to the working of our civilization' (p. xi). Given its importance, although the literature on strategic management in the hospitality industry is developing rapidly much still needs to be done. Additional work should be conducted to further develop the relationships among the key elements of the co-alignment principle, not as independent investigations of each element but of synthesized views of how they interact in producing successful strategies. Further examination of the most appropriate research methodologies to be employed must also be done in order to match the most appropriate methods to the types of research problems needing answering. The global nature of the business must also be considered as a more mitigating variable in strategic decisions. Lastly, efforts must also turn to improved investigations on the concepts and skills that the future manager must possess in order to succeed in a more complex and dynamic environment.

As a final epitaph, whilst it is clear that there is scope for significant development in strategy research as applied to the hospitality industry, the extent of literature reviewed for this paper proves that the area is hardly 'embryonic' (an accusation made by Taylor and Edgar, 1996). Nevertheless, all hospitality researchers in strategic management do need to contribute more to the furtherance of theoretical knowledge, by providing new insights into mainstream strategic theories given their different industrial applications. Saying this, recent research by McGahan and Porter (1997) has emphasized that industry does matter. In their research these two scholars found that industry does have a powerful direct and indirect influence on profitability and that 'it would be misguided to disconnect the influence of organization from the industry and competitive contexts in which firms operate' (p. 30). In conclusion, there is real empirical evidence that it remains appropriate for us to be industry-specific strategic management researchers!

References

Alexander, N., Lockwood, A., 1996. Internationalisation: a comparison of the hotel and retail sectors. The Service Industries Journal 16 (4), 458–473.

Barge, P., 1993. International management contracts. In: Jones, P., Pizam, A. (Eds.), The International Hospitality Industry: Organizational and Operational Issues, Pitman, London, pp. 117–125.

Baum, J.A.C., Haveman, H.A., 1997. Love they neighbor? Differentiation in the manhattan hotel industry, 1898–1990. Administrative Science Quarterly 42, 304–338.

Beattie, R., 1991. Hospitality internationalization – an empirical investigation. International Journal of Contemporary Hospitality Management 3 (4), 14–24.

Bradach, J.L., 1997. Using the plural form in the management of restaurant chains. Administrative Science Quarterly 42, 276–303.

Brotherton, B., Leslie, D., 1991. Critical information needs for achieving strategic goals. In: Teare, R., Boer, A. (Eds.), Strategic Hospitality Management: Theory and Practice for the 1990s. Cassell, London, pp. 33–44.

Brotherton, B., Shaw, J., 1996. Towards an identification and classification of critical success factors in UK hotels plc. International Journal of Hospitality Management 15 (2), 113–135.

Burgess, C., Hampton, A., Price, A., Roper, A., 1995. International hotel groups: what makes them successful? International Journal of Contemporary Hospitality Management 7 (2/3), 74–80.

Byrne, A., 1993. International hotel consortia. In: Jones, P., Pizam, A., (Eds.), The International Hospitality Industry: Organizational and Operational Issues. Pitman, London, pp. 126–134.

Canas, J., 1982. Strategic corporate planning. In: Pizam, A., Lewis, R.C., Manning, P. (Eds.), The practice of hospitality management. AVI Publishing, Westport, CT, pp. 31–36.

Chandler, A.D., 1962. Strategy and Structure: Chapters in the History of the Industrial Enterprise. The M.I.T. Press, Boston, MA.

Cho, W., 1996. A case study: creating and sustaining competitive advantage through an information technology application in the lodging industry. Unpublished doctoral dissertation. Virginia Polytechnic Institute and State University, Blacksburg, Virginia.

Chon, K.S., Singh, A., 1993. Current economic issues facing the US lodging industry. International Journal of Contemporary Hospitality Management 5 (3), 3–9.

Clark, A., 1987. A comparative analysis of corporate structures of hotel groups in the UK. Unpublished MPhil dissertation, Huddersfield Polytechnic, Huddersfield, West Yorkshire, UK.

Clifton, W.J., Johnson, K., 1994. A structural analysis of the European hotel sector: a simple case of deja-vu?. International Journal of Contemporary Hospitality Management 6 (4), vii–viii.

Costa, J., Teare, R., 1994. Environmental scanning and the Portuguese hotel sector. International Journal of Contemporary Management 6 (5), 4–7.

Costa, J., Teare, R., 1997a. Environmental scanning: a tool for competitive advantage. In: Kotas, R., Teare, R., Logie, J., Jayawardena, C., Bowen, J. (Eds.), The International Hospitality Business. Cassell, London, pp. 12–20.

Costa, J., Teare, R., 1997b. A review of the process of environmental scanning in the context of strategy making. In: Teare, R., Farber Canziani, B., Brown, G. (Eds.), Global Directions: New Strategies for Hospitality and Tourism. Cassell, London, pp. 5–38.

Crawford-Welch, S., 1990. Empirical examination of mature service environments and high performance strategies within those environments: the case of the lodging and restaurant industries. Unpublished doctoral dissertation, Virginia Polytechnic Institute and State University, Blacksburg, Virginia.

Crawford-Welch, S., Tse, E., 1990. Mergers, acquisitions and alliances in the European hospitality industry. International Journal of Contemporary Hospitality Management 2 (1), 10–16.

Dave, U., 1984. US multinational involvement in the international hotel sector – an analysis. Service Industries Journal 4, 48–63.

De Chabert, J., 1997. Core competencies and competitive advantage in the casual theme restaurant industry: a case study. Unpublished doctoral dissertation, Virginia Polytechnic Institute and State University, Blacksburg, Virginia.

DeNoble, A., Olsen, M.D., 1982. The relationship between the strategic planning process and the service delivery system. In: Pizam, A., Lewis, R.C., Manning, P. (Eds.), The Practice of Hospitality Management. AVI Publishing, Westport, CT, pp. 229–236.

Dev, C., 1988. Environmental uncertainty, business strategy and financial performance: a study of the lodging industry. Unpublished doctoral dissertation, Virginia Polytechnic Institute & State University, Blacksburg, Virginia.

Dev, C., Klein, S., 1993. Strategic alliances in the hotel industry. Cornell Hotel and Restaurant Administration Quarterly 34 (1), 42–45.

Dev, C., Olsen, M.D., 1989. Environmental uncertainty, business strategy and financial performance: an empirical study of the U.S. Lodging industry. Hospitality Education and Research Journal 13 (3), 171–186.

Dunning, J.H., Kundu, S.K., 1995. The internationalization of the hotel industry – some new findings from a field study. Management International Review 35 (2), 101–133.

Dunning, J.H., McQueen, M., 1981. Transnational Corporations in International Tourism, United Nations Commission on Transnational Corporations (UNCTC), New York.

Dunning, J.H., McQueen, M., 1982. Multinational Corporations in the international hotel industry. Annals of Tourism Research 9, 48–63.

Eccles, G., Teare, R., Costa, J., 1997. The relationship between organizational structure and strategy. In: Teare, R., Farber Canziani, B., Brown, G. (Eds.), Global Directions: New strategies for Hospitality and Tourism. Cassell, London, pp. 39–65.

Edgar, D.A., Nisbet, L., 1996. A matter of chaos – some issues for hospitality business. International Journal of Contemporary Hospitality Management 8 (2), 6–9.

Edgar, D., Taylor, S., 1996. Strategic management research in hospitality: from slipstream to mainstream? Proceedings of 5th Annual CHME Research Conference. Nottingham Trent Polytechnic, Nottingham, U.K., 10–11 April, pp. 264–278.

Elwood-Williams, C., Tse, C-Y., 1995. The relationship between strategy and entrepreneurship: the US restaurant sector. International Journal of Contemporary Hospitality Management 7 (1), 22–26.

Gannon, J., Johnson, K., 1995. The global hotel industry: the emergence of continental hotel companies. Progress in Tourism and Hospitality Research 1, 32–42.

Go, F.M., Pine, R., 1995. Globalization Strategy in the Hotel Industry. Routledge, London.

Go, F.M., Pine, R., 1997. Globalization in the Hotel Industry. In: Kotas, R., Teare, R., Logie, J., Jayawardena, C., Bowen, J., (Eds.), The International Hospitality Business. Cassell, London, pp. 96–104.

Griffin, R.K., 1994. Critical success factors of lodging yield management systems: an empirical study. Unpublished doctoral dissertation, Virginia Polytechnic Institute and State University, Blacksburg, Virginia.

Hamel, G., Prahalad, C.K., 1994. Competing for the Future. Harvard Business School Press, Boston, MA.

Hazard, R., O'Rourke-Hayes, L., Olsen, M.D., 1992. Going global-acting local: the challenge of Choice International. In: Teare, R., Olsen, M.D. (Eds.), International Hospitality Management. Pitman, London, UK, pp. 91–94.

Heller, F., Drenth, P., Koopman, P., Rus, V., 1988. Decisions in Organization – A Three Country Comparative Study. Sage, London.

Ingram, P., Baum, J.A.C., 1997. Opportunity and constraint: organizational' learning from the operating and competitive experience of industries. Strategic Management Journal 18, 75–98.

Jogaratnam, G., 1996. Environmental munificence, strategic posture and performance: an exploratory survey of independent restaurant establishments. Unpublished doctoral dissertation, Virginia Polytechnic Institute and State University, Blacksburg, Virginia.

Johns, N., Lee-Ross, D., 1996. Strategy, risk and decentralisation in hospitality operations, International Journal of Contemporary Hospitality Management 8 (2), 14–16.

Khan, M., 1993. International restaurant franchises. In: Jones, P., Pizam, A. (Eds.), The International Hospitality Industry: Organizational and Operational Issues. Pitman, London, pp. 104–116.

Kim, C.Y., 1992. Development of a framework for identification of political environmental issues faced by multinational hotel chains in newly industrialized countries in Asia. Unpublished doctoral dissertation, Virginia Polytechnic Institute and State University, Blacksburg, Virginia.

Knowles, T., 1995. Corporate Strategy for Hospitality. Longman, Harlow, Essex.

Langton, B.D., Bottorff, C., Olsen, M.D., 1992. The strategy, structure, environment co-alignment. In: Teare, R., Olsen, M.D. (Eds.), International Hospitality Management. Pitman, London, pp. 31–35.

Littlejohn, D., Beattie, R., 1992. The European hotel industry: corporate structures and expansion strategies. Tourism Management 27–33.

Littlejohn, D., Roper, A., 1991. Changes in international hotel companies' strategies. In: Teare, R., Boer, A. (Eds.), Strategic Hospitality Management: Theory and practice for the 1990s. Cassell, London, pp. 194–212.

Littlejohn, D., Slattery, P., 1993. Macro analysis techniques: an appraisal of Europe's main hotel markets. International Journal of Contemporary Hospitality Management 3 (4), 6–13.

McGahan, A.M., Porter, M.E., 1997. How much does industry matter? Strategic Management Journal 18, (Summer Special ed.), 15–30.

Miles, R.E., Snow, C.C., 1978. Organization Strategy, Structure and Process. McGraw-Hill, New York.

Mintzberg, H., 1994. The Fall and Rise of Strategic Planning. Prentice Hall International, Hemel Hempstead.

Monga, R., 1996. Strategic alliances in the lodging industry: a multi-case study. Unpublished doctoral dissertation, Virginia Polytechnic Institute and State University, Blacksburg, Virginia.

Moutinho, L., McDonagh, P., Peris, S.M., Bigne, E., 1995. The future development of the hotel sector: an international comparision. International Journal of Contemporary Hospitality Management 7 (4), 10–15.

Murthy, B., 1994. Measurement of the strategy construct in the lodging industry and the strategy-performance relationship. Unpublished doctoral dissertation, Virginia Polytechnic Institute and State University, Blacksburg, Virginia.

Nebel, E., Schaffer, J.D., 1992. Hotel strategic planning at the business and unit level in the USA. In: Teare, R., Olsen, M.D.; (Eds.), International Hospitality Management. Pitman, London, pp. 228–254.

Okumus, F., 1997. An investigation into the strategy implementation process of international hotel groups, Workshop session. Proceedings of 6th Annual CHME Research Conference, Oxford Brookes University, Oxford, 2–3 April, pp. 244–245.

Olsen, M.D., 1991. Structural changes: the international hospitality industry and firm. International Journal of Contemporary Hospitality Management 3 (4), 21–24.

Olsen, M.D., 1993. Accommodation: international growth strategies of major US hotel companies. Travel and Tourism Analyst 3, 51–64.

Olsen, M.D., 1995. Into the New Millennium: The IHA White Paper on the Global Hospitality Industry: The performance of the Multinational Industry. International Hotel Association, Paris, 24pp.

Olsen, M.D., 1996. Events shaping the future and their impact on the multinational hotel industry. Tourism Recreation Research 21 (2), 7–14.

Olsen, M.D., Bellas, C.J., 1980. Managing growth in the 1980s: a blue print for food service survival. Cornell Hotel and Restaurant Administration Quarterly 21 (2), 23–26.

Olsen, M., Crawford-Welch, S., Tse, E., 1991. The global hospitality industry of the 1990s. In: Teare, R., Boer, A. (Eds.), Strategic Hospitality Management: Theory and practice for the 1990s. Cassell, London, pp. 213–225.

Olsen, M.D., DeNoble, A., 1981. Strategic planning in a dynamic environment. Cornell Hotel Restaurant and Administration Quarterly 21 (4), 75–80.

Olsen, M.D., Merna, K.M., 1993. The changing character of the multinational hospitality firm. In: Jones, P., Pizam, A. (Eds.), The International Hospitality Industry: Organizational and Operational Issues. Pitman, London, pp. 89–103.

Olsen, M.D., Murthy, B., Teare, R., 1994. CEO perspectives on scanning the global hotel business environment. International Journal of Contemporary Hospitality Management 6 (4), 3–9.

Olsen, M.D., Tse, E., West, J., 1992. Strategic Management in the Hospitality Industry. Van Nostrand Reinhold, New York.

Peng, W., Littlejohn, D., 1997. Managing complexity: strategic management of hotel chains, Proceedings of EuroCHRIE/IAHMS Conference. Sheffield Hallam University, Sheffield, 13–14 November, pp. 283–288.

Phillips, P.A., 1996. Strategic planning and business performance in the quoted UK hotel sector: results of an exploratory study. International Journal of Hospitality Management 15 (4), 347–362.

Phillips, P.A., 1997. A review of strategic planning and performance: challenges for hospitality managers. In: Teare, R., Farber Canziani, B., Brown, G. (Eds.), Global Directions: New strategies for hospitality and tourism. Cassell, London, pp. 67–104.

Porter, M., 1980. Competitive Strategy, Chapter 2. Free Press, New York, NY.

Quinn, J.B., 1980. Strategies for Change: Logical Incrementalism. Irwin, Homewood, IL.

Reichel, A., 1982. Corporate strategic planning for the hospitality industry: a contingency approach. In: Lewis, R.C., Beggs, T.J., Shaw, M., Croffoot, S.A. (Eds.), The practice of hospitality management II. AVI Publishing, Westport, CT, pp. 49–63.

Reichel, A., 1986. Competition and barriers to entry in service industries: the case of the American lodging industry. In: Pizam, A., Lewis, R.C., Manning, P. (Eds.), The Practice of Hospitality Management II. AVI Publishing, Westport, CT, pp. 79–89.

Reid, R., Olsen, M.D., 1981. A strategic planning model for independent food service operators. Journal of Hospitality Education 6 (1), 11–24.

Rispoli, M., 1997. Competitive analysis and competence based strategies in the hotel industry. In: Sanchez, R., Heene, A., Thomas, H. (Eds.), Dynamics of Competence Based Competition. Pergamon, London, pp. 119–137.

Rispoli, M., Tamma, M., 1995. Risposte Strategiche Alla Complessita: le forme di offerta dei prodotti alberghiere. G. Giappichelli Editore, Torino.

Roberts, C., Shea, L., 1996. Core capabilities in the hotel industry, Hospitality Research Journal 19 (4), 141–153.

Roper, A., 1992. Hotel consortia strategies and structures: an analysis of the emergence of hotel consortia as transorganizational forms. Unpublished doctoral dissertation, University of Huddersfield, Huddersfield, West Yorkshire, U.K.

Roper, A., 1995. The emergence of hotel consortia as transorganizational forms, International Journal of Contemporary Hospitality Management 7 (1), 4–9.

Roper, A., Brookes, M., Hampton, A., Price, L., 1997. Towards an understanding of centricity: profiling international hotel groups. Progress in Tourism and Hospitality Research 3 (3), 199–212.

Rumelt, R.P., Schendel, D.E., Teece, D.J., 1995. Fundamental Issues in Strategy: A Research Agenda. Harvard Business School Press, Boston, MA.

Schaffer, J.D., 1987. Competitive strategies in the lodging industry. International Journal of Hospitality Management 6 (1), 33–42.

Schaffer, J.D., 1987. Strategy, structure and performance in the lodging industry. Unpublished doctoral dissertation, Virginia Polytechnic Institute and State University, Blacksburg, Virginia.

Schmelzer, C., 1992. A case study investigation of strategy implementation in three multi-unit restaurant firms. Unpublished doctoral dissertation, Virginia Polytechnic Institute and State University, Blacksburg, Virginia.

Schmelzer, C., Olsen, M.D., 1994. A data based strategy implementation framework for companies in the restaurant industry. International Journal of Hospitality Management, 13 (4), 347–359.

Slattery, P., 1997. International development of hotel chains. In: Kotas, R., Teare, R., Logie, J., Jayawardena, C., Bowen, J. (Eds.), The International Hospitality Business. Cassell, London, pp. 30–36.

Slattery, P., Boer, A., 1991. Strategic developments for the 1990s: implications for hotel companies. In: Teare, R., Boer, A. (Eds.), Strategic Hospitality Management. London, pp. 161–165.

Slattery, P., Johnson, S.M., 1993. Hotel chains in Europe. Travel and Tourism Analyst 1, 65–80.

Stacey, R.D., 1996. Strategic Management and Organizational Dynamics. Pitman, London.

Taylor, S., Edgar, D., 1996. Hospitality research: the emperor's new clothes? International Journal of Hospitality Management 15 (3), 211–227.

Todd, G., Mather, S., 1995. The International Hotel Industry. The Economist Intelligence Unit Ltd., London.

Tse, E., 1988. Defining corporate strengths and weaknesses: is it essential for successful strategy implementation? Hospitality Education and Research Journal 12 (2), 57–72.

Tse, E., 1991. An empirical analysis of organizational structure and financial performance in the restaurant industry. International Journal of Hospitality Management 10 (1), 59–72.

Tse, E., Olsen, M.D., 1988. The impact of strategy and structure on the organizational performance of restaurant firms. Hospitality Education and Research Journal 12 (2), 57–72.

Tse, E., Olsen, M.D., 1990. Business Strategy and organisational structure: a case of US restaurant firms. International Journal of Contemporary Hospitality Management 2 (3), 17–23.

Tse, E., West, J., 1992. Development strategies for international markets. In: Teare, R., Olsen, M.D. (Eds.), International Hospitality Management. Pitman, London, pp. 118–134.

Turnbull, D., 1996. The influence of political risk events on the investment decisions of multinational hotel companies in caribbean hotel projects. Unpublished doctoral dissertation, Virginia Polytechnic Institute and State University, Blacksburg, Virginia.

Webster, M.M., 1994. Strategic management in the context at Swallow hotels. International Journal of Contemporary Hospitality Management 6 (5), 3–8.

Webster, M., Hudson, T., 1991. Strategic management: a theoretical overview and its application to the hospitality industry. In: Teare, R., Boer, A. (Eds.), Strategic Hospitality Management. Cassell, London, pp. 9–32.

West, J., Anthony, W.P., 1990. Strategic group membership and environmental scanning: their relationship to firm performance in the foodservice industry. International Journal of Hospitality Management 9 (3), 247–267.

West, J., Olsen, M.D., 1988. Environmental scanning and its effect upon firm performance: an exploratory study of the foodservice industry. Hospitality Education and Research Journal 12 (2), 127–136.

West, J., Olsen, M.D., 1989. Competitive strategies in food service: are high performers different? Cornell Hotel Restaurant and Administration Quarterly 31 (1), 68–71.

West, J., Olsen, M.D., 1990. Grand strategy: making your restaurant a winner. Cornell Hotel Restaurant and Administration Quarterly 31 (2), 72–75.

Whittington, R., 1993. What is Strategy-and does it Matter? Routledge, London.

Wise, B., 1993. Hotel chains in the Asia Pacific rim. Travel and Tourism Analyst 4, 57–73.

Zhao, J.L., 1992. The antecedent factors and entry mode choice of multinational lodging firms: the case of growth strategies into new international markets. Unpublished doctoral dissertation, Virginia Polytechnic Institute and State University, Blacksburg, Virginia.

Zhao, J.L., Merna, K., 1992. Impact analysis and the international environment. In: Teare, R., Olsen, M.D. (Eds.), International Hospitality Management. Pitman, London, pp. 3–32.

22
Choice between Non-Equity Entry Modes: An Organizational Capability Perspective

M. Krishna Erramilli, Sanjeev Agarwal and Chekitan S. Dev

Introduction

Non-equity modes, defined as modes that do not entail equity investment by a foreign entrant, are becoming increasingly popular among service firms for organizing overseas ventures/operations. Non-equity modes are especially popular among consumer-services firms (such as hotel and restaurant firms) as compared to professional-services firms (such as consulting firms) (Erramilli, 1990). Non-equity modes are essentially contractual modes, such as leasing, licensing, franchising, and management-service contracts (Dunning, 1988).

For many service firms desirous of entering foreign markets, an important question is not how to choose between different equity and non-equity modes but how to choose between different non-equity modes for organizing their operations in the foreign markets. While several previous studies have examined the choice between equity and non-equity modes for manufacturing (e.g., Gatignon and Anderson, 1988; Agarwal, 1994; Tse, Pan, and Au, 1997; Arora and Fosfuri, 2000; Pang and Tse, 2000) as well as service firms (e.g., Agarwal and Ramaswami, 1992; Erramilli and Rao, 1993; Fladmoe-Lindquist

Source: *Journal of International Business Studies*, 33(2) (2002): 223–242.

and Jacque, 1995; Erramilli, 1996; Contractor and Kundu, 1998a; Contractor and Kundu, 1998b), the extant literature does not offer a theoretically sound – and empirically corroborated – framework for how service firms could choose between different types of non-equity modes. The present study attempts to address this issue in the context of the multinational hotel industry. The reason for choosing this industry is that hotels are renowned for their use of non-equity modes (Contractor and Kundu, 1998b). In the hotel industry, non-equity modes account for 65.4% of multinational properties worldwide (Contractor and Kundu, 1998b). The two most commonly employed non-equity modes by the hotel industry are franchising and management-service contracts (MSC). Hotel firms typically do not make any equity investment in either of these modes, although some firms may combine non-equity arrangements with equity investments (Dunning, 1988). Although both franchising and MSCs are non-equity modes, there are important differences between them.

First, in franchising, the foreign entrant (the franchiser) receives royalties from the host-country collaborator (the franchisee) and supply-chain markups. In MSCs, the foreign entrant may receive some combination of royalties, supply-chain markups, management fees, and a share of profits. Second, under the franchising mode, the franchiser typically leases its brand name, and provides marketing support, technical advice and training, to the franchisee. However, the day-to-day involvement of the franchiser in the running of the franchised hotel property in the host country is rather minimal. Although many exceptions abound due to the manner in which franchising contracts are written, the franchiser typically enjoys some strategic control but relatively little operational control in most franchising agreements. In contrast, under MSCs, the foreign entrant not only leases its brand name to a host-country collaborator, but secures a contract to provide extensive onsite technical and management support. Its managers are assigned to the specific hotel property in the host country on deputation to run it on a day-to-day basis. They often enjoy complete *de facto* strategic and operational control (Contractor and Kundu, 1998b; Dunning, 1988). Such deputation of senior managers on a long-term basis, however, renders a MSC mode more expensive to operate relative to a franchising mode. Third, while franchising is not a pure arm's length market transaction, given the long-term and ongoing nature of the partnership (Shane, 1996), and MSCs are not pure hierarchical arrangements in the classical sense, it may be appropriate to treat franchising as a quasi-market transaction, and MSC as a quasi-internalized transaction (Contractor and Kundu, 1998a; Dunning, 1988; and Fladmoe-Lindquist and Jacque, 1995).

The purpose of this study is to develop a theoretical model to explain the choice between franchising and MSC, and to empirically test the model with data from hotel properties belonging to multinational hotel chains. Traditional international business theories have asserted that firms enter foreign host markets to exploit ownership advantages, presumably developed in their home markets or third-country markets (Dunning, 1988; Agarwal and Ramaswami, 1992). In doing so, they must choose a mode that affords them a higher degree of control. In the context of non-equity modes, entry modes are viewed as *conduits* for transferring resources and capabilities from a firm to its foreign venture; a role recognized by Root (1994), but not emphasized in entry-mode investigations. The theoretical underpinnings for the framework are rooted in the organizational capability (OC) perspective. The OC approach is more appropriate than the traditional international business theories (including transaction cost theory) because the choice between different types of non-equity modes is rooted in the *effectiveness of capability transfer*, not just concern for control. The paper does not wish to discuss the relative merits and demerits of the OC and transaction cost perspectives, a subject that has received excellent coverage in Kogut and Zander (1993) and Madhok (1997). In line with the general conclusions by these authors that the two perspectives complement each other, we draw on some transaction-cost and internalization arguments in the course of developing the hypotheses.

Theory and Hypotheses

Every firm is thought to be a bundle of resources and capabilities. Resources include all assets, organizational processes, firm attributes, information, and knowledge controlled by a firm that enable it to conceive and implement strategies efficiently and effectively (Barney, 1991). Capabilities refer to a combination of resources that creates higher-order competencies (Madhok, 1997). For example, brand reputation, customer base, and ability to create repeat business, can be viewed as independent resources which, when combined with organizational routines and technology in a judicious manner, could create a capability (say, "customer competence").

As mentioned earlier, the choice between MSC and franchising could be viewed as a choice between a quasi-internal mode and a quasi-market mode. Whereas franchising requires transfer of resources *across firm boundaries*, MSC involves transfer of capabilities *within firm boundaries*. Thus an understanding of the factors that affect these transfers would help us understand how firms choose between MSC and franchising. Five factors that affect these external and internal transfers are discussed below.

Imperfect Imitability

In line with the OC perspective, the present study defines value of a resource or capability in terms of its contribution to a firm's competitive advantage (Collis and Montgomery, 1995; Madhok, 1997). Obviously, when a firm enters a foreign market, it must transfer the resources and capabilities to its foreign operations. Consequently, a firm should choose an entry mode that can best transfer its resources or capabilities from the home country operations to the host country operations without eroding their value (i.e., without affecting the firm's ability to generate the desired competitive advantage). The question, therefore, is when does it make sense to transfer resources and capabilities via franchising (i.e., a quasi-market mode) and via MSC (i.e., a quasi-internal mode).

In line with the OC perspective, it can be argued that transfer of a resource or capability need not be internalized unless the resource or capability being transferred is *imperfectly imitable* (Madhok, 1997). When the foreign entrant's resource or capability is imperfectly imitable, the host-country collaborator is unable to absorb or replicate it and perform the needed activities without incurring a substantial loss in value (that is, loss in competitive advantage). Under such circumstances, the entrant undertakes internal transfer to preserve the value of the resource or capability.

Note that the traditional Resource Based View examines the problem of *competitors* imitating a firm's resources and capabilities and eroding its competitive advantage. The OC approach outlined here is more concerned with *collaborators* being able to imitate or replicate the foreign entrants capabilities in order to facilitate across-firm transfer. However, the underlying factors responsible for imperfect imitability are identical regardless of whether one is dealing with competitive or collaborative replication.

What causes imperfect imitability? Barney (1991) suggests that the unique historical paths, causal ambiguities, and complex social interactions that underlie creation of a firm's resources and capabilities render it difficult for other firms to imitate them. To other scholars, it is the tacitness of the resource that makes it difficult to transfer and imitate (Teece, 1998). Hu (1995) suggests that transfering tacit knowledge is difficult because it is complex, acquired through experience, and through trial and error, taught and learnt through demonstration, observation, imitation, practice and feedback, and continuously evolving. According to Kogut and Zander (1993), the less codifiable, less teachable, and more complex the knowledge is, the more difficult it is to replicate and transfer across firm boundaries.

From the perspective of the OC approach, imperfect imitability results from *embeddedness*, i.e., when the capability is deeply embedded within organizational routines and becomes specific to a firm (Madhok, 1997). Lam (1997) explains that embedded knowledge is not owned by any specific individual, but is embedded in complex social interactions and team relationships within an organization. It cannot be systematically coded and it can be transferred only through intimate social interaction. Furthermore, transfer of embedded knowledge requires the use of established routines and organizational processes. For these reasons, the OC perspective suggests that internal modes are more effective than market modes to transfer imperfectly imitable capabilities (Madhok, 1997). Note that internal and market modes are, perhaps, equally effective in transfering capabilities that are *imitable*. However, the additional costs and risks associated with internal modes may tilt the choice in favor of market modes. Recent studies that have empirically examined the choice between an equity-based internal mode, like wholly-owned subsidiary, and a non-equity based market mode, such as licensing, in the manufacturing sector (Hennart, 1987; Kogut and Zander, 1993; Arora and Fosfuri, 2000), have corroborated the expectation that firms favor internal modes (wholly-owned subsidiaries or joint ventures) when transferring tacit (i.e., imperfectly imitable) capabilities, and market modes (licensing) when transferring codified (i.e., readily imitable) capabilities.

One could extend these arguments to the choice between two non-equity modes. Both MSC and franchising could be equally effective in transferring *perfectly imitable* capabilities. However, as argued before, MSC is often associated with greater costs and risks than franchising. But it is unclear whether the difference in costs and risks between the two non-equity modes is as great as that between an equity and a non-equity mode. Consequently, one may not observe a clear choice between MSC and franchising when the capabilities being transferred are perfectly imitable. The ultimate choice under these circumstances may be contingent on the presence of other factors, such as the availability of managerial staff, development of franchising infrastructure in the host market, and the enforcement of intellectual property laws.

It should be noted that imperfect imitability, as described by the OC framework, is only one approach to sustain a firm's competitive advantage. The OC approach argues that it is the characteristics of these capabilities, principally their embeddedness, that makes them imperfectly imitable. But firms can protect their resources and capabilities through legal means as well, that is, through copyrights, trademarks, patents and licensing. In other words, firms can enjoy a sustainable competitive advantage even though their capabilities are classified as perfectly imitable. Not surprisingly, companies employing franchising show a great deal of concern for the presence and enforcement of intellectual property laws in the host markets. In short, sustainability is a broader concept than "imperfect imitability", as employed by the OC approach.

The transfer of *imperfectly imitable* capabilities would clearly favor MSC. Any attempted transfer of such capabilities to local franchisees may lead to serious value-erosion and loss of competitive advantage for the foreign entrant, for reasons described earlier. But the influence of these imperfectly imitable capabilities on modal choice depends upon the strength of the competitive advantage generated by them. When they do not generate value for the firm, they may not be transferred to the host market, and are not likely to influence the firm's choice of entry modes. On the other hand, when these capabilities are critical to the firm's competitive advantage, they will dominate modal choice. Thus:

> **Hypothesis 1:** Greater the competitive advantage generated by "imperfectly imitable" capabilities, higher is the firm's probability of choosing a management service contract relative to franchising.

Availability of Management Capabilities in Host Market

In addition to the local firm's organizational capacity to replicate the foreign entrant's capabilities, the OC perspective stresses the role of supporting infrastructure within and outside the firm that may facilitate or impede the transfer (Hu, 1995; Madhok, 1997). For example, even if the core resources and capabilities could be transferred through market mechanisms, what happens if the host market lacks good management talent? Franchising becomes a sub-optimal mode to exploit the firm's advantages if host country franchisees lack adequate access to competent managerial staff. Rather than risk destroying the value of its capabilities under such circumstances, the firm may decide to use MSC in an effort to transfer critical managerial capabilities from home country to the host market. Thus:

> **Hypothesis 2:** Lesser the availability of qualified managerial staff in the host market, higher is the firm's probability of choosing a management service contract relative to franchising.

Availability of Investment Partners in Host Market

For management service contracts to become reality, there must exist qualified and trustworthy partners in the host market with complementary capabilities, that is, partners who can make the necessary capital investments (Dunning, 1988; Contractor and Kundu, 1998b). These complementary capabilities free up the foreign entrant to focus on managing the hotel. Lack of such qualified and trustworthy investment partners impedes establishment of MSCs. Thus:

> **Hypothesis 3:** Greater the availability of qualified and trustworthy investment partners in the host market, higher is the firm's probability of choosing a management service contract relative to franchising.

Development of Host Country Business Environment

As mentioned earlier, for effective transfer of resources and capabilities to occur, not only are its characteristics important, but the capabilities of the local collaborator are also important. Cohen and Levinthal (1990) underscore the importance of the "absorptive capacity" of receiving firms. Contractor and Kundu (1998a) argue that, generally speaking, franchising, as a system, is more developed and franchisees, as individual entities, are more capable in more developed countries than in less developed ones. They also note that the use of franchising in developed nations is promoted by the existence and enforcement of intellectual property laws. Based on this reasoning, they find that the propensity to franchise increases (in relation to company-run operations) as the host market becomes more developed. Extending this logic to the present study, it appears that franchising becomes more viable in relation to MSC when the host market business environment is more developed. Thus:

Hypothesis 4: Greater the level of development of the host country business environment, lower is the firm's probability of choosing a management service contract relative to franchising.

Cultural Distance of Host Country

Traditional entry-mode literature holds that firms minimize the high information costs associated with operating in culturally unfamiliar countries by seeking collaborative modes (Gatignon and Anderson, 1988; Agarwal, 1994). While no apparent relationship between sociocultural distance and modal choice has been found in the hotel sector (Contractor and Kundu, 1998a; Contractor and Kundu, 1998b), empirical evidence in the general service sector (Erramilli and Rao, 1993; Fladmoe-Lindquist and Jacque, 1995) and in the manufacturing sector (Gatignon and Anderson, 1988; Agarwal, 1994), supports the prediction that collaborative modes are preferred in culturally distant markets.

In general, all non-equity modes are collaborative because they necessarily involve a local partner. However, the role of the collaborator can shed some light on the degree and strength of the collaboration. Franchising involves a strong local collaborator who essentially manages the entire interface with local labor, suppliers, regulatory authorities, customers and the community. MSCs involve a sleeping or passive collaborator, and the interface with all external entities in the host market is the management company's responsibility. Consequently, while franchising resembles a joint-venture type collaboration, a MSC tends to have characteristics of a sole venture.

One of the OC arguments supports the traditional perspective on cultural distance, although for different reasons. According to this view, organization routines that are effective in the home country may not be so in the host market when high cultural distance exists. This impedes capability transfer *within firm boundaries* (Madhok, 1997). To prevent value erosion, firms must collaborate with host country entities whose routines are better adapted to the local conditions.

It must be noted that the relationship between cultural distance and ownership is far from certain. As Brouthers and Brouthers (2001) and Shenkar (2001) have noted, the empirical evidence is ambiguous, even contradictory. They cite studies that have found no relationship, positive relationship, as well as, negative relationship between cultural distance and the desire to establish collaborative modes.

Even the OC approach offers a very intriguing counterview. High socio-cultural distance could result in ineffective resource transfer *across firm boundaries* because of (a) a mismatch in the foreign entrant's and local collaborator's routines and capabilities, and/or (b) the local collaborator's lower absorptive capacity (Contractor and Kundu, 1998a; Madhok, 1997; Lam, 1997). Therefore, when cultural distance is large, the foreign entrant may actually prefer to internalize the transfer to preserve the value of its capabilities (and the resulting competitive advantage). However, given the preponderance of the evidence in favor of the collaborative modes, the following hypothesis is offered:

Hypothesis 5: Larger the cultural distance between home and host countries, lower is the firm's probability of choosing a management service contract relative to franchising.

Control Variables

Four firm-specific factors and one market-specific factor are included in the analysis to control for possible extraneous variation: (a) size of the foreign entrant, (b) international experience of the foreign entrant, (c) size of the subsidiary hotel property, (d) reputation of the foreign entrant in the host market, and (e) service-sensitivity of the hotel's target audience. The entry-mode literature predicts that the likelihood of establishing internal, company-run modes is *higher* for firms that are larger and more experienced, and have strong reputation (to prevent collaborators from free-riding). On the other hand, the likelihood of establishing internal, company-run modes, is *lower* for foreign entrants that establish larger subsidiaries (Gatignon and Anderson, 1988; Erramilli and Rao, 1993; Contractor and Kundu, 1998a; Contractor and Kundu, 1998b). Also, extraneous variation in modal choice could arise between hotels serving highly service-sensitive markets (in which customers are very particular about the quality of service they receive) and those targeting less service-demanding markets.

Interaction Effects

Following other entry-mode studies that have underscored the importance of interaction effects (Agarwal and Ramaswami, 1992; Erramilli and Rao, 1993), we propose to include some interaction effects in the model. One of the objectives is to understand how firms make tradeoffs when pulled in opposite directions. The specific interaction effects will be identified subsequently.

Methodology

Data Collection and Sample

A questionnaire was developed and pre-tested on a sample of 30 Hotel General Managers who attended an executive program at Cornell University. The questionnaire was modified based on their feedback. The questionnaire was mailed to managers of five hundred and thirty hotels belonging to the Global Hoteliers Club. A reminder was sent two weeks later and a second reminder was sent four weeks later with the copy of the questionnaire. Two hundred and one usable questionnaires were received. The response rate was a respectable 39 percent.

Thirty-eight non-respondents (hotels that did not respond even after the two reminders) were later faxed a short one-page form with some particulars about the background of the hotel and requested to complete the form and fax it back. Eleven hotels responded. Information provided by these hotels was compared with comparable data from the respondents. Also, the background information of the early respondents was compared to that of the late respondents (Armstrong and Overton, 1977). Taking these results together, it was concluded that non-response bias is negligible.

Respondents were asked to indicate the description that best captured the foreign entrant's involvement in their property. Based on the responses, entry modes other than pure franchising and pure management contracts were removed from the analysis, resulting in a sample of 139 observations. Table 1 summarizes the salient characteristics of the analysis sample. The vast majority of the respondents are General Managers of the hotels surveyed (which helps improve the quality of data). Also, there are 46 countries represented in the sample, assuring the representation of a diversity of environments.

Variables

The Appendix lists the variables and their measures used in the study. The primary dependent variable, *Y1, MODE* is assigned a value of 0 for franchising and 1 for MSC. Franchising accounted for 25.2% of the observations. The second dependent variable *Y2, INIMIT*, is used to identify imperfectly inimitable capabilities.

Variables Needed to Test H1: To test this hypothesis, one needs to identify the "imperfectly imitable" capabilities that drive a firm's competitive advantage. As defined by the OC approach, capabilities are combinations of resources and skills. Therefore, a list of 22 resources was drawn from a variety of sources: Chandler & Hanks' (1994) list of resources, the researchers' industry knowledge and interactions with hotel managers. Survey respondents were asked to rate the extent to which the foreign entrant enjoyed a competitive advantage in each of the 22 resources (1 = No advantage, 5 = Great advantage). Their responses were factor analyzed (using the principal components method with varimax rotation) resulting in five factors. This led to the identification of five capabilities for the foreign entrant. Organizational Competence (*X1, ORGCOMP*) embraces a range of organizational skills and resources that enable the hotel to compete better, such as corporate culture, empowerment, operating policies and procedures, and reservation systems.

Table 1: Salient characteristics of hotels in sample for analysis (N = 139)

(1)	Location of Hotel	
	➢ City Centre	63.3%
	➢ Suburban	9.4%
	➢ Airport	4.3%
	➢ Resort	21.6%
	➢ Miscellaneous	1.4%
(2)	Positioning of Hotel	
	• Luxury/5 Star	38.1%
	• Upscale/5 Star	30.9%
	• First Class/4 Star	27.3%
	• Others	3.6%
(3)	Mean Number of Hotels in Worldwide Chain = 351.6	
(4)	Mean Percentage of International Revenues for Parent = 57.4%	
(5)	Mean Number of Rooms Per Hotel Property = 359.2	
(6)	Mean Number of Employees Per Hotel Property = 420.4	
(7)	Number of Countries in Sample = 46	
(8)	Major Countries Represented in Sample	
	• China	10.8%
	• Australia	10.1%
	• Singapore	5.8%
	• USA	5.0%
	• Thailand	5.0%
	• Indonesia	4.3%
	• Canada	3.6%
	• Germany	3.6%
(9)	Developing versus Developed Country Representation	
	• Developing Countries	55%
	• Developed Countries	45%

Quality Competence (*X2, QUALCOMP*) includes skills and resources needed to offer high quality service and ensure customer satisfaction. Customer Competence (*X3, CUSTCOMP*) encompasses a variety of skills that help the hotel to create brand reputation, establish a customer base, and build customer loyalty. Entry Competence (*X4, ENTRCOMP*) taps the hotel's abilities to find good locations and to time its entry into a certain market. Physical Competence (*X5, PHYSCOMP*) captures the hotel's skills to design and build physical facilities that are of desirable quality, comfort and ambience.

We defined *imperfectly imitable* capabilities as those that contribute significantly to the "*inimitability*" of a hotel's overall competitive advantage. First, we created a variable called *INIMIT (Y2)*, which measures the perceived degree to which other firms can copy or imitate the foreign entrant's overall competitive advantage in the host market. This is not specific to individual capabilities, but represents a global measure of inimitability of the foreign entrant's competitive advantage, as perceived by the respondent. Although this variable measures imitation by competitors, it can be equally effective to explain imitation by host-country collaborators, because the underlying causes for imperfect imitability are identical, as argued above.

We regressed the five capabilities, described above, against *INIMIT*, and compared their standardized beta coefficients. The results are summarized in Table 2. The larger the coefficient, the more the specific competence contributes to the inimitability of the hotel's competitive advantage. Clearly, Organizational Competence (*ORGCOMP*) and Quality Competence (*QUALCOMP*) are not only statistically significant, but are also the largest contributors to *INIMIT*. In other words, the greater the competitive advantage generated from *ORGCOMP* and *QUALCOMP*, the more inimitable is the hotel's overall competitive advantage. On the other hand, Customer Competence (*CUSTCOMP*), Entry Competence (*ENTRCOMP*), Physical Competence (*PHYSCOMP*) are not statistically significant, suggesting that they do not contribute to the inimitability of the hotel's competitive advantage. Based on this evidence, we conclude that *ORGCOMP* and *QUALCOMP* represent capabilities that are *imperfectly imitable*.

To further test the validity of the above results, respondents were asked to rate each of the underlying 22 resources in terms of the difficulty of transferring them from the foreign entrant's operations to the local operation through franchising (1 = very easy to transfer, 5 = very difficult to transfer). Using this data, the mean difficulty of transfer was calculated for the five capabilities. Results reported in Table 2, generally support the expectation that *ENTRCOMP* and *PHYSCOMP* appear to be the easiest to transfer, while *QUALCOMP, CUSTCOMP* and *ORGCOMP* are more difficult to transfer via arms-length modes. This evidence supports the general thesis in this study that *imperfectly imitable* capabilities are more difficult to transfer via market mechanisms than the *imitable* ones.

Table 2: Capabilities and their characteristics (N = 139)

Capability	Regression results[a] for dependent variable = Y2, INIMIT Standardized Beta Coefficients[b]	Perceived degree of difficulty in transferring via franchising (1 = Very easy, 5 = Very difficult) Mean
Physical Competence PHYSCOMP	−0.04	2.61
Entry Competence ENTRCOMP	0.07	2.82
Customer Competence CUSTCOMP	−0.17	3.01
Quality Competence QUALCOMP	0.20[c]	3.29
Organization Competence ORGCOMP	0.27[d]	2.96

Notes: (a) Regression Model: F = 3.21 (p = 0.009), R^2 = 0.10.
(b) The larger the coefficient, greater is the capability's contribution to the inimitability of the hotel's competitive advantage.
(c) Two-tail test, significant at $p < 0.05$.
(d) Two-tail test, significant at $p < 0.01$.

Variables Needed to Test H2-H5: The Appendix provides a detailed description of the other variables used in the study. Where appropriate, the reliability coefficients are also reported. *MGMTAVAIL (X6)* measures the availability of managerial staff in the host market, whereas *PRTNRAVAIL (X7)* indicates the availability of investment partners in the host country. *BUSENV (X8)* represents the level of development of the host-country market, and *CULTDIST (X9)* captures the cultural differences existing between home and host countries, as perceived by the respondents. In order to examine the face validity of these measures, Table 3 compares means of these four variables for developed (OECD countries) and developing host countries. As expected, the means for *MGMTAVAIL, PRTNRAVAIL,* and *BUSENV* are larger for developed countries. The mean for *CULDIST* is lower for developed countries, since most of the hotel firms (foreign entrants) are from developed countries. This evidence provides considerable face validity for the measures.

Control Variables: *FIRMSIZE (X10)* measures the size of the hotel firm (i.e., the foreign entrant) in terms of the number of hotels in the chain worldwide, whereas *FIRMEXP (X11)* captures the firm's international experience in years. The size of the hotel property in the host market is captured by *HTLSIZE (X12),* and its reputation is represented by *HTLREPUTE (XI3).* Finally, the dergee to which customers in the host market are sensitive to high-quality service, is measured by *SRVCSENS (X14).*

Interaction Effects: Four interaction terms are included in the model to understand how firms make modal choices, particularly when pulled in opposite directions. First, the *ORGCOMPXBUSENV* interaction will answer

Table 3: Comparison of some research variables: Developed vs developing countries (N = 139)

Research variable	Developed countries (OECD countries) (N = 66) Mean values	Developing countries (All other countries) (N = 73) Mean values	F Test for difference in means
Availability of Management Staff MGMTAVAIL	3.03	2.18	24.9 (p = 0.000)
Availability of Partners PRTNRAVAIL	2.85	2.53	3.6 (p = 0.067)
Development of Business Environment BUSENV	4.23	3.03	87.9 (p = 0.000)
Cultural Distance CULTDIFF	3.32	4.08	14.2 (p = 0.000)

the question "will the firm serving developed markets prefer franchising (as posited in H4), even when its capabilities are imperfectly imitable (H1)?" Second, the *HTLREPUTEXPHYSCOMP* interaction will address the question, "Given the fact that imitable capabilities like *PHYSCOMP* may not, by themselves, discriminate well between non-equity modes, will combination with a contingent factor, like hotel reputation, do so?" Third, an answer to the question, "will the firm's preference for MSC when transferring Quality Competence become stronger in service-sensitive markets?" will be provided by the *QUALCOMPXSRVCSENS* interaction. Finally, the *QUALCOMPXHTLSIZE* intraction term is included to gain insights into the issue of transferring and managing capabilities to produce high-quality customer service for larger hotel properties. Extending the arguments made by some scholars (e.g., Shane, 1996), will the resultant problem of monitoring and controlling employees represent such a management challenge that the firm would sacrifice value and switch to franchising when host-country hotel properties are large?

Analysis and Results

The independent variables are standardized to mean zero and standard deviation one. The correlation matrix (not reported here due to space constraints] revealed that most of the correlations among the 14 variables are relatively small. Further, an examination of the variance-inflation factors (VIF) (which were calculated for all of the independent variables) reveals that most of these are close to 1. The largest VIF value is 2.15, which is well below the cut-off of 10 recommended by Neter, Wasserman, and Kutner (1985). The evidence suggests that multicollinearity is, perhaps, not a serious problem with this data.

Table 4 summarizes the results for two logistic regression models explaining the choice between franchising (MODE = 0) and MSC (MODE = 1). Model 1 reports the results for the main effects only, whereas Model 2 includes interaction effects as well. The hypotheses are evaluated based on Model 1 results, since the predictions involve main effects.

Hypotheses Testing: Model 1 enjoys good fit ($\chi^2 = 31.25$, p = 0.005). Note that a positive sign on a coefficient suggests that the likelihood of choosing MSC *increases* relative to franchising, and a negative sign implies that it *decreases*, as the value of the associated predictor increases.

As described earlier, Organizational Competence (*X1*) and Quality Competence (*X2*) have been identified as the *imperfectly imitable* capabilities. In Table 4, both coefficients are statistically significant with positive signs suggesting that the likelihood of MSC increases as the contribution to the firm's competitive advantage from these two capabilities increases. Incidentally, the three other capabilities, Customer Competence (*X3*), Entry Competence (*X4*) and Physical Competence (*X5*), which are *imitable* capabilities, do not have any impact on the choice between franchising and MSC. In combination, the results provide powerful support for H1. The statistically significant negative and positive coefficients for *MGMTVAIL* (*X6*) and *PRTNRAVAIL* (*X7*), respectively, suggest that the likelihood of choosing MSC relative to franchising *increases* as managerial talent becomes scarcer and

Table 4: Logistic regression results

Variable	Reference hypothesis	Model 1	Model 2
Dependent Variable: Y1, MODE (0 = Franchising, 1 = Management Service Contract)			
Intercept		1.503[d]	2.069[d]
Main Effects			
Organizational Competence (X1, ORGCOMP)	H1	0.593[c]	0.633[b]
Quality Competence (X2, QUALCOMP)	H1	0.417[a]	0.923[b]
Customer Competence (X3, CUSTCOMP)	H1	0.269	0.604[b]
Entry Competence (X4, ENTRCOMP)	H1	−0.227	0.037
Physical Competence (X5, PHYSCOMP)	H1	−0.216	−0.408
Availability of Managers (X6, MGMTAVAIL)	H2	−0.531[b]	−0.625[b]
Availability of Partners (X7, PRTNRAVAIL)	H3	0.364[a]	0.797[c]
Development of Business Env. (X8, BUSENV)	H4	−0.578[b]	−0.308
Cultural Distance (X9, CULTDIST)	H5	0.222	0.508[a]
Control Variables			
Size of Foreign Entrant (X10, FIRMSIZE)		0.325	0.631[a]
Intl. Experience of Foreign Entrant (X11, FIRMEXP)		0.065	0.279
Hotel Size (X12, HTLSIZE)		0.137	0.815[c]
Hotel Reputation (X13, HTLREPUTE)		0.134	−0.308
Service Sensitivity of Market (X14, SERVCSENS)		−0.347	−0.357
Interaction Effects			
ORGCOMP × BUSENV			0.653[c]
PHYSCOMP × HTLREPUTE			−0.896[d]
QUALCOMP × HTLSIZE			2.200[d]
QUALCOMP × SRVCSENS			1.270[d]
MODEL STATISTICS			
N		139	139
Model Chi-square		31.25	58.4
Probability		.005	.000
Classification Rate		78.4%	85.6%

Note: One-tail p-value: a = 0.10, b = 0.05, c = 0.01, d = 0.001.

investment collaborators become more abundant in the host country. These results support hypotheses H2 and H3, respectively. *BUSENV (X8)* has a significant negative sign, suggesting that franchising is preferred as the level of development of the host-country business environment is greater, as predicted by H4. *CULTDIST (X9)* is not a significant predictor, however, and so H5 has to be rejected.

Interaction Effects: The Model 2 results reveal that the four interaction terms are highly significant. Although interaction effects can be interpreted in more than one way, the following interpretations are offered in view of the questions raised earlier. First, although foreign entrants seem to generally prefer franchising as the host business environment becomes more developed, they switch to MSC when Organizational Competence, an imperfectly imitable capability, makes an increasingly greater contribution to their competitive advantage. Second, while Physical Competence, by itself, may not influence the selection of the franchising mode (because it is imitable), it can become a powerful predictor in conjunction with strong firm reputation. Third, the firm's proclivity to employ MSC with rising importance of the Quality Competence becomes stronger in larger hotels. Finally, the influence of Quality Competence on modal choice becomes stronger when the hotel's market tends to be service-sensitive.

Model 2 results also show that *CULTDIST* and *CUSTCOMP*, which were both insignificant in the main-effects only model, are significant with positive signs in the model including interactions. Evidently, the propensity for MSC is higher when cultural distance between home and host countries is higher. The propensity for MSC is also higher when the advantage generated by customer competence is higher.

Discussion and Conclusion

While a significant amount of research has been devoted to understanding the choice between equity and non-equity modes, relatively little is known about how firms choose *between different types of non-equity modes*. The paper attempts to address this gap in the literature. It describes a study of modal choices in 139 hotels based in 46 different countries. It develops several hypotheses, based largely on the Organizational Capability (OC) perspective, to explain the hotel firm's choice between a franchising and management service contract. Four out of the five hypotheses were strongly supported.

First, the significant, positively signed intercept term in both models (Table 4), supports the often-observed phenomenon that firms *intrinsically* prefer the internal, high-control mode (Gatignon and Anderson, 1988; Erramilli and Rao, 1993). This is an interesting piece of evidence that fails to support the transaction-cost contention that market modes are the *default* modal choice.

Second, the results provide strong support for the OC-based proposition that imperfectly imitable capabilities, like Organizational Competence and Quality Competence, cannot be transferred effectively through market modes (Madhok, 1997). Imperfect imitability not only protects the firm from its competitors, it thwarts efforts to transfer the needed capabilities to associates and collaborators in the host market, "forcing" it to adopt internal modes. This finding is generally consistent with studies demonstrating that difficult-to-codify tacit know-how is transferred internally (e.g., Kogut and Zander, 1993; Arora and Fosfuri, 2000).

On the other hand, the transfer of easy-to-replicate capabilities (e.g., Physical Competence) does not appear to directly influence non-equity modal choice since they can be transferred equally effectively by the internal non-equity mode (MSC) as well as the market non-equity mode (franchising). This is at variance with studies contrasting an internal *equity* mode (wholly-owned subsidiary) with a market *non-equity* mode (licensing), where the latter mode is clearly preferred when codified know-how is transferred (e.g., Kogut and Zander, 1993; Arora and Fosfuri, 2000). The finding, perhaps, suggests that the difference in transfer costs between non-equity modes is not large enough to produce unambiguous choices. However, the significant interaction between *PHYSCOMP* and *HTLREPUTE* sheds some light on the conditions under which clear choices could result when transferring imitable capabilities. While the transfer of Physical Competence, by itself, does not clearly favor any one mode, it unambiguously favors franchising when combined with a strong brand.

The *QUALCOMP* and *HTLSIZE* interaction is interesting in that it underscores the importance of scale effects on modal choice. Other scholars have observed that firms shift to collaborative modes when the scale of operation grows larger, either to reduce risks (Gatignon and Anderson, 1988) or to minimize management problems (Shane, 1996). Our result suggests that as Quality Competence (imperfectly imitable capability) becomes more important as a source of competitive advantage, the firm's desire for internal modes becomes even stronger as the size of the planned hotel property is larger. Evidently, the know-how needed to offer quality service becomes more complex (and even less imitable) as the hotel property expands in size, thus making MSC all the more necessary to transfer key capabilities to the host market.

The interaction between *QUALCOMP* and *SRVCSENS* highlights the interplay between internal capabilities and external market requirements, a noted strength of the resource-based and capability-based approaches (Collis and Montgomery, 1995). As the hotel's customers become more service-conscious and demand greater service, hotels stronger in quality competence become even more committed to internal modes like MSC.

The results also corroborate the OC contention that firms cannot exploit their advantages without the benefit of a whole range of internal and external support capabilities (Madhok, 1997; Hu, 1995). Franchising becomes more attractive as the availability of managerial staff (*MGMTAVAIL*) increases in the host market. When this external capability is scarce, firms have to make up for the shortfall through internal transfers (i.e., via MSCs). Similarly, the finding for *PRTNRAVAIL* implies that the MSC option becomes increasingly attractive with greater availability of reliable investment partners in the host market.

In addition to the *availability* of certain resources in the environment, the *effectiveness* of these resources is also critical. The result for *BUSENV* suggests that, as potential collaborators (e.g., franchisees) with high levels of competence and "absorptive capacity" become more abundant in the host market, entrant firms become more comfortable with franchising. This is generally consistent with findings reported by other researchers (Contractor and Kundu, 1998a; Fladmoe-Lindquist and Jacque, 1995). On the other hand, the interaction between *ORGCOMP* and *BUSENV* also emphasizes the fact that firms will be primarily driven by the transfer characteristics of their-advantage generating capabilities when making modal decisions. When these capabilities are imperfectly imitable, they not only shun franchising, but also become stronger advocates for MSC in developed markets (perhaps, to gain a bigger share of the revenue streams). In other words, while external support capabilities are important, modal choice appears to be primarily driven by internal capability considerations.

The non-significant result for *CULT-DIST* (perceived cultural distance between home and host countries) in Model 1 is in line with the results reported for hotels in Contractor and Kundu (1998a and 1998b). However, there may well be some confounding influences suppressing the relationship. When these are apparently removed in Model 2 (most likely due to the strong interaction terms), the effect becomes significant and positively signed. Apparently, the preference for internal modes, like MSC, *increases* (relative to collaborative modes) as cultural distance becomes larger. Obviously, this contradicts findings on cultural distance in traditional entry-mode studies (e.g., Gatignon and Anderson, 1988; Agarwal, 1994), but is quite consistent with one of the OC perspective's arguments that internal modes may be more effective in culturally distant markets because differences in partner capabilities and routines make transfers across firm boundaries ineffective (Madhok, 1997).

None of the control variables apparently has any direct impact on modal choice. It is worth noting that firm characteristics, like size of the foreign entrant, size of the host country property, the entrant's international experience and brand reputation, all of which have been found to significantly influence choice between different types of equity modes and between equity and non-equity modes (e.g., Gatignon and Anderson, 1988; Agarwal and Ramaswami, 1992; Contractor and Kundu, 1998b), apparently have no direct influence on the choice between non-equity modes. Firms are seemingly indifferent to costs and risks associated with the two non-equity modes.

The present study is perhaps the first empirical study exclusively focused on the choice between different non-equity modes. It is also one of a few recent attempts to examine a mode's *effectiveness in transferring capabilities* as the basis for explaining modal choice. The results help provide support and corroboration to the emerging OC framework. Madhok (1997) identifies the lack of measurement for key constructs, like imperfect imitability, as a stumbling block for development of the OC perspective. The procedure outlined here to identify capabilities characterized by imperfect imitability is a useful step forward in alleviating this problem.

Although the study focuses on the hotel industry, its key findings are generalizable to non-equity modal choices in other service industries and in manufacturing firms. In a more general sense, they are relevant to any modal choice, equity or non-equity, as long as one is able to frame the choice as a contrast between internal and market-based modes. The ideas that capabilities generating competitive advantage influence modal choice, that imperfectly imitable capabilities push firms towards internal modes, and that the availability of a support infrastructure is critical to the type of mode chosen, are all universally applicable to any OC-based explanation of entry-mode choice.

Future research could aim to further improve the measures discussed in this study. Also, a wider range of non-equity modal choices could enrich the analysis. Replications in other industry settings would obviously serve to test the generalizability of these findings.

Note

The authors thank Jeff Weinstein of the Global Hoteliers Club and Vikram Mujumdar for their assistance in this research, and acknowledge the support of the summer research program of the Cornell School of Hotel Administration. The authors also acknowledge the comments of the three anonymous reviewers who provided valuable guidance.

References

Agarwal, Sanjeev. 1994. Socio-cultural Distance and the Choice of Joint Ventures: A Contingency Perspective. *Journal of International Marketing,* 2(2): 63–80.

―――― & Sridhar N. Ramaswami. 1992. Choice of Foreign Market Entry Mode: Impact of Ownership, Location, and Internalization Factors. *Journal of International Business Studies,* 23(1): 1–27.

Anderson, Erin & Hubert Gatignon. 1986. Modes of Foreign Entry: A Transaction Cost Analysis and Propositions. *Journal of International Business Studies,* 17 (Fall): 1–26.

Armstrong, Scott J. & Terry S. Overton. 1977. Estimating Non-Response in Mailed Surveys. *Journal of Marketing Research,* 14(August): 396–402.

Arora, Ashish & Andrea Fosfuri. 2000. Wholly-owned Subsidiary Versus Technology Licensing in the Worldwide Chemical Industry. *Journal of International Business Studies*, 31(4): 555–572.

Barney, Jay. 1991. Firm Resources and Sustained Competitive Advantage. *Journal of Management*, 17(March): 99–120.

Brouthers, Keith D. & Lance Eliot Brouthers. 2001. Explaining the National Cultural Distance Paradox. *Journal of International Business Studies*, 32(1): 177–189.

Chandler, Gaylen N. & Steven H. Hanks. 1994. Market Attractiveness, Resource-based Capabilities, Venture Strategies, and Venture Performance. *Journal of Business Venturing*, 9(July): 331–349.

Chang, Sea Jin. 1995. International Expansion Strategy of Japanese Firms: Capability Building Through Sequential Entry. *Academy of Management Journal*, 38(2): 383–407.

Cohen Wesley M. & Daniel A. Levinthal. 1990. Absorptive Capacity: A New Perspective on Learning and Innovation. *Administrative Science Quarterly*, 35: 128–152.

Collis, David J. & Cynthia A. Montgomery. 1995. Competing on Resources: Strategy in the 1990s. *Harvard Business Review*, (July–August): 118–128.

Contractor, Farok J. & Sumit K. Kundu. 1998a. Franchising Versus Company-run Operations: Modal Choice in the Global Hotel Sector," *Journal of International Marketing*, 6(2): 28–53.

——— & ———. 1998b. Modal Choice in a World of Alliances: Analyzing Organizational Forms in the International Hotel Sector. *Journal of International Business Studies*, 29(2): 325–358.

Dunning, John H. 1988. *Explaining International Production*. London: Unwin Hyman.

Erramilli, M. Krishna. 1990. Entry Mode Choice in Service Industries. *International Marketing Review*, 7(5): 50–62.

———. 1996. Nationality and Subsidiary Ownership Patterns in Multinational Corporations. *Journal of International Business Studies*, 27(2): 225–248.

——— & C.P. Rao. 1993. Service Firms' International Entry Mode-choice: A Modified Transaction-Cost Analysis Approach. *Journal of Marketing*, 57(July): 19–38.

Fladmoe-Lindquist, Karin & Laurent L. Jacque. 1995. Control Modes in International Service Operations: The Propensity to Franchise. *Management Science*, 41(7): 1238–49.

Gatignon, Hubert & Erin Anderson. 1988. The Multinational Corporations' Degree of Control over Foreign Subsidiaries: An Empirical Test of a Transaction Cost Explanation. *Journal of Law, Economics, and Organization*, 4(2): 305–336.

Gomes-Casseres, Benjamin. 1989. Ownership Structures of Foreign Subsidiaries. *Journal of Economic Behavior and Organization*, 11: 1–25.

Hennart, Jean-Francois. 1987. A Transaction Costs Theory of Equity Joint Ventures. *Strategic Management Journal*. 9: 361–374.

Hu, Yao-Su. 1995. The International Transferability of the Firm's Advantages. *California Management Review*, 37(4): 73–88.

Kogut, Bruce & Udo Zander. 1993. Knowledge of the Firm and the Evolutionary Theory of the Multinational Corporation. *Journal of International Business Studies*, 24(4): 625–646.

Lam, Alice. 1997. Embedded Firms, Embedded Knowledge: Problems of Collaboration and Knowledge Transfer in Global Cooperative Ventures. *Organization Studies*, 18(6): 973–996.

Madhok, Anoop. 1997. Cost, Value and Foreign Market Entry Mode: The Transaction and the Firm. *Strategic Management Journal*. 18: 39–61.

Neter, John, William Wasserman, & Michael H. Kutner. 1985. Applied Linear Statistical Models: Regression, Analysis of Variance, and Experimental Designs, 2nd Edition. Homewood: Richard D. Irwin, Inc.

Pan, Yigang & David Tse. 2000. The Hierarchical Model of Market Entry Modes. *Journal of International Business Studies,* 31(4): 535–554.

Root, Franklin R. 1994. *Entry Strategies For International Markets.* New York: Lexington Books.

Shane, Scott A. 1996. Hybrid Organizational Arrangements and Their Implications for Firm Growth and Survival: A Study of New Franchisers. *Academy of Management Journal,* 39(1): 216–234.

Shenkar, Oded. 2001. Cultural Distance Revisited: Towards a More Rigorous Conceptualization and Measurement of Cultural Differences. *Journal of International Business Studies,* 32(3): 519–535.

Teece, David J. 1998. Capturing Value from Knowledge Assets: The New Economy, Markets for Know-How, and Intangible Assets. *California Management Review.* 40(3): 55–79.

Tse, David K., Yigang Pan, & Kevin Y. Au. 1997. How MNCs Choose Entry Modes and Form Alliances: The China Experience. *Journal of International Business Studies,* 28(4): 779–805.

Appendix: Variables Used in the Study

Y1 Non-Equity Entry Mode (MODE)
Takes value of 0 for franchising and 1 for management service contracts

Y2 INIMITABILITY of Competitive Advantage (INIMIT) $\alpha = 0.76$
6-item scale based on following question: Indicate the degree to which you agree/disagree with the following statements concerning your hotel's competitive advantage in this market. (1 = Strongly Disagree, 5 = Strongly Agree).
(a) It is difficult for our competitors to imitate us
(b) Our services are unique and nobody but our company can offer them
(c) It took us years to build our brand reputation – nobody can easily copy it
(d) Our advantages are embodied in the company and not in individuals– nobody can copy us by stealing our employees away from us
(e) We pre-empt our competitors by building our properties in prime locations.
(f) Nobody can copy our corporate routines, processes and culture

X1 Organizational Competence (ORGCOMP) $\alpha = 0.87$
6-item scale based on following question: Indicate the degree to which your parent company has competitive advantage in the following areas (1 = No Advantage, 5 = Great Advantage).
(a) Company culture
(b) Employee empowerment
(c) Information technology system
(d) Operating policies and procedures
(e) Quality of reservation system
(f) Establishing a chain operation

X2 Quality Competence (QUALCOMP) $\alpha = 0.92$
6-item scale based on following question: Indicate the degree to which your parent company has competitive advantage in the following areas (1 = No Advantage, 5 = Great Advantage).
(a) Quality of guest-contact staff
(b) Quality of managerial staff
(c) Ensuring service quality
(d) Ensuring customer satisfaction
(e) Teamwork among employees
(f) Providing appropriate services

X3 Customer Competence (CUSTCOMP) $\alpha = 0.83$
3-item scale based on following question: Indicate the degree to which your parent company has competitive advantage in the following areas (1 = No Advantage, 5 = Great Advantage).
(a) Creating brand reputation
(b) Creating customer base
(c) Creating repeat business

X4 Entry Competence (ENTRCOMP) $\alpha = 0.77$
2-item scale based on following question: Indicate the degree to which your parent company has competitive advantage in the following areas (1 = No Advantage, 5 = Great Advantage).
(a) Finding good locations
(b) Knowing the right time to enter

X5 Physical Competence (PHYSCOMP) $\alpha = 0.93$
4-item scale based on following question: Indicate the degree to which your parent company has competitive advantage in the following areas (1 = No Advantage, 5 = Great Advantage).
(a) Décor/design of physical properties
(b) Ambience/atmosphere of properties
(c) Comfort of physical facilities
(d) Quality of physical facilities

X6 Availability of Managerial Staff in Host Country (MGTAVAIL)
1-item scale based on responses to following statement measured as (1 = Very Low, 5 = Very High)
(a) Availability of qualified managerial staff in the host country

X7 Availability of Investment Partners in Host Country (PRTNAVAIL) $\alpha = 0.82$
2-item scale based on responses to following statements measured as (1 = Very Low, 5 = Very High)
(a) Availability of qualified local investment partners to parent company
(b) Availability of trustworthy local investment partners to parent company

X8 Attractiveness of Host Country Business Environment (BUSENV) $\alpha = 0.81$
3-item scale asking respondent to rate the business conditions in the host-country on 5-point scale (1 = Very Poor, 5 = Very Good)

(a) Political stability
(b) General business conditions
(c) Quality of infrastructure

X9 Cultural Distance Between Host & Home Countries (CULTDIST)
1-item scale based on responses to following statement measured as (1 = Very Small, 5 = Very Large).
(a) Differences in culture between this country and the parent's home country

X10 Size of the foreign entrant (FIRMSIZE)
Number of Hotels Worldwide in Chain. (Actual number reported by respondents).

X11 International Experience of the Foreign Entrant (FIRMEXP)
No. of Years Engaged in International Operations. (Actual number reported by respondents).

X12 Size of Subsidiary Hotel (HTLSIZE)
Number of Rooms in the Subsidiary Hotel in the Host Market. (Actual number reported by respondents).

X13 Reputation of Hotel's Brand in Host Country (HTLREPUTE)
1-item scale asking respondent to rate the reputation of the hotel's brand in the host country on 5-point scale (1 = Very Poor, 5 = Very Good)

X14 Service Sensitivity of Hotel's Customers (SRVCSENS) $\alpha = 0.71$
3-item scale asking respondent whether he/she agrees with the following statements on 5-point scale (1 = Strongly Disagree, 5 = Strongly Agree)
(a) Our customers belong to a very exclusive class whose needs are unique
(b) Our customers are very particular about the service they receive
(c) We would not succeed in this market without providing excellent service

23

Stock Market Reactions to Entry Mode Choices of Multinational Hotel Firms

Nicolas S. Graf

1. Introduction

As the hotel industry continues its global expansion, several organizational forms have appeared to be favored in entering foreign markets. Contractual agreements such as franchise and management contracts have for long been widespread means of entry (Dunning and McQueen, 1981). Joint-ventures, minority equity interests and wholly owned subsidiaries have also been used, yet to a lesser extent (Olsen and Zhao, 2000).

An increasing amount of studies have attempted to delve into the determinants of choice of entry modes in the hotel industry. For the most part, these scholarly endeavors have tried to provide answers to the questions of which mode is preferred, why it is preferred, and what determines that choice (e.g. Contractor and Kundu, 1998). These determinants appear to be well understood as the findings of these efforts consistently emphasized similar determinants, especially factors related the host country's risk profile and to the need for control over the assets and operations (e.g. Dev et al., 2002).

What is less clear at this stage is whether the association between these determinants and the chosen organizational form is actually related to the performance of the foreign operation. Indeed, little attention has been paid

Source: *International Journal of Hospitality Management*, 28 (2009): 236–244.

to the performance consequences of entry mode choices in the general management literature, and no study thus far has ever investigated such relationships in the context of the hotel industry.

As the hotel industry faces an increasingly competitive environment, especially for capital and growth opportunities (Olsen et al., 2007), improving upon our understanding of market entry strategies and their influence on firm performance appears to be an important undertaking. Based upon the current understanding of the determinants of entry mode choices, and the lack of research on the influence of such modal choices on performance, an initial attempt to investigate how investors value entry mode strategies in developed and developing countries appears to be a worthy task. Thus, the present research effort was designed to answer the following questions:

1. Are the entry mode choices in the international hotel industry different for developed and developing host countries?
2. Are the combinations of entry mode choices and the development stages of the host countries valued by investors?

2. Review of Literature

The advent of internationalization of business firms has sparked a fair amount of research on means of expansion in foreign markets. For the most part, studies on international development have attempted to investigate the determinants of entry mode choices (e.g. Blomstermo and Sharma, 2006). These efforts have essentially used theoretical arguments obtained from the general market entry literature (e.g. Dunning and McQueen, 1981), transaction cost economics (e.g. Anderson and Gatignon, 1986), the organizational capabilities theory (e.g. Chandler, 1992), or the agency theory (e.g. Shane, 1996) to explain such modal choices. A number of typologies have been suggested, but only a few works have tested the relationships between the mode of entry, its determinants, and the performance outcomes (e.g. Sharma, 1998).

A variety of organizational forms have been included in these studies, ranging from fully owned subsidiaries to licensing and franchising. Sharma (1998) suggested that entry mode strategies could be viewed along a continuum based on the degree of equity investment. Specifically, the range of entry modes can be encapsulated by the following five organizational forms (from the lowest level of equity investment to the highest): (1) licensing/franchising, (2) management service agreements, (3) joint-ventures, (4) partially owned subsidiaries, and (5) fully owned subsidiaries (Cateora and Graham, 1986).

2.1. Determinants of Entry Mode Choices

The choice between these organizational forms has been viewed as dependent on several factors. The initial works on the internationalization of business firms essentially concentrated on the choice between exporting goods from the home country and producing in the host country via foreign direct investment (FDI).

In these early works, a number of factors related to the host country, the companies themselves, as well as environmental conditions, have been presented as key determinants. McCarthy et al. (1993) surveyed 42 companies active in the former USSR, and reported that the entry mode choice (i.e. licensing versus FDI) was affected not only by the perceived level of risk, but also by the type of business activities carried in host nation. These findings were echoed by Shama (1995) who found that entry strategies were influenced by the perceived risks, companies past entry mode experience and activities, and perceived growth opportunities in the host market. The author also suggested that the timing of entry was an important consideration as the evolution of the host country's political and economic environment alters the risk–reward relationship, making some entry modes more adequate in later stages of the development than in earlier stages.

Root (1987) proposed a generic framework of the factors affecting entry mode decisions. He suggested that the modal choice of entry was contingent upon three major factor groups: (1) company factors, (2) host country factors, and (3) host country environmental factors. Company factors included the type of products or services, the technological intensity, and the firm's resources. Host county factors comprised variables such as market potential, degree of competition, production costs and the state of the labor market. Finally, the host country's environmental factors encompassed economic, political and socio-cultural factors in addition to the geographical distance to the home country.

Shama (2000) empirically investigated the relative importance of a number of these factors on the choice of entry mode made by U.S. multinational firms in eastern European countries. Based on the responses of executives from 101 U.S. companies to a mailed questionnaire, the author found that the economic outlook of the host country, the level of competition, the year of entry of the firm in the host market, as well as the type of activities performed by these firms were the most important factors influencing the choice of entry mode. Specifically, he found that, as firms become more experienced in a foreign market they tend to adopt more risky organizational forms and make additional equity investments. His results also suggested that the type of activities conducted affected the choice between exporting and licensing versus joint-ventures and partial or full ownership. In particular, the degree of interaction with the consumers appeared to play a major role as firms offering services with a high degree of interaction tended to favor more equity investment modes in an attempt to ensure strict control over the service process.

2.2. Transaction Cost Perspective

A number of studies have concentrated on transaction costs as primary factors affecting the entry mode choice. The transaction cost economics (TCE) analysis framework suggests that firms will select the modal choice that minimizes the sum of their production and transaction costs to enter in new markets (Williamson, 1975). These costs essentially refer to the expenses incurred for preparing and enforcing contractual agreements. Anderson and Gatignon (1986) formalized the TCE approach in their theory of choice of entry mode. The authors made a series of propositions linking the mode of entry choice to the specificity of the assets being operated or transferred abroad, the external uncertainty in the host country, the internal uncertainty related to operating the assets in a foreign country, and the "free-riding" potential of the foreign operation.

Several empirical efforts have been made to test these proposed relationships. Anderson and Coughlan (1987) surveyed firms in the semiconductor industry and investigated the extent to which the specificity of the assets transferred abroad dictated the choice of internalization versus externalization of the companies' distribution channels. Using logistic regression analysis, the authors found that high degrees of asset and product specificity were associated with highly integrated channels of distribution.

Contractor and Kundu (1998) used a number of TCE determinants in their study of the hotel industry. By means of mailed questionnaires, the authors surveyed 1131 hotel properties established in foreign markets. Using a generalized logit regression model, they investigated the determinants of choice between four entry modes: franchise, management contract, partly owned, and fully owned. The authors found that a majority of determinants were significantly different in the hotel industry than in manufacturing sectors. Yet, they also found similarities, principally with regards to the influence of external and internal uncertainties. Specifically, their results suggested that high external uncertainty, operationalized by a country risk index, favored the use of low equity involvement entry modes, such as franchising or management contracts. They also found that the low internal uncertainty, resulting from the control hotel chains could maintain over their key strategic assets, enabled hotel chains to expand without much equity investment. They argued that contractual relationships (i.e. franchise and management agreements) could effectively substitute for the increased control that normally results from equity involvement, and that the de facto control of the reservation systems and brand names sufficiently lowered internal uncertainties.

In their review of TCE studies on factors influencing entry mode choices, Zhao et al. (2004) examined the consistency of the results found in 38 TCE based studies on entry mode choice. The authors expressly considered the signs and significance of factors related to the four constructs of the TCE theory, which included variables such as the asset specificity, the country risk, the cultural distance, the international experience, and the advertising intensity. The results of their meta-analysis suggested a high degree of consistency amongst studies and with TCE theoretical arguments for the asset specificity construct. Findings on the influence of the other determinants were more ambiguous. The authors found high consistency when the modal choices were polarized (i.e. wholly owned versus licensing), but more conflicting evidences when intermediate modes (e.g. joint-venture, partly owned) were considered. They also found that a number of other factors not accounted for by the TCE theory moderated these relationships. For instance, they found that other industry and firm specific factors had an important moderating role.

2.3. Agency Theory Perspective

The TCE studies have for the most part attempted to investigate how firms were making the tradeoff between the risks and returns associated with various modes of entry under different circumstances captured by the specificity of the assets and the internal and external uncertainty. The notion of control has been viewed as one of the most critical elements to this tradeoff (Arora and Fosfuri, 2000). Yet, the TCE theory has not provided much detail about how organizations may actually implement effective control mechanisms though various organizational forms. Typical TCE studies have assumed that the internalization of foreign operations through high equity involvement was the prime means of control (Zhao et al., 2004). In contrast, agency theory has provided more complex explanations of how firms attempt to control the behaviors of the managers in charge of foreign operations. Specifically, the agency theory suggests that a number of organizational forms and agreements exists that enable firms to align managers and owners' goals (Shane, 1996).

The agency theory is based on the concept of a principal–agent relationship, where the principal (i.e. owner or parent company) hires an agent (i.e. the professional manager) to carry out the day-to-day operations of the business (Jensen and Meckling, 1976). One of the fundamental aspects of the agency theory is the notion of information asymmetry between the principal and the agent, and the consequent monitoring costs. Information asymmetry appears to be a particularly relevant concept in the entry mode choice as it considers not only the external and internal factors affecting the decision, but also the nature of the relationship between the participants in the home and host countries (Quinn and Doherty, 2000).

More specifically, the notion of information asymmetry has been viewed as an explanation to the increasing importance of franchising as a mode of international expansion in retail industries. Indeed, franchising has emerged as a special organizational form that combines the low level of risk of licensing and a fair amount of control normally exhibited by entry modes involving some degree of equity investment. The agency explanation of such low risk, yet high control form of organization resides in the fact that franchisees in the retail sector must commit a significant investment in assets that are specific to the business model and brand name of the franchisor (Lafontaine, 1992). Such investments make the franchisee's return on investment dependent on retaining the franchise agreement, which consequently forces him to align its business goals to those of the franchisor (who may terminate the contract if the franchisee does not comply with contract's terms). These theoretical arguments shed new light on the differences between apparently closely related entry mode choices which were not much differentiated by the TCE theory.

Despite the apparent theoretical appeal of the agency theory, only little empirical attention has been placed on the influence of agency costs on the determinants of organizational mode choices, and even fewer have investigated the entry mode choices. These efforts, principally conducted in the context of the hospitality industry, are discussed next.

2.4. Entry Mode Choices in the International Hotel Industry

The international hotel industry has been a fertile environment for research in the entry mode literature. Driven in part by the early work of Dunning and McQueen (1981), but also by the rapid international expansion of the major hotel chains and their use of all forms of entry, a number of scholars have empirically examined the determinants of entry mode choice in this industry context.

Dunning and McQueen (1981) investigated the reasons for, and patterns of foreign involvement in the international hotel industry using the eclectic theory of international production. The authors argued that the key determinants of entry mode choice were to be found in the ownership, location and internalization advantages (OLI). Specifically, the authors suggested that brand image was a crucial element in the ownership advantage of international firms, and that such intangible assets gave the international hotel chains an advantage over local firms when competing for international customers. They also posited that the issue of internalization was a prime determinant of entry. The traditional notion of internalization suggests that the importance of controlling the assets drives the amount of equity investment. In this view, high equity involvement is regarded as highly related to the degree of control of the assets. Yet, the authors suggested that, in the context of the hotel industry, international firms could preserve enough control over their key assets through the use of specific contractual agreements as opposed to direct equity investment.

Zhao and Olsen (1997) delved into the antecedent factors affecting the entry mode choices of multinational hotel firms. Using the case study approach, the authors collected data from multiple primary and secondary sources (including interviews and company documentation) for five of the world's major international hotel companies. They specifically attempted to identify the major dimensions considered by these companies when deciding on an entry mode. The authors were able to make 15 propositions related to these antecedents.

Notably, these findings suggested that hotel firms used predetermined entry mode choices, and then searched for an existing or new market that was well suited for their preferred entry mode choice. They also found that environmental factors related to the development stage of the target host were of the utmost importance, especially the taxation and repatriation aspects. In addition, the authors stressed the fact that hotel chains did not share their key assets (e.g. capacity management system) with host partners, thereby maintaining a total control over these assets, no matter what entry mode was selected. The authors also concluded that, in general, the most common entry modes were non-equity involvement via management contracts and franchise agreements. Additionally, the choice between these two organizational forms, and the wholly owned subsidiary mode, was suggested to be dependent on the development stage of the host country.

Dev et al. (2002) concentrated on the determinants of choice between franchising and management contract modes in the international hotel industry. The authors surveyed 201 managers of hotels belonging to the Global Hotelier Club, and tested a number of hypotheses related principally to arguments developed by the TCE, the agency theory and the organizational capabilities approach. In particular, they expected that "(1) the presence of irreproducible resources and capabilities favors management contracts over franchising agreements; (2) the availability of management resources in the host market favors franchising agreements over management contracts; (3) the availability of qualified local investment partners in the host market favors management contracts over franchising agreements; and (4) a highly deve-loped business environment favors franchising agreements over management contracts" (p. 96).

The authors found that most of their contentions were strongly supported. Their results indeed corroborated the arguments that franchise was the preferred mode when the operations could be codified and standardized, and when the host country was sufficiently developed and offered an acceptable degree of managerial capabilities. In contrast, when the resources and capabilities required at the property level were crucial to the brand's establishment and survival, and when the host country was less developed, hotel chains favored management contracts.

In a later study, Brown et al. (2003) argued that the theory of entry mode choices in the hotel industry needed to differentiate between the notions of ownership and control which have usually been treated as a single dimension in prior studies. The authors suggested that some of the conflicting results found in the context of the hotel industry could be explained by the fact that several low ownership modes (e.g. franchise and affiliated hotels with or without management contracts) could still provide strong control to the company in the home country over the assets and operations in the host country. The authors sent questionnaires to 558 hotel managers and received 124 usable responses. They tested their contentions by means of multinomial logistic regression. Their results provided strong support to the notion that ownership is not necessarily required to ensure the control of the key assets and capabilities in the hotel industry. They also found that the entry choice was dependent upon the ability of the firm to find qualified and trustworthy partners in the host country, which was seen as consistent with the influence of the development stage of the host country on the entry mode choice selection reported in several prior studies.

2.5. Entry Mode Choices and Performance

The extent of empirical research on the performance consequences of entry mode choices is extremely limited (e.g. Nitsch et al., 1996; Sharma, 1998; Woodcock et al., 1994). These studies showed significant performance differences associated with the various entry modes, especially between wholly owned subsidiaries and joint-ventures. Yet, with the exception of the works of Brouthers et al. (2003) and Lopez-Duarte and Garcia-Canal (2007), none of these studies has investigated the linkages between the determinants of entry mode choices and their subsequent performance levels.

Brouthers et al. (2003) attempted to fill this gap by studying the differences in performance of modes of entry based on the TCE theory and entry strategies not associated with TCE determinants. The authors surveyed 158 European firms and measured the performance and TCE-related variables using managers' perceptions. The authors classified the responding firms into two groups using probit analysis; a group of firms exhibited a good match between their entry mode choices and the TCE determinants, and a group with a lower fit. Then, they used OLS regression to test whether the fit was a significant predictor of ventures' performance. Their results suggested that the firms determining their entry strategies based on TCE arguments performed significantly better than the other firms. The authors acknowledged the fact that managers were not necessarily objective when providing information about entry mode choice determinants and performance, and they concluded that more research with more objective measures were required to validate their findings.

Lopez-Duarte and Garcia-Canal (2007) attempted to provide such validation by measuring the performance of entry mode choices using the event-study methodology. Specifically, the authors argued that, if a mode of entry was superior to another under certain circumstances, the investors would value it more. Thus, when an unexpected entry is announced, and when it is deemed as superior, the price of the stock of the company should increase more than expected. Using this reasoning, the authors tested the influence of a number of determinants and entry choices on the abnormal returns following the entry announcement. Their results suggested that the interaction effect between the entry mode and the location of the investment had the most influence on the abnormal returns. Yet, the authors did not conduct any cross-sectional test to statistically assess the abnormal returns' differences. Therefore, they could not establish any significant relationship between the entry mode, the determinants of entry mode, and the abnormal returns.

2.6. Synthesis and Hypotheses

The literature reviewed thus far emphasizes the role of a number of determinants in the entry mode choice decision. The essential tradeoff in that decision appears to be the weighing of the risks and returns associated with each organizational form in a given external and internal context. When retaining control of the assets and operations is vital, firms appear willing to commit some degree of equity investment even when the perceived risk level is high. Yet, when firms are able to maintain enough control over their key strategic assets and resources (e.g. distribution channels, corporate culture) without directly investing in the host country, other contractual arrangements are likely to be preferred, principally management contracts or franchising agreements. In the full service sector of the hotel industry, the choice between these two contractual agreements is then seen as dependent upon the extent to which the host country offers the managerial capabilities to properly operate the assets, as well as on the experience of the firm in dealing with these contracts.

The primary purpose of the present effort is to investigate the performance levels of entry mode choices in the hotel industry, or more specifically, the stock market reactions resulting from the entry mode announcements. As such, it is not the intent of this study to investigate all the determinants of choice. Rather, the study concentrates on testing hypotheses suggesting that some modes of entry are more valued by investors than other modes when they exhibit superior risk-adjusted returns' expectations. The risk-adjusted returns offered by the various entry modes have been presented as dependent on the alignment between the type of external environment in the host country, the nature of the assets, and the chosen organizational form. In order to simplify the potential sets of alignments, this study solely focuses on full-service hotels in an attempt to control for the nature of the assets and the complexity of the operations. Full-service hotels were defined as offering at least the following services: (1) full-service restaurant and bars, (2) room service, (3) turndown service, and (4) fitness center. This definition broadly corresponds to 3–5-star hotel classes of the Mobil Star Rating.

The development stage of the host country has been the most widely reported determinant of entry mode choice. Dimensions, such as external uncertainties (Anderson and Coughlan, 1987), political and economic risk (Zhao and Olsen, 1997), are examples of approaches taken to describe and differentiate host countries based on their degree of development (Zhao et al., 2004). Consequently, it is posited that the choice of entry mode varies as a function of the development stage of the host country. This hypothesis has already been tested in many settings, yet it is viewed as important initial step prior to investigating the performance consequences of the alignment between the development stage of the host counts and the mode of entry. Formally, the following hypothesis will be tested:

H1. The choice of mode of entry is dependent upon the development stage of the host country.

A number of studies have suggested that developing countries exhibited more economic and political risk than developed countries, and that they offered fewer managerial capabilities due to lower educational levels and less experience in international business (e.g. Contractor and Kundu, 1998). Dev et al. (2002) suggested that hotel companies would favor management contracts over other modes of entry in developing countries as they would not necessarily be able to find the necessary competencies in the host country. Alternatively, they argued that firms would prefer franchising in developed countries as they would be able to find the required managerial capabilities. Franchising would be preferred when competencies are available as it reduces the administrative and agency costs associated with management contracts and equity investment.

If these arguments hold true, the risk-adjusted return expectations for various entry mode choices should be dependent upon the fit between the entry modes and the development stage of the host country. In this case, investors should value entry mode announcements differently depending on the fit between the modal choice and the development stage of the host country. Therefore, we hypothesize that:

H2a. The Cumulative Abnormal Returns (CAR) following the announcements of entry mode choices depends on the interaction between the entry modes and stages of development of the host country.

Also, for the same reasons, management contracts in developing countries and franchise agreements in developed countries should exhibit higher risk-adjusted return expectations. If that is the case, then investors are likely to respond more positively to these announcements as opposed to other expansion-related announcements as demonstrated by Lopez-Duarte and Garcia-Canal (2007). Consequently, the abnormal returns following such announcements should be greater than those following other announcements involving other entry modes. Hence, it is hypothesized that:

H2b. The CAR following the announcements of expansion in developing countries is greater for the management contract entry modes than it is for other entry modes.

Whereas developing countries are expected to provide a low level of managerial capabilities and a high level of external uncertainties, developed countries are expected to exhibit opposite characteristics (Anderson and Coughlan, 1987). Under these contextual constraints, it has been suggested that the firms should favor some equity investment as opposed to contractual agreement, as it would facilitate the generation of higher returns with low external and internal uncertainties. Hence, in developed countries, it is hypothesized that:

H2c. The CAR following the announcements of expansion in developed countries is greater for the entry modes involving some equity involvement than it is for other entry modes.

Similarly, as developed countries offer more managerial capabilities than developing countries, the importance of the control of the operations and service processes is not crucial as other key assets may remain under the control of the parent company and serve as incentives to ensure the proper alignment between the managers in the host country and the corporation (Quinn and Doherty, 2000). Consequently, franchising is expected to offer a better risk-adjusted return potential than management contracts in developed countries. Therefore, the following hypothesis is made:

H2d. The CAR following the announcement of expansion in developed countries is greater for the franchising entry mode than it is for the management contract entry mode.

3. Methodology

3.1. Event Study Method

Estimating the stock market reaction to news announcements is typically achieved by conducting event studies, in which the signs and significance of the abnormal returns following the announcements are evaluated. The event study method relies on the assumption that the returns of individual stocks and portfolios of stocks can be predicted by measuring their relationships with the evolution of the market return (e.g. Ross et al., 2003). In this approach, the expected return of individual stock is estimated by Ordinary Least Square (OLS) regression and takes the following form:

$$E(R_{it}) = \alpha_i + \beta_i R_{mt} + \varepsilon_{it} \qquad (1)$$

where $E(R_{it})$ is the expected return of stock i at time t, β_i is the slope coefficient for stock i, R_{mt} is the market return at time t, α_i is a constant, and ε_{it} is the error term, which is assumed to be normally distributed with a mean of zero. Because the residuals are expected to be zero under normal conditions (and thus, producing normal returns), the effect of news announcements can be assessed by computing the residuals following the announcement, which are termed abnormal returns. These abnormal returns are calculated as follow:

$$AR_{it} = R_{it} - (\hat{\alpha}_i + \hat{\beta}_i R_{mt}) \qquad (2)$$

where AR_{it} is the abnormal return for stock i at time t, R_{it} is the actual return for stock i at time t, and $(\hat{\alpha}_i + \hat{\beta}_i R_{mt})$ is the expected return of stock i at time t using the parameters estimated by OLS and the actual return on the market at time t.

For a sample of firms, the abnormal returns are then averaged (Average Abnormal Returns; ARR) using the following formula:

$$AAR_t = \frac{\sum_{i=1}^{N} AR_{it}}{N} \qquad (3)$$

In order to test the significance of these AAR over a response window, the AAR are cumulated. The Cumulative Average Abnormal Returns (CAAR) are calculated as follow:

$$CAAR_{T_1,T_2} = \frac{\sum_{i=1}^{N} \sum_{t=T_1}^{T_2} AR_{it}}{N} \qquad (4)$$

As suggested by Berman et al. (2000) and Veraros et al. (2004), abnormal returns may exhibit cross-sectional dependence. When such dependence is suspected, Peterson (1989) advocated the standardization of the abnormal returns. The Standardized Abnormal Returns are calculated by

$$SAR_{it} = \frac{AR_{it}}{S_{AR_{it}}} \quad (5)$$

where $S_{AR_{it}}$ is the standard prediction error of the stock returns.

Standardized cross-sectional tests can then be performed to assess the significance of the abnormal returns over the response window. The test, reported in this paper as Patell (1976) Z test, is an adjusted version of the initial Patell test (Sanders and Robins, 1991). The standardized test for the null hypothesis CAAR = 0 is

$$z_t = \frac{\sum_{i=1}^{N} SCAR_{T_{1j}, T_{2j}}}{N^{1/2} s_{SCAR \cdot t}} \quad (6)$$

Due to concerns over the lack of normality in stock returns' distributions, it is common to provide additional non-parametric tests to confirm the results of the parametric alternatives. Consequently, a generalized sign test was also conducted which uses the normal approximation of the binomial distribution, and tests whether the proportion of positive and negative abnormal returns in the post event window significantly differs from the proportions found in the estimation period. Formally, the test statistic is

$$z = \frac{w - n\hat{p}}{[n\hat{p}(1 - \hat{p})]^{1/2}} \quad (7)$$

where

$$\hat{p} = \frac{1}{N} \sum_{i=1}^{N} \frac{1}{T} \sum_{t=E_1}^{E_T} S_{it} \quad (8)$$

$$S_{it} = \begin{cases} 1 & \text{if } AR_{it} > 0 \\ 0 & \text{otherwise} \end{cases}$$

In order to test the hypotheses presented, the procedure introduced above was implemented as follows. First, six types of groups were constructed based on their (1) entry mode choices (i.e. franchising, management contract, or equity involvement), and (2) stage of development of the host country (i.e. Organization for Economic Co-operation and Development (OECD) countries versus non-OECD countries).

Then, the market model parameters were estimated for each announcement within each group using OLS. The estimation period included 200 days (−210 to −10 days prior to the announcement) and the event period considered included the day of the announcement and the next day (days 0 and +1). In order to ensure that no leakage occurred before the announcement, the abnormal returns of the day prior to the announcement were also considered, and expected to be insignificant.

Once the coefficients were estimated, we proceeded to the estimation of the expected returns and abnormal returns by applying Eqs. (1) and (2). We then carried on the parametric and non-parametric tests detailed above.

All stock returns used in the study were retrieved from Center for Research in Security Prices (CRSP) database. We used daily continuously compounded stock returns as recommended by Brown and Warner (1980) and Peterson (1989). For the market return (R_m), we used the value-weighted index of the NYSE, AMEX and NASDAQ.

3.2. Cross-sectional Tests

In order to test various hypotheses, three cross-sectional tests are required. For hypothesis 1, the Chi-Square test of independence is appropriate. For the hypotheses 2a–2d, a two-way and two one-way ANOVAs are carried out, including the interaction term between the entry modes and the development stage of the host country as well as post hoc tests for multiple comparisons. The dependent variable in the ANOVA procedure is the CAR over the event period (days 0 and +1).

3.3. Measures

The CAR, the dependent variable, is estimated using daily stock returns (McWilliams and Siegel, 1997). The development stage of the host countries is estimated using the binomial categorization suggested by Root and Contractor (1981). Specifically, developing countries are non-OECD countries and developed countries are OECD members. The mode of entry choice measure is also categorical, and is based on the categories proposed by Brown et al. (2003). Indeed, given the current nature of the organizational forms used by hotel companies, and in an attempt to obtain sufficient data for each groups, the entry modes will only include franchising, management contract and equity involvement. The latter measure includes all equity involvement related modes, such as wholly and partly owned subsidiaries and joint-ventures.

3.4. Sample

The selection of the sample is one of the most critical components of event-studies. Indeed, in order to reliably assess the stock reaction to an announcement, one has to ensure that the announcement is well specified;

that is, the announcement must be unanticipated, and it must be isolated from other firm specific events that may also create abnormal responses and confound the effects (McWilliams and Siegel, 1997). In this study, all available company news and trade journal news have been reviewed between January 1, 2003 and December 31, 2006 in an attempt to ensure the unexpected nature of the announcement. Specifically, the name and location of the hotel for which the entry mode choice was announced was tracked over time and across sources to ensure that the announcement date represented the first announcement. All trade journal data were retrieved from the Factiva database. Company news were retrieved from the company's website and the press releases published by Business Wires. In addition, the following criteria were applied to develop the sample:

1. The announcement date must be an active trading day.
2. There was no confounding factor within plus or minus 5 days of the announcement. Confounding factors included dividend announcements, other relevant financial and non-financial news (e.g. issuance of large debt, lawsuit settlement), and other entry mode choices' announcements.
3. The entry mode choice and host country were clearly stated; there were no announcement including a mix of entry mode (e.g. management contract and equity involvement) or a mix of entered country (e.g. OECD with non-OECD countries).

The initial sample included 648 announcements, of which only 133 complied with the inclusive criteria. The descriptive statistics for the sample are presented in Table 1. The evolution of the number of these announcements per entry mode type is presented in Fig. 1.

Typical announcements included the entered country, the entry mode, and the type of property (full-service vs. limited service), as well as the number of rooms. The following is an example of announcements retained in the sample (see Table 2).

Table 1: Sample description

Sample size (# of announcements)		133
Average # of hotels per deal (maximum/minimum)		1.73 (3/1)
Average # of rooms per deal (maximum/minimum)		515 (3243/74)
Average # of rooms per hotel (maximum/minimum)		298 (1295/74)
Total number of hotels involved		233
Mode of entry	Count	Percentage
Franchise agreements	25	18.8
Management contracts	98	73.7
Equity investments	10	7.5

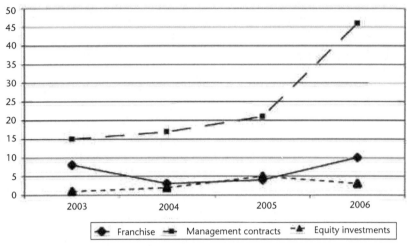

Figure 1: Entry announcements by mode of entry

Table 2: Sample announcement (excerpt)

"MARRIOTT INTERNATIONAL TO MANAGE NEW MARRIOTT HOTEL IN NINGBO, CHINA Washington, DC – 20 April 2005 Marriott International, Inc. (NYSE:MAR) will manage a 311-room Marriott hotel in Ningbo, China, under an agreement reached with Haicheng Investment Development Co., Ltd. When opened in 2007, it will be the 11th Marriott-flagged hotel in China. The project architect is GMP Architects, and Hirsch Bednar Associates is the interior design firm. The property will be located in the heart of the central business district of Ningbo within a mixed-used project containing a 38-story building that will house the hotel and office space. The hotel will face the southern tip of Jiangbei across the Yuyao River, which is now home to a newly redeveloped historic neighborhood housing trendy restaurants and entertainment spots. Within walking distance is Tianyi Square, Ningbo's main shopping area." *Source:* Retrieved from http://www.marriott.com/news/detail.mi?marrArticle=90354 on December 10th, 2007.

4. Results

Overall, the CAR following entry mode choice announcements was positive and significant. These overall results are presented in Table 3. Over the event window (days 0 and +1), the Average CAR (ACAR) is 0.27% and is significant with an alpha of 0.04 using the parametric test (Patell Z), and nearly significant with the generalized sign Z test (alpha of 0.07). It is also worth noting that the CAR prior to the announcement (day –1 and 0) is not significant, suggesting that the announcements identified were truly unexpected and that no significant information leakage occurred.

When considering each combination of the entry mode choice and development stage of the host country, five out of six CAR are significant. Table 4 shows the results at the group level. Equity involvement in developed countries and management contracts in developing countries have the two

Table 3: General test of CAR

Event window (days)	N	CAR(%)	Positive:negative	Patell Z	p-value	Generalized sign Z	p-value
–1, 0	133	0.21	69:64	1.228	0.1097	0.929	0.1765
0, +1	133	0.27	72:61	1.744	0.0406	1.450	0.0736

Table 4: CAR means by mode of entry choice and coutnry type

CAR (0, +1) (positive:negative) sub-sample size	Franchising	Management contract	Equity involvement
OECD	0.22%** (8:7) N = 15	–0.13% (7:9) N = 16	0.61%*** (5:1**) N = 6
Non-OECD	0.32%** (4:6*) N = 10	0.44%*** (48:34***) N = 82	–0.46%* (1:3) N = 4

Note: Significance of Patell Z test reported for one-tail tests (i.e. CAR greater than 0 or less than 0).
* Significant CAR at 0.1.
** Significant CAR at 0.05.
*** Significant CAR at 0.01.

highest CAR, 0.61% and 0.44% respectively. Franchise agreements offer positive CAR in both stages of development of the host country, yet the CAR in developing countries is slightly higher than in developed countries. In contrast, equity involvement in developing countries is not well perceived by investors as the CAR is significantly negative using the parametric test (–0.46%). The result for the management contract announcements in developed countries shows that the CAR is not significantly different from zero.

Hypothesis 1 was a general test of independence between the mode of entry choice and the development stage of the country. No specific preference for the modal choice was expected for OECD and non-OECD countries at this stage; however, the literature suggests that the entry mode choice will be associated with the nature of the host country. The Chi-Square test of independence was chosen as it permits testing whether such association exists.

The Chi-Square value of 24.497 reported in Table 5 is highly significant (sig. 0.000), and provides strong support to the expected association. Hypothesis 1 is thus not rejected; the choice of the mode of entry appears to be dependent upon the development stage of the host country.

The next series of hypotheses related the association of entry mode choice and development stage of the host country, to the CAR. Hypothesis 2a specifically suggested that there was an interaction effect between the entry

Table 5: Chi-Square test of independence

	Value	df	Asymp. Sig. (2-sided)
Person Chi-Square	24.497	2	0.000
Likelihood ratio	22.930	2	0.000
No. of valid cases	133		

Table 6: ANOVA table (dependent variable: CAR (0, +1))

Source	Type III sum of squares	df	Mean square	F	Sig.
Correct model	0.002	5	0.000	2.915	0.016
Intercept	0.000	1	0.000	3.399	0.068
Development stage of host country	9.162E–05	1	9.162E–05	0.692	0.407
Mode of entry choice	9.646E–05	2	4.823E–05	0.364	0.695
Country × Mode of entry	0.002	2	0.001	5.816	0.004
Error	0.017	127	0.000		
Total	0.023	133			
Corrected total	0.019	132			

mode and the development stage in explaining the abnormal returns. Table 6 presents the results of the two-way ANOVA performed (adjusted for unbalanced design). As can be seen in the ANOVA table, as well as in the chart in Fig. 2, the main effects are not significant, while the interaction between the mode of entry and country type is highly significant ($F = 5.816$ and sig. of 0.004), providing support to hypothesis 2a.

Hypothesis 2b argues that the CAR following the announcements of entry using management contracts in developing (i.e. non-OECD) countries are greater than the CAR following the announcements of other entry modes in similar countries. A one-way ANOVA followed by a Tukey's post hoc procedure was conducted to assess the proposed relationship. The results, showed in Table 7, endorse the hypothesized difference, which was also expected from the reading of Fig. 2.

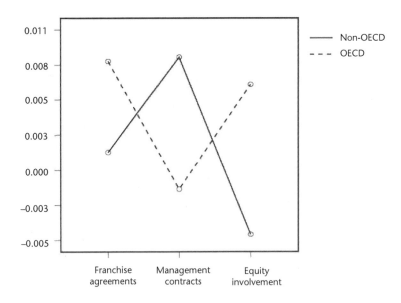

Figure 2: Interaction term; estimated marginal means of CAR(0, +1)

Table 7: Summary of multiple comparisons (Tukey HSD procedure)

Hypotheses	Comparisons	Test statistics	Conclusions
H2b	In non-OECD countries:		
	CAR management contracts > CAR franchise agreements	Sig. at 0.05*	Do not reject
	CAR management contracts > CAR equity investments	Sig. at 0.02*	Do not reject
H2c	In OECD countries:		
	CAR equity involvement > CAR management contracts	Not significant at 0.1	Reject
	CAR equity investmetns > CAR franchise agreements	Not significant at 0.1	Reject
H2d	In OECD countries:		
	CAR franchise agreements > CAR management contracts	Sig. at 0.07	Inconclusive

* Test adjusted for unequal variances.

Hypothesis 2c suggests that investors value entry modes in developed countries that involve some degree of equity investment more than other modes of entry. As expected from the estimated marginal means plotted in Fig. 2, the hypothesis is rejected; the CAR following the announcements of equity involvement in developed countries are not significantly different than those of the other entry mode choices. This result may partly be due to the limited amount of announcements found for this group.

The last hypothesis contends that, in developed countries, investors would react more positively to announcements involving the franchising entry mode than to announcement involving management contracts. The one-way ANOVA and multiple comparison procedure (Tukey's HSD) results bring some support to this contention, but fail to provide conclusive evidences. Indeed, the difference between the CAR following the announcements of franchise agreements and management contracts in developed countries is not significant (sig. of 0.07 for CAR of 0.22% for franchise agreements and –0.13% for management contracts).

5. Discussion and Conclusions

Prior empirical works have demonstrated the significant influence of the development stage of the host country on the entry mode choices made by multinational firms (e.g. Zhao et al., 2004). In general, a low development level has been viewed as a risk factor that deters equity investments. Yet, as developing countries have also been perceived as providing less skilled labor and weaker managerial capabilities than developed nations, firms have been encouraged to maintain a fair amount of control over the conduct of their operation in such environment. In the hospitality industry literature, Dev et al. (2002) showed that under such circumstances, international hotel chains favored management contracts in an attempt to limit the amount of equity at stake, and to maintain operational control. Alternatively, in developed countries, equity investments have been considered as the preferred entry mode as the investment risk associated with such strategy was deemed as low, and the return potential superior to other entry modes (Anderson and Coughlan, 1987). In the context of the hotel industry, franchising agreements have also been seen as superior to management contracts in developed countries, principally as it permits a stronger alignment of goals between the unit managers (i.e. franchisees) and the corporation (i.e. franchisor), thereby minimizing the agency costs (Contractor and Kundu, 1998; Brown et al., 2003; Dev et al., 2002).

This study tested several arguments pertaining to the dependence of the modal choices on the development stages of the host country, and to the performance consequences of the alignment between choices of entry modes and host countries development levels. It was hypothesized that the alignment between the choice of entry and the host country's characteristics would result in superior performance, as measured by the abnormal returns following the announcement of market entry. Several more detailed hypotheses were also posited, arguing that the announcements of some modes of entry in some specific countries would result in higher abnormal returns. A number of the suggested relationships were supported; specifically, that the abnormal returns following the announcement of an entry in a foreign market was dependent upon the degree of alignment between the entry mode choice and the development stage of the host country. Also, the announcements of management contracts in developing countries resulted in higher abnormal returns than the other modes of entry, and that the announcements of franchise agreements in developed countries produced higher abnormal returns than the management contract mode. Conversely, the hypothesis suggesting that the announcement of equity investment in developed countries would result in superior abnormal returns was not confirmed.

These results highlight several key points related to the perceived performance consequences of entry mode choices in the international hotel industry. First, as suggested by prior studies, there is no universally superior modal choice; the performance of foreign market entry is contingent upon the modal choice and the development stage of the host country. It is likely that the alignment of the choice with other internal and external factors would also be important to the performance of the venture. Further research should be conducted to test more complex alignment forms.

Secondly, the arguments brought forward by Dev et al. (2002) and Brown et al. (2003), which essentially suggest that one of the key differences between the management contract and franchise agreement modes of entry reside in the availability of managerial capabilities in the host country, appears to be mostly verified. Management contracts are indeed apparently more valued when used in developing countries, whereas franchise agreements are more prized when used in developed countries, yet only nearly significantly.

Thirdly, the various claims regarding equity investments in developed countries appear not to hold in the context of the hotel industry. While the limited amount of announcements found for such entry mode choice reduces the extent to which one may generalize from the findings of this study, it also shows that such modal choice is not favored in the industry. More detailed characteristics of these transactions could shed more light on these announcements. However, it is worth noting that the abnormal returns following the announcements of equity involvement entry modes in developed and developing countries are the highest and lowest significant CAR respectively. This large difference in CAR (from 0.61% to –0.46% as shown in Table 2) calls for more investigation for this mode of entry.

From a managerial standpoint, the results of this study indicate that equity investors do value entry mode choices differently when the entry is made in developed or developing countries. While the results do not provide a decision framework as to exactly which entry mode should be favored in a given country, they do offer a number of generic guidelines. Indeed, when the entered market is defined by a lower level of development as per the OECD criteria, then management contracts appear to be more appropriate as equity investors would price the decision better than other entry modes. In addition, when the entered market is deemed as more developed in OECD terms, then franchising appears to be better priced than management contracts. For managers of publicly traded companies, such guidelines are likely to be important even if the operational performance of the venture is not guaranteed.

Overall, the results presented above provide answers to the research questions that triggered this study. However, it is worth noting a number of limitations. First, the nature of the sample, driven by the current trend toward management contracts, has potentially limited the extent to which the results can be generalized. Specifically, the limited amount of announcements related to equity involvement (i.e. 10) may not be sufficient to fully grasp what investors' value when equity investment is involved. A more fined grained analysis of each announcement, coupled with additional cases, would certainly yield more specific recommendations, especially on the effect of the magnitude of equity invested on the expected risk-adjusted performance. Secondly, the binary classification of the host country, OECD versus non-OECD countries, does not permit a detailed evaluation of the environment of the entered countries. It is indeed likely that wide variations in these environments exist within each of the two groups and that such variations could alter the relationships reported in this study. Future research could thus aim to further refine the measure of country profile.

References

Anderson, E., Coughlan, A.T., 1987. International market entry and expansion via independent or integrated channels of distribution. Journal of Marketing 51 (1), 71–82.

Anderson, E., Gatignon, H., 1986. Modes of foreign market entry: a transaction cost analysis and propositions. Journal of International Business Studies 17 (3), 1–26.

Arora, A., Fosfuri, A., 2000. Wholly owned subsidiary versus technology licensing in the worldwide chemical industry. Journal of International Business Studies 31 (4), 555–572.

Berman, G., Brooks, R., Davidson, S., 2000. The Sydney Olympic games announcement and Australian stock market reaction. Applied Economic Letters 7, 781–784.

Blomstermo, A., Sharma, D.D., 2006. Choice of foreign market entry mode in service firms. International Marketing Review 23 (2), 211–229.

Brouthers, K.D., Brouthers, L.E., Werner, S., 2003. Transaction cost-enhanced entry mode choices and firm performance. Strategic Management Journal 24 (12), 1239–1248.

Brown, J.R., Dev, C.S., Zhou, Z., 2003. Broadening the foreign market entry mode decision: separating ownership and control. Journal of International Business Studies 34, 473–488.

Brown, S.J., Warner, J.B., 1980. Measuring security price performance. Journal of Financial Economics 8 (September), 205–258.

Cateora, P.R., Graham, J.L., 1986. International Marketing, 10th ed. McGraw-Hill, New York.

Chandler, A.D., 1992. Organizational capabilities and the economic history of the multinational enterprise. Journal of Economic Perspectives 6 (3), 79–100.

Contractor, F.J., Kundu, S.K., 1998. Modal choice in a world of alliances: analyzing organizational forms in the international hotel sector. Journal of International Business Studies 29 (2), 325–356.

Dev, C.S., Erramilli, M.K., Agarwal, S., 2002. Brands across borders: determining factors in choosing franchising or management contracts for entering international markets. Cornell Hotel and Restaurant Administration Quarterly 43 (6), 91–104.

Dunning, J.H., McQueen, M., 1981. The eclectic theory of international production: a case study of the international hotel industry. Managerial and Decision Economics 2 (4), 197–210.

Jensen, M., Meckling, W., 1976. Theory of the firm: managerial behavior, agency costs, and ownership structure. Journal of Financial Economics 4, 305–360.

Lafontaine, F., 1992. Agency theory and franchising: some empirical results. Rand Journal of Economics 23 (1), 263–283.

Lopez-Duarte, C., Garcia-Canal, E., 2007. Stock market reaction to foreign direct investments: interaction between entry mode and FDI attributes. Management International Review 47 (3), 393–422.

McCarthy, D.J., Puffer, S.M., Simmonds, P.J., 1993. Riding the Russian roller coaster: U.S. firms' recent experience and future plans in the former USSR. California Management Review 36 (1), 106–109.

McWilliams, A., Siegel, D., 1997. Event studies in management research: theoretical and empirical issues. Academy of Management Journal 40 (3), 626–657.

Nitsch, D., Beamish, P., Makino, S., 1996. Entry mode and performance of Japanese FDI in western Europe. Management International Review 36 (1), 27–43.

Olsen, M.D., West, J., Tse, E., 2007. Strategic Management in the Hospitality Industry, 3rd ed. John Wiley & Sons, New York.

Olsen, M.D., Zhao, J.L., 2000. Competitive Methods of Multinational Hotel Companies – A Five Year Review, 1995–99. International Hotel and Restaurant Association, Paris, pp. 31–45.

Patell, J.M., 1976. Corporate forecasts of earnings per share and stock price behavior: empirical test. Journal of Accounting Research 14 (2), 246–276.

Peterson, P.P., 1989. Event studies: a review of issues and methodology. Quarterly Journal of Business and Economics 28 (3), 36–66.

Quinn, B., Doherty, A.M., 2000. Power and control in international retail franchising – evidence from theory and practice. International Marketing Review 17 (4/5), 354–366.

Root, F.R., 1987. Entry Strategies for International Markets. Lexington Books, Lexington, MA.

Root, F.R., Contractor, F.J., 1981. Negotiating compensation in international licensing agreements. Sloan Management Review 22 (2), 23–32.

Ross, S.A., Westerfield, R.W., Jaffe, J., 2003. Corporate Finance, 6th ed. McGraw-Hill, Boston.

Sanders, R.W., Robins, R.P., 1991. Discriminating between wealth and information effects in event studies in accounting and finance research. Review of Quantitative Finance and Accounting 1 (3), 307–329.

Shama, A., 1995. Entry strategies of U.S. firms to the newly independent states, Baltic states, and eastern European countries. California Management Review 37 (3), 90–109.

Shama, A., 2000. Determinants of entry strategies of U.S. companies into Russia, the Czech Republic, Hungary, Poland, and Romania. Thunderbird International Business Review 42 (6), 651–676.

Shane, S.A., 1996. Hybrid organizational arrangements and their implications for firm growth and survival: a study of new franchisors. Academy of Management Journal 39 (1), 216–234.

Sharma, A., 1998. Mode of entry and *ex-post* performance. Strategic Management Journal 19 (9), 879–900.

Veraros, N., Kasimati, E., Dawson, P., 2004. The 2004 Olympic games announcement and its effect on the Athens and Milan stock exchanges. Applied Economic Letters 11, 749–753.

Williamson, O.E., 1975. Market and Hierarchies: Analysis and Antitrust Implications. Free Press, New York.

Woodcock, C.P., Beamish, P., Makino, S., 1994. Ownership-based entry mode strategies and international performance. Journal of International Business Studies 25 (2), 253–273.

Zhao, H., Luo, Y., Suh, T., 2004. Transaction cost determinants and ownership-based entry mode choice: a meta-analytical review. Journal of International Business Studies 35 (3), 524–544.

Zhao, J.L., Olsen, M.D., 1997. The antecedent factors influencing entry mode choices of multinational lodging firms. International Journal of Hospitality Management 16 (1), 79–98.

24

Hotel Management Contracts – Past and Present

Jan A. deRoos

Hotel management contracts have become a fixture in the hotel industry for most full-service, upscale, luxury, resort, and convention properties. The American Hotel & Lodging Association (AH&LA; 2009) estimates that there are eight hundred management companies managing 12,000 properties worldwide. More than one-third of that number, 4,370 hotels, were managed by the nine largest hotel companies in 2006 (Eyster and deRoos 2009). This article provides a historical overview of hotel management contracts and serves as a benchmark for management contract practice in 2009. A subsequent article will examine future trends.

The earliest definitive analysis of hotel management contracts appeared in a series of *Cornell Quarterly* articles written in 1977 by Professor James Eyster of Cornell's School of Hotel Administration (For example, see Eyster 1977). By this time, management contracts had achieved a notable presence in the industry.

Management contracts were developed starting in the 1950s, when the large hotel operators, particularly Hilton, InterContinental, Sheraton, and Hyatt, expanded internationally. By separating ownership from the operation of the asset, both parties were better off. The property owner, employing the services of a professional operator and the brand for a fee, could generate significant value and cash flows without having to invest in the expertise of

Source: *Cornell Hospitality Quarterly,* 51(1) (2010): 68–80.

the hotel business. The operator, by agreeing to manage the property on behalf of the property owner, could generate significant fee income, expand the reach of its brand, and earn profits without having to invest in the property needed to support the operation. The provisions of these early contracts, which were relatively straightforward, are now characterized as being favorable to the operator, given their lengthy duration and limited rights by the owner to terminate the contract.

The relationship of owner and operator began to change in the 1980s, when international interests invested heavily in the U.S. hotel industry. During this period, hotel management contracts were in widespread worldwide use, and there was a significant body of literature and legal expertise on the topic, including the seminal Eyster book of 1988. The crash of the commercial real estate bubble in 1990 exposed the lodging market to significant distress. The resulting hotel bankruptcies provoked two long-lasting developments in management contracts. First, when management contracts were tested in the courts, the results were generally favorable to owners (for an excellent summary, see Renard and Motley 2003). Second, due to financial distress issues and a perceived misalignment between owners and operators, the hotel asset management discipline arose to provide professional services to hotel owners. Contracts signed in this era are generally characterized as favorable to the owner, with significant rights of termination and a clearly established set of duties for operators.

Contracts grew much more complicated in the 1980s and 1990s. What were once straightforward clauses were transformed to tiered provisions and multiple contracts as a result of owners' and operators' growing experience with the positive and troublesome aspects of contracts. Examples include

- incentive fee structures based on achieving certain levels of cash flow or certain levels of profitability as measured by (for example) gross operating profit (GOP) margins;
- performance termination clauses;
- owner's rights to approve operating; furniture, fixture, and equipment (FF&E) replacement; and capital expenditure budgets;
- owner's right to have input on personnel decisions;
- owner's right to terminate – at will, upon sale, and upon foreclosure;
- restrictions on blanket indemnification of the operator;
- operator's rights to enforce brand standards; and
- operator's expansion of rights to collect sums for centrally provided services such as loyalty programs, accounting, training, marketing, and reservations.

On the strength of another real estate bubble, the period from 2000 through 2009 has been characterized by an explosion of hotel management contracts, especially by the branded operators. The demand for management services outstripped the supply in many markets, primarily driven by the success of the brands in meeting the owners' objectives and the fact that operators were able to engage in auction-like behavior. Given the limitations of real estate markets, the best brands have had the ability to select which of several prospective projects they would manage in a given market. This ability, combined with the expansion of the lending market and competition among lenders for good hotel loans, provided a window of opportunity for hotel operators to obtain contracts on particularly favorable terms from 2000 through 2008.

No longer. At this writing, both owners and operators are faced with unprecedented dreadful performance, possibly for an extended period, causing enormous stress between the parties. Management contracts will certainly be tested again, with the likely consequence of changes in recent practice. Litigation is expected to spike significantly over the next two years. Disagreements between owners and operators may escalate, as has occurred at the Four Seasons Aviara, where the parties have resorted to changing locks, engaged in personal confrontations, and filed competing lawsuits (see Segal 2009).

In this article, I analyze the state of hotel management contracts in 2009, drawing heavily on a review of contracts written during the past ten years, my work with practitioners in the course of teaching and consulting, and a review of recent writings on the topic (see Eyster and deRoos 2009; Wales and Ferroni 2008; McDaniel 2008). My intent is to provide a benchmark for management contracts as the industry moves into the next decade and to offer a context for the negotiation of new contracts, as well as the administration of existing contracts.

Contract Fundamentals

In negotiating a management contract, owners and operators keep an eye on five fundamental issues. While some are more important to one party than the other, they form the essence of all contracts. On these five points, I have observed a greater level of balance between the owner and operator than at any point in history. These five fundamentals form the outline for this article, as follows:

- the legal framework;
- investment by the operator in the relationship;
- term, renewal, and termination rights;
- fees and system reimbursable charges; and
- reporting and controls.

The Legal Framework

The legal framework defines the parties, their relationships, and their rights. Far from being a single document, a management contract involves negotiations that can include up to eight concurrent agreements (i.e., preopening management agreement, postopening management agreement, brand license, royalty or franchise agreement, marketing agreement, technology agreement, employment agreement, and technical services agreement).

Separation of the Management Contract from the Contract for Brand Services

Separation of the postopening management agreement into two contracts (management contract and brand license agreement) is an innovation that favors the operator. This practice has grown steadily in recent years. In a typical negotiation of the two contracts, little fee payments are associated with the management contract itself, typically a base-only fee of less than 1 percent of revenues. The brand license agreement, by contrast, provides for base royalty fees of approximately 2 percent and an incentive royalty fee that mirrors contemporary incentive fee practice in a more traditional contract where the management and brand are bundled. The effect is to shift the source of fees from the management contract to the brand license agreement. For international operators, this structure produces lower taxes for the operator due to differential treatment of management fees and license fees. In most cases, the two agreements are cross-defaulted, but this is not necessarily true in all cases. Owners should be careful not to expose themselves to a situation in which they have the right to terminate the management contract but are obligated to take brand services (and pay the corresponding fees) under the brand license agreement.

The Parties to the Contract

In a contemporary management contract, each party often incorporates a special-purpose company; the operating entity is a single-asset subsidiary of the operator, while the owning entity is a "bankruptcy remote" special-purpose entity controlled by the owner. The intent of creating these entities is to limit liability and to provide lenders with a clear foreclosure path should the owner default on the hotel loan. It is clear that the liability management aspects of the special-purpose companies work as intended.

However, in the current environment, I observe that the lender's desire to prevent owners from using bankruptcy and instead force hotels into foreclosure may not be in the best interests of any party. I say this because the foreclosure process is handled in the state courts and its outcomes are uncertain, depending on the judge and the appointed receiver. On the other hand, hotels that have gone through a bankruptcy typically use the federal court system, which is well equipped to handle a hotel failure in relatively predictable fashion. It is clear that the bankruptcy process favors borrowers as long as the hotel loan is nonrecourse to the borrower; in addition, the bankruptcy process provides a lender (the new owner) with significant power to terminate or modify the management contract. The foreclosure process, by contrast, is so unpredictable that it would be unfair to characterize it as favorable to the operator, but in general, it is more likely that the operator's contract would survive a foreclosure process than a bankruptcy process.

Two additional legal matters relate to the contract; first, the owner and operator must consider the matter of whether the owner, the operator, or some third party is the employer. The second relates to the name of the holder of permits, licenses, and other rights to do business as hotel. For permits, licenses, and other authorizations, it is in the owner's best interests to stipulate that the operator is responsible for obtaining and maintaining these on behalf of the owner.

With regard to employees, until recently, neither the owner nor the operator has wished to carry the employees on its payroll (see Eyster and deRoos 2009). Each has been reluctant to assume the continuing business obligations for keeping payroll and pension records and for negotiating and adhering to labor agreements. Also, neither has wanted to be liable for potential tort actions or discrimination claims (for a discussion of discrimination issues, see Sherwyn 2010 [this issue]). Recently, though, several operators have expressed a preference for employing all property-level staff, because that gives the operator specific competitive and strategic advantages. The most significant of these is the ability of the operator to transfer personnel to another property in the case of a contract termination, depriving the owner of the ability to simply terminate a contract under the assumption that the hotel will continue to operate with the existing staff. In addition, operators can provide employees with long-term career paths, strengthening the operator and providing employees with career options not available within a given property. An innovation found in recent contracts is employee leasing or professional employment organizations (PEOs), in which the owner or operator leases employees from a third-party company, which sometimes is affiliated with the owner or operator. These companies handle the management of human resources, employee benefits, payroll, and workers' compensation.

The Status of the Agency Relationship in Management Contracts

The third major component of the legal framework is that of agency, a topic that has attracted considerable attention (Renard and Motley 2003).[1] The relationship between the owner and operator is one of principal and agent. If the contract and the actions of the parties have in fact the substance of a principal-agent relationship, the courts have affirmed this relationship – even in the presence of contract language specifically stating that the relationship is not one of agency. The agency relationship is decidedly in favor of owners, because it provides a mechanism for owners to terminate contracts that do not otherwise provide for termination. The principal in an agency relationship can terminate a contract if the agent breaches its fiduciary duty to the principal, irrespective of the contract language.

While this matter remains a matter for courts to assess, many owners insist on a principal-agent relationship. On the other hand, some operators insist on language establishing an independent contractor relationship and specifically disclaiming agency. Again, only time will tell whether this language survives a court test. The State of Maryland has addressed the matter with Commercial Law §23-102, which removes the remedy of at-will termination of agency unless that is explicit in the agreement. Instead of the common law understanding regarding agency, Title 23 states that the "four corners" of the contract govern its enforcement, in recognition of the meeting of the minds of the parties to the contract.

Dispute-Settlement Mechanisms

Dispute-settlement mechanisms are an important component of the legal framework – the most common being arbitration or use of experts. Absent any language to the contrary, the parties have full access to the courts at any time in matters under dispute. Operators usually insist on language that creates formal dispute settlement mechanisms that have the effect of preserving the status quo while the dispute is under consideration, are uncertain in outcome, and place decisions outside of the contract parties (Wales and Ferroni 2008; McDaniel 2008).[2] As an example of current practice in the United States, contract provisions are found along a continuum. At one end of the continuum, contracts use arbitration for some, but not all, contract disputes. Arbitration or the use of experts would apply typically to disputes over the budget, budget definitions, performance termination, and capital expenditures. At the other end of the continuum are the few contracts in which the use of experts or arbitration is the sole remedy of the parties in all disputes.

Real Property Rights and Personal Property Rights

The last major component of the legal framework is the matter of property rights. As a rule, the owner owns the real estate. Thus, contracts have long been written with the understanding that all real property and physical personal property remained with the owner. In addition, since the operator was doing business on behalf of the owner, all records, data, and other matters relating to the hotel business were the property of the owner. The courts have made it clear that the work performed by the operator does not create an interest in the hotel and that the contract does not create any partnership, joint venture, or tenant rights. This position favors owners in termination disputes by clearly identifying property rights of the parties.

A new practice gives branded operators considerable rights to withhold operating information from the owner. In particular, guest history and marketing data, as well as systems used to operate the hotel, are, in essence, owned by the operator. In a minority of cases, the operator has secured rights to control cash flows in the event of the owner's default on capital obligations. While federal bankruptcy law would take precedence over this language in a bankruptcy procedure, the language could stand in a foreclosure procedure.

Investment by the Operator in the Relationship

Operators are often asked to invest in the relationship as evidence of their commitment to a project, and operators often invest strategically to create an interest in the deal, to gain favorable provisions, or to limit the owner's ability to terminate the contract.

Operators may invest with one or more of five financial tools. I list them below in the order of preference most often cited by owners.

- *Key money.* Generally framed as an up-front rebate of fees in the amount of less than 5 percent of the capital structure, this arrangement often has "claw-back" mechanisms for repayment if contract does not run the entire initial term.
- *Second mortgage loan.* Not often used due to first-mortgage restrictions, this approach was found in a few contracts in the 1970s and 1980s. It has since fallen into disfavor.
- *Mezzanine loan.* This investment is treated as any other piece of the capital stack. Amounts are most often between 5 and 10 percent of the capital structure. Generally structured with a cash sweep and a look-back return calculation.
- *Cash flow guarantees.* Not a cash investment in the property, these guarantees generally are structured to provide the owner with cash flow

of between 80 and 100 percent of the budgeted cash flow for a specific number of years (generally less than five). The guarantee is calculated on an annual basis, with an overall cap on the guarantee in an amount that is less than 5 percent of the capital structure. These also often have a claw-back mechanism to recover sums paid if cash flow exceeds certain thresholds.
- *Equity investment.* Many owners consider this approach unacceptable. The equity investment by the operator has the effect of creating a partnership relationship between the owner and operator and certainly would alter any principal-agent relationship. Consequently, the use of equity investment by the operator has fallen into disfavor.

When the operator makes a meaningful investment in the relationship, the owner is expected to recognize the investment by agreeing to certain terms that favor the operator. Depending on the parties' objectives, those terms may take the form of fees that are a bit higher than market, a long initial term and renewal term(s), weak termination rights, limited access to the courts, or designating Maryland as the governing jurisdiction for the contract.

Term, Renewal, and Termination Rights

Once the nature of the operator's investment is clear, the parties can substantively negotiate the contract term, renewal, and termination rights. Any discussion of fees must wait until the operator has some notion of provisions relating to term and termination. Exhibit 1 presents statistics for term and renewal (Eyster and deRoos 2009).

Exhibit 1: Initial terms and renewals

	Initial term (median years)	Number of renewals (median)	Length of renewals (median years)
Brand operators			
Full-service	16	2	10
Independent operators			
Full-service (no equity)	6	2	4
Select service	9	2	5
Caretaker operators[a]			
Full-service	1	1	1

Source: Adapted from Eyster and deRoos (2009, Exhibit III-3).
a. Caretaker operators are usually independent operators. Frequently, initial contract terms state that the contract continues indefinitely until notice of cancellation is given either with or without cause by either owner or operator. If the contract is terminated before the end of the initial term, the owner is usually obligated to pay management fees for the remainder of the current term; thus, initial terms are quite short.

As has been true for many years, the term and renewals for branded operators is substantially longer than those for independent operators. Similarly, independent operators have weaker termination rights than do branded operators, as shown in Exhibit 2.

Since most brand operator contracts do not provide for termination without cause, performance-related termination is generally seen to be in the owner's favor. The original intent was to give the owner rights to terminate the contract during the initial or renewal term should the operator perform poorly. Interestingly, a contemporary performance termination clause operates primarily as a cash flow guarantee and not a termination device. A typical performance termination clause operates as follows:

- Poor performance is defined as a failure to achieve some fraction of the budgeted GOP, generally between 80 and 100 percent.
- The poor performance must continue for more than one year. Many different forms of time measurement are in place, including a rolling twelve-month period, two of three consecutive years, and two (or even three) consecutive years.
- If there is a terminable event, the operator is given the opportunity to cure the performance failure and avoid termination by giving (or lending) the owner the difference between the actual GOP and the benchmark. There may be a claw-back provision on the cures in the event that future

Exhibit 2: Owner termination

	All properties except caretaker[a]	
	Brand	Independent
Without cause		
Frequency in contracts		
At any time	0%	42%
After predetermined period[b]	15%	2%
Required notice period (days)	90–365	30
Termination fee multiple[c]	3–5	1–5
On-sale		
No operator option to purchase	35%	67%
Operator option to purchase[d]	56%	22%
Operator option to continue with new operator	72%	38%
Termination fee multiple[c]	2–5	0.5–2.5
On-foreclosure		
Frequency in contracts	80%	80%
Termination fee multiple[c]	0–2	0–1

Source: Adapted from Eyster and deRoos (2009, Exhibit III-7).
a. Caretaker operators: when an owner terminates a contract before the end of the initial term, most contracts require the owner to pay the caretaker operator management fees for the remainder of the contract term.
b. Usually from between one to three years.
c. Multiple of most recent twelve-months' basic plus incentive management fee. Multiple decreases as remaining period of contract term decreases.
d. Combination of right of first offer, right of first refusal.

performance exceeds the benchmark or the contract is terminated prematurely.
- In addition, there is a force majeure clause that makes any terminable event subject to a market test. In general, as long as the hotel is achieving its long-term market share of room revenues, no termination is possible.

Operators often have unlimited cure rights and can unilaterally decide whether to cure or be terminated. In addition, the use of a performance termination clause provides a mechanism for operators to keep owners from exerting too much control over budgeting and operations. Since the operator is at all times responsible for the budget via the performance clause, the operator should make its best possible effort to produce an accurate, defensible budget and then achieve that budget. Owners are reluctant to allow operators to avoid performance termination liability by taking control of the budget away from the operator.

No discussion of termination rights would be complete without noting the role of subordination, nondisturbance, and attornment agreements (SNDA), or tri-party agreements, which limit the lender's rights and which represent a sea change in contract status. Over the past ten years, operators have been increasingly successful at binding the lender to the operator by using SNDA language from commercial real estate. Using this agreement, the operator seeks the status of an important tenant, whose rights survive a foreclosure procedure. The acceptance of these agreements in foreclosure and ability of the management contract to survive a foreclosure is a fundamental change in management contracts and will be more vigorously negotiated in the future. While there is a possibility that the management contract is voided by a receiver in a foreclosure, any receiver who does so must believe that it represents the entire business of the borrower, with the operator but a part of the overall business that is being foreclosed upon.

Fees and System Reimbursable Charges

Simple in concept, fees and system reimbursable charges can be complex in implementation. The idea of combining a base fee and an incentive fee was meant to align the interests of owner and operator. Operator fees could be based on both revenues and profits. Historically, the base and incentive fees were of roughly equal magnitude for a hotel in a good economy with a solid management team. In general, base fees are a straightforward percentage of gross revenues. Some contracts define gross revenues tightly so as to exclude revenues that are not the result of the operator's efforts (e.g., a parking concession). A few operators have accepted contracts that have no base fee but must be assured that the incentive fees provide for a reasonable fee stream over the term of the contract.

Incentive fee structures involve greater complexity and have a wide variety of forms in practice. At their root, incentive fees are the fundamental financial risk-shifting device in the contract. With incentive fees, the operator bears some risk for poor results and has an incentive to maximize the profit measure that serves as the incentive fee basis, typically GOP, generally calculated as gross revenues less operating expenses. However, the operating expenses do not include property taxes, insurance, reserves to replace FF&E, or any capital charges such as debt service, ground lease payments, or an owner's preferred return. Thus, GOP is larger than the cash flow to the owner. Over time, owners sought various means to establish the incentive fee on cash flow after a return on capital and to subordinate the incentive fee to this return, a change meant to further align the owner's and operator's interests.

A summary of base and incentive fees is presented in Exhibit 3, which describes the two most common types of incentive fees. A fee based on GOP is common in Asia and most of Europe and the Middle East. When this incentive fee structure is used, the incentive fee percentage is often tiered, based on the achieved GOP margin of the property in any given year.[3] An incentive fee subordinate to and based on cash flow after a return on assets, called an owner's priority return, is commonly employed in North America.[4]

Note that while base fees are higher for select-service hotels operated by branded operators, they are lower for independent operators. This is due to

Exhibit 3: Base and incentive management fee structures

	Basic fee (percentage of gross revenues)			Incentive fee	
	Low	Median	High	Fee base	Ranges (percentage of fee base)
Brand operators					
Full-service	2.0	3.25	3.5	GOP	6–10
				Owner's priority return	10–30
Select-service	3.0	5.0	7.0	GOP	8–12
				Owner's priority return	10–30
Independent operators					
Full-service	1.5	4.0	6.0	GOP	5–10
				Owner's priority return	10–20
Select-service	2.5	2.75	3.0	GOP	8–12
				Owner's priority return	10–30
Caretaker operators					
All hotels	3.0	4.0	6.0	GOP	5–8
				Improved GOP	10–25

Source: Adapted from Eyster and deRoos (2009, Exhibit III-4).
Note: GOP = gross operating profit as defined in the Uniform System of Accounts for the Lodging Industry. Owner's priority return = cash flow after owner's priority (the owner's priority is a return on total property investment, generally in the range of 8 to 12 percent).

the fact that the select-service hotels are rarely independent hotels, and the brand itself is usually bundled with the management contract. For a hotel operated by an independent company, the owner often pays franchise fees in addition to the management fees.

Always a matter of some contention, system reimbursable charges have become the most controversial area of fees to emerge over the past ten years. These charges are for services provided by third-party affiliates of the operator or by the operator itself for centralized services, including fees for international marketing, group marketing, regional sales and revenue management teams, frequent traveler programs, the operation of reservation systems, purchasing fees, training fees, fees for providing hardware and software, centralized accounting services, and travel expenses of corporate personnel.

Operators feel that properly structured and administered centralized services increase the efficiency, pricing power, and effectiveness of their delivery of management and brand services. They argue that their service to owners would be less effective at greater cost if the services were provided locally. Operators also argue that consistent implementation of a global brand network demands regional and central services that are beyond the reach of individual hotels. Owners recognize the value created by centralized services but have concerns in three areas: whether the charges are fair (that is, the services are provided at their true marginal cost), the ability of the operator to impose new and expensive mandates over the term of the contract for programs not anticipated during contract negotiations, and whether the effectiveness of centralized services applies equally from hotel to hotel.

Owners have heretofore granted broad rights to operators to define and impose system reimbursable charges, typically amounting to 2.5 to 5.0 percent of total revenues. However, these charges continue to grow to the point that they are equal in magnitude to management fees in some cases. Moreover, they are difficult to total at any particular property as these fees are associated with almost every aspect of hotel operations and purchasing. Two paths regarding system reimbursable charges are emerging in contracts today. The first approach is advantageous for operators and continues the existing trend toward broad rights to define and allocate system charges to hotels. Some operators have inaugurated a different approach, in response to owners' concerns, that involves a single charge that serves as the payment for all operator provided services over the term of the contract. In these cases, the system reimbursable fee is most commonly a fixed percentage of revenues, with some additional fees associated with the traditional fee per transaction for reservations.

Reporting and Controls

Two important topics are generally found in the category of reporting and controls: territorial protection and the broad topic of financial reporting and budgets. Regarding territorial protection, owners feel that they should have the right to a reasonable trade area for their hotels and should not have to compete with the operator or the operator's brands for business within the trade area. Operators know that the hotel business is highly competitive and that new entries are inevitable as hotel demand develops within a market. Their position is that they should not be precluded from adding hotels to a market – especially newly developed districts in that market – once a given hotel is successfully established.

In the past, owners were given little territorial protection, but over the years operators have added territorial protection devices in response to owner demands. Over the past ten years, such protections have generally precluded the operator from operating the same brand in a defined geographic area for a term of years, generally the initial contract term or ten years, whichever is less. Almost universally, the operator has the right to open hotels from the operator's brand family without violating the territorial protection (Dev et al. forthcoming). Most contracts shrink the geographic area over time, and some provide tests for adding new, same-brand properties in the market. Some operators have been successful in obtaining contracts that allow new competitors as long as the existing hotel is proven to be unharmed or that compensate the existing hotel even if it is harmed (sometimes referred to as impact provisions). Compensation can take the form of first rights to develop new hotels in the market or cash payments.

Financial reporting and the budgeting process are, in most cases, straightforward matters. Operators have long recognized that the hotel is being managed on behalf of the owner and that the owner needs timely and accurate reports to comply with accounting requirements. Owners that are publicly listed firms or that have fiduciary responsibility to their investors are responsible for producing the audited records of the hotel; this requires the close cooperation of the operator. In cases where the owner is a partnership or private company, the operator often produces the audited records. A recent concern has arisen for operators that are publicly listed firms in the United States. As a result of the Sarbanes-Oxley requirements, these firms no longer wish to have the liability of producing the audited records. In these cases, the owner is asked to take records prepared by the operator; the owner retains the services of an independent auditor to certify the records. While a bit more complicated, these procedures recognize the reality of contemporary liability-management practices.

Budgets are the most contentious issue between owners and operators. Budgets are the benchmark for bonuses, for incentive fees, and for performance clauses; and they serve as a set of goals to be achieved. Owners have traditionally had the right to approve the annual budgets for operating, FF&E replacement, and capital expenditures. Recent contracts, however, have restricted these rights to the favor of the operator. Examples include changing the owners' right to approve budgets to the right simply to review the budget. This is intended to remove the owner's incentive to use annual budget approval as a negotiating weapon. This change is found in many contracts with performance termination provisions. Other changes include the right to exceed agreed-upon limits to FF&E replacement and capital expenditures when these changes are framed as changes to brand standards. Increasingly, owners focus on the definitions of items that might variously be handled as a maintenance expense, an FF&E replacement, or a capital expenditure. In addition, owners are insisting on contract language and cooperation from operators to create and implement long-term furniture replacement and capital expenditure budgets, due to the large sums involved and uncertainty over whether reserve funds would be sufficient to handle anticipated expenditures. It is becoming common for the contract to acknowledge a three- to five-year planning cycle for these items to facilitate strategic and cash planning.

Summary

Management contracts have become much more substantive and sophisticated over the past fifty years – and particularly in the past two decades. What was once a relatively straightforward agreement for one company to manage a hotel on behalf of another has become a multiple-contract set of agreements that require significant experience to negotiate and understand. Management contract practice has advanced substantially, and contemporary contracts deal with a myriad of issues – notably, real property rights; intellectual property rights; hotels as financial assets; hotels as operating businesses; and the needs of owners, operators, and (increasingly) lenders. Contract provisions must be written to anticipate the needs of a property over a long time horizon – an average of twenty-five years for branded hotels and frequently as long as fifty years or more. As case law has modified the interpretation of management contracts, the parties have revised them to reflect those legal precedents. The many influences, issues, and parties involved make hotel management contracts among the most complex property management contracts in commercial real estate.

Decisions made during the negotiation and administration of a management contract can have large, lasting effects on a hotel, especially since those contract provisions are essentially the defining relationship for any given hotel. The rapid evolution of management contracts and the quick response of the parties to changing market conditions make careful study of contemporary management contracts an important topic for every hotel owner, operator, and lender. The next issue of *Cornell Hospitality Quarterly* will extend the analysis of this article to examine future trends in management contracts.

Notes

1. It should be noted that the agency matter is the most contentious issue between owners and operators, as evidenced by the spirited discussion at the May 2009 Management Contracts Roundtable at Cornell's Hotel School.
2. McDaniel (2008) presents tables showing that arbitration or the use of experts is found in 81 percent of North American contracts, 72 percent of contracts in EMEA (Europe, Middle East, Africa), and 72 percent of contracts in the Asia-Pacific region.
3. As an example, the incentive fee could be structured as follows: a gross operating profit (GOP) percentage of less than 35 percent would earn an incentive fee of 6.0 percent, a GOP percentage between 35 and 40 percent would earn an incentive fee of 7 percent, and a superior performance of a GOP percentage exceeding 40 percent would trigger an incentive fee of 8 percent.
4. A typical contract would call for the incentive fee to be 10 to 30 percent of cash flow available after an owner's priority return of 10 percent assets.

References

American Hotel and Lodging Association (AH&LA). 2009. *Directory of hotel & lodging companies*. Washington, DC: AH&LA.

Dev, Chekitan, Thomas, John H., Buschman, John and Eric Anderson. 2009. "Brand rights and management contracts: Lessons from Ritz-Carlton Bali's lawsuit against the Ritz Carlton hotel company." Working Paper. Ithaca, NY: School of Hotel Administration.

Eyster, James. 1977. Factors influencing the adoption of management contracts in the lodging industry. *Cornell Hotel and Restaurant Administration Quarterly* 17 (4): 17-26.

Eyster, James. 1988. *The negotiation and administration of hotel and restaurant management contracts*. Ithaca, NY: Cornell University Press.

Eyster, James, and Jan deRoos. 2009. *The negotiation and administration of hotel management contracts*. 4th ed. London: Pearson Custom Publishing.

McDaniel, K. C. 2008. Current issues in the negotiation of hotel management agreements. In *Modern real estate transactions*. Philadelphia: American Law Institute and the American Bar Association.

Renard, James, and Kristi Motley. 2003. The agency challenge: How *Woolley, Woodley*, and other cases rearranged the hotel-management landscape. *Cornell Hotel and Restaurant Administration Quarterly* 44 (3): 58-76.

Segal, David. 2009. Pillow fights at the Four Seasons. *New York Times*, Business Section, June 28, p. 1.

Sherwyn, David. 2010. How employment law became a major issue for hotel operators. *Cornell Hospitality Quarterly*, 51.

Wales, Karen, and Lauro Ferroni. 2008. *Hotel management contracts*. New York: Jones Lang LaSalle Hotels.

25

Real Estate Investment Trusts: Performance, Recent Findings, and Future Directions

Peng (Peter) Liu

Created by the U.S. Congress in 1960, real estate investment trusts (REITs) have become an important segment of the U.S. economy and investment markets. REITs have seen their equity market capitalization soar from $5 billion to roughly $271 billion in just the past twenty-five years. In the process, that growth has set the stage for the adoption of the REIT approach to securitized real estate across the globe. The REIT industry has evolved dramatically over the past twenty years, so that major REITs today are actively engaged in operations through vertically integrated asset management. A typical vertical articulation in a single firm may span such functions as raw land acquisition and development, portfolio management, and operational-level property-tenant services.

REITs deserve our attention because studying their performance helps us understand better the value of commercial properties, which account for a significant proportion of the world's wealth. In addition, REIT stocks are often not covered in the finance literature. Even though REITs are traded on public exchanges, many finance researchers specifically exclude REITs from their samples, in part perhaps because REITs behave differently from other stocks in general financial markets.

The objective of this article is to summarize recent findings regarding REITs. The scope of research involving REITs has expanded substantially in recent years, and REITs provide a laboratory in which to study long-standing issues in financial markets and corporate finance. More than 140 articles on REITs were summarized by Corgel, McIntosh, and Ott (1995), and that work has been updated by Zietz, Sirmans, and Friday (2003). H. Chan, Erickson, and Wang (2003) have also done an intensive literature survey on the structure and performance of REITs. Recent studies examining REITs are organized into two major categories: (1) corporate financing decisions of REITs and (2) REIT pricing, performance, and financial market implications. This article examines previous studies with an emphasis on post-2003 publications in finance and real estate journals, and offers a brief discussion of lodging REITs. In the course this discussion I lay out a research agenda for this sector. After introducing the REIT institutional background, I review the literature on corporate finance–related issues and then pricing and financial market implications. Finally, I focus specifically on lodging REITs, which own and often operate hotels, motels, and resorts.

Institutional Background of REITs

REITs make it possible for investors at all levels to invest in large-scale, income-producing real properties by offering shares that function much like other liquid securities. To make REITs a more attractive investment, Congress waived corporate-level income taxes on REITs if they qualify under certain tax provisions – chiefly, that they disburse nearly all of their earnings as dividends. REITs are not taxed directly on their earnings, but the distributed earnings do represent taxable dividend income to shareholders.

Regulatory Constraints on REITs

A firm must meet several requirements to become a REIT. Although these requirements change over time, they can be grouped roughly into the following four categories:

- *Distribution requirements:* At least 90 percent of a REIT's annual taxable income must be distributed to shareholders as dividends.[1]
- *Asset requirements:* In each quarter, at least 75 percent of the value of a REIT's assets must consist of real estate properties, mortgages, cash, and government securities.[2]
- *Income requirements:* Annually, at least 75 percent of a REIT's gross income must be derived from income related to real estate, such as rents from

real property, mortgage interest, dividends from other REIT holdings, or gains from property sales. Additionally, at least 95 percent of the gross income must be derived from the above-listed sources, but it can also include other passive forms of income such as dividends and interest from non–real estate sources, such as bank deposit interest.[3]

- *Ownership requirements:* A REIT cannot be a closely held corporation. Shares in a REIT must be transferable and must be held by a minimum of one hundred persons. No more than 50 percent of a REIT's stock may be held by five or fewer distinct shareholders.[4] This is known as the 5/50 rule.

A company is prohibited from repeatedly switching its REIT status to minimize taxes. If a company loses its qualified status, the IRS can demand back taxes and interest on those taxes, and perhaps penalties. The company will also be barred from becoming a REIT for at least five years.

REITs are categorized into these three types:

1. equity REITs (investing in real properties, such as industrial, office, retail, multifamily, lodging, and other types);
2. mortgage REITs (lending or investing in mortgage/mortgage-backed securities); and
3. hybrid REITs (a combination of the above two types).

Becoming a REIT is simply a tax status election. Publicly traded REITs are governed by the same SEC and listing regulations as other publicly traded stocks. Going public is a separate decision from the decision to become a REIT. Exhibit 1 shows the evolution of public REITs in term of numbers of firms and total assets.

Corporate Finance Issues Involving REITs

Capital Structure

The academic corporate finance literature has explored the effects of taxes on a firm's capital structure in great detail. Theory suggests that there is a significant tax gain to be realized from corporate borrowing. Firms balance benefits (e.g., tax savings) against costs (e.g., deadweight bankruptcy costs) from debt. Howe and Shilling (1988) claim that there is a strong tax disadvantage to the use of debt for non-tax-paying firms, since these firms must compete in debt markets with firms for which interest expenses result in tax savings. Because they can count on a tax deduction, tax-paying firms can afford to pay higher interest on debt. Due to their tax-exempt status, the

Exhibit 1: Historical REIT industry market capitalization: 1971–2009

End of year	Composite		Equity		Mortgage		Hybrid	
	Number of REITs	Market capitalization	Number of REITs	Market capitalization	Number of REITs	Market capitalization	Number of REITs	Market capitalization
1971	34	1,494.30	12	332.00	12	570.80	10	591.60
1972	46	1,880.90	17	377.30	18	774.70	11	728.90
1973	53	1,393.50	20	336.00	22	517.30	11	540.20
1974	53	712.40	19	241.90	22	238.80	12	231.70
1975	46	899.70	12	275.70	22	312.00	12	312.00
1976	62	1,308.00	27	409.60	22	415.60	13	482.80
1977	69	1,528.10	32	538.10	19	398.30	18	591.60
1978	71	1,412.40	33	575.70	19	340.30	19	496.40
1979	71	1,754.00	32	743.60	19	377.10	20	633.30
1980	75	2,298.60	35	942.20	21	509.50	19	846.80
1981	76	2,438.90	36	977.50	21	541.30	19	920.10
1982	66	3,298.60	30	1,071.40	20	1,133.40	16	1,093.80
1983	59	4,257.20	26	1,468.60	19	1,460.00	14	1,328.70
1984	59	5,085.30	25	1,794.50	20	1,801.30	14	1,489.40
1985	82	7,674.00	37	3,270.30	32	3,162.40	13	1,241.20
1986	96	9,923.60	45	4,336.10	35	3,625.80	16	1,961.70
1987	110	9,702.40	53	4,758.50	38	3,161.40	19	1,782.40
1988	117	11,435.20	56	6,141.70	40	3,620.80	21	1,672.60
1989	120	11,662.20	56	6,769.60	43	3,536.30	21	1,356.30
1990	119	8,737.10	58	5,551.60	43	2,549.20	18	636.30
1991	138	12,968.20	86	8,785.50	28	2,586.30	24	1,596.40
1992	142	15,912.00	89	11,171.10	30	2,772.80	23	1,968.10
1993	189	32,158.70	135	26,081.90	32	3,398.50	22	2,678.20
1994	226	44,306.00	175	38,812.00	29	2,502.70	22	2,991.30
1995	219	57,541.30	178	49,913.00	24	3,395.40	17	4,232.90
1996	199	88,776.30	166	78,302.00	20	4,778.60	13	5,695.80
1997	211	140,533.80	176	127,825.30	26	7,370.30	9	5,338.20
1998	210	138,301.40	173	126,904.50	28	6,480.70	9	4,916.20
1999	203	124,261.90	167	118,232.70	26	4,441.70	10	1,587.50
2000	189	138,715.40	158	134,431.00	22	1,632.00	9	2,652.40
2001	182	154,898.60	151	147,092.10	22	3,990.50	9	3,816.00
2002	176	161,937.30	149	151,271.50	20	7,146.40	7	3,519.40

2003	171	224,211.90	144	204,800.40	20	14,186.51	7	5,225.00
2004	193	307,894.73	153	275,291.04	33	25,964.32	7	6,639.37
2005	197	330,691.31	152	301,490.98	37	23,393.73	8	5,806.61
2006	183	438,071.10	138	400,741.40	38	29,195.30	7	8,134.30
2007	152	312,009.00	118	288,694.60	29	19,054.10	5	4,260.30
2008	136	191,651.00	113	176,237.70	20	14,280.50	3	1,132.90
2009	142	271,199.20	115	248,355.20	23	22,103.20	4	740.80

Source: National Association of Real Estate Investment Trusts.
Note: This table shows historical real estate investment trust (REIT) equity market capitalization outstanding at year-end from 1971 to 2009. Numbers are in millions of dollars.

researchers argue, REITs should involve little or no debt financing. Jaffe (1991) disputes that reasoning and shows that the tax code is only one factor explaining leverage. Under general conditions, Jaffe's model shows that the values of REITs do not vary with leverage.

Rather than simply focus on total debt, Brown and Riddiough (2003) provide a detailed examination of the debt structure of REITs. They believe that firms adjust their leverage ratios towards optimal target levels and that each incremental financing activity is undertaken to adjust a firm's overall leverage to reach its target level. Brown and Riddiough find in addition that public debt is typically used to reconfigure a REIT's liability structure to maintain its credit rating, while equity offerings are more likely to fund investment. Consistent with Brown and Riddiough, Hardin and Wu (2009) find that REITs with banking relationships tend to operate with lower leverage.

Another popular explanation of a firm's capital structure is the "pecking order" theory, which states that firms prioritize their sources of financing. The order is as follows: internal funds are used first; when that source is depleted, debt is issued; and when the debt capacity is reached, equity is issued. Feng, Ghosh, and Sirmans (2007) find that REITs with historically high market-to-book ratios tend to have persistently high leverage ratios. In essence, REITs enjoying strong growth opportunity and high market valuation raise funds through debt issues.

Using a sample of REIT issuance decisions, Boudry, Kallberg, and Liu (forthcoming) conclude that REITs strategically time the market when they adjust their capital structures. REITs operate in one of the few industries in which a firm's underlying assets trade in a secondary market. Therefore, analysts are able to obtain a mark-to-market measure of a firm's assets, the net asset value (NAV), as an alternative measure on the equity market. Boudry, Kallberg, and Liu find that a REIT is more likely to issue equity when its price-to-NAV ratio is high. Consistent with traditional market timing, REITs are more likely to issue equity after experiencing large price increases. Counter to the results of Feng, Ghosh, and Sirmans (2007), though, Boudry, Kallberg, and Liu find no evidence that the static pecking order plays an important role in REIT financing decisions.

The illiquidity of corporate assets represents a significant private cost to firms that choose to finance with debt. When a firm is in distress and has to liquidate its assets, potential industry buyers in the same industry are likely experiencing similar business difficulties and thus cannot pay full value for the assets. This effect of liquidation values on corporate debt capacity predicts that firms with relatively more liquid assets will prefer debt financing to equity. Giambona, Harding, and Sirmans (2008) find that evidence from the REIT industry supports the above hypothesis and report that REITs specializing in shorter lease maturity assets (higher liquidation value) use more leverage and longer debt maturity.

Corporate Governance

In the past few years, corporate governance issues have attracted considerable attention, particularly as they relate to issues of managers as agents. REITs offer a natural experiment through which to test corporate governance hypotheses due to their special legal and organizational structure. One of the most restrictive legal requirements is the 90 percent mandatory payout, which leaves little free cash flow for management. This legal obligation limits the opportunities for managerial expropriation and reduces agency problems. Hartzell, Kallberg, and Liu (2005) find that REITs with stronger governance structures have high initial public offering (IPO) valuations and better long-term operating performance than do their peers.

Another hypothesis states that the legal setting in which REITs operate should be complemented by internal corporate governance mechanisms to prevent managerial entrenchment and thus reduce agency problems. The 5/50 rule is designed to prevent the entrenchment of a small block of holders. Eichholtz and Kok (2008) argue that the 5/50 rule deters the formation of large block holders and protects REIT managers from the scrutiny of the market for corporate control.

Bauer, Eichholtz, and Kok (2009) investigate the governance-performance relation using the corporate governance quotient index. They find that corporate governance does not matter for firm value and operating performance in a sample of U.S. REITs. This is in contrast to the strong positive relationship between governance and performance found in other industries. They also find that, for a subsample of REITs with relatively low payout ratios, governance is important. They attribute the weakening relationship to the mandatory payout rule and operational restrictions, which reduce the cost of deviations from the optimal governance structure.

Hartzell, Sun, and Titman (2006) study the effect of corporate governance on REIT investment decisions. They find that REITs with stronger corporate governance respond more positively to their real estate investment opportunities after controlling for other factors. Specifically, investment choices are more closed tied to Tobin's q (the ratio of stock market value to equity book value) if a REIT has greater institutional ownership or if it has lower director and officer stock ownership. Those results are consistent with the hypothesis that the independent directors and institutions serve a monitoring role and act as a check on managers' tendency to overinvest.

Dividend Payout Policy

Although the 2001 tax regulations state that REITs are required to pay out 90 percent of earnings, this regulation constraint does not seem to be entirely binding. Bradley, Capozza, and Seguin (1998) report that dividend payouts in their sample are on average about twice the net income. One reason for the requirement that REITs pay out most earnings to shareholders is that this reduces agency costs. It is a well-documented fact that managers have incentives to invest in negative net present value (NPV) projects if their compensation is related to company size. With limited retained earnings, REIT managers have to issue new debt or equity securities if they want to acquire a new building. Then the capital market will provide an effective monitoring function. Wang, Erickson, and Gau (1993) support the above hypothesis and find that REITs with high debt-to-asset ratios or low asset growth rates tend to pay out more dividends.

Another reason that REITs pay high dividends is to signal a firm's future cash flows. Standard finance textbooks say that managers should maintain a stable or increasing dividend-payment stream, as dividend cuts will be penalized by the capital market. If the 90 percent dividend payout constraint is really binding, we should observe dividend payouts fluctuating with REIT earnings. Therefore, by paying more dividends, the manager is essentially signaling to capital markets that future earnings will be higher. Bradley, Capozza, and Seguin (1998) find that REITs with greater leverage, smaller asset bases, or undiversified asset bases offer lower dividend payout rates. Because such firms have high cash flow volatility, it is more difficult for them to maintain a high dividend payout ratio.

Ghosh and Sirmans (2006) examine the influence of managerial performance, ownership, and governance on REIT dividend policies. Their analyses demonstrate that shareholders demand bigger dividends from poorly performing firms out of concern that managers would otherwise waste corporate assets on value-destroying projects. Dividends are a negative function of CEO stock ownership and are positively affected by board independence and a CEO's length of service.

Departing from the extant dividend policy literature, which does not differentiate between mandatory and nonmandatory dividend payments, Hardin and Hill (2008) study the determinants of excess dividend payments above mandatory requirements in REITs. They conclude that excess dividend payments are related to factors associated with reduced agency costs, such as the acquisition of short-term bank debt that subjects the firm to additional monitoring, the use of stock repurchase programs, and strong operating performance.

Initial Public Offerings

Investors in IPOs of common stocks in the United States earned, on average, about an 18 percent return on the first day of trading during the 1970 to 2000 period, indicating significant underpricing for industrial firm IPOs.

However, REIT IPOs provided their investors only a 0.21 percent gain during the same period, according to Wang, Chan, and Gau (1992) and H. Chan, Erickson and Wang (2003). Noting this phenomenon, researchers sought to determine what is special about REIT IPOs and what contributes to REITs' overpricing for IPOs. Ling and Ryngaert (1997), using a later time frame, document underpricing for REIT IPOs and find positive abnormal performance up to one hundred days after the offering. They indicate the following three possible reasons for REIT IPOs to behave differently from industrial firm IPOs: (1) the REITs have greater valuation uncertainty, (2) the REIT market comprises more institutional investors than does the industrial market, and (3) the organizational structure of REITs makes them more like a mutual fund IPO.

Buttimer, Hyland, and Sanders (2005) analyze the long-term performance of REIT IPOs. They find no evidence of the volatile post-IPO stock market performance that is typically found for other stocks. Taking a different approach, Hartzell, Kallberg, and Liu (2005) focused on the degree to which the characteristics of the underlying real estate markets, such as returns on unsecuritized commercial real estate, dividend payout, vacancy rates, and space market supply and demand, can help explain REIT IPO volume and long-term operating performances. They find no relationship between the heat of the IPO market and post-IPO operating performance.

REIT Pricing and Performance

Because REIT shares represent securitized real estate, their pricing may diverge from that of shares of industrial companies, because REITs may have different risk and return performance. Moreover, since REITs represent an alternative form of investment, investors might seek to know the extent to which REIT stocks are integrated into the general stock market. In short, the question is whether REITs are a form of real estate or stocks.

REIT Pricing

Gentry, Kemsley, and Mayer (2003) find that a firm's value is positively related to a firm's tax basis, indicating that future dividend taxes are capitalized into share prices. They estimated that each dollar of tax basis increases a REIT's share prices by nine to twenty-six cents, conditional on the fair market value of properties.

In the finance literature, classical dividend pricing (or present value) models are rejected using only dividends but accepted when share repurchases are included. The REIT mandate to pay out no less than 90 percent of earnings provides a test of those models. Using an index of REITs, Kallberg, Liu, and Srinivasan (2003) reexamine those models and conclude that the dividend-pricing models cannot be rejected.

Barkham and Geltner (1995) show that securitized real estate markets lead direct markets and conclude that direct markets are to some extent informationally inefficient. MacKinnon and Al Zaman (2009) find that REIT returns and returns to direct real estate both revert to the mean, which is caused by a tendency on the part of commercial property transaction prices to overshoot inflation. However, at all horizons REITs remain riskier than direct real estate. REITs play little or no role in optimal portfolios when both REITs and direct real estate are available, especially for large, long-horizon investors.

Glascock, Lu, and So (2000) believe that there was a structural change in the early 1990s due to increased participation by institutional investors. They find that equity REITs have behaved more like traditional stocks than like real estate since 1992. In contrast, Clayton and Mackinnon (2003) show that equity REIT returns become increasingly sensitive to the performance of the underlying real estate and that REIT stocks have behaved more like real estate since 1992. They also find that small-cap REITs behave more like real estate than do large-cap REITs. Finding the opposite result, Lee, Lee, and Chiang (2008) show that large-cap REITs behave more like real estate than do small-cap REITs. They interpret the above results as evidence that institutional investors provide information-gathering services and strengthen the linkage between REIT returns and underlying real estate factors.

The development of a multifactor model in real estate has seen an increasing focus on macro-factor approaches. One of the earliest works, K. C. Chan, Hendershott, and Sanders (1990), examines equity REIT returns using the capital asset pricing model (CAPM) and arbitrage pricing theory (APT) approaches. Chen, Hsieh, and Jordan (1997) compare multifactor models using macro-economic variables with principal component analysis (PCA) for REIT returns and conclude that the macro-factor model outperforms a statistical PCA model. Ling and Naranjo (1997, 1999), Ling, Naranjo and Ryngaert (2000), and others are all in favor of macro-factor approaches. However, the macro-factor model requires proxies for the key systematic risk factors to be priced fairly in high-frequency trading. Furthermore, the normality assumption is frequently rejected when measuring commercial real estate return. Lizieri, Satchell, and Zhang (2007) revisit the statistical approach and explore an independent component analysis (ICA) approach. Their examination of individual REIT returns suggests that the ICA procedure performs better than the PCA by considering skewness and kurtosis of return distribution.

Chui, Titman, and Wei (2003a, 2003b) examine the determinants of REIT returns in a multifactor framework and also find a structural break in the early 1990s. Before 1990, REIT returns were associated with the following four factors: momentum, size, turnover, and analyst coverage. However, only momentum was a significant factor in the post-1990 sample.

REIT Performance

Real estate firms can choose among a several organizational forms, such as REIT, master limited partnership (MLP), business trust, and corporation. As I explained above, the REIT has tax advantages over the other organizational forms, but REITs also have tighter restrictions, notably, the mandatory payout requirement. Damodaran, John, and Liu (1997) examine changes by real estate firms among these four types of organizational forms: REIT, MLP, business trust, and corporation. They classify these forms according to whether changing from one to another is to a looser or a tighter structure; and they document the associated changes in profitability, free cash flow, debt, and dividends from one form to another. They find that firms under financial distress at the time of organizational form change move to a more flexible structure, with subsequent reductions in dividends, improvements in performance, and increases in asset sales and investment.

Several studies have explored whether predictability improves the performance for an investor with a short investment horizon – that is, an investor who exploits only market timing and contemporaneous diversification opportunities. Liu and Mei (1994) analyzed the out-of-sample performance of investment REITs with predictable returns and found that active strategies outperform passive ones, even after deducting transaction costs. This is no longer the case in more recent studies, such as Nelling and Gyourko (1998) and Ling, Naranjo, and Ryngaert (2000), who find it difficult to exploit predictability, particularly in the 1990s. While these studies focus on short-term portfolio strategies, Fugazza, Guidolin, and Nicodano (2009) investigate the welfare gains of time diversification in a multiperiod setting. They find that diversification into REITs increases both the Sharpe ratio (a ratio of excess return to investment riskiness) and the certainty equivalent of wealth for all investment horizons.

Information and REIT Performance

Damodaran and Liu (1993) study the way in which private information of real estate value spreads to the stock market via insider trading. REITs that choose to have their assets appraised provide an opportunity to examine how private information is used by insiders of the firm and how the private information signal operates to general stock market participants. There is substantial evidence that insider trading is present around corporate announcements and that insider trading generates abnormal stock returns. However, the timing and contents of private information are hard to measure and normally unobservable by researchers. Since REIT assets are mostly real properties, the REIT managers often hire an independent appraiser to value the firm's assets. Damodaran and Liu find that REIT insiders seem to trust the appraised value and trade on it for a profit and, in the process, reveal their information to outsiders. They attribute the informational value of appraisals to that fact that the independent appraisers combine the data from comparable properties with the internal data from the performance measures of REIT being appraised.

Capozza and Israelsen (2007) show evidence that levels of predictability vary with firm size, leverage, and investment focus. They find that momentum is stronger for larger, more leveraged REITs; while reversion is faster for focused, leveraged REITs. Those findings are consistent with the hypothesis that REIT information is either less costly to acquire or has less impact on fundamental value and should therefore exhibit less predictability.

Ambrose, Lee, and Peek (2007) study the information spillover effect after a REIT is included in a Standard & Poor's index. Even though REITs have been in existence for more than four decades, they play only limited roles in asset allocation for general investors. Beginning October 2001, twenty-one REITs were included in an S&P market index (i.e., S&P500, S&P400, and S&P600). Ambrose, Lee, and Peek use the index inclusion as a natural experiment as a nonfundamental event. They find that returns on REITs that remain outside those indexes tend to become more highly correlated with returns on general market indexes after other REITs join the indexes.

Subrahmanyam (2007) examines the liquidity and order flow spillover effect across New York Stock Exchange stocks and REITs using Granger causality tests and impulse-response functions. They find that (1) there are persistent liquidity spillovers running from REITs to non-REITs; (2) non-REIT effective spreads forecast shifts in REIT spreads at both daily and monthly horizons, and this effect is economically significant; and (3) order flows and returns in the stock market negatively forecast REIT order flows, which is consistent with the view that a REIT is a substitute investment for the stock market investors.

Lodging REITs

Lodging REITs have had a substantial effect on the ownership and operation of lodging properties, but one could ask whether REITs are a good ownership form for the lodging industry. Hotels and other such properties push the bounds of the internal revenue code's attempts to constrain REITs to a passive role. The intensive daily operations in the hotel industry pose a challenge to

Exhibit 2: Lodging REIT descriptions

Company name	Ticker	Property focus	Headquarters	Description
Ashford Hospitality Trust	AHT	Full service	Dallas, TX	Owns and has interests in more than 100 upscale hotels across 24 states and Washington, D.C.; most operate under the Hilton, Hyatt, Marriott, and Sheraton
FelCor LodgingTrust	FCH	Full service	Irving, TX	Owns upscale all-suite hotels, hotels, and resorts, located in 23 states
Host Hotels&Resorts	HST	Full service	Bethesda, MD	The largest lodging REIT, owns upscale and luxury full-service hotel properties in the U.S. and worldwide
LaSalle Hotel Properties	LHO	Full service	Bethesda, MD	Owns upscale and luxury full-service hotels in 11 states and D.C.
MHI Hospitality Cor.	MDH	Full service	Williamsburg, VA	Owns midscale, upscale, and upper-upscale full service hotels in the mid-Atlantic, Midwest and southeastern states
Strategic Hotels&Resorts	BEE	Full service	Chicago, IL	Owns luxury hotels and resorts in the U.S., Mexico and Europe
Sunstone Hotel Investors	SHO	Full service	San Clemente, CA	Owns upscale hotels mostly in New York and California
DiamondRock Hospitality	DRH	Full service	Bethesda, MD	Owns premium hotels in New York, Los Angeles, Chicago, Boston, and Atlanta. Hotels are operated under brands owned by Marriott, Starwood, and Hilton.
Pebblebrook Hotel Trust	PEB	Full service	Bethesda, MD	IPO in Dec. 2009, Pebblebrook plans to buy full-service and select-service luxury properties that don't need a major renovation
Hersha Hospitality Trust	HT	Limited service	Philadelphia, PA	Owns primarily midscale, upscale, and extended-stay properties in central business districts. The properties are operated under such brands as Comfort Inn, Fairfield Inn, Hampton Inn, Hilton Garden Inn, and Holiday Inn Express.
Hospitality Properties Trust	HPT	Limited service	Newton, MA	Owns midscale mostly suite hotels located in 38 states in the United States; Puerto Rico; and Ontario, Canada
Supertel Hospitality	SPPR	Limited service	Norfolk, NE	Owns limited-service hotels in 23 midwestern and eastern states

Source: SNL financial, Hoovers.
Note: As of January 1, 2010. REIT = real estate investment trust.

Exhibit 3: Lodging REIT statistics

Company name	Ticker	Hotels owned	Rooms owned	Market capitalization	IPO year
Ashford Hospitality Trust	AHT	103	23,255	99.5	2003
FelCor Lodging Trust	FCH	89	25,656	118.2	1994
Host Hotels&Resorts	HST	243	63,076	3,976.5	1953
LaSalle Hotel Properties	LHO	31	8,494	453.8	1998
MHI Hospitality Cor.	MDH	9	2,199	8.8	2004
Strategic Hotels&Resorts	BEE	19	8,347	125	2004
Sunstone Hotel Investors	SHO	44	15,029	296.3	2004
DiamondRock Hospitality	DRH	20	9,586	456.6	2005
Pebblebrook Hotel Trust	PEB	NA	NA	NA	2009
Hersha Hospitality Trust	HT	76	9,556	144.8	1999
Hospitality Properties Trust	HPT	289	42,881	1,397.7	1995
Supertel Hospitality	SPPR	123	10,702	35.6	1994

Source: SNL financial.
Note: As of end of 2008. REIT = real estate investment trust.

the use of REITs to securitize real estate properties. On the positive side, REITs offer protection from the corporate taxes (and provide an income stream to shareholders). Moreover, REITs can spread the risk of hotel ownership over a wider financial and geographic base.

Although REITs have received considerable attention, little research has focused directly on lodging REITs. The first comprehensive discussion on lodging REITs was written by Paul Beals and John Arabia and published in *Cornell Hotel and Restaurant Administration Quarterly* in 1998. They provide an overview of REIT history and discuss a variety of REIT forms that have been used for hotel industry – in particular, the paired-share REIT, which is unique to hotel REITs. A paired-share REIT is a combination of a REIT and a C Corporation that trades as a single investment unit and has the same shareholders. The REIT owns real estate that is leased to the C Corporation, a fully taxable entity that operates the property. At the time of the 1998 *CQ* article, four paired-share REITs were extant. They were Starwood W Lodging Trust (which had bought out California Jockey Club/Pay Meadows Operating Co in July 1997), Patriot American Hospitality, First Union Real Estate Investments, and Meditrust Corp (which had purchased Santa Anita Realty Enterprises Inc in November 1997). These four companies did have their activities restricted, but since then the REIT Modernization Act of 1999 has loosened some of the restrictions and allowed REITs to own taxable REIT subsidiaries.

Based on a sample of sixteen hotel REITs and fifty-one non-REIT corporations from 1993 to 1999, Mooradian and Yang (2001) find the significant differences for the two types of company. The non-REIT companies are more heavily leveraged, pay lower dividends, and retain a larger amount of free cash flow than do the REITs.

Kim, Mattila, and Gu (2002) compare the performances of hotel REITs with six other REIT sectors, as well as the overall stock market. They find that hotel REITs carry the highest market risk and underperformed office, industrial, and diversified REIT sectors.

Gu and Kim (2003) extend the Kim, Mattila, and Gu (2002) study and further research the determinants of the unsystematic risk of U.S. hotel REIT firms. They show that high leverage and high dividend payout tend to magnify the unsystematic risk, where large capitalization helps mitigate the unsystematic risk. Their results suggest that hotel REITs should use less debt financing and should consolidate via mergers and acquisitions.

Conclusions

The research record of REITs for the lodging industry is all too short. Given that hospitality REITs are well established, one question is whether public REITs are, in fact, a good form of ownership for hotels; and another is what factors should apply as one compares a lodging REIT with a hotel operating company. Given the diversity of ownership forms, the lodging industry is a fruitful area for research in this area. In this regard, Sunstone Hotel Investors has an interesting story to tell. Formed in 1985, Sunstone became a publicly trade REIT in 1995. Four years later, Sunstone was taken private in a management buyout with Westbrook Partners, a private equity firm. The company made an IPO again five years later, in October 2004, when the equity market was more favorable. Clearly, the principals saw a benefit to these changes. Their experience raises the questions of whether the REIT's tax benefits offset the regulatory requirements. Research might examine the pros and cons of REIT ownership versus that of a regular corporation and how performance under different ownership structures varies in different phases of the economic cycle. Those are potential research areas that have not explored in the lodging industry.

Notes

1. Before 2001, the minimum dividend payout ratio was constrained at 95 percent.
2. Since 2001, real estate investment trusts (REITs) have been allowed to own taxable REIT subsidiaries (TRSs), which engage in servicing tenants. However, no more than 25 percent of a REIT's assets can consist of TRS.
3. No more than 30 percent of the gross income can be derived from the sale of stocks or securities held for less than six months or the disposition of real properties held for less than four years other than properties involuntarily converted or foreclosed on.
4. With the "look-through" provision enacted in 1993, pension funds are considered for the purpose of this rule to represent as many owners as there are pension plan members. Thus, in effect, institutional investors are not limited by this ownership requirement.

References

Ambrose, Brent W., Dong Wook Lee, and Joe Peek. 2007. Industry comovement after joining an index: Spillovers of nonfundamental effects. *Real Estate Economics* 35 (1): 57–90.

Barkham, R., and D. Geltner. 1995. Price discovery in American and British property markets. *Real Estate Economics* 23 (1): 21–44.

Bauer, R., Eichholtz, P., and Kok, N. 2010. Corporate governance and performance: The REIT effect. *Real Estate Economics* 38 (1), 1–29.

Beals, Paul, and John V. Arabia. 1998. Lodging REITs. *Cornell Hotel and Restaurant Administration Quarterly.* 39 (6): 52–59.

Boudry, W., J. Kallberg, and C. Liu. Forthcoming. An analysis of REIT security insurance decisions. *Real Estate Economics.*

Bradley, Michael, Capozza, Dennis R., and Seguin, Paul J. Dividend policy and cash-flow uncertainty. *Real Estate Economics* 26 (4): 555–580.

Brown, David T., Brian A. Ciochetti, and Timothy J. Riddiough. 2006. Theory and evidence on the resolution of financial distress. *Review of Financial Studies* 19 (4): 1357–97.

Brown, David T., and Riddiough, Timothy J. 2003. Financing Choice and Liability Structure of Real Estate Investment Trusts. *Real Estate Economics* 31 (3): 313–346.

Buttimer, R. J., D. C. Hyland, and A. B. Sanders. 2005. REITs, IPO waves, and long-run performance. *Real Estate Economics* 33:51–87.

Capozza, D., and Israelsen, R. 2007. Predictability in Equilibrium: The Price Dynamics of Real Estate Investment Trusts. *Real Estate Economics* 35 (4): 541–567.

Clayton, J., and G. Mackinnon. 2003. The relative importance of stock, bond, and real estate factors in explaining REIT returns. *Journal of Real Estate Finance and Economics* 27:39–60.

Chan, H., J. Erickson, and K. Wang. 2003. *Real estate investment trusts: Structure, performance, and investment opportunities.* Oxford: Oxford University Press.

Chen, S. J., C. H. Hsieh, and B. D. Jordan. 1997. Real estate and the arbitrage pricing theory: Macrovariables vs. derived factors. *Real Estate Economics* 25 (3): 505–523.

Chiang, Kevin C. H., Kirill Kozehvnikov, Ming-Long Lee, and Craig H. Wisen. 2008. Further evidence on the performance of funds of funds: The case of real estate mutual funds. *Real Estate Economics* 36 (1): 47–61.

Chui, A. C., S. Titman, and John Wei. 2003a. The cross-section of expected REIT returns. *Real Estate Economics* 31:451–79.

Chui, A. C., S. Titman, and John Wei. 2003b. Intra-industry momentum: The case of REITs. *Journal of Financial Markets* 6:363–87.

Corgel, John B., W. McIntosh, and S. H. Ott. 1995. Real estate investment trusts: A review of the financial economics literature. *Journal of Real Estate Literature* 3:13–43.

Damodaran, Aswath, Kose John, and Crocker H. Liu. 1997. The determinants of organizational form changes: Evidence and implications from real estate. *Journal of Financial Economics* 45:169–92.

Damodaran, Aswath, and Crocker H. Liu. 1993. Insider trading as a signal of private information. *Review of Financial Studies* 6 (1): 79–119.

Eichholtz, Piet M., and Nils Kok. 2008. How does the market for corporate control function for property companies? *Journal of Real Estate Finance and Economics* 36 (2): 141–63.

Feng, Z., C. Ghosh, and C. F. Sirmans. 2007. On the capital structure of real estate investment trusts (REITs). *Journal of Real Estate Finance and Economics* 34:81–105.

Fugazza, Carolina, Guidolin, Massimo and Nicodano, Giovanna. 2009. Time and Risk Diversification in Real Estate Investments: Assessing the Ex Post Economic Value. *Real Estate Economics* 37 (3): 341–381.

Gentry, William M., Deen Kemsley, and Christopher J. Mayer. 2003. Dividend taxes and share prices: Evidence from real estate investment trusts. *Journal of Finance* 57 (1): 261–82.

Ghosh, C., and C. F. Sirmans. 2006. Do managerial motives impact dividend decisions in REITs? *Journal of Real Estate Finance and Economics* 32:327–55.

Giambona, Erasmo, John P. Harding, and C. F. Sirmans. 2008. Explaining the variation in REIT capital structure: The role of asset liquidation value. *Real Estate Economics* 36 (1): 111–37.

Glascock, John L., Chiuling Lu, and Raymond W. So. 2000. Further evidence on the integration of REIT, bond, and stock returns. *Journal of Real Estate Finance and Economics* 20 (2): 177–94.

Gu, Zheng, and Hyunjoon Kim. 2002. An examination of the determinants of hotel REITS' unsystematic risk. *Journal of Hospitality & Tourism Research* 27 (2): 166–84.

Hardin, William, III, and Matthew D. Hill. 2008. REIT dividend determinants: Excess dividends and capital markets. *Real Estate Economics* 36 (1): 349–69.

Hardin, William, III, and Wu, Z. 2009. Banking Relationships and REIT Capital Structure, *Real Estate Economics* Forthcoming.

Hartzell, J., J. Kallberg, and C. H. Liu. 2005. The role of underlying real asset market in REIT IPOs. *Real Estate Economics* 33:27–50.

Hartzell, J. C., L. Sun, and S. Titman. 2006. The effect of corporate governance on investment: Evidence from real estate investment trusts. *Real Estate Economics* 34 (3): 343–76.

Howe, John S., and James D. Shilling. 1988. Capital structure theory and REIT security offerings. *Journal of Finance* 43 (4): 983–93.

Jaffe, Jeffrey F. 1991. Taxes and the capital structure of partnerships, REIT's, and related entities. *Journal of Finance* 46 (1): 401–7.

Kallberg, Jarl G., Liu, Crocker H., and Srinivasan, Anand. 2003. Dividend Pricing Models and REITs. *Real Estate Economics* 31 (1): 435–450.

Kim, Hyunjoon, Anna S. Mattila, and Zheng Gu. 2002. Performance of hotel real estate investment trusts: A comparative analysis of Jensen indexes. *International Journal of Hospitality Management* 21 (1): 85–97.

Lee, Ming-Long, Ming-Te Lee, and Kevin C. H. Chiang. 2008. Real estate risk exposure of equity real estate investment trusts. *Journal of Real Estate Finance and Economics* 36 (2): 165–81.

Ling, D. C., and A. Naranjo. 1997. Economic risk factors and commercial real estate returns. *Journal of Real Estate Finance and Economics* 14:283–307.

Ling, D. C., and A. Naranjo. 1999. The integration of commercial real estate markets and stock markets. *Real Estate Economics* 27:483–515.

Ling, D., A. Naranjo, and M. Ryngaert. 2000. The predictability of equity REIT returns: Time variation and economic significance. *Journal of Real Estate Finance and Economics* 20:117–36.

Ling, David C., and Michael D. Ryngaert. 1997. Valuation uncertainty, institutional involvement, and the under-pricing of IPOs: The case of REITs. *Journal of Financial Economics* 43:433–56.

Liu, C., and J. Mei. 1994. An analysis of real estate risk using the present value model. *Journal of Real Estate Finance and Economics* 8:5–20.

Lizieri, Colin, Stephen Satchell, and Qi Zhang. 2007. The underlying return-generating factors for REIT returns: An application of independent component analysis. *Real Estate Economics* 35 (4): 569–98.

MacKinnon, Gregory H., and Ashraf Al Zaman. 2009. Real estate for the long term: The effect of return predictability on long-horizon allocations. *Real Estate Economics* 37 (1): 117–53.

Mooradian, Robert, and Shiawee Yang. 2001. Dividend policy and firm performance: Hotel REITs vs. non-REIT hotel companies. *Journal of Real Estate Portfolio Management* 7 (1): 79–87.

Nelling, Edward, and Gyourko, Joseph. 1998. The predictability of equity REIT returns. *The Journal of Real Estate Research* 16 (3): 251–268.

Ott, S., T. Riddiough, and H. Yi. 2005. Finance, investment and investment performance: Evidence from the REIT sector. *Real Estate Economics* 33:203–35.

Wang, K., J. Erickson, and G. W. Gau. 1993. Dividend Policies and Dividend Announcement Effects for Real Estate Investment Trusts. *Journal of the American Real Estate and Urban economics Association* 21 (2): 185–201.

Wang, K., S. H. Chan, and G. Gau. 1992. Initial public offerings of equity securities: Anomalous evidence using REITs. *Journal of Financial Economics* 31:381–410.

Zietz, E. N., G. S. Sirmans, and S. H. Friday. 2003. The environment and performance of real estate investment trust. *Journal of Real Estate Portfolio Management* 9 (2): 127–165.

26

Hotel Brand Strategy
John W. O'Neill and Anna S. Mattila

In the past twenty-five years, the hotel industry has firmly embraced and accepted the value of branding as an essential component of its marketing strategy (Dev et al. 2009), especially given extensive hotel brand segmentation. Beginning with Quality International (now Choice Hotels International) in 1981, most lodging companies have developed multiple brands to serve multiple market segments (Jiang, Dev, and Rao 2002). Beside Choice, companies that offer numerous product tiers include Starwood, Marriott, Hilton, and Accor. This strategy seems to be an accepted aspect of hotel operation.

This segmentation strategy is based on the idea that a brand name is part of the process of giving tangibility to what is essentially intangible, providing a "shorthand" method of establishing a particular property's quality by giving the customer important information about its product and service, sight unseen (Brucks, Zeithaml, and Naylor 2000). In this regard, the brand's value is based on potential guests' awareness of the brand, their perception of its quality, and overall customer satisfaction (O'Neill and Mattila 2004).

The remarkable growth of hotel branding rests on the concept that brands provide added value to both guests and hotel companies, in large part because they foster brand loyalty (O'Neill and Xiao 2006). From a corporate strategy viewpoint, well-managed hotel brands tend to gain increasing market share (O'Neill and Mattila 2004), even though different parent companies take diverse approaches to managing their individual brand identity. Marriott

International, for instance, is careful to include its corporate name on most of its brands. One exception to this approach is Ritz-Carlton, which was a well-established brand before being acquired by Marriott. Other firms, such as Starwood and Choice Hotels International, employ a house-of-brands strategy. The individual brand names for each hotel concept stand on their own, typically without including the parent company name (O'Neill and Mattila 2006). Hilton and Wyndham have used both approaches, depending on the nature of their various hotel brands.

Similarly, various chains take different approaches to logos and identifying information for their various product brands. Choice Hotels International, for example, uses similar and consistent sign designs for its Comfort Inn, Comfort Suites, Quality Inn, Sleep Inn, and Clarion brands. This family approach to design simultaneously distinguishes the brands from each other, identifies them as all being part of a unified organization, and differentiates them from their competition. As a brand represents the company itself, its presentation generally should be consistent. Though there are cases where companies have changed their positioning or strategies, their corporate colors, and even their logos, few have abandoned an established brand name for a new one (Vaid 2003). Indeed, long-established brand names continue in operation after being reinvented and reinvigorated, including Holiday Inn, Ramada Inn, and Howard Johnson.

By establishing a set of promises to consumers, a brand creates a differentiated identity in hotels where functional characteristics of the products are not substantially differentiated. Consequently, brand personality may be a salient reason for selecting one brand over another (Siguaw, Mattila, and Austin 1999). A vivid brand personality, such as W and Palomar, is likely to make the brand more concrete in the minds of the consumers and, hence, reduce the degree of intangibility associated with a hotel brand.

Given the idea that it creates a personality for an intangible entity, a brand relates to consumer emotions (Kim and Kim 2004). Gobé (2001) has posited that the biggest misconception in branding strategies is that people focus on branding in the context of market share, when a brand really involves the mind and emotion "share." This does not negate the superficial aspects of branding that we have already touched on, including ubiquity, visibility, and function, but the brand's major significance is to establish in a consumer's mind an emotional connection. This emotional connection to a brand arises in part from the promise that we mentioned above. Hotel guests rely on brand names to reduce the risks associated with staying at an otherwise unknown property (O'Neill and Xiao 2006). Beyond that, brands are supposed to be intense and vibrant, to connect on multiple levels of the senses, and to be a reminder of a pleasant experience. Brands consistently interact with consumers and should not disappoint them, since that constitutes a broken promise. Thus, a brand is something for consumers to feel good about (Vaid

2003), and successful brand organizations promote themselves as such. For example, Marriott International has recently promoted its winning the 2009 "Tourism for Tomorrow Award for Sustainability" in the Global Tourism Business category by the World Travel and Tourism Council (see www.marriott.com).

In sum, a hotel brand represents a relationship with guests. This relationship is built as consumers get to know a brand (even if they initially choose their accommodation at random), use its facilities, evaluate their experience, and begin the relationship; and it becomes cemented as guests continue using its services. Ultimately, the brand represents the consumer's experience with its organization. The intense competitive landscape has forced hotel brands to focus on providing memorable experiences to their guests rather than simply selling services (Gilmore and Pine 2002). Thus, even though Hilton operates both the Waldorf-Astoria and the New York Hilton, and both are first-class hotels, staying at one should be a different experience from staying at the other.

What We Know about the Value of Hotel Brands

A hotel's brand drives the operating ratios that are correlated with a hotel property's market value. Some brands consistently have stronger net operating incomes (NOIs) than do others (O'Neill and Mattila 2006), while other brands report consistently stronger average daily rates (ADRs) than others do. In an earlier study, we found that ADR (an indicator of a hotel's "top line") is a better predictor of a hotel's market value than is its NOI (an indicator of a hotel's "bottom line"), but hoteliers would nevertheless wish to drive both (O'Neill and Mattila 2006). In fact, a study published in this journal has shown that for certain product tiers, hotel brand affects hotel market value above and beyond the important effects of NOI, ADR, occupancy rate, and number of guest rooms (O'Neill and Xiao 2006). That same study found that this positive brand effect occurs only in the middle chain scale categories (upper upscale, upscale, and midscale), but not in the top (luxury) and bottom (economy) categories.

We further examined how brand affiliation affects hotel revenue. The branding literature has demonstrated that consumers use brand name as an important quality cue. Our study indicated that consumers are typically willing to pay a price premium for brands they view as being high in quality (O'Neill and Mattila 2006). A concurrent study found that brand affiliation, name recognition, and reputation for high-quality service together can contribute as much as 20 to 25 percent of the going-concern value of a successfully operating hotel (O'Neill and Xiao 2006). In addition, a well-managed brand can discourage competition (Dev, Morgan, and Shoemaker 1995).

What We Know about How Brands Create Value

Let us look more closely at the source of customer-based brand equity. One study suggested that the following four components underlie this equity: brand awareness, brand loyalty, perceived quality, and brand image (Kim and Kim 2004). Prasad and Dev (2000) developed a numerical brand equity index that captures brand awareness and consumer perceptions of brand performance. Beyond the advantage of awareness and image, brand equity results from benefits of marketing efficiency and enhanced performance associated with that brand and long-term brand effect based on customer loyalty (Prasad and Dev 2002). Brand equity also allows a chain to expand the brand in a variety of markets (Mahajan, Rao, and Srivastava 1994). For example, in the hotel industry, the level of brand equity may be related to the brand's ability to geographically expand, to expand via franchising, and to develop subbrands. These issues are particularly salient for global lodging organizations such as Marriott or Accor.

Well-established brands are intangible assets that serve as a source of strategic advantage and create financial value due to their ability to generate cash flows via relatively higher margins (O'Neill and Mattila 2006). In general, major contributors of generating cash flows are customer loyalty, brand extension including licensing opportunities, and enhanced marketing efficiency (Rao, Agarwal, and Dahlhoff 2004).

Hotel brands first create value for guests by helping to assure them of a uniform level of quality (O'Neill and Xiao 2006). As customers' loyalty grows, the brand owner can capitalize on the brand's value through price premiums, decreased price elasticity, increased market share, and more rapid brand expansion. Finally, companies with successful brands benefit in the financial marketplace by improving shareholders' value (O'Neill and Xiao 2006). Although it is important for hotel owners to be able to recognize the effects of a brand on a hotel's market value, other benefits associated with a brand, such as guest satisfaction and loyalty, should be considered to fully assess the brand's total value (O'Neill and Xiao 2006).

What We Know about the Relationship between Guest Satisfaction and Hotel Brands

With the increasing focus on customers over the past twenty-five years, guest satisfaction has served as a measure of operational success for branding strategies (O'Neill and Mattila 2004). The strategic management of satisfaction is of utmost importance in today's crowded marketplace, where customers are overwhelmed with lodging choices (O'Neill and Mattila 2004). For example, in 2008, Kim identified at least twenty-five different brands in the extended-stay segment alone (Kim 2008). Such a competitive environment requires attention to guest satisfaction. Research over the past two decades has shown that guest satisfaction leads to repeat purchases (Oh 1999), favorable word-of-mouth behavior (Gunderson, Heide, and Olsson 1996), and loyalty (Dubé and Renaghan 2000).

Among the factors that drive hotel guests' satisfaction are guest room cleanliness, hotel maintenance, employee friendliness, and knowledgeable employees (Oh 1999; Mattila and O'Neill 2003), as well as the hotel's physical environment (Mattila 1999; Mattila and O'Neill 2003). Our research also has shown that hotel brands with higher levels of guest satisfaction achieve not only higher ADRs but significantly greater percentage increases in their ADRs over time as well (O'Neill and Mattila 2004).

What We Know about Hotel Brand Extension

Since the first blush of product tiers in the 1980s, the hotel industry has embraced the concept of marketing new products and services as extensions of the original brand name (Lane and Jacobson 1995). In 2006, the *Cornell Hotel and Restaurant Administration Quarterly* reported some 285 lodging brands worldwide (O'Neill and Xiao 2006). Long-established brands such as Hilton, Hyatt, InterContinental, Marriott, and Wyndham have all grown through brand extensions over the past twenty-five years. The brand-extension strategy works for the hotel industry in part because guests choose different types of hotels depending on their purpose of travel, and a brand extension with a familiar name allows consumers who depend on trusted brands to economize on time and search costs (Lane and Jacobson 1995). This approach is successful when consumers immediately conceive similar attributes and benefits for the extended concept based on the established brand name. According to Keller (1993), favorable, strong, and unique brand associations are stored in memory when the consumer possesses familiarity with a brand.

Consideration sets are a set of alternatives that the consumer evaluates in making a decision (Peter and Olson 2005). Consumers choose products and services that are familiar to them more often than they try those with which they are unfamiliar. Therefore, the extensions of familiar brand names, such as Hilton developing the Hilton Garden Inn brand, should find themselves in potential guests' consideration sets; and those extended brands are highly likely to be chosen by consumers using peripheral cues, particularly when consumers are without specific product knowledge in the purchase situation, because the family name on an unfamiliar property serves as a heuristic to guide product choice (Lane and Jacobson 1995).

Having said that, one study identified the disadvantages of a multibrand strategy. Brand extensions often add complexities to the corporate structure, positioning of the brand might be challenging due to cannibalization issues, and it might be difficult to maintain brand-specific service quality standards (Jing, de Ruyter, and Wetzels 2002). That study suggested that the ideal number of brand extensions is three, because that number provides the consumer with a sufficient menu of choices, still under the trusted brand name, without the threat of brand dilution (Jing, de Ruyter, and Wetzels 2002).

The financial advantage of brand extension is that it provides firms not only with higher revenues but with savings in marketing expenditures (Lane and Jacobson 1995). In addition, more highly familiar brands tend to generate greater future revenues because of opportunities in expanding markets (Lane and Jacobson 1995). However, due to the previously discussed negatives of brand extension, when a firm is to launch a new product or service connected to its original brand, the strategic decisions are critical regarding the types of branding strategies it adopts (Rao, Agarwal, and Dahlhoff 2004).

What We Know about the Relationship between Hotel Branding and Franchising

Franchising presents a set of special considerations for brand management. When the owner of the brand is not the property operator, issues may arise, both in terms of consumer perceptions and a franchisee's willingness to sign or stay with a particular hotel brand (Prasad and Dev 2000). Since hotel franchisees are quick to change their brand loyalty, it may be more important than ever for hotel brand executives to maintain consistent brand quality (O'Neill and Mattila 2004). To that end, most lodging firms, when entering new markets, prefer to control high-risk activities such as branding decisions while they might be willing to leave other, lower-risk marketing decisions (e.g., pricing) to local partners (Dev, Brown, and Zhou 2007).

As markets change and properties age, owners must consider the possibility of repositioning their properties. Sometimes the decision is forced on them when a facility can no longer meet brand requirements. In either case, rebranding can be a positive event. A study in the *Cornell Hospitality Quarterly* found that although hotel rebranding generally has a negative effect on short-term financial performance of the hotel, the long-term financial effect is positive. Scale changes from a lower to a higher scale tend to have a significant positive effect on ADR, as would be expected. However, hotel rebranding without rescaling to a different level seems to have no significant effect on hotel financial performance (Hanson et al. 2009). While such factors as location and facilities have a greater effect on individual hotel financial performance than brand name or franchise affiliation, it is clear that the brand must be appropriate for the property.

In general, lenders are more comfortable underwriting a branded hotel than one that is independent. Since franchise affiliation is incorporated in lenders' tight underwriting formulas, obtaining financing for an independent hotel is generally more difficult than for a branded one (O'Neill and Xiao 2006). Owners need to examine a franchise firm's brand portfolio to ensure that the chain's branding strategies are appropriate to the owner's property (O'Neill and Mattila 2006). In short, different hotel brands deliver different levels of profitability. Given their prior brand relationships, owners generally do not hesitate to seek brands that are in conformance to their financial goals (O'Neill and Mattila 2006).

Part of the owners' franchising decision involves choosing a brand name that will maximize the value of their asset by correctly positioning the property. For hotel companies' brand-management teams, consequently, effectively assessing brands' effects on hotel market values can strengthen the overall value of the brands and possibly improve the brands' franchise sales (O'Neill and Xiao 2006). Such rational analysis can signal weaknesses and assist with the development of reimaging, retrenchment, or remedial brand strategies, when necessary. Furthermore, such analysis can assist corporate brand managers in evaluating whether their intended brand strategies are being achieved (O'Neill and Xiao 2006).

One issue that arises with franchising is the potentially adverse effect on the brand perception in a property that is operated by a third-party manager (O'Neill and Mattila 2004). The percentage of franchised units within a hotel brand has been shown to be negatively correlated with both guest satisfaction and occupancy percentage (O'Neill and Mattila 2004). This matter could become more salient as hotel brand executives continue to focus their growth strategies to a greater extent on brand management and franchising rather than actual property management.

The issue of guest satisfaction could become an increasingly important factor in determining the ultimate revenue success of hotel brands (O'Neill and Mattila 2004). We were involved in a study that investigated satisfaction, ADR, and occupancy between 2000 and 2003 for a total of twenty-six hotel brands (O'Neill, Mattila, and Xiao 2006). Our findings present a cautionary tale for those relying on guest satisfaction as a driver of ADR. This study found that twenty-three out of twenty-six brands studied achieved guest satisfaction improvements, while at the same time many of them were experiencing ADR and occupancy decreases. We can only conclude that this study captured the effects of the sharp recession of that time. Eighteen brands suffered from ADR decreases during the recessionary study period.

Although reducing ADR was partly a competitive response, such reductions may serve different strategic goals for brands in different market environments. We participated in a study of hotels' rate positioning after September 11, 2001, in which we concluded that some hotel operators and brand managers voluntarily chose to reduce their ADRs to maintain or enhance the level of guest satisfaction. This study indicated that lower prices might increase customers' value perceptions, thus having a positive effect on satisfaction. For example, Marriott reduced its rates by 14 percent in the study period and saw guest satisfaction rise 2.5 percent, while Wyndham's ADR dropped 13.7 percent and its customer satisfaction rate increased 4.0 percent (O'Neill, Mattila, and Xiao 2006).

Several specific cases further clarify the possible effect of franchising on guest satisfaction. The study examined the case of La Quinta Inn & Suites, which was virtually a franchise-free brand in 2000. By 2003, however, 25.8 percent of its hotels were franchised. While there is no direct indication of causality, the growth in franchise expansion correlated with a decrease of 2.6 percent in guest satisfaction at La Quinta during the study period. By contrast, Westin increased its percentage of franchised properties by 9.6 percent during this study but saw a 6.4 percent increase in guest satisfaction. Westin also recorded minimal decreases in ADR (–0.5 percent change) and occupancy rate (–4.4 percent change). Its widely touted "Heavenly Bed" program, which it implemented during the course of the study period, may have contributed to its enhanced guest satisfaction and probably acted as a buffer to downward ADR and occupancy pressure (O'Neill, Mattila, and Xiao 2006). With a different take on a franchising strategy, Hampton Inn & Suites was essentially a purely franchised brand in that study, with 99.3 percent of its properties being franchised in 2003. During the course of that investigation, Hampton increased its room inventory by 16.1 percent, but the brand experienced concurrent improvements in occupancy (3.7 percent), ADR (6.6 percent), and guest satisfaction (2.5 percent). Clearly, Hampton Inn understands how to execute a franchising strategy as it relates to branding, service, and quality strategies.

Suggestions for Future Research

While we have learned much about hotel branding over the past twenty-five years, interesting research questions remain. For example, with the growth of boutique hotels over the past several years, a fascinating research question would be, How small can a brand be in terms of the number of hotel units and still be a brand? W and Palomar, for instance, have few properties, but those are in key locations, suggesting that certain types of brands can be successful with relatively few well-chosen hotels. The same principle might apply to an upscale extended-stay brand such as Starwood's Element, because such a brand by design is intended to thrive by giving its guests a sense of exclusivity. Knowing the variables that drive successful smaller brands would be valuable to researchers and practitioners alike.

Although hotel brands have become ubiquitous in the United States over the past twenty-five years, they are much less widespread in other parts of the world. Future research could investigate the factors that might encourage brand growth in countries in Asia and the Middle East. Moreover, existing research regarding hotel branding is heavily focused on U.S. brands. It would be interesting to examine branding issues from more cross-cultural perspectives by incorporating potential country-of-origin effects into the research agenda.

Related to the issue of studying hotel brands are the issues of subbranding and cobranding, which have evolved over the past decade. Examples include subbrands developed by hotel companies themselves, as in the case of Starwood's Heavenly Bed, as well as brands developed by others that hoteliers have taken as cobrands, such as Starbucks. As we study hotel branding in the future, we should consider the role and effects of subbrands and cobrands when evaluating such factors as consumer loyalty and brand equity.

Until recently, we have seen only limited research relating to guest loyalty programs, even though they are essentially universal. While research in the *Cornell Hospitality Quarterly* has suggested that loyalty programs appear to increase hotel unit revenues and profit, we do not really know whether they help to create brand loyalty. Now that virtually every major Western hotel chain has a loyalty program, one could argue that such programs have ceased to be significant competitive advantages for hotel brands. It would be worthwhile, therefore, to test this proposition and to determine the extent to which brand loyalty would remain in the absence of such programs. In other words, what truly bonds the customer to a brand? For example, is the emotional connection the key to creating brand loyalty in today's crowded marketplace?

Returning to the matter of rebranding and rescaling, given the study that found that hotel brand changes generally result in short-term negative financial results but long-term gains, it would be helpful for hotel owners to know about the corresponding capital requirements related to such positive financial effects (i.e., property improvement plan). This information would help owners to proactively estimate the level of return on investment (ROI) based on different types and locations of hotel brand changes.

Conclusions

Finally, although the value of hotel brands is widely accepted, one frequently sees the complaint that brands are often being mismanaged. Simon and Sullivan (1993) argued, for instance, that too much emphasis is being placed on short-term performance rather than the long-term value of brand equity. Future research should strive to measure and analyze not only short-term but also long-term brand equity.

References

Brucks, M., V. Zeithaml, and G. Naylor. 2000. Price and brand name as indicators of quality dimensions for consumer durables. *Journal of the Academy of Marketing Science* 28 (3): 359–74.

Dev, C., J. Brown, and K. Z. Zhou. 2007. Global brand expansion: How to select a market entry strategy. *Cornell Hospitality Quarterly* 48 (1): 13–27.

Dev, C., M. S. Morgan, and S. Shoemaker. 1995. A positioning analysis of hotel brands. *Cornell Hotel and Restaurant Administration Quarterly* 36 (6): 48–55.

Dev, C., K. Z. Zhou, J. Brown, and S. Agarwal. 2009. Customer orientation or competitor orientation: Which marketing strategy has a higher payoff for hotel brands? *Cornell Hospitality Quarterly* 50: 19–28.

Dubé, L., and L. Renaghan. 2000. Creating visible customer value: How customers view best-practice champions. *Cornell Hotel and Restaurant Administration Quarterly* 41 (1): 62–72.

Gilmore, J. H., and J. Pine. 2002. Differentiating hospitality operations via experiences. *Cornell Hotel and Restaurant Administration Quarterly* 43 (3): 87–96.

Gobé, M. 2001. *Emotional branding: The new paradigm for connecting brands to people.* New York: Allworth.

Gundersen, M., M. Heide, and U. Olsson. 1996. Hotel guest satisfaction among business travelers. *Cornell Hotel and Restaurant Administration Quarterly* 37 (2): 72–81.

Hanson, B., A. S. Mattila, J. W. O'Neill, and Y. H. Kim. Forthcoming. Rebranding and rescaling: Effects on hotel performance. *Cornell Hospitality Quarterly*.

Hanson, B., A. S. Mattila, J. W. O'Neill, and Y. H. Kim. Hotel rebranding and rescaling: Effects on financial performance. *Cornell Hospitality Quarterly* 50 (3): 360–370.

Jiang, W., C. Dev, and V. Rao. 2002. Brand extension and customer loyalty: Evidence from the lodging industry. *Cornell Hotel and Restaurant Administration Quarterly* 43 (4): 5–16.

Jing, L., K. de Ruyter, and M. Wetzels. 2008. Consumer responses to vertical service line extensions. *Journal of Retailing* 84 (3): 268–80.

Keller, K. L. 1993. Conceptualizing, measuring, and managing customer-based brand equity. *Journal of Marketing* 57 (1): 1–22.

Kim, W. G. 2008. Branding, brand equity and brand extensions. In *Handbook of hospitality marketing management*, ed. H. Oh and A. Pizam, 87–118. New York: Elsevier.

Kim, W. G., and H. B. Kim. 2004. Measuring customer-based restaurant brand equity: Investigating the relationship between brand equity and firms' performance. *Cornell Hotel and Restaurant Administration Quarterly* 45 (2): 115–31.

Lane, V., and R. Jacobson. 1995. Stock market reactions to brand extension announcements. *Journal of Marketing* 59:63–77.

Mahajan, V. V., V. R. Rao, and R. Srivastava. 1994. An approach to assess the importance of brand equity in acquisition decisions. *Journal of Product Innovation Management* 11:221–35.

Mattila, A. S. 1999. Consumers' value judgments. *Cornell Hotel and Restaurant Administration Quarterly* 40 (1): 40–46.

Mattila, A. S., and J. W. O'Neill. 2003. Relationships between hotel room pricing, occupancy, and guest satisfaction: A longitudinal case of a midscale hotel in the United States. *Journal of Hospitality & Tourism Research* 27 (3): 328–41.

Oh, H. 1999. Service quality, customer satisfaction, and customer value: A holistic perspective. *International Journal of Hospitality Management* 18:67–82.

O'Neill, J. W., and A. S. Mattila. 2004. Hotel branding strategy: Its relationship to guest satisfaction and room revenue. *Journal of Hospitality & Tourism Research* 28 (2): 156–65.

O'Neill, J. W., and A. S. Mattila. 2006. Strategic hotel development and positioning: The effect of revenue drivers on profitability. *Cornell Hotel and Restaurant Administration Quarterly* 47 (2): 146–54.

O'Neill, J. W., A. S. Mattila, and Q. Xiao. 2006. Hotel guest satisfaction and brand performance: The effect of franchising strategy. *Journal of Quality Assurance in Hospitality & Tourism* 7 (3): 25–39.

O'Neill, J. W., and Q. Xiao. 2006. The role of brand affiliation in hotel market value. *Cornell Hotel and Restaurant Administration Quarterly* 47 (3): 210–23.

Peter, J. P., and J. C. Olson. 2005. *Consumer behavior & marketing strategy*. New York: McGraw-Hill/Irwin.

Prasad, K., and C. Dev. 2000. Measuring hotel brand equity: A customer-centric framework for assessing performance. *Cornell Hotel and Restaurant Administration Quarterly* 41 (3): 22–31.

Prasad, K., and C. Dev. 2002. Model estimates financial impact of guest satisfaction efforts. *Hotel and Motel Management* 217 (14): 23.

Rao, V. R., M. Agarwal, and D. Dahlhoff. 2004. How is manifested branding strategy related to the intangible value of a corporation? *Journal of Marketing* 68:126–41.

Siguaw, J. A., A. S. Mattila, and J. Austin. 1999. The Brand Personality Scale: An application for restaurants. *Cornell Hotel and Restaurant Administration Quarterly* 40 (June): 48–55.

Simon, C., and M. Sullivan. 1993. The measurement and determinants of brand equity: A financial approach. *Marketing Science* 12:28–52.

Vaid, H. 2003. *Branding: Brand strategy, design, and implementation of corporate and product identity*. New York: Watson-Guptill.

27

Post-merger Stock Performance of Acquiring Hospitality Firms

Jing Yang, Woo Gon Kim and Hailin Qu

The hotel and real estate investment trusts (REITs) sectors have experienced profound transformation in recent years. One of the major developments has been consolidation in the hospitality industry at various scales and levels. With the fast growth of the US and global economy in the past several years, the hotel industry has enjoyed steady improvement in its operating revenues and profit margin, resulting in strong stock performance. The ascent in real estate values has also attracted a broad range of investors interested in the underlying assets of hotel companies. Consequently, the combination of unprecedented appreciation in hotel assets and strong cash flows has led to an abundance of consolidation in the industry and most recently, a number of leveraged buy-out transactions such as Fairmont Hotel and Four Seasons. The industry today appears much less fragmented. However, the trend of consolidation is likely to continue in the foreseeable future (Hsu and Jang, 2007).

Although the financial success of a company can be measured by many parameters, the stock performance of a public company remains the most important and often most objective barometer. For a company that has gone through a merger and acquisition (M&A), the financial benefit for the acquiring company often takes an extended period of time to become apparent, as the change in management and integration of businesses is often accomplished over time. The transformation adjustment is often highly dependent on the scale and nature of the merging companies.

It is difficult to separate the pure impact of a merger from any shift in the general business environment. This is particularly common for hotel and REITs companies, since their business cycles are highly correlated with the general health of the economy and the economic cycle. Therefore, it is important to study beyond the performance of the acquiring companies themselves. Their performance should be measured against not only the overall market but also their respective industry sectors. In this paper, we extend the study of Hsu and Jang (2007) by examining the stock performances of acquiring hotel/casino and lodging REITs companies in the long run. The previous study (Hsu and Jang, 2007) selected the S&P 500 index as the benchmark portfolio. In this study, the authors adopted sector indices rather than the S&P 500. The authors propose that the sector indices offer a more appropriate measure of abnormal gains since the indices help isolate the impact from the volatilities of the hospitality industry as a whole.

Literature Review

The Federal Trade Commission (FTC) classifies a merger into four categories: horizontal, vertical, product and market concentric or conglomerate categories. Past literature contributed primarily to the fundamental understanding of synergy. Synergy was created when two companies were better off together than apart (Lubatkin, 1983). The universally acknowledged rule for mergers by finance theorists is prescribed by Michel and Shaked (1985) as follows: as long as the prospective returns of the combining enterprises are not perfectly correlated, the surviving firm will yield an income stream for its owners having less dispersion per dollar of expected return than would be attainable by holding only one of its predecessors. On the other hand, to claim that 'the market will pay premium for the new income stream ignores the opportunity which individual investors had prior to the merger to combine the predecessor shares in their own portfolios' (Michel and Shaked, 1985, p. 109).

Intuitively, acquiring firms benefit from the merger due to technical, pecuniary and diversification synergies. However, empirical studies of various industries, especially the financial industry using a capital asset pricing model, reported gains mainly for the acquired firms (Lubatkin, 1983). In general, most studies applied an 'event-study' framework or 'residual analysis'. Relatively large samples of mergers were required. The return on common stock of both the acquiring and acquired firms prior to the 'event' date was studied. Event date is a reference date from which an analysis is made. The procedure begins with an adjustment of the stock risk by using modern portfolio theory (MPT) to calculate beta. This theory suggested that the expected return on a security was the sum of the risk-free rate of interest using Treasury bill rate and a risk premium (Michel and Shaked, 1985). Abnormal residual occurred when there was a difference between the actual return and the return predicted by MPT. For each firm in the sample, daily residuals were averaged and for each day, the residuals were averaged for all firms in the sample.

A technique called cumulative average residuals (or CARs) was applied by cumulating these average residuals over a period of time to study the impact of the merger on the shareholders' wealth. A study by Michel and Shaked (1985) indicated that stockholders of acquired firms earned abnormal gains from the mergers, while acquiring firms gained less than comparable non-acquisitive companies or the average of the acquiring firms' home-base industries. Industry-specific empirical research shared some commonalities (Dodd and Ruback, 1977; Asquith et al, 1983; Canina, 2001), while others indicated opposite results (Dodd, 1980; Asquith, 1983; Sheel and Nagpal, 2000; Hsu and Jang, 2007). It is noticeable that studies differ in the sample time periods, definitions of event date, models used to generate abnormal returns, time frames prior to and post merger and specific industries.

Dodd and Ruback (1977) studied a sample of 172 bidding firms and 172 target firms to analyse the stock market reaction to both successful and unsuccessful tender offers. The results indicated that target firm stockholders gained positive and significant abnormal returns of 20.58% for successful offers and 18.96% for unsuccessful offers. The stockholders of the acquiring firms also earned positive abnormal gains in the month of announcement, but their gains were smaller compared to those of the target firms.

Dodd (1980) continued to study a comprehensive sample of the public announcement of proposals to acquire. In total, the author studied 151 proposals during the period 1971–1977. The study showed that there was a swift and positive reaction to the approval of completed proposals and a negative reaction to cancelled proposals. The stockholders of the target firms generally earned large positive abnormal returns from the announcement of the proposals, regardless of the completion of the proposal. For shareholders of bidder firms, a negative abnormal return of –7.22 to –5.50% was reported.

Asquith (1983) studied stock returns for the entire merger process for both successful and unsuccessful merger bids. The researcher suggested that target firms created synergy by providing unique resources; however, the shareholders of the acquiring firms gained insignificant benefit from the merger, if any. Asquith et al (1983) focused exclusively on the gains for the stockholders of the acquiring firms. To test the hypothesis of whether shareholders of bidding firms benefitted from mergers, the study examined bidding firms for the period 1955–1979. Their research showed significant gains to the acquiring firms during the 21 days prior to the announcement of bids.

While others (for example, Dodd, 1980; Asquith et al, 1983) focused on the effect of the announcement gains, Franks et al (1991) studied the post-merger performance. They examined share-price performance of 399 post-corporate takeovers during 1975–1984 using multifactor benchmarks (Lehmann and Modest, 1987; Grinblatt and Sheridan, 1989). They further analysed the subgroups of the sample to evaluate potential determinants of post-merger performance such as payment in the merger, the relative sizes of the target and the bidder, the level of opposition by incumbent management and the presence of competing bidders. With cross-sectional analysis in event time and portfolio analysis in calendar time, the authors found that different benchmarks generated significantly different measures of abnormal performance.

Canina (2001) found significant positive unexpected returns for both the acquired and acquiring lodging firms on the merger announcement day. She argued that M&A in the lodging industry involved companies with similar core business. Moreover, the senior managers possessed a large portion of shares in the equity; thus, they shared ultimate interest with the owners of the business. These characteristics made M&A in the lodging industry different from other industries. Hence, it was rational to see acquisitions in the lodging industry increase the equity value for the shareholders.

Using the Jensen measure and market model, Hsu and Jang (2007) were among the first to investigate both the short- and long-term post-merger financial performance of acquiring firms in the hospitality industry. In addition, they tested the accounting measures of financial performance with return on equity (ROE) and return on assets (ROA). Studying a pool of 17 lodging firms, the authors suggested that merger did not create abnormal gains to shareholders of the acquiring firms in the short term but, instead, led to a negative effect on profitability in the long term.

In general, it is acknowledged that target firms receive more abnormal returns than bidding firms. However, the effect of merger on acquiring firms has yet to be decided. The impact of mergers on acquiring firms over the long term was found to be negative in the hospitality industry. Yet previous researchers suggested that the results from a limited sample size were often specific to the studied acquirers and sensitive to the period studied (Sheel and Nagpal, 2000; Hsu and Jang, 2007). This inconclusiveness is also attributed to diverse research focuses and the different benchmarks selected.

Research Methodology

Research Hypotheses

Based on previous literature, this paper proposes the following hypotheses:

> H1: Shareholders of the acquiring hospitality firms receive significant gains from the M&As in the long run.

H2: Shareholders of the acquiring hotel/casino firms receive significant gains from the M&As in the long run.
H3: Shareholders of the acquiring lodging REITS firms receive significant gains from the M&As in the long run.

Data Collection

The authors chose merger events that were completed between 2000 and 2006. There was a proliferation of merger and divesture activities during this period in which the US economy went through the volatile technology boom and bust of the early 2000s. The fact that the overall stock performance was not directional helped isolate merger impact. This paper used the secondary data extracted from the Bloomberg database.

The data-filtering process took the following steps. First, all hotel/casino and lodging REITs related M&As were queried from the Bloomberg database between January 2000 and March 2006. Second, only 505 completed M&A deals were chosen. The total value of the deals was approximately US$92 billion. Third, 195 deals with an individual value above US$50 million were retained. Fourth, only hospitality acquirers publicly traded in the New York Stock Exchange (NYSE), America Stock Exchange (AMEX) and National Association of Security Automated Quotations (NASDAQ) were included, resulting in 81 deals with a total deal value of US$44 billion. Fifth, 38 firms whose SIC codes were other than 7011(hotel and motel) and 6798 (REIT) were excluded.

Certain acquirers made multiple acquisitions in the period studied. To isolate the correlation from each merger, the authors used the following criteria to filter out the multiple deals: (i) only the highest valued deals were kept; (ii) if multiple deals had comparable sizes, only the most recent deals were kept; and (iii) if a company made multiple acquisitions separated by over 2 years in time, the authors kept both deals, effectively treating each transaction as independent of one another. This procedure removed seven transactions. Finally, the authors filtered out international acquiring hotel/casino and/or lodging REITs companies. The filtering process led to a final sample of 15 US hospitality acquirers with 7 hotel/casino companies and 8 lodging REITs companies.

Analytical Models

Previous literature (Frank *et al*, 1991; Sheel and Nagpal, 2000; Hsu and Jang, 2007) suggested that the Jensen measure, expressed as the intercept of the regression of the excess return of the acquiring firms on the excess return of the market index, offered a reasonable measure of merger performance (Jensen, 1968). In the study, monthly data of stock returns, T-bill yields, market and sector indices were extracted from Bloomberg beginning the month after the M&A announcement date.

The Jensen measure of the portfolio p ($\alpha_{p,t}$) is expressed in Equation (1). In the previous study (Hsu and Jang, 2007), the S&P 500 index was selected as the benchmark portfolio. The excess return for company p, the excess return of the market portfolio and the Jensen index were expressed using Equation (1) (Jensen, 1968):

$$(R_{p,t} - R_{f,t}) = \alpha_{p,t} + \beta_{p,t}(R_{m,t} - R_{f,t}) + \varepsilon_{p,t} \qquad (1)$$

where

$\alpha_{p,t}$ = the Jensen index of company p measuring abnormal performance;
$\beta_{p,t}$ = volatility coefficient of company p to the S&P 500 index;
$R_{p,t}$ = shareholder return for acquirer p in month t, which is the spread of the return on month t and $t-1$ divided by the return on month $t-1$;
$R_{f,t}$ = monthly US Treasury bills, which is 1/12th of the yearly yield;
$R_{p,t} - R_{f,t}$ = the excess return for company p in month t;
$R_{m,t}$ = return on market index in month t, which is expressed as the spread of the S&P 500 index return on month t and $t-1$ divided by the return on month $t-1$;
$R_{m,t} - R_{f,t}$ = the excess return for the S&P 500 market portfolio;
t = month relative to the announcement date ($t = 0$ is the announcement month);
$\varepsilon_{p,t}$ = a random and serially independent error with mean zero.

The regression of the shareholders' excess returns on the general market excess return was not sufficient to isolate merger impact. It is necessary to isolate the impact caused by the volatility of the hospitality industry to the general economy on the studied M&A activities. By adopting sector indices instead of S&P 500 index as the market benchmark, this study attempts to calculate more accurate abnormal returns.

Further comparison of the S&P 500 index with the Bloomberg hotel/casino index and Bloomberg lodging REITs index indicated that the hospitality sectors in the past 6 years have clearly outperformed the general market, as shown in Figure 1. In addition, the hotel/casino sector has outperformed the lodging REITs companies. All three indices were converted by equalizing their starting points to facilitate comparison.

The paper incorporated both hotel/casino and lodging REITs indices in Equation (2) for the modified Jensen measure. There were 2 subgroups, 7 hotel/casino companies and 8 lodging REITs companies. The hotel/casino index and lodging REITs index were applied for each subgroup. The Bloomberg

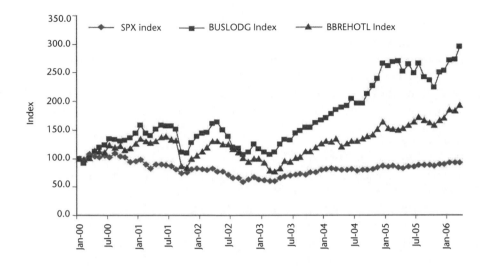

Figure 1: The S&P 500 index versus the Bloomberg lodging REITS and hotel/casino index

US hotel/casino index is a capitalization-weighted index of 16 leading US hotel/casino stocks. The Bloomberg lodging REIT index is a capitalization-weighted index of leading lodging REITs companies with at least 75% of assets invested in hotel properties.

$$(R_{p,t} - R_{f,t}) = \alpha'_{p,t} + \beta'_{p,t}(R'_{m,t} - R_{f,t}) + \varepsilon'_{p,t} \tag{2}$$

where

$\alpha'_{p,t}$ = the modified Jensen index of company p measuring abnormal performance;

$\beta'_{p,t}$ = volatility coefficient of company p to the hotel/REITs index;

$R_{p,t}$ = shareholder return for acquirer p in month t, which is the spread of the return on month t and $t-1$ divided by the return on month $t-1$;

$R_{f,t}$ = monthly US Treasury bills, which is 1/12th of the yearly yield;

$R_{p,t} - R_{f,t}$ = the excess return for company p in month t;

$R'_{m,t}$ = return on the market index in month t, which is expressed as the spread of the sector index return on month t and $t-1$ divided by the return on month $t-1$;

$R'_{m,t} - R_{f,t}$ = the excess return for the sector portfolio;

t = month relative to the announcement date ($t=0$ is the announcement month);

$\varepsilon'_{p,t}$ = a random and serially independent error with mean zero.

Results

Table 1 indicates the results of the regression on the S&P 500 index. It provides the long-term post-merger performance of 15 acquiring hospitality firms using the Jensen measure. There is a total of 15 hospitality companies' data available, with 8 in lodging REITs and 7 in hotel/casino, comprising 376 valid observations. The intercept (alpha) of the regression provides the abnormal returns of post-merger, while the slope (beta) indicates the volatility to the S&P 500 index.

In general, the Jensen measures of 5 acquirers are negative and 10 acquirers are positive. The Jensen measures for 2 REITs out of a pool of 8 are negative, compared to 3 out of 7 in the hotel/casino group.

Additionally, the authors pooled all the data of the 15 acquirers: the data of the 8 lodging REITs acquirers and the data of the 7 hotel/casino acquirers. The Jensen measure of the hotel/casino acquirers is 2.5% and the p-value is 0.002. The positive alpha and the significant p-value suggest that the hotel shareholders receive positive gains from 2000–2006, supporting Hypothesis 2. The Jensen measure of the REITs acquirers is 0.59% and the p-value is 0.20. The positive alpha and the insignificant p-value suggest that the lodging REITs shareholders do not receive significant positive gains from 2000–2006, which fails to support Hypothesis 3.

The Jensen measure of all the pooled data is 1.7% and the p-value is 0.0006. The positive alpha and the significant p-value at the 0.05 level indicated that, overall, the hospitality acquirers experienced significant positive equity increase from 2000–2006. The results support Hypothesis 1.

Table 1: Jensen measure analysis (regression on the S&P 500): 2000–2006

Acquirer	Industry group	Alpha	t-Statistic	p-Value
All lodging REITs		0.59%	1.29	0.20
Ashford Hospitality Trust (AHT)	REITs	–0.07%	–0.03	0.973
Eagle Hospitality Properties (EHP)	REITs	0.76%	0.19	0.856
Sunstone Hotel Investors (SHO)	REITs	0.46%	0.49	0.625
Highland Hospitality Corp (HIH)	REITs	0.10%	0.07	0.945
Innkeepers USA (KPA)	REITs	0.29%	0.33	0.740
Hospitality Properties Trust (HPT)	REITs	–0.15%	–0.16	0.879
Diamondrock Hospitality Co (DRH)	REITs	0.69%	0.79	0.453
Host Marriott Corp (HST)	REITs	1.58%	1.62	0.122
All hotels/casinos		2.5%	3.166	0.002*
All hotels/casinos excluding an outlier		1.5%	2.017	0.045*
MGM Mirage (MGM)	Casino	–0.50%	–0.22	0.82
Harrah's Entertainment Inc (HET)	Casino	–1.33%	–0.71	0.498
MGM Mirage (MGM)	Casino	2.01%	1.60	0.116
Red Lion Hotels Corp (RLH)	Casino	1.46%	0.98	0.331
Ameristar Casinos Inc (ASCA)	Casino	5.04%	2.51	0.015*
La Quinta Corp-Paired (LQI)	Hotel	1.15%	0.52	0.610
Marriott International-Cl A (MAR)	Hotel	–0.85%	–0.69	0.510
All acquirers		1.7%	3.449	0.0006*
All acquirers excluding an outlier		1.07%	2.494	0.0006*

Note: Alpha = abnormal returns. *$p < 0.05$.

One hotel firm in the sample received greater positive gains (5.04%) over the years compared with the rest of the sample (1.7%). This score might be an outlier that affected the analysis adversely; therefore, the authors also created new pooled data after excluding the outlier. The result is a smaller return (1.07%). The studies on M&A have generated mixed results (Dodd and Ruback, 1977; Dodd, 1980; Asquith, 1983; Asquith et al, 1983; Sheel and Nagpal, 2000; Canina, 2001; Hsu and Jang, 2007). The results are consistent with Dodd and Ruback (1977), Asquith et al (1983) and Canina (2001), yet differ from Asquith (1983), Sheel and Nagpal (2000) and Hsu and Jang (2007). In contrast to most of the results, the authors found positive alpha and significant p-value, which indicates that the equity values of acquiring hospitality firms have significant positive gains in the long term for 2000–2006.

However, the authors generated different results when comparing the acquirers' performance against their respective sector indices. As shown in Figure 1, both hotel/casino and lodging REITs sectors outperformed the general market for the period studied and the hotel/casino sector outperformed the lodging REITs sector. This paper measured 7 hotel/casino acquirers against the Bloomberg US lodging index and 8 lodging REITs companies against the Bloomberg lodging REITs index. The results are presented in Table 2.

Franks et al (1991) suggested that different benchmarks generated significantly different abnormal returns. In the study, a much lower average of abnormal returns from both groups are expected. In general, the modified Jensen measures of 7 acquirers are negative and 8 acquirers are positive. The

Table 2: Modified Jensen measure analysis (regression on the sector indices): 2000–2006

Acquirer	Industry group	Alpha	t-Statistic	p-Value
All lodging REITs		−0.2%	−0.602	0.548
Ashford Hospitality Trust (AHT)	REITs	−0.54%	−0.29	0.774
Eagle Hospitality Properties (EHP)	REITs	0.07%	0.02	0.986
Sunstone Hotel Investors (SHO)	REITs	−0.20%	−0.23	0.818
Highland Hospitality Corp (HIH)	REITs	−0.67%	−0.52	0.606
Innkeepers USA (KPA)	REITs	−0.65%	−1.08	0.288
Hospitality Properties Trust (HPT)	REITs	−1.00%	−1.00	0.338
Diamondrock Hospitality Co (DRH)	REITs	0.03%	0.04	0.972
Host Marriott Corp (HST)	REITs	0.39%	0.66	0.517
All hotels/casinos		1.4%	1.872	0.06
All hotels/casinos excluding an outlier		0.6%	0.885	0.377
MGM Mirage (MGM)	Casino	0.87%	0.37	0.718
Harrah's Entertainment Inc (HET)	Casino	−1.25%	−1.41	0.201
MGM Mirage (MGM)	Casino	0.55%	0.50	0.622
Red Lion Hotels Corp (RLH)	Casino	1.05%	0.69	0.49
Ameristar Casinos Inc (ASCA)	Casino	3.43%	1.87	0.066
La Quinta Corp-Paired (LQI)	Hotel	1.29%	0.62	0.574
Marriott International-Cl A (MAR)	Hotel	−0.53%	−0.49	0.632
All acquirers		0.7%	1.516	0.130
All acquirers excluding an outlier		0.2%	0.582	0.560

Note: Alpha = abnormal returns.

modified Jensen measures of 5 out of 8 lodging REITs firms are negative, while only 2 out of 7 hotel/casino firms are negative.

The authors also pooled all the 15 acquirers' data, the 8 REITs acquirers' data and the 7 hotel/casino acquirers' data. The modified Jensen measure (against respective sector indices) of the hotel/casino acquirers is 1.4% and the p-value is 0.06. It fails to support Hypothesis 2, which is inconsistent with the previous result with the Jensen measure. Compared to Table 1, the result is less significant, as the sector outperforms the general market, as expected and seen in Figure 1.

The modified Jensen measure of the REITs acquirers is –0.2% and the p-value is 0.548, failing to confirm Hypothesis 3. The result is consistent with the previous model. The negative alpha and insignificant p-value indicate that when compared within the sector itself, REITs mergers fail to generate gain for their shareholders. REITs acquirers receive positive gains when compared with the general market, yet their equity values decrease when the sector is selected as the benchmark. The sharp contrast indicates that REITs firms invested in M&A activities underperformed other REITs firms from 2000 to 2006.

The modified Jensen measure of all the pooled data is 0.7 and 0.2% of the data excluding an outlier. The positive alpha and the insignificant p-value indicated that the studied hospitality acquirers experienced an insignificant positive equity increase from 2000 to 2006. It fails to support Hypothesis 1. The result is contradictory to that of the previous model. Again, the results can be reasonably interpreted by Figure 1. Since the hospitality industry as a whole outperformed the market from 2000 to 2006, the sample portfolios' excess return against the sectors was expected to be much smaller than that against the market. The modified Jensen measure provides a more accurate overview on post-merger performance for hospitality M&A.

Conclusion and Implications

The value-maximization behaviours of acquiring firms warrant that M&A activities create synergy for the acquired and acquiring firms. In the study, the authors generate mixed results using the Jensen measure and the modified Jensen measure. When compared with the S&P 500 index, the results showed significant positive gains for the acquiring hospitality firms. Yet when compared with the sector indices, REITs acquirers failed to increase the equity value for their shareholders, while the hotel/casino acquirers accrued rather nominal gains.

Despite the mixed results of the previous empirical research (for example, Sheel and Nagpal, 2000; Canina, 2001; Hsu and Jang, 2007), the hospitality industry continues to witness more firms diversifying their portfolios through

M&A activities. One possible explanation is that the industry itself usually outperforms the general market; thus, shareholders support management decisions to accomplish greater market shares. On the way, hospitality acquirers are striving to adjust to the highly saturated market, post-merger management problems and the higher beta of the industry to the broad market. Ultimately, hospitality top management needs to take into consideration that the goal is to maximize shareholders' value and to make prudent investment decisions.

As this study drew to an end, the US financial market experienced a massive crisis, despite the approval of the bailout plan. On 29 September 2008, the Dow Jones Industrial Average had its biggest closing decline with a 777.68 point drop, surpassing the loss caused by the 9/11 terrorist attack; and the S&P 500 fell 8.6% the same day. In the current market environment, the credit crunch is posing a serious threat to the overall economy. M&A among hotels will become more difficult due to concerns over a slowing economy and high leverage used in such transactions. Highly leveraged hotel companies in particular will find additional financing extremely difficult. M&A activities are expected to cool down substantially in the near term due to acquiring firms' financing difficulties.

However, hotel company valuations, among other types of real estate investment (for example, residential, office complex), have generally become more resilient during this distressed period. Great opportunities are available for those acquiring companies with unused leverage capacity, high credit ratings, strong balance sheets and funding options with selective targets which have been significantly undervalued. The bigger winners will be the acquiring companies who can purchase undervalued hotel properties and manage those properties as long-term investment portfolios. When the economy recovers and hotel demand increases, these acquiring companies could realize large gains from selling the properties.

This paper has made some contribution to the study of M&A in the hospitality industry. Future studies should select not only the market portfolio (NASDAQ, the S&P 500 index, etc) as the benchmark, but also respective sector indices. In the meantime, the study has its own limitations, due to the limited sample size. Future studies can extend time duration and increase sample size to yield more significant results, and may also examine the relationship between payment method and post-merger performance.

References

Asquith, P. (1983), 'Merger bids, uncertainty, and stockholder returns', *Journal of Financial Economics*, Vol 11, pp. 51–83.

Asquith, P., Bruner, R.F., and Mullins, D.W. (1983), 'The gains to bidding firms from merger', *Journal of Financial Economics*, Vol 11, pp 51–83.

Canina, L. (2001), 'Acquisitions in the lodging industry: good news for buyers and sellers', *Cornell Hotel and Restaurant Administration Quarterly*, Vol 42, No 6, pp 47–54.

Dodd, P. (1980), 'Merger proposals, management discretion and stockholder wealth', *Journal of Financial Economics*, Vol 8, pp 105–138.

Dodd, P., and Ruback, R. (1977), 'Tender offers and stockholder returns', *Journal of Financial Economics*, Vol 5, pp 351–373.

Franks, J., Harris, R., and Titman, S. (1991), 'The postmerger share-price performance of acquiring firms', *Journal of Financial Economics*, Vol 29, pp 81–96.

Grinblatt, M., and Sheridan, T. (1989), 'Mutual fund performance: an analysis of quarterly portfolio holdings', *Journal of Business*, Vol 62, pp 393–417.

Hsu, L., and Jang, S. (2007), 'The post-merger financial performance of hotel companies', *Journal of Hospitality and Tourism Research*, Vol 31, pp 471–485.

Jensen, M.C. (1968), 'The performance of mutual funds in the period 1945–1964', *Journal of Finance*, Vol 23, pp 389–416.

Lehmann, B., and Modest, D. (1987), 'Mutual fund performance evaluation: a comparison of benchmarks', *Journal of Finance*, Vol 42, pp 233–265.

Lubatkin, M. (1983), 'Mergers and performance of the acquiring firm', *The Academy of Management Review*, Vol 8, No 2, pp 218–225.

Michel, A., and Shaked, I. (1985), 'Evaluating merger performance', *California Management Review*, Vol 27, No 3, pp 109–118.

Sheel, A., and Nagpal, A. (2000), 'The post-merger equity value performance of acquiring firms in the hospitality industry', *The Journal of Hospitality Financial Management*, Vol 8, No 1, pp 37–45.

28

Hotel Reform in China: A SWOT Analysis

Larry Yu and Gu Huimin

China's dynamic economic growth has attracted business and investment interests from around the world over the past decade. Corporate demand for travel and lodging services will increase as additional international corporations establish operations in China. Increasing corporate demand will put great pressure on four- and five-star hotels to maintain international service standards. In addition, China's long history and diverse tourism resources will attract both international and domestic leisure tourists to visit different parts of China, creating demand for different types of hotel products and services. The 2008 Beijing Olympics and the 2010 World Exposition in Shanghai will drive and sustain tourism and hotel development in this decade.

Since China's accession to the World Trade Organization (WTO) on December 11, 2001, China has been gradually opening its hotel market to international development and competition.[1] By December 2005, China will completely open its market to international investors for hotel, restaurant, and other mixed-used real estate development projects.[2] Intensified competition from international developers and operators will pose great challenges to domestic hotel operations, of which 57 percent are owned by various government entities. The performance of many domestic hotels lags behind that of internationally managed operations due to management inefficiency, a lack of corporate governance, and inferior service quality.[3] To prepare domestic hotels – particularly state-owned hotels – for global competition, the Chinese government has initiated fundamental reforms in the hotel industry. These reforms are designed to weed out nonperforming hotels by transferring state ownership to nongovernmental business enterprises. The purpose of this study is to offer a strategic SWOT (strengths, weaknesses, opportunities, and threats) analysis of China's hotel industry by analyzing its strengths and weaknesses and identifying the opportunities and potential threats to both domestic and international hotel developers and operators.

Strengths

China has witnessed the rapid development of its hotel properties over the past two decades. The strengths of China's hotel industry rest in (1) the growing popularity of China as a major international business market and tourism destination, (2) the diversity and quality of China's hotel products, (3) the efforts to standardize operations and improve service quality, and (4) increased development by global hotel corporations.

In the first instance, the growth of hotels appealing to international tourists has been fueled by aggressive economic reforms in the past decade. This growth has paralleled rapid national economic expansion and the emergence of China as one of the leading tourist destinations in the world, from the eleventh most visited international destination in 1990 to the fourth most visited destination in 2002.[4] The World Tourism Organization estimates that China will become the leading tourist destination in the world by 2020. Therefore, sustained economic development and China's rising popularity will provide a hotel market conducive to development.

Second, China's hotel industry is now characterized as having diverse products that cater to various market segments. As Exhibit 1 shows, tourist-oriented hotels in China have grown steadily, from 1,987 hotels in 1990 to 8,880 hotels in 2002.[5]

China's hotels operate under several ownership structures. Exhibit 2 describes ten types of hotel ownership in China and the distributions of star-ranked hotels in 2002. State ownership represents state-owned hotels at all levels, comprising 5,061 hotels, or 57 percent of the country's 2002 hotel inventory. Nongovernment, collective enterprises owned 893 hotels, or 10 percent of the total hotel count. Foreign investors accounted for the development of 279 hotels (just more than 3 percent); and investors from Hong Kong, Macau, and Taiwan owned 407 hotels (4.6 percent). In addition, 2,240 hotels were owned by Chinese partnerships, private owners, and strategic alliances (just more than 25 percent).[6]

China developed its five-star hotel ranking system in the early 1990s to standardize its fledgling hotel operations and services.[7] In the past decade,

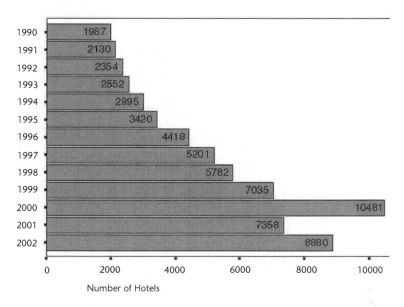

Source: China National Tourism Administration, *The Yearbook of China Tourism Statistics* (Beijing: China Travel and Tourism Press, 2003).
Note: The year-2000 figures are not directly comparable to those of other years. Hotel data included both star-ranked and nonstar tourism hotels in 2000 as the China National Tourism Administration changed its reporting format in that year. Only star-ranked tourism hotels were reported in its annual statistical yearbook for 2001 and 2002.

Exhibit 1: Hotel development in China, 1990–2202

the number of star-ranked hotels has increased phenomenally to include hotels under all types of ownership. Exhibit 2 illustrates the distribution of the star-ranked hotels in each of the five star categories.

Five-star hotels made up 2 percent of the total star-ranked properties in 2002; 7.2 percent of those hotels held four-star ratings. One-third of China's tourist hotels were ranked as three-star hotels, and half were classified as two-star hotels. One-star hotels accounted for 9 percent of the total tourism hotels in China. There is no clear relationship between ownership patterns and star-ranking status since both state-owned hotels and privately owned hotels were found in all star categories.

The star-ranking system constitutes the third strong point for the nation's hotels because it assures guests of hotels' quality. In a more recent effort to enhance domestic hotel operation standards, the China National Tourism Administration (CNTA) enacted in March 2002 the first regulation governing hotel operating standards.[8] The regulation, formulated after extensive research in international hotel operations, consists of eight parts. It calls for credibility in hotel management, protection of the legitimate interests of guests and hotels, and the standardization of the hotel operations in line with international practice.

Exhibit 2: Hotel ownership and star-ranking distributions in China, 2002

Ownership	Hotels	Percentage of total	Rooms	Percentage of total	Beds	Percentage of total
State owned	5,061	57.0	487,100	54.3	975,400	56.4
Collective	893	10.1	71,000	7.9	139,900	8.1
Shareholding cooperative	172	1.9	15,600	1.7	28,100	1.6
Alliance	90	1.0	9,500	1.06	18,100	1.1
Limited liability	734	8.3	75,000	8.4	141,300	8.2
Limited liability shares	327	3.7	41,100	4.6	76,900	4.5
Private owned	556	6.3	36,000	4.0	68,900	4.0
Others	361	4.1	26,400	2.9	51,600	3.0
Foreign funded	279	3.1	60,700	6.8	103,100	6.0
Hong Kong, Macau, and Taiwan	407	4.6	74,800	8.3	126,000	7.3

Star ranking	Hotels	Percentage	Rooms	Percentage	Beds	Percentage
5 Star	175	2.0	64,900	7.2	102,400	5.9
4 Star	635	7.2	143,500	16.0	248,400	14.4
3 Star	2,846	32.1	346,500	38.6	680,000	39.3
2 Star	4,414	49.7	306,000	34.1	622,100	36.0
1 Star	810	9.1	36,400	4.1	76,500	4.4
Total	8,880		897,300		1,729,500	

Source: China National Tourism Administration, *The Yearbook of China Tourism Statistics* (Beijing: China Travel & Tourism Press, 2003), 7–8.

Fourth, increased involvement by international hotel companies represents yet another strength of China's hotel development. Market entry by international hotel companies has brought not only competition but also management know-how from developed countries. With that added expertise, the gap between domestically operated hotels and those run by international companies has narrowed substantially. Moreover, by example, hotels operating under international standards have contributed to enhancing the productivity and efficiency of domestically operated hotels.

Many international hotel corporations have established their presence in China in the past decade, and consolidation and brand development among domestic companies have also been accelerating. Exhibit 3 lists the top domestic and international hotel companies in China and the portfolio of properties owned, managed, or franchised by these companies. Clearly, many international hotel brands are now represented in China, and other international hotel companies, such as Days Inn and Four Seasons, are currently developing or converting new projects. It is also revealing that many Chinese domestic hotel brands have been developed to compete with the global lodging giants, particularly the Jinjiang International Hotel Management Corporation in Shanghai, which is currently ranked as the thirty-fifth largest hotel group in the world and is headed by an American president who has a strategic vision for international growth.[9]

The strengths of China's hotel industry are therefore identified as popularity for business and leisure travelers, diverse hotel products,

Exhibit 3: International and domestic hotel companies in China

Company	Hotels	City, Country
Jingjiang International Hotels	120	Shanghai, China
InterContinental Hotels	41	Berkshire, United Kingdom
Jianguo Hotels International	40	Beijing, China
Marriott International	24	Washington, D.C., United States
Accor	22	Paris, France
Rujia Hemei Hotel Management Group	22	Beijing, China
Hong Kong CTS Hotel Management Group	19	Hong Kong, China
Shangri-la Hotels	16	Hong Kong, China
Conifer International Hotel Group	15	Hong Kong, China
China Travel Service Hotel Company	15	Beijing, China
Starwood Hotels and Resorts	14	White Plains, New York, United States
Howard Johnson Hotel Management Group	14	Parsippany, New Jersey, United States
Oriental Hotel Management Company	12	Beijing, China
Kai Yuan Tourism Enterprise Group	12	Hangzhou, China
Gloria Plaza International Hotels	11	Hong Kong, China
Best Western International	10	Phoenix, Arizona, United States
Hua Tian International Hotel Group	9	Changsa, China
Hilton International	5	Watford, Herts, United Kingdom
Hyatt Corporation	4	Chicago, Illinois, United States

Source: *China Tourism News*, February 26, 2003; and China Tourist Hotel Association (2004), data collected by personal interview in Beijing.
Note: Statistics are as of July 30, 2004, except for Accor, Gloria Plaza, Hilton, InterContinental, Oriental, and Shangri-la, which are as of 2003; and Hyatt, which is as of 2002.

government and industry efforts to improve operations to match international standards, increased international development, and the emergence of domestic hotel groups. With adequate hotel infrastructure and two decades of development and management experience, China's hotel industry can now prepare for new global and domestic challenges.

Weaknesses

As China's hotel industry prepares for the international challenges ahead, its operators are keenly aware of the weaknesses that have been hindering effective management in domestic hotel operations. These weaknesses are particularly evident in (1) certain ownership structures, (2) debt issues, and (3) financial performance.

To begin with, operation and ownership of most state-owned properties have not kept pace with the past two decades of Chinese economic reform. Furthermore, the distinction between ownership and management is often blurred in many state-owned hotels. Therefore, management deficiencies, including bureaucratic controls, lack of fiscal discipline, low operating efficiency, and lack of innovation are characteristic of state-owned hotels.[10] These weaknesses significantly limit those hotels' competitiveness.

Second, excessive indebtedness is a national problem that has been plaguing not only the hotel industry but all businesses in China. China's banks are carrying an estimated US$500 billion in bad loans.[11] The magnitude of bad loans by state-owned banks is attributable to poor lending policies, which forgo the vigorous assessment of project viability, and to corrupt lending practices between banks and borrowers. The national banks could face a liquidity shortage as China opens the financial sector to international competition as part of its commitments to the WTO. Given the banks' dearth of cash reserves, the Chinese government has required state banks to reduce the ratio of underperforming loans. It was reported that major banks had slashed more than $25 billion in bad loans from their balance sheets, reducing the ratio of bad loans by more than 5 percent to an estimated 18 percent of total loans in 2003.[12] However, the $45 billion bailout of two state banks, the Bank of China and the Construction Bank of China, announced on January 6, 2004, clearly indicated the inefficiency of China's banking system. It also showed that the government was trying to prepare national banks to sell shares on foreign stock markets to raise new capital and improve their management structure.[13]

Many of the bad loans underwritten by state-owned banks were made in the past twenty years and have resulted in the banks' owning hotels, in whole or in part. For instance, the Bank of China formerly owned five hotels solely, and had partial investment interests in approximately two hundred hotels.[14] The bank's ownership interest occurred chiefly as a result of the Chinese currency devaluation and poor hotel performance of the 1980s. When China first opened to international tourism in the late 1970s, there was a pent-up demand for building hotels to international standards by importing elevators and modern bathroom facilities. The Bank of China was at that time the only bank in China designated for managing foreign exchange and handling international business transactions. Consequently, many hotel developers had to turn to the Bank of China for foreign currency to purchase building materials and equipment from overseas. To facilitate those purchases, the Bank of China made loans of foreign exchange to many hotel developers in the 1980s.

However, the exchange rate between the U.S. dollar and the Chinese yuan changed substantially after these hotel projects were completed. After several devaluations, the yuan went from $1:¥1.7 in 1978 to $1:¥8.7 in 1994.[15] Devaluation of the Chinese yuan immediately squeezed operating cash flows of hotels with poor financial performance, as a greater revenue percentage was required to pay for dollar-denominated debt. As a result, many hotels defaulted on their loans, and the Bank of China had to foreclose – becoming sole or part owner of the failing hotels. The foreclosure of the Olympic Hotel in Beijing by the Bank of China is an example of a hotel's failure due to foreign-exchange volatility and inefficient management.[16]

Third, increased competition at home and from abroad has tested management efficiency among all types of domestic hotels. Three types of management are commonly found in China's hotel industry: international management, domestic chain management, and domestic independent management. Hotels with international management are owned by various interests and are typically ranked with four or five stars. Examples of internationally managed hotels include the five-star Grand Hyatt Shanghai and Palace Hotel in Beijing (managed by the Peninsula Group), the four-star Traders Hotel (managed by Shangri-la), and the Beijing Peace Hotel (managed by Accor).

Domestic chain management refers to hotels managed by domestic Chinese management companies. As illustrated in Exhibit 3, several domestically branded hotel management companies have been developed over the past decade, with Jinjiang International Hotel Management Corporation currently representing the largest hotel management company in China. The Nanjing Jinling Hotel managed by the Jinling Group and the Beijing Kunlun Hotel, managed by the Jinjiang Group, are both five-star hotels. Examples of four-star domestic-chain managed hotels include the Jianguo Hotel in Beijing (managed by the Jianguo International Hotel Group) and the Zhejiang World Trade Center Hotel in Hangzhou (managed by the Zhejiang World Trade Center Hotel Group).

Domestic-independent management refers to independent operations without international or domestic management affiliations. Most state-owned hotels are independently managed and are distributed across all the star categories. For example, the five-star Beijing Yanshan Hotel and the Shenzheng Yangguang Hotel are both state-owned and independently operated. The four-star Beijing Friendship Hotel and the Shanghai Yinghe Hotel are also state-owned and independently managed. Most independent hotels that are state owned do not separate ownership and management.

Hotel performance tends to vary according to management type. Many nonperforming hotels are identified as independent hotels. Since 1998, the hotel industry in China has been losing money overall. Total industry losses were an estimated ¥5.364 billion in 1999 and ¥2.346 billion in 2000.[17] These losses were attributed to the overprovision of high-end luxury hotels and inefficient management at many independent hotels. Hotel performance for the past three years was crippled by the 9/11 terrorist attacks in 2001 and the SARS epidemic in 2003.[18] Only 20 percent of all Chinese hotels were profitable in 2003, of which 85 percent were internationally managed.[19] A recent hotel industry survey conducted by Horwath Asia Pacific for China Tourist Hotel Association from a sample of 248 hotels provided revealing information on hotel performance by comparing the five-star and four-star hotels operated by the three different types of management (Exhibit 4).

Exhibit 4: Hotel financial performance by management type, 2002

	4-Star hotels			5-Star hotels		
Performance	International management	Domestic chain management	Independent management	International management	Domestic chain management	Independent management
Occupancy	71.4%	72.7%	67.9%	70.4%	74.6%	64.8%
ADR	¥485	¥366	¥330	¥727	¥604	¥518
RevPAR	¥346	¥266	¥224	¥512	¥450	¥336

Source: *China Hotel Industry Study 2003* (Beijing: China Tourist Hotel Association, 2003).
Note: ADR (average daily rate, measured by rooms revenue divided by the number of rooms sold) and RevPAR (revenue per available room) were reported in Chinese yuan. As of this writing, the exchange rate between U.S. dollar and Chinese yuan is: $1:¥8.28.

The analysis found that four- and five-star hotels operated by international companies had the best RevPAR (revenue per available room) performance. RevPAR for five-star hotels operated by domestic independent operators was 12 percent lower than that of five-star hotels operated by international management. This difference in RevPAR was even more considerable for four-star hotels. Four-star properties operated by domestic hotel-management companies recorded RevPAR 23 percent lower than those operated by international management. When comparing RevPAR between hotels operated by international management and those operated by domestic independent management, international management outperformed domestic independent management by better than 35 percent for four-star hotels and 34 percent for five-star hotels. The performance gaps in both ranking categories were considerable, particularly between international management and domestic-independent management.

The inefficiencies of independent local management also fell to the bottom line, as shown in Exhibit 5. Measured by earnings before income tax, depreciation and amortization (EBITDA), four-star domestically managed chain hotels achieved a respectable EBITDA of 27.9 percent in 2002, while internationally managed hotels had an EBITDA of 23.3 percent. Comparing these two types of management, each had similar departmental expenses: 42.3 percent for international management and 42.4 percent for domestic management. However, domestic chain management had higher administrative and general expenses, even though many international management companies employed expatriate managers who normally received higher compensation and benefits. International management firms also spent more on marketing and energy compared to domestic chain management but had lower fixed charges in their operations.

Domestic-independent management showed the lowest EBITDA – just 13.5 percent – of the three types of management. This group had the highest expenditures in every spending category. Domestic-independent expenditures on administrative expenses were 5.6 percent higher and on general operations

Exhibit 5: Comparison of operation performance by management type (in percentages)

	4-Star hotels			5-Star hotels		
	International management	Domestic chain management	Independent management	International management	Domestic chain management	Independent management
Department revenues						
Rooms	60.7	56.6	44.4	55.2	52.1	44.7
Food	23.9	23.6	31.2	22.3	23.7	31.6
Beverage	5.1	4.9	6.0	6.8	5.5	5.4
Catering	2.2	2.7	4.7	5.0	4.5	4.7
Telephone	0.9	0.8	0.3	0.8	0.1	0.6
Spa	0.9	1.4	4.9	1.3	5.5	3.9
Rent	3.9	9.8	9.7	4.1	8.1	8.6
Other	2.9	5.8	6.4	5.0	3.8	3.8
Total	100	100	100	100	100	100
Department expenses						
Rooms	25.7	25.0	23.7	19.4	19.1	19.6
F&B	74.3	80.8	71.2	63.5	69.3	65.3
Telephone	117.4	190.5	177.7	101.8	–	148.7
Spa	57.1	54.2	56.8	52.0	101.2	38.4
Rent	12.4	9.4	20.7	13.3	29.0	25.6
Other	60.1	74.9	93.3	32.4	91.1	127.8
Total	42.3	42.4	44.6	35.6	38.9	43.0
Undistributed expenses						
Administrative	9.7	12.8	15.3	8.4	13.4	11.3
Marketing	4.4	2.9	2.0	5.4	2.0	2.4
Energy	9.0	6.8	7.3	7.4	6.7	7.2
POM	4.7	4.4	7.9	4.1	4.0	5.6
Total	27.9	22.6	28.4	25.3	23.4	25.3
IBFCMF	29.7	35.0	27.1	39.0	37.8	31.8
Management fee (basic and incentive)	3.0	3.1	6.7	3.5	3.0	3.5
Fixed charges	3.8	6.4	12.1	6.3	10.5	7.8
EBITDA	23.3	27.9	13.5	30.4	26.5	23.5

Source: China Hotel Industry Study 2003 (Beijing: China Tourist Hotel Association, 2003).
Note: Corporate income taxes levied by the Chinese government are as follows: 33 percent for taxable income greater than ¥100,000, 27 percent for taxable income between ¥30,000 and ¥100,000, and 18 percent for taxable income less than ¥30,000. F&B = food and beverage; POM = property operation and maintenance; IBFCMF = income before fixed charges and management fees; EBITDA = earnings before income tax, depreciation and amortization.

2.5 percent higher than those of both international management and domestic management. Property operations and maintenance costs were substantially higher in domestic independent operations than those of internationally managed hotels and domestically managed chain hotels. It is interesting to note that domestic independent hotels paid more than twice as much in management fees as did international management and domestic management companies. This group's fixed charges were almost three times those of international management and about twice those of domestic management companies.

Internationally managed five-star hotels returned higher EBITDA than either of the other groups. Internationally managed hotels had EBITDA of

30.4 percent, while domestic chain hotels obtained an EBITDA of 26.5 percent, and that of domestic independent hotels was 23.5 percent. International management maintained relatively lower departmental expenses and fixed charges, while domestic chain management reported the highest administrative and general expenses, at 13.4 percent of total sales, and domestic independent hotels incurred administrative and general expenses of 11.3 percent of total sales. Both domestic groups had higher fixed charges than those of international management. Again, international management spent the most in marketing and energy consumption.

The financial-performance data demonstrate that, in the four-star category, domestic management and international management performed much better than did domestic independent hotels. The main reason for this performance gap was the extremely high management fees and fixed charges of domestic independent hotels. These operational differences can be attributed to inefficient management, lack of strict corporate governance, and in some cases, accounting irregularities that hide income to avoid taxes. The low EBITDA for domestic independent hotels clearly indicates unsatisfactory financial performance by domestic hotels (most of which, as we pointed out above, are owned and managed by government agencies). In the five-star category, international management achieved superior financial performance despite high marketing and energy costs. Domestic chain management performed better than did domestic independent hotels, but domestic chains had the highest fixed costs and administrative and general expenses. Domestic independent hotels again had the lowest financial performance due to the highest department expenses and relatively high fixed charges. Clearly, international management not only achieved the highest RevPAR but also effectively controlled operating costs. In contrast, domestic hotels had lower RevPAR and incurred higher operating costs. This situation was especially pronounced with independently managed hotels. Such poor performance eventually exerted great pressure on the owners and lending institutions to make critical decisions on many non-performing and failing hotel assets.

Hotel Reforms and Opportunities

In response to the poor performance of domestic hotel operations, fundamental reforms in China's hotel industry have been initiated. These reforms are intended to transform domestic hotels into profitable and competitive operations by shifting hotel ownership from the state to nongovernment business enterprises. This reform is intended to liquidate the nonperforming assets held by state-owned banks and further reduce the proportion of bad loans. It is hoped that these reforms will make domestic hotels more competitive by late 2005, in time for China to open its hotel development under the WTO agreement. The following section discusses the current reform models and identifies potential opportunities for hotel development and management.

Several hotel-industry-reform models have been applied in various parts of the China. These include

- internal transfer of ownership,
- partnership between current management and new investors,
- exiting joint-venture projects,
- selling hotels to nonhospitality companies,
- hotel auctions, and
- creating domestic hotel holding and management groups.[20]

Internal transfer. An internal transfer of ownership is essentially a management-led buyout. The property is sold to its management and those employees who are interested in continuing the hotel's operation. This model permits the transfer of state-owned hotels to limited-liability companies owned by the hotel's management and its employees. Normally, the general manager holds the majority stake in the new company, the assistant general manager and department managers also participate in stock ownership, and employees can participate in stock ownership if they wish. For instance, Suzhou's municipal government recently transferred the ¥63 million Lexiang Hotel to its management and employees. As a result, the management company now owns 45 percent of the hotel, the assistant general manager owns 10 percent, the department managers hold shares that range from 2 to 5 percent each, and a number of employees have stakes of up to 1 percent apiece.[21]

New investment. In a variant of the management buyout, if the existing management does not have sufficient financial resources to assume ownership of the hotel through internal transfer, it can seek new investors as partners to invest in the hotel. In this case, ownership is determined by the shares of investment in the property, normally divided among the new investor, the hotel management, and various department managers and hotel employees.

Unwinding joint ventures. Some hotels were originally developed by joint partnerships between Chinese government entities and international investors. By exiting these joint ventures, Chinese partners completely withdraw from the joint-venture project and transfer their shares to the international partners. Therefore, the international partners become the sole owners.

Outright sale. Some state-owned hotels have been sold to domestic nonhospitality companies as these companies seek business diversification through real estate development and expansion into the hospitality industry. In such cases, the ownership of state hotels is completely transferred to the purchaser.

Auctions. Hotel auctions have been on the rise as the state hotel owners want to maximize the value of their properties when they exit the hotel business. Some auctions have ended happily. For example, the Friendship Hotel in Suzhou, which was originally owned by the city's Workers' Union and was offered at auction starting at ¥22 million, eventually fetched ¥37 million.[22] However, some hotels have been sold for less than the requested starting bid. The Olympic Hotel in Beijing, for example, owned by the Bank of China, was auctioned for just ¥225 million, even though the property was appraised at ¥350 million.[23] In addition, many hotels were auctioned to nonhospitality companies to be converted to other commercial use, such as the purchase of failing hotels by two of China's leading hospital management groups.[24]

New holding companies. Creating a large domestic hotel holding and management group is one of the reform strategies, particularly in major cities. Municipal governments separate their hotel assets from the city treasury and allocate them to the newly independent hotel companies. Most resulting firms are now listed on the stock market and are actively traded on China's financial markets. Two hotel operations that were formerly owned by the Shanghai government, for instance, Jinjiang International Hotel Management and New Asia Hotel Group, merged to form the largest hotel holding and management company in China.[25] The new company, under the Jinjiang International name, is now the largest publicly listed hotel group in China, with 120 hotels operating under the brands of Jinjiang Star, Jinjiang, New Jinjiang, Huating, and Heping. This merger is what put it at thirty-fifth in the *Hotels* magazine listing in 2003.[26]

These various types of reforms have been implemented with relative speed and will only accelerate as China continues preparations for the 2005 hotel-market opening. Indeed, some cities have been pursuing hotel reform for several years with marked results. Suzhou, for instance, had twenty-eight star-ranked hotels and one state guesthouse before reforms were instituted. Of these twenty-nine hotels, twenty-one were owned by various agencies of the city government (including two joint-venture hotels), two hotels were owned by private Chinese businesses, and six hotels were owned by companies from other parts of China. At this writing, twelve city-owned hotels have changed ownership, one hotel was converted for other commercial uses, and three other hotels are in the process of transferring ownership. This transfer of ownership has returned total capital of ¥1.37 billion to the city treasury.[27]

With ownership transfers like those in Suzhou, state capital is withdrawn from the hotel business and the ratio of bad loans plaguing state-owned banks is reduced. At the same time, the reform is intended to improve domestic hotel-management efficiency and prepare the hotels for international competition by transforming state-owned and operated hotels into professional, for-profit hotel companies. These reforms, therefore, present many potential opportunities to both domestic and international hotel companies.

Operators of ancillary services will also benefit. The transfers of hotel ownership create demand for hotel appraisal and valuation services, for instance. To ensure that state assets are not just given away to hotel companies or individual investors, the government wants to transfer hotel properties at a fair market value. At present, most hotel-valuation appraisals are performed by domestic accounting firms. While these accounting firms are knowledgeable in general accounting and valuation procedures, their limited expertise in hotel operations restricts them from accurately estimating the fair market value of a hotel operation in terms of future operating cash flows. This shortcoming was reflected in the wide gap between opening bids and final bids on the auction market. To prevent additional unpleasant bidding surprises, opportunities exist for hotel market analysts and appraisers to perform valuation services and for Chinese hotel-management-education programs to introduce hotel market analysis and valuation into their curriculum.

At present, the hotel reforms that we have been discussing primarily involve domestic transactions. An open and transparent real estate market for hotel transactions is almost absent in China, particularly for transactions involving hotels operated by international companies. Few transactions to date in China have involved internationally managed hotels.[28] Given the 2005 WTO deadline, a market mechanism is needed to facilitate increased transactions of hotels and restaurants that involve both domestic Chinese and international owners. Systematic and standard services involving hotel real estate agents, appraisers, lending institutions, and escrow companies are expected to provide professional consultation and services for potential hotel developers and buyers. In addition, reliable data on hotel operations and financial performance need to be made available for potential investors and buyers. The annual China Tourism Hotel Study, started in 2003 by China Tourist Hotel Association and Horwath Asia Pacific, is an encouraging effort in this direction. Gradually, hotel sales data on lending rates, equity dividends, equity yields, and capitalization rates should be compiled and provided to potential developers and buyers for decision making.

One immediate opportunity stemming from current hotel reform is brand development for both domestic and international hotel companies. After assuming control of hotel operations, the new management typically engages in strategic planning and continues to invest in renovating and enhancing hotel facilities and services to increase services and upgrade their star-ranking status. Other owners are intent on joining well-established international or domestic hotel brands. Following this pattern, for example, the Suzhou International Hotel rebranded itself after a management buyout, becoming the Holiday Inn Crowne Plaza Hotel by InterContinental Hotel Group. Another reformed hotel, Shengjiang Hotel, also in Suzhou, joined the Jinjiang Star brand and will focus on the economy market for domestic business tourists.[29] Because only a small proportion of Chinese hotels are currently branded, China's hotel reform therefore creates great opportunities for brand development.

Many newly formed hotel companies have pursued new development opportunities. Mixed-use development projects, including office-residential-hotel developments, have been built in many cities. Some hotel companies have diversified their lines of business and ventured into fast-food restaurants and teahouse operations to increase sales and diversify business risk. For example, the strategic objective of the publicly traded Capital Travel Corporation in Beijing is to form a joint-venture hotel-management company with Nikko Hotels International that will manage four- and five-star hotels in twelve cities served by Japan Airlines. The firm has also embarked on an ambitious, ¥1 billion mixed-used project of offices and hotel accommodations, known as Beijing Palace, which will be used as the command center for the 2008 Beijing Olympic Games.[30]

As more state-owned hotels are converted to private ownership, competition for hotel-management professionals has intensified. An increasing number of expatriate managers is employed by both international and domestic hotel companies. On top of expatriate hiring, a steady return of Chinese hotel-management professionals, who were educated and have been working in the hotel business in North America and Europe, is adding to the number of competent hotel managers in China. In addition, many hospitality-management programs offered in Chinese universities have boosted the flow of well-educated professionals for entry-level management positions. However, competent managerial professionals remain in short supply in many critical management areas, such as conference and exhibition management, brand management, yield management, asset management, e-commerce, and strategic development. Demand for executive education and training programs in these areas will increase as hotel reform in China accelerates.[31] Therefore, professional, corporate, and academic education-and training-program providers are presented with potential opportunities for training competent hotel professionals in China.

Threats

Impediments to the future development of China's hotel industry need to be evaluated and analyzed for contingency planning. The external threats facing China's hotel industry include (1) the overprovision of hotels, (2) an economic slowdown, (3) intensified competition from neighboring countries, and (4) political disruptions in the region.

First, overbuilding of hotels can be a major threat to profitable operations for both domestic and international hotel companies. In a rush to capitalize on potential hotel-market development, foreign and domestic hotel companies will continue to jockey for market position by developing new hotel projects. This development may be further fueled by the 2008 Olympic Games and 2010 World Expo. Development without sound market research and planning will lead to overbuilding of hotel properties, a lesson painfully learned by hotel developers in the United States in the latter part of the 1980s.

Second, China's impressive economic growth is the envy of the whole world. However, concerns about the sustainability of the economic boom are often debated in academe and the international business community, particularly in view of the bad-loan problem faced by state-owned banks.[32] If the Chinese government cannot engineer a soft landing for its fast-growing economy, a potential economic slowdown may be triggered by sudden, unforeseeable, and uncontrollable forces – and certainly would hurt the hotel industry.

Third, China's neighboring countries will continue to compete for the international tourism market. Aggressive marketing by established and emerging destinations in the region will challenge China's position and may draw potential international visitors away from China.

Finally, existing political tension between mainland China and Taiwan and the possible escalation of the nuclear weapons threat from North Korea may pose additional potential threats to the political stability of the region. These threats, though remote, should be included in contingency planning by hotel developers and investors.

Implications for Future Development

China's hotel industry experienced phenomenal growth in the past decade. This rapid development was fueled by robust economic expansion, and China now enjoys the world's sixth largest economy. The concomitant growth in demand for business and leisure travel by both Chinese and international visitors and the prospects of the Olympic Games and the World Exposition have stimulated sustained development of lodging accommodations in China. Driven by these economic and tourism forces, China's hotel industry has great potential for future growth. However, China's hotel industry also faces internal weaknesses and potential external threats. Exhibit 6 summarizes our SWOT analysis of China's hotel industry and presents global hotel companies and developers a matrix for strategic planning for future hotel development in China.

With a well-developed hotel infrastructure, China now offers a wide range of hotel products to serve all segments of the travel market. The facilities of

Exhibit 6: SWOT (strengths, weaknesses, opportunities, and threats) analysis – China hotel reform

Strengths	Leading world destination
	Growing international hotel brands
	Improving domestic brands
	Star-ranking system
	New hotel regulation
Weaknesses	State ownership
	Debt problem
	Unprofitable operations
	Inefficiency in management
Opportunities	Hotel reform
	Hotel appraisal and valuation
	Hotel real estate market
	Hotel brand development
	Mixed-use projects
	Education and training
Threats	Overprovision
	Potential economic slowdown
	Regional political tensions
	Intensified competition (both international and domestic)

most star-ranked hotels meet international standards of construction and furnishing. The entry by international hotel corporations has introduced global hotel brands to China, raising the bar for the quality of services and influencing the development of domestic hotel groups. The five-star ranking system and CNTA's newly established hotel regulations call for the accountability of management, protection of guest and operator interests, and the standardization of hotel operations in line with international practice. These are positive developments that will create an environment conducive for hotel development and competition.

The weaknesses that we identified above were reflected in the ownership structure, debt problems, and unprofitable operations that resulted from inefficient management. The urgent need for reform of the state ownership and management model was validated by the comparison of operating performance among companies operating under international management, domestic chain management, and domestic independent management.

The current reforms that target non-performing and debt-laden state-owned hotels have created new opportunities for both domestic and international hotel companies and ancillary businesses. Ongoing reforms will also create growing demand for brand development and management. Since a relatively small proportion of the hotels in China are currently branded, opportunities abound for expanding brands by international and domestic hotel corporations, through both franchise and management-contract agreements. The emergence of branded Chinese management and franchise companies will encourage competition among domestic firms and well-established international brands operating in China.

As consolidation and branding continue, developers will pursue complex mixed-use development projects, such as the Foreign Trade Tower in Shanghai, which encompasses commercial, lodging, and residential functions. Multifaceted development projects will attract attention from foreign and domestic developers. As competition in hotel business grows, the competition for competent management professionals will intensify, and such competition will create great demand for academic education and professional training programs. Programs that can integrate advanced management know-how with Chinese service culture will most effectively produce competent managerial professionals for Chinese hotels.

Perhaps the greatest threat to China's future hotel development is the prospect of overbuilding, followed by a slowdown in the overheated economy. While that eventuality cannot be foreseen with precision, it is almost certain that Chinese hotels will feel intensified competition from neighboring countries for international tourists. Finally, we can only hope that conflict in the region remains only a remote possibility.

Endnotes

1. Matthew Tapson, *Hotels in China: A Market Analysis* (Bucks, UK: Access Asia Ltd., 2002); and China Economic Information Network, *China's Tourism Industry in 2003* (Beijing, China: State Information Center, 2003).
2. Jones Lang LaSalle Hotels, *China's Hotel Investment Market* (New York: Jones Lang LaSalle Hotels, 2003).
3. Ray Pine, "China's Hotel Industry: Serving a Massive Market," *Cornell Hotel and Restaurant Administration Quarterly* 43, no. 3 (June 2002): 61–70.
4. World Tourism Organization, *Tourism Highlights, Edition 2003* (Madrid, Spain: World Tourism Organization, 2003).
5. The sharp drop in the number of hotels from 2000 to 2001 was due to changes in statistical reporting by the China National Tourism Administration (CNTA). In 2000, CNTA changed its compilation method for hotel statistics by counting both star-ranked and nonstar tourism hotels. However, CNTA soon realized the difficulty and complexity of accurately counting nonstar hotels throughout China because of the multifunctional uses of these properties. Since 2001, CNTA returned to reporting only star-ranked tourism hotels in its statistical yearbook.
6. CNTA, *The Yearbook of China Tourism Statistics* (Beijing: China Travel and Tourism Press, 2003).
7. For detailed information on hotel star ranking system, see Larry Yu, "Seeing Stars: China's Hotel Ranking System," *Cornell Hotel and Restaurant Administration Quarterly* 33, no. 5 (October 1992): 24–27.
8. *People's Daily*, "China Issues Hotel Regulation," April 2, 2002, p. 3.
9. "China's Jin Jiang Readies for Next Chapter," *Hotels*, July 2004, p. 28.
10. Ray Pine, Hanqin Qiu Zhang, and Ping-Shu Qi, "The Challenges and Opportunities of Franchising in China's Hotel Industry," *International Journal of Contemporary Hospitality Management* 12, no. 5 (2000): 300–307.
11. Peter S. Goodman, "Loans Feed Inflation in China, Regulators Say," *Washington Post*, March 12, 2004, pp. E1, E2.

12. Ibid., E2.
13. Dexter Roberts, "Worrying about China," *Business Week*, January 19, 2004, pp. 28–31.
14. Wei Xiaoan, "On State-Owned Hotel Enterprise Reform: A Macro Analysis," *China Travel and Tourism Press*, March 3, 2004, p. A9.
15. Li Jianwei and Yu Ming, "The Effective Fluctuation and Its Impacts on the Chinese Economic Growth," *World Economy* 11 (2003): 21–34.
16. Zhang Xiuli and Gu Huimin, "The Recapitalization of Olympic Hotel," *Hotel Modernization* 2, no. 2 (2003): 20–23.
17. Ibid.
18. Wang Zihua and Chen Guangbing, "An Analysis of SARS's Impact on Tourism Development in China," *Travel and Tourism Economy* 8 (2003): 65–66.
19. Bai Rendong and Li Guojun, "Two Hospital Management Groups Purchased Adjacent Hotels: Failing Hotels Rescued," *Beijing Business Today*, February 18, 2004, p. A13.
20. Larry Yu, "Critical Issues in China's Hotel Industry," in *Tourism in China*, ed. Alan Lew, Larry Yu, John Ap, and Guangrui Zhang (New York: Haworth Hospitality Press, 2003), 129–41; Wei Xiaoan, "On State-Owned Hotel Enterprise Reform"; and Lu Ju, "Models for Reforming City-Owned Hotels in Suzhou," *China Travel and Tourism Press*, February 18, 2004, p. A9.
21. Lu, "Models for Reforming City-Owned Hotels in Suzhou," A9.
22. Ibid., A9.
23. Bai and Li, "Two Hospital Management Groups Purchased Adjacent Hotels," A13.
24. Ibid.
25. Wei Xiaoan, "On State-Owned Hotel Enterprise Reform."
26. Sally Wolchuk and Mary Scoviak, "*Hotels*' 325," *Hotels*, July 2004, pp. 36–52.
27. Lu, "Models for Reforming City-Owned Hotels in Suzhou," A9.
28. Jones Lang LaSalle Hotels, *China's Hotel Investment Market*, 8.
29. Lu, "Models for Reforming City-Owned Hotels in Suzhou," A9.
30. Bai Rendong and Wang Dongliang, "Capital Travel Corporation Raising ¥1-Billion Yuan to Build Beijing Palace as Command Center for Beijing Olympic Games," *Beijing Business Today*, February 19, 2004, p. A1.
31. Ken Moritsug and Tim Johnson, "Possible Slowdown in China's Economy Has Global Impact," *Knight Ridder Newspapers*, May 27, 2004, p. 1; and *The Economist*, "Is the Chinese Economy Overheating?" November 13, 2003, p. 12.
32. Jiang Du, "Reforms and Development of Higher Tourism Education in China," *Journal of Teaching in Travel and Tourism* 3, no.1 (2003): 103–13.

29

China's Hotel Industry: Serving a Massive Market

Ray Pine

According to at least one forecast, by 2020 the People's Republic of China will be the world's number-one tourist destination, with annual arrivals of 130 million.[1] This is an impressive statistic considering that China's international tourism industry got underway only as recently as 1979, as a result of the country's Open-door Policy. Just 21 years later, in 2000, China welcomed 31-million tourists, who spent US$16.2 billion.[2]

In addition to inbound visitors, China's own increasingly affluent population is traveling more within the country. The nation's affluence stems from average annual economic growth of 9.8 percent between 1979 and 1997. Even with a predicted slowdown, annual growth should still average 7 percent over the next 10 years.[3] China's growing economy stimulates more internal business travel, and those business travelers need hotel rooms. Concurrently, the government has boosted leisure travel by loosening travel restrictions and introducing a five-day workweek and substantial vacation time. Given that there were 744-million domestic travelers in 2000, it is clear that domestic tourism no longer suffers from the stigma of being a politically and socially unacceptable bourgeois activity, as was formerly the case.[4] To encourage tourism the government has provided nearly US$97 million to upgrade travel-related infrastructure, including roads, seaports, and airports, as well as to improve tourist sites.

Source: *Cornell Hotel and Restaurant Administration Quarterly*, 43(3) (2002): 61–70.

Exhibit 1: Year-to-year increases in hotels, rooms, and tourist volume, 1990–2000

Year	Hotels No.	Δ	Rooms No.	Δ	Occ.	Travelers Int'l*	Δ	Domestic*	Δ
1990	1,987	11.1%	293,827	9.8%	59.4%	27.5	12.1%	280	16.6%
1991	2,130	7.1%	321,116	9.3%	62.5%	33.4	21.4%	290	3.6%
1992	2,354	10.5%	351,044	9.3%	67.0%	38.1	14.3%	330	13.8%
1993	2,552	8.4%	386,401	10.1%	67.7%	41.5	9.0%	410	24.0%
1994	2,995	17.4%	406,280	5.1%	62.2%	43.7	5.2%	520	27.8%
1995	3,720	24.2%	486,114	19.6%	58.1%	46.4	6.2%	620	19.2%
1996	4,418	18.8%	594,196	22.3%	55.3%	51.1	10.2%	640	3.0%
1997	5,201	17.7%	701,736	18.1%	53.8%	57.6	12.6%	644	0.6%
1998	5,782	11.2%	764,797	8.9%	51.7%	63.5	10.2%	694	7.8%
1999	7,035	21.6%	889,430	16.2%	53.4%	72.8	14.7%	719	3.6%
2000	10,481	49.0%	948,185	6.6%	55.9%	83.4	14.6%	744	3.4%

Notes: *Traveler numbers in millions. Δ = year-to-year change.
Source: Yearbooks of China Tourism Statistics (Beijing: China National Tourism Administration, China Travel and Tourism Press, 1990–2001).

Entry into the World Trade Organization (WTO) will be a significant event for China. Internally, in addition to infrastructure investments, work is progressing to improve the legal system, liberalize foreign-investment restrictions, and enhance the rights and privileges of foreign investors. Moreover, to take maximum advantage of China's WTO entry, multinational corporations contracted for investments totaling US$38 billion during the first nine months of 2000, 28 percent above the same period in the previous year. Those multinationals include the world's top hotel firms, many of which already have a foothold in this potentially massive market.[5] WTO membership should fuel continued economic growth and stimulate increased movements of both domestic and international travelers, thereby increasing hotel business and creating more opportunities for hotel developments.

In 2000 China's stock of hotels stood at 10,481, comprising 948,185 rooms.[6] The hotel industry will need to expand further to meet the growing demand from both international and domestic travelers.

China's own hotel companies are relatively small and immature when compared to foreign multinational hotel companies, most of which have already declared China as a key target for expansion. To date, overseas involvement in China's hotel business, although encouraged and even supported by the government, has still been much under government control. However, China's WTO entry should mean the eventual removal of such controls and expose the local industry to greater competition from foreign companies. For example, the government will need to forgo its hotel-ownership hegemony, because the WTO agreement provides that China will have hotels that will be 100-percent foreign owned within three years after WTO entry.

The question I examine in this article is whether indigenous or foreign-owned hotel firms are better positioned to benefit most from China's hotel-industry growth, or whether international partnerships will become the norm. I examine China's relatively small hotel industry within its complex home environment, and in relation to the global hotel industry. I identify some of the advantages and disadvantages held by local and foreign companies, bearing in mind the peculiar business context existing during China's transitional stage as it moves from a politically dominated, centrally planned economy toward a market economy.

Profile of China's Hotel Industry

Before 1978 China offered few accommodation facilities of international standard. What existed was of poor quality and was insufficient to satisfy the sudden influx of overseas tourists to China under its Open-door Policy.[7] The top priority of the tourism sector at that time was to build hotels that met international standards. From 1986 to 1991 the Chinese government invested RMB 6 billion into its hotel industry (about US$1.25 billion at 1990 exchange rates).[8] The government's investment and restructuring of the hotel industry, plus its encouraging external investment and allowing the entry of foreign-owned hotel companies, resulted in 2,354 newly opened hotels by 1992.

In 1992 China widened its economic reform and Open-door Policy. Increased business activity and international tourist arrivals stimulated hotel investment. In just four years, from 1993 to 1997, China doubled its hotel capacity to 5,201 hotels and 701,736 rooms. As shown in Exhibit 1, however, the annual increase of hotels and rooms often exceeded the increases of inbound travelers and domestic tourists. As a consequence, since 1996 occupancy rates have been around 55 percent. Oversupply combined with the effects of the Asian economic crisis that started in 1997 handed the Chinese hotel industry a financial loss in 1998. That first-ever loss totaled RMB 4.656 billion – or about US$0.6 billion.[9] Despite this setback, the stock of hotel rooms still grew by 16.2 percent from 1998 to 1999, although annual room growth slowed to 6.6 percent in 2000. Thus, in 2000 China had a total of 10,481 hotels with 848,145 rooms and achieved 55.85-percent occupancy.[10]

The oversupply I just mentioned was the result of early steps to ease China's initial hotel shortage stemming from the Open-door Policy in 1978, when the government implemented a diversification and decentralization policy for hotel investment. While this policy did accelerate hotel development,[11] decentralization resulted in a melange of hotel-ownership structures, including the state itself, collectives, private entities, alliances, stock companies, and foreign investors, as well as investors from Hong Kong, Macau, and Taiwan.[12] In 2000 the government subdivided the stock-company category into shareholding cooperatives, limited-liability companies, limited-liability shares, and "others."[13] The complicated ownership structures resulted in a lack of coordination in decision making in hotel construction,[14] while at the same time hotel developers had no business experience with hotel-chain operation. Available management systems are equally varied. This complexity of ownership and management creates unusual problems for expansion and growth, as I explain next.

Hotel Ownership. State ownership (which might be national, provincial, regional, or municipal) is still the dominant mode, accounting for 63 percent of all hotels and rooms. The chief problems occasioned by state ownership are the failure to separate hotel management and ownership[15] and effective monitoring of the state's assets. One might think that the government could create some sort of group or chain among hotels that are owned by a particular state entity, but most state-owned properties exist as independent units, giving them the combined disadvantages of being small and facing the bureaucratic restrictions attached to state ownership. An example of the difficulties of such a situation is the China Post & Telecom Tourism Group, a newly organized holding company under the Ministry of Information Industry (MII) with the specific purpose of bringing MII hotels together under one group. Most of the hotels under the MII, however, are owned in the name of local bureaus, and they are unwilling to shift their assets to the holding company.[16]

Past studies attribute the slow growth of Chinese hotel chains mostly to the business environment and the distinctive aspects of the Chinese political, economic, and social systems – in particular, the protectionism of local authorities.[17] I am not the only observer who believes that creation of hotel chains in China needs to start with reform of the ownership system. One idea is to establish an ownership-trading market[18] to allow a restructuring of China's hotel assets.[19]

Performance. Performance varies according to ownership type (see Exhibit 2). Hotels funded by outside interests, including foreign investors and those in Hong Kong, Macau, and Taiwan, have realized the highest revenues but have also involved the biggest investments in fixed assets. These high levels of investment are not surprising as all "foreign" hotels are in the 4- and 5-star categories.

Hotel Groups. In 1999 China's 7,035 hotels involved 30 foreign hotel companies and 39 local hotel-management companies. The diverse ownership structure, however, renders the relationship between owner and operator even more tenuous than one might typically find outside of China. The issues involved in ownership and control over assets and operations is a central difficulty in hotel agreements universally.[20] The complexities of hotel ownership in China make such negotiations even more problematic, and thus chain formation is difficult.

Today only 16 percent of China's hotels are chain operated, most of those being 3-star or higher.[21] By contrast, as long ago as 1987 it was estimated

Exhibit 2: Overview of China's hotels by ownership type – 2000

Ownership	Hotels	Rooms	Mean rooms per hotel*	Mean occupancy	Total revenue (000 RMB)	Revenue per room RMB*	Revenue per room US$	Fixed assets (000 RMB)	Fixed assets per room RMB*	Fixed assets per room US$
State-owned	6,646	593,361	89	54.34%	4,650,009	78,367	9,610	12,752,749	214,924	26,355
Collective	1,280	79,218	62	53.11%	559,597	70,640	8,662	1,673,610	211,266	25,906
Share-holding co-operative	69	10,766	156	61.03%	82,049	76,211	9,345	185,903	172,676	21,174
Alliance	176	27,711	157	55.33%	125,351	45,235	5,547	475,209	171,487	21,029
Limited liability	383	31,016	81	59.24%	325,117	104,822	12,854	853,714	275,250	33,752
Limited liability shares	395	37,440	95	60.16%	401,073	107,124	13,136	1,382,020	369,129	45,264
Private-owned	324	12,872	40	54.88%	100,438	78,028	9,568	273,938	212,817	26,097
Others	375	24,185	64	56.62%	212,772	87,977	10,788	537,188	222,116	27,237
Foreign funded	414	73,659	178	63.64%	1,388,582	188,515	23,116	4,065,748	551,969	67,685
HK, Macau, Taiwan funded	419	57,957	138	58.89%	777,666	134,180	16,454	3,117,414	537,884	65,958
Total	**10,481**	**948,185**	**90**	**55.85%**	**8,622,653**	**90,939**	**11,151**	**25,317,492**	**267,010**	**32,742**

Notes: *Figures calculated from Yearbook data. Currency conversion is RMB 8.155 to US$1.
Source: The Yearbook of China Tourism Statistics (Beijing: China National Tourism Administration, China Travel and Tourism Press, 2001), pp. 92–93.

Exhibit 3: Top 10 hotel operators in China (2000)

Company	China			World		
	Rank	Hotels	Rooms	Rank	Hotels	Rooms
Jin Jiang International*	1	34	11,077	51	50	13,598
Bass Hotels & Resorts	2	26	9,169	2	3,096	490,531
Shangri-La Hotels & Resorts	3	15	7,734	46	37	19,202
Marriott International	4	15	6,252	3	2,099	390,469
Starwood Hotels & Resorts	5	10	3,881	8	738	227,042
Jian Guo International*	6	7	3,257	–	NA	–
China Travel*	7	12	3,239	–	NA	–
Gloria International*	8	10	3,228	219	10	3,216
Zenith Hotels International	9	10	3,140	200	10	3,708
Nikko Hotels International	10	4	1,860	49	51	16,820

Notes: *Denotes a domestic Chinese firm. Bass Hotels and Resorts is now known as Six Continents Hotels. In 2000 Zenith became a partner with Accor, which is ranked fourth in the world with 3,488 hotels and 389,437 rooms.
Sources (for China): Jones Lang LaSalle Hotels, 2000, from *Hotel Asia Pacific*, Vol. 1, No. 8 (November 2000), p. 20; and (for the world): J. Marsan and S. Wolchuck, "*Hotels'* 325," *Hotels,* July 2001, pp. 52–60.

that 64 percent of hotel rooms in the United States were controlled by or affiliated with hotel chains.[22] In 1998 over five million of the total of 15.4-million hotel rooms worldwide – or about one-third – were controlled by the top-300 hotel chains.[23] Thus, one could easily argue that there is potential for more hotel-chain development in China.

Hotel Operators. The list of China's top-ten operators in 2000, found in Exhibit 3, indicates two things. First, the biggest single operator is based in China, but foreign firms dominate the top ten, having 80 out of the 143 hotels (60 percent) and 32,036 out of the 52,837 rooms (61 percent). Second, most of the indigenous companies are small compared to the total size of some of the foreign operators. I would argue that foreign companies have on their side all the advantages of large size, along with experience in developing and managing chains.

Ownership and Management Mechanisms

The Chinese government has been able to control the number of and conditions of entry for foreign hotel companies, sometimes helping and sometimes hindering entry or subsequent operations. Unhelpful were high import taxes on essential operating equipment and furnishings, and the requirement that foreign general managers have a "shadow" local general manager (a communist-party official). Policies that have provided advantages to joint-venture hotels include tax breaks and other financial incentives, plus permission to apply market-based employment policies – that is, managers may hire and fire at their discretion.

Despite China's protectionist history, its barriers to the entry of foreign companies and restrictions on indigenous companies should eventually disappear with China's entry into the WTO, thereby creating opportunities for hotel-industry growth. The following sections describe China's current ownership and management mechanisms, indicate some global-industry influences, and suggest barriers to and support for future growth.

After 20 years of development, China's hotel industry is characterized by a complicated scenario of fierce competition, multiform ownership and management systems, and geographically imbalanced distribution – meaning that some areas are oversupplied while others need hotel rooms.[24]

Independent Hotels. Chinese hotel owners generally prefer to manage themselves rather than losing control by hiring a management company. The decision of whether to be part of a group or to stay independent is normally based on a comparison of the conditions and benefits of both systems. In other countries the validity of the group brand, a well-targeted marketing effort, and suitable packages of specific operating procedures are strong attractions for independent hotel owners to affiliate with a chain. Such market-based points fail to apply to the many Chinese hotels owned by the state or collectives, which traditionally are not motivated by profit. What does motivate China's independents to affiliate, however, is the prospect of technology transfer. It is not uncommon for a hotel in China to revert to independent operation at the end of a contract period, having gleaned the requisite management expertise during the time of the contract.

Joint-venture Hotels. One key approach for alleviating China's hotel shortage in the early 1980s was to attract foreign investment to build hotels. One result of this initiative was the Beijing Jianguo Hotel, a Sino-U.S. joint-venture property, which opened in 1982 under a management contract with Hong Kong's Peninsula Group. Afterward more foreign companies entered China to invest in and manage hotels.[25]

The foreign-owned hotel companies expanded gradually, concentrating on China's key business and tourist destinations. This foreign involvement greatly changed the operation of Chinese hotels,[26] particularly through technology transfer.[27] As most joint-venture hotels were part of a chain, the concept and practice of hotel chains and branding were introduced to China. Indigenous hotel-management companies adapted the methods of those foreign companies.

Technology transfer is by no means a one-way street. A recent example of joint-venture activity is Accor's partnership in 2001 with Zenith Hotels International, which is a Hong Kong–based firm that operates eight hotels in key Chinese cities and has another four under development. This relationship provided both partners with coverage of the Beijing-Shanghai-Guangzhou triangle, along with secondary cities in between. A key advantage for Accor was gaining valuable China experience from the Zenith team.

Domestic Hotel Chains. Ironically, even as China experienced a glut of high-end hotels, the situation was reversed at the low end of the market. The rise of domestic tourism and the lack of suitable economy and budget hotels caused an imbalance between supply and demand in that market segment. In 2000 China recorded 744-million domestic travelers, but only 600 1-star and 3,061 2-star properties.[28] Some domestic groups are already developing budget brands. The well-established luxury-hotel chain Shanghai Jin Jiang Group has created a "Jin Jiang Star" brand of 1- and 2-star hotels, with five properties already open and two more being developed. Gloria Hotels, which currently has mainly 4- and 5-star hotels, is likewise planning a 3- or 2-star brand, to be called Gloria Inn. It will later develop a 1-star brand specifically for the domestic market.[29]

In addition to the immediate business advantages to be gained by domestic or foreign companies that can fill the gap in the low-end sector are the potential advantages of brand recognition when large numbers of Chinese travel abroad. China is already Asia's second-largest source of international travelers, with 9.2 million leisure trips in 1999. Observers expect China to take over first place from Japan this year (2002), with outbound numbers of 25 million, increasing to 50 million by 2010.[30] By 2020, Chinese traveling abroad will likely number as many as 100 million.[31] Thus, there are clear benefits of creating brands within China that would be recognized and used by travelers both within and beyond China.

Mergers and Acquisitions. According to the *Hotels'* 325 survey, "The big are getting bigger, but the small are getting bigger too."[32] Merger and acquisition activity is the norm within the world's top-300 hotel companies. Of the five million hotel rooms included in the *Hotels* magazine 1997 annual survey, the ten biggest companies controlled more than 100,000 rooms each, for a total of 2.7 million rooms.[33] By 2000 just nine companies each controlled more than 100,000 rooms, but due to mergers their total room count was 2.89 million of the 5.72 million rooms listed in the 2000 survey.[34]

A significant acquisition from the China perspective was the US$1-billion purchase by Marriott International of the Renaissance Hotel Group, including New World Hotels International, which has a strong presence and a long history in China.[35] Not many other operators can follow Marriott's lead in this instance, however, because China has few other potential targets for large-scale acquisitions or mergers. The local chains that do exist, such as Jin Jiang, Gloria, and Kingdom, are probably "not for sale," being keen to further develop their own businesses. Most of the remaining hotels are those independents that I have already discussed, with their peculiar ownership and generally poor quality, along with almost total dependence on domestic business. Thus, for the near term, expansion of foreign companies inside China will probably involve investment to develop new properties rather than acquisition.

Management Contracts. To reduce the reliance on foreign companies and gain some share of the domestic hotel-management market, the White Swan Hotel Management Company was set up in Guangzhou in 1988.[36] Since that time, 39 hotel-management companies have started in China, operating about 100 hotels nationwide.[37] I am told, however, that the growth of these indigenous companies has been slow, and that they are mainly located in a few highly developed areas such as Beijing (twelve companies) and the Guandong Province in southern China, bordering Hong Kong (nine companies). When one considers that of the 100 hotels just two companies have 41 hotels between them (Jian Guo has seven hotels, and Jin Jiang operates 34), it becomes clear that the majority of companies manage just one or two properties. Indeed, many of China's operators are not management companies in the accepted sense of operating a hotel chain. Instead, the firms are often created to look after a specific property in an effort to separate ownership from management, and contract periods are commonly for just one or two years.

Hotel franchising. American-style franchising is uncommon in China. One of the greatest obstacles to the expansion of franchising is China's legal system, which many franchisors believe does not adequately protect their contractual rights.[38] Nevertheless, franchising is making some headway. Most notably, Cendant's Days Inn brand announced the opening in China of ten franchised hotels totaling 1,500 rooms. This is the largest single addition to their brand at any one time, and the company's first hotel venture in China.

Consortia. Several hotel consortia have developed in China. The first three were the Lianyi Hotel Group, sponsored by Beijing Xiyuan Hotel with ten other hotels; the Hualong Tourist Hotel Group; and the Friendship Tourist Hotel Group.[39] More consortia or referral systems were formed in later years: VIP Hotel Club, the Friendship Hotels, and CITIC Hotels Affiliation. None of these has expanded to a large scale, but they do provide some joint marketing, reservations, and purchasing services. It seems likely that the existing indigenous consortia will grow to serve the increasingly complex needs of China's independent hotels and smaller groups, which sorely need access to global distribution systems, technology solutions, and the ability to process data. In particular, consortium membership may be attractive to many state-owned independent hotels that do not want to relinquish ownership or management control.

Contrasts: China and Everyone Else

While China does not have the same economic profile or infrastructure developments as those found in North America and Europe, I consider such developments to be just a matter of time. Right now, however, the differences are considerable, most notably in terms of the economy and government policies, but also simply in the industry's size and market mix.

Industry Size. China's hotel industry is small compared to those of other countries. China moved from a position of virtually zero hotels in 1979 to having over 10,000 just 20 years later. Today, there's still considerable room for growth, both at home and abroad. Chinese officials are trying to ensure that overseas hotel companies do not dominate the market and crowd out local companies. Concurrently, to counteract leakage, Chinese operators may try to locate hotels in foreign countries for Chinese people to use. For instance, China Travel Service (Hong Kong) Limited, the biggest travel company in China, has set up CTS (HK) Ltd. to develop and operate four hotels in Hong Kong and several others around Asia to accommodate Chinese mainland outbound travelers. (Affiliations among Chinese hotels, Chinese airlines, and other Chinese companies could ensure that even more money is retained when Chinese people travel abroad.)

Guest Mix. At the moment, China's hotel industry is bifurcated, with a set of (high end) hotels typically used by international visitors and another (low end) set frequented by domestic travelers. This stands in contrast to most countries, and it means that high-end hotels cannot rely much on local travelers to fill rooms. It also means that the type and quality of products and services available in the two groups of hotels is different. While this situation will change over time, just as it has in other countries, at present the bifurcation greatly influences the potential for affiliation between hotels in China. So the government faces the major policy decision of determining whether expanded hotel groups and alliances will exist within or across these now-distinct international and domestic markets.

Political and Business Environment. China's political system and business environments are in flux. Heretofore, the centrally controlled economy has meant that most owners were bureaucrats rather than business people. Employment conditions were based more on social needs than on business reality (e.g., the "iron rice bowl" that guarantees employment for life). Also complicating matters is territoriality. Even if it's locally successful, a Chinese company may not be able to expand outside of its home city or province because of protectionist policies maintained by other locations. In fact, a foreign company has an easier time establishing itself nationwide than does a Chinese company.

Furthermore, business in China is typically done through personal relationships and networks, a system called "*guanxi,*"[40] and it is virtually impossible for a foreigner to become part of this network. *Guanxi* can be more powerful than the profit motive, and it can circumvent legal controls or international trade rules, thus making it difficult if not impossible for a foreign company to be successful without the support of a local Chinese partner.

Having said that, some of the government and economic factors are changing. China's policy of creating special economic zones is being expanded.

These zones have a business environment akin to western market economies. However, the pace of change will need to accelerate if China is to take full advantage of WTO membership. Such changes will be key factors in helping or hindering indigenous hotel companies' growth in relation to foreign companies' expansion. While it's now possible for foreign companies to take majority or full ownership in hotel properties, there remain subtle (and not-so-subtle) means to ensure the need for local partners – even without the effects of *guanxi*. No matter who owns a property, its managers have to rely on the availability of local labor, reliable water and power, and a host of peripheral – but essential – services for which having a local partner may pay high dividends.

Operating in a Chinese Context

The formation of hotel groups or chains might appear to be a logical way to develop China's hotel industry, but any policy for developing groups or chains must occur within a Chinese context. Indigenous hotel companies are making progress in adapting overseas hotel concepts and initiating their own ideas, and the few companies that are now established should be able to grow once they can overcome the problems of local protectionism. Domestic operators have the knowledge of the internal workings of the Chinese political, regulatory, financial, and social systems, and a natural affinity with local cultural norms and Chinese-based business practices. These domestic operators, however, do not enjoy the technological and marketing advantages accruing to foreign firms, and access to financing is an additional problem for local operators.

As I explained earlier, foreign hotel companies already enjoy the advantages of economies of scale, global recognition and networking, and well-established managerial and technological expertise. They also have the advantage of being able to bypass local protectionist policies. To prosper, however, international firms will have to appreciate China's political, social, and cultural frameworks, in particular the need to work with local partners who are part of the *guanxi* network. I have found that even foreign companies with a history of working in China still encounter frustrations in their efforts to do business there.

In short, I conclude that partnerships between local owners and foreign operators should have the most potential for success within the short- to medium-term, combining international-companies' expertise with the local knowledge and connections of domestic operators. Indigenous companies will probably become stronger in the medium- to long-term as they continue to glean as much information as possible from foreign partners and competitors for use in their own businesses. Forecasts and expectations aside, it will be interesting to see how China's hotel industry actually evolves in this complex but potentially rewarding market.

Notes

1. WTO, *Tourism 2020 Vision, Intraregional and Long-haul Flows*, Vol. 3, East Asia–Pacific (Madrid, World Tourism Organization, April 1999), p. 8. Note that "China" as it is used throughout this paper refers to mainland China and excludes Hong Kong, Macau, and Taiwan.
2. CNTA, *The Yearbook of China Tourism Statistics* (Beijing: China National Tourism Administration, China Travel and Tourism Press, 2001), p. 21 (quoting World Tourism Organization figures).
3. State Statistic Bureau, "A Comparison of Economy-increase Rate between China and Other Countries and Regions in the World," *People's Daily*, September 25, 1998, p. 1.
4. CNTA, p. 57.
5. S. Shellum and P. Lui, "Entering the Dragon," *Hotel Asia Pacific*, Vol. 1, No. 8 (November 2000), p. 17.
6. CNTA, pp. 92–93.
7. See: "Foreign Investment in China's Hotel Sector," *EIU Travel and Tourism Analyst*, No. 3 (1989), pp. 17–32; J. Zhao, "Overprovision in Chinese Hotels," *Tourism Management*, March 1989, pp. 63–66; and L. Yu, "Hotel Development and Structures in China," *International Journal of Hospitality Management*, Vol. 11, No. 2 (1992), pp. 99–110.
8. R. Pine, H.Q. Zhang, and P. Qi, "The Challenges and Opportunities of Franchising in China's Hotel Industry," *International Journal of Contemporary Hospitality Management*, Vol. 12, No. 5 (2000), pp. 300–307.
9. CNTA, *The Yearbook of China Tourism Statistics* (Beijing: China National Tourism Administration, China Travel and Tourism Press, 1999), p. 93.
10. CNTA, 2001, pp. 92–93.
11. Z.Q. Liu and J.C. Liu, "Assessment of the Hotel Rating System in China," *Tourism Management*, December 1993, pp. 440–452.
12. CNTA, 2000, p. 92.
13. CNTA, 2001, p. 92.
14. C. Tisdell and J. Wen, "Foreign Tourism as an Element in PR China's Economic Development Strategy," *Tourism Management*, March 1991, pp. 55–67.
15. C. Tisdell, "Separation of Ownership and Management, Markets, Their Failure and Efficiency: Possible Implications for China's Economic Reforms," *Asian Economies*, June 1990, pp. 41–55.
16. P.S. Qi, "Growth of China's Hotel Chains and Their Future Expansion," master's thesis (2001), The Hong Kong Polytechnic University, Hong Kong SAR.
17. J. Du and B. Dai, "Market Base and Development Strategies of the National Hotel Groups," and T.Q. Zou, "Strategies of Chinese Hotel Groups: Development Model and Policy Guidance," both from Seminar on Theories and Practices of Conglomerates in Chinese Hotels, Beijing, November 20–22, 1998.
18. Y.Z. Wang, "Study on the Trading System of Property Rights for Chinese Hotel Conglomeration," Seminar on Theories and Practices of Conglomerates in Chinese Hotels, Beijing, November 20–22, 1998.
19. See: K. Xu, "Restructuring Assets and Management: Views on National Hotel Conglomeration," Y.Z. Wang, *op. cit.*, and Y.Z. Wang, "The Development of Chinese National Hotel Groups and Market Competition," all from: Seminar on Theories and Practices of Conglomerates in Chinese Hotels, Beijing, November 20–22, 1998.

20. H.A. Saunders and L.M. Renaghan, "Southeast Asia: A New Model for Hotel Development," *Cornell Hotel and Restaurant Administration Quarterly,* Vol. 33, No. 5 (October 1992), pp. 16–23.
21. J. Li and T. Feng, "Economy Hotel Market Awaits Exploration," *Hotels China and Overseas,* Vol. 5 (1997), pp. 5–6.
22. S.F. Leonard, "Hotel Chains in the USA: Review of an Industry in Transition," *Travel and Tourism Analyst,* October 1987, pp. 43–53.
23. See: WTO, *Tourism Market Trends: Europe, 2000* (Madrid: World Tourism Organization, 2000), p. 25; and T.D. Cruz and S. Wolchuck, *"Hotels' 325,"* Hotels, July 1998, p. 51.
24. See: J. Zhao, *op. cit.*; G.R. Zhang, "Ten Years of Chinese Tourism: Profile and Assessment," *Tourism Management,* March 1989, pp. 51–62; and L. Yu, *International Hospitality Business: Management and Operations* (Englewood Cliffs, NJ: Prentice-Hall, 1999).
25. P.S. Qi, *op. cit.*
26. L. Yu, *op. cit.*
27. R. Pine, "Technology Transfer in the Hotel Industry," *International Journal of Hospitality Management,* Vol. 11, No. 1 (1992), pp. 3–22.
28. CNTA, 2001, pp. 57, 92.
29. P.S. Qi, *op. cit.*
30. R. Hecker, "Outbound Set to Soar," *Hotel Asia Pacific,* Vol. 1, No. 8 (November 2000), p. 23.
31. WTO, 1999, p. 8.
32. J. Marsan and S. Wolchuck, *"Hotels' 325,"* Hotels, July 2001, p. 49.
33. T.D. Cruz and S. Wolchuck, *"Hotels' 325,"* Hotels, July 2000, p. 51.
34. T. D. Cruz and S. Wolchuck, p. 43.
35. See: "Training China's Hospitality Industry," *Cornell Hotel and Restaurant Administration Quarterly,* Vol. 28, No. 4 (February 1988), pp. 17–18.
36. Z.T. Yuan, *A Road of Development of Chinese Tourist Hotels* (Beijing: China Travel and Tourism Press, 1998).
37. X.A. Wei, *Competition and Development of the Chinese Hotel Industry* (Guangzhou: Guangdong Tourism Press, 1999).
38. R. Pine, H. Zhang, and P.S. Qi, "The Challenges and Opportunities of Franchising in China's Hotel Industry," *International Journal of Contemporary Hospitality Management,* Vol. 12, No. 5 (2000) pp. 300–307.
39. Z.T. Yuan, *op. cit.*
40. H. Davies, "Interpreting Guanxi: The Role of Personal Connections in a High Context Transitional Economy," in *China Business: Contexts and Issues,* ed. H. Davies (Hong Kong: Longman, 1995).

30

The Future of Small Firms in the Hospitality Industry
Alison Morrison and Rhodri Thomas

Introduction

There is no agreement in the literature about how "small firms" in the hospitality industry should be defined. Some commentators adopt quantitative criteria – notably numbers of employees – whereas others prefer qualitative approaches. Although the justifications for, and implications of, these diverging perspectives are important, since they have been discussed in detail elsewhere (Thomas, 1998a), it is unnecessary to repeat the arguments here. Of over-riding significance is the observation that whatever definition is adopted, the most commonly found hospitality enterprise is small.

Yet, until recently, those engaged in hospitality management research had all but ignored small enterprises or, arguably, misunderstood their dynamics by treating them as scaled down versions of larger firms. There is a growing consensus, however, that the size of firm and its sectoral context are likely to be important influences on the phenomenon being studied (Thomas, 1998a). As a consequence, more rigorous research is emerging relating to the management of such organisations and how they engage with the economy.

Following an assessment of the sometimes conflicting evidence regarding the structure and related trends in the industry, this paper offers a critical review of what is currently understood about small hospitality firms. In addition, it concentrates particularly on the notion of entrepreneurship as evidenced in small firms.

The Structure of the Industry

The case is frequently made – from as early as Pickering et al. (1971) to, more latterly, Litteljohn (1993) and Mogendorff (1996) – that key sectors of the hospitality industry are becoming more concentrated. Moreover, it is suggested by some, notably Slattery (1994), that structural shifts in the UK economy have precipitated this development, at least as far as the hotel sector is concerned. In essence the argument is that smaller firms are being squeezed out of the market.

To some extent, the evidence – represented by the growth of multiples, especially in the fast-food and accommodation sectors over recent decades – is incontrovertible. However, the extent to which multiples have taken market share and will continue to grow at the expense of smaller operators is more questionable. As several commentators have pointed out (for example Morrison, 1998), many of the most widely cited statistics on the structure of the industry are partial in their coverage. Indeed, some go further, arguing that it is only since the creation of the DTI's *Statistical Bulletin* series some two years ago that it has become possible to gauge the structure of the industry with any degree of confidence (Thomas, 1998a). Thus, assertions about the demise of the small business sector must be treated with extreme caution. This is particularly the case since some of the theoretical constructs that inform explanations and predictions of future structural change have also been sensibly challenged on the grounds of their crudeness (Hughes, 1993).

Peacock (1993) provides an alternative outlook in terms of the dynamics of the small business sector. He argues that standardisation – inherent in chain operations – stifles innovation. As a consequence, dynamic small firms might continue to thrive, even in prime locations. Given the low barriers to entry, and the highly segmented nature of demand (Morrison, 1996), such an argument is not implausible. Certainly, recent survey evidence (Thomas et al., 1997) – which included a broad range of small tourism and hospitality firms – found that the majority of almost all the 1,400 firms sampled had experienced stability or growth in revenues, profits and employment during the 12 months prior to questioning and were optimistic about the future. In addition, comparison between the second and third *DTI Statistical Bulletin* (DTI, 1996, 1997) suggests that in the case of hotels and restaurants, the proportion of employment and turnover accounted for by small firms has remained relatively constant. Clearly this is an issue which will require careful monitoring.

The Management of Small Hospitality Firms

It is important to recognise that a distinct and significant range of management issues confronts small hospitality firms. Specifically, the following section considers: the role of marketing; quality management; the value and application of information technology; the relationship of business planning and small firm success; strategic management and growth; and entrepreneurship. Of necessity, the discussion of each issue is circumscribed by available space; readers are referred to Thomas (1998b) for a more comprehensive assessment. What follows draws heavily on the reviews contained in the text.

Marketing

The role of marketing in small firm management has latterly received growing attention. Friel (1998) in his discussion of the topic begins by reinforcing the differences between small and large enterprises, but with specific reference to marketing. This is instructive for it establishes the inappropriateness of assuming that marketing techniques developed in the context of large enterprises may be replicated to good effect in small firms.

To some extent, Friel's work challenges some common perceptions relating to marketing activities in small hospitality firms. Although he is cautious – as a result of the limited research on which he is able to draw – he suggests that the majority of small businesses in these industries undertake some kind of research into customer needs and formulate a marketing plan, even if only on a short-term basis. Moreover, a variety of promotional methods are used and there is some evidence of market-orientated pricing even though the "cost-plus" approach remains most dominant. His impression, therefore, is that there is greater dynamism in terms of marketing among small hospitality firms than is generally considered to be the case.

Quality Management

In recent years there has been an explosion of interest in quality management. The debates surrounding the most appropriate means of ensuring and enhancing the quality of products or services has recently been examined in the context of small hospitality firms by Church and Lincoln (1998). They begin by arguing that if small firms addressed the issue of quality management, they might expect to gain advantages over their competitors that should result in a more secure financial future.

A central tenet of Church and Lincoln's work is the rejection of retrospective methods of quality control. They argue that such approaches, with their emphasis on comparing outputs with a given standard, are both expensive and highly intrusive in the context of services. As a result, they promote preventative systems of quality control. Their proposition is that if the various stages of the process of production and/or service delivery are controlled, little, if any, testing of the final product or service is required. Against this background, they examine the potential of two methods: Hazard Analysis Critical Control Points (HACCP) and Failure Modes and Effects Analysis (FMEA). Both are seen as potentially valuable, but two limitations are recognised by the authors. First, there has so far been little systematic evaluation of these systems in small hospitality firms. Consequently, their strengths and weaknesses in such environments remain to be tested. The second is that the approaches are partial; they do not necessarily produce the holistic approach to quality management that many commentators now advocate.

In order to overcome the second of these limitations, Church and Lincoln (1998) review a range of alternatives: Investors in People (IiP), benchmarking, BS EN ISO 9000, total quality management (TQM) and quality costing. They see potential merit in both IiP and quality costing. Notwithstanding possible marketing advantages, they display more ambivalence towards the remainder; unless small firms have already established preventive quality control mechanisms, benchmarking, BS EN ISO 9000 and TQM, they argue, are not likely to be as effective as their proponents would claim.

Information Technology

Mutch (1998) has examined the potential value of information technology (IT) for small hospitality firms. He argues that smaller enterprises can gain significant benefits from IT. However, there needs to be a clear distinction between the information requirements of organisations and their technology needs. In too many cases, the technology used is inappropriate and reorganisation of manual systems in the light of an enhanced awareness of information needs may well prove to be more productive.

Nevertheless, in some cases, IT may play a significant role in supporting business development. In addition to a review of the relevant literature, Mutch (1998) uses the findings of his own research in the tourism industry to illustrate his case. It is clear from his analysis that the growth of one case study company examined – Country Holidays – can be partially attributed to its careful management of information needs and the appropriate use of technology. However, while the case study may illustrate potential benefits, such effective use of IT currently remains relatively isolated among small tourism and hospitality firms.

Business Planning

As Margerison (1998) points out, business planning is one of the most widely advocated aspects of small firm management. In providing an outline of the planning process, he emphasises both financial considerations – such as cash flow and profit forecasting – and the non-financial, such as matters relating to employment, product or service development and marketing. In order to illustrate the principles of this process, he provides an example of how it has been operationalised by a small restaurant firm. The descriptive case study is useful as it draws attention to the informal as well as the formal process of planning that is sometimes neglected.

Arguably, the key element of Margerison's contribution, however, is its critical evaluation of any connections between business planning and small firm success. The potentially ambiguous notion of "success" is used merely to enable the author to be inclusive in his review of available research. In practice, most of the studies referred to relate to the search for an articulation between business planning and small firm growth. Perhaps the two most important aspects of the review are its demonstration of the complexity of establishing causality between business planning and growth and its revelation that relatively little robust research has been undertaken in this area. The latter is disappointing, given the importance currently attached to the topic by banks and a wide range of private and public sector advisory agencies. The somewhat inevitable conclusion of his work is that although business planning appears to play a role in the "success" of small businesses, it is not possible at this stage to be confident of its importance *vis-à-vis* other variables.

Strategic Planning and Growth

Such a perspective is supported by Webster (1998) when she considers the role that strategic management plays in the growth of small tourism and hospitality firms. Her focus of attention is, therefore, on the minority of businesses that have aspirations to grow and those which have actually grown since their inception.

Webster takes Storey's (1994) position as her starting point. Thus, she argues that small firms appear to grow when three influences on growth overlap: a particular blend of ownership characteristics discussed in more detail below, the features of the firm itself, e.g. age, size, location, and the strategic decisions taken by the firm. To that extent, she argues that although strategic decisions are important for growth, they are unlikely to be effective if they are taken in a context where other factors that are necessary for growth are absent.

In summary, it has been argued that:

- small firm marketing is distinctive and often more dynamic than many commentators acknowledge;
- the incorporation of quality management, which is sensitive to the operational and financial characteristics of small firms, may be a means of achieving competitive advantage and a more secure financial future;
- astute information technology application can enhance small business performance provided operators accurately identify organisational requirements;
- there is an inconclusive link between business planning and growth; and
- business growth occurs when there is an appropriate blend of ownership and firm characteristics, and strategic decisions made.

Entrepreneurship and Small Firms

From the foregoing, it is clear that if the small hospitality firm sector in general is to retain an element of stability and flourish into the next century, a wide range of management challenges require to be addressed. For some, the application of entrepreneurial principles may represent one way forward. This section considers the role and impact of "entrepreneurship" which has its origins in small firm creation within the context of the hospitality industry. For a more extensive treatise of this subject area refer to Morrison *et al.* (1998).

Timmons (1994) defines entrepreneurship as creating and building something of value from practically nothing. It is the process of creating or seizing an opportunity, and pursuing it regardless of the resources currently personally controlled. Traditionally, entrepreneurship has been associated with the solo entrepreneur, but more recently the value of entrepreneurial teams has been recognised. These persons are intensely, directly, creatively and actively involved in the entrepreneurial process creating firms that McCrimmon (1995) describes as glorified by independence, creativity, improvisation and rebellious opportunism. These entrepreneurs face challenges of uncertainty, calculated risk-taking, and risk minimisation. Typically they retain almost total control and remain at the centre of the decision-making web (Goffee and Scase, 1995). The following section summarises and illustrates within the context of the hospitality industry the key elements that are generally associated with entrepreneurship (Kirzner, 1980; Timmons, 1994; Carson *et al.*, 1995; Goffee and Scase, 1995; Deakins, 1996).

Key Elements of Entrepreneurship

- *Change initiation*: capability of identifying an opportunity for creation or innovation, and ability to turn it into a reality.

Illustration: Holiday Inn

Kemmons Wilson founded what is now called Holiday Inn Worldwide in 1952. In 1951 he and his family of five children decided to visit Washington on holiday. Everywhere they went they found that while a room cost $6 to $8 each child was to be charged $2 extra. This annoyed Wilson and he vowed to develop a chain of hotels where children could stay free as long as they slept in the same room as their parents. Wilson's hotels would also feature free parking, air-conditioning, free in-room TV and swimming pool. By the late 1970s Wilson and his associates ran a hotel chain of more than 400,000 rooms. Wilson changed the rules of the "hotel game", innovating in the development of a radically new concept.

- *Commitment to employees*: application of appropriate management practices and reward systems designed to exact employee loyalty, retention and efficiency.

Illustration: Browns Restaurants

Over a period of 24 years, Jeremy Mogford created Browns Restaurants, a chain of seven. In 1998 he sold it to Bass for £35 million. As an employer, Mogford was widely regarded as being one of the industry's best and most enlightened. This is particularly well reflected in an exceptionally low turnover of staff, and the 15 or more years with the company that many of them had served. Mogford attributed this remarkable stability to his policy of promoting from within, and to his management practices and conditions of service. The company trains staff and encourages them to be involved with the business through monthly meetings, where policy and performance figures are discussed and ideas welcomed. As an incentive, staff receive bonuses based on turnover and monthly results. After a year's service, they are eligible for accident insurance and after two years' employment they also get private health-care cover, plus a private pension plan to which both parties contribute. Senior managers are also given permanent health insurance. "It is incredible just how many of the people who leave return to us within just two or three years. It's simply because they've compared us with other employers and realise how much we have to offer", said Mogford. Mogford provides an illustration of industry good practices that benefit employees and employer alike.

- *Creative resourcing*: ingeniously marshalling resources, of both a financial and managerial nature, from a complex set of sources in order to mobilise and realise the opportunity.

Illustration: Highland Mysteryworld

Laurence Young is the entrepreneur behind the development of the Highland Mysteryworld visitor centre on the banks of Loch Leven in Scotland, which first opened in 1996. The Young family, under the company name of Glencoe Adventure, owns it. The investment of £1.2 million in the project came from the Young family's personal resources of £100,000, a bank loan of £600,000, and £180,000 from a local development company, Lochaber. A further £350,000 was secured because of delays in planning permission. While the permission was being processed the European Union designated the Highlands and Islands as being worthy of receiving Objective One funding, some of which Young managed to secure for Highland Mysteryworld. Young ingeniously marshalled the resources necessary for him to realise his dream, using but a fraction of the family's money.

- *Entrepreneurial learning*: motivation to acquire the necessary knowledge and expertise through relevant exploration and reflection, in order to excel.

Illustration: Pied à Terre

Pied à Terre is the 35-seat London restaurant of Richard Neat. It opened in 1991 and achieved two stars in the 1996 Michelin Guide. When Neat describes his background in catering his accomplishments seem incredible. He started out as a washer-up at a nearby Little Chef "because it paid more money than a paper round". But, at 15 he decided he was seriously interested in the industry and gained experience in the kitchens of Pennyhill Park, Bagshot. In 1984 Neat joined London's Savoy Hotel, moving to the South Lodge country house hotel in West Sussex in 1985. While there, he set his sights even higher. He sent seven letters to various gastronomic havens in France and one letter to Raymond Blanc, who was the only chef to respond. He spent two years at Le Manoir, leaving in 1989 to work with Robuchon at Jamin for a couple of years. He then returned to England and worked under Marco Pierre White at Harvey's Wandsworth for 12 months before opening Pied à Terre. Neat's knowledge and expertise was not gained through any formal education system. The acquisition illustrates a dedication and tenacity of a person determined to achieve his entrepreneurial goals.

- *Innovation and creativity*: renewal of products or services by adding value through application of expertise and imagination.

Illustration: Planet Hollywood

Planet Hollywood is a themed restaurant concept that was the brainchild of entrepreneur Robert Earl and movie producer Keith Barish in 1991. They own the majority of the company, but investors include movie stars Arnold Schwarzenegger, Sylvester Stallone, Bruce Willis, Demi Moore, All Stars and Pelican chains. The outlets sell burgers against a backdrop of movie clips, loud theme tunes, and other memorabilia. In 1996, according to *The Sunday Times*' eighth annual survey of Britain's 500 wealthiest people, Earl was the richest man in leisure. The survey valued him at £350 million compared to £80 million in 1995. The increase is due to the success of the Planet Hollywood chain. Earl took a basic core food and beverage product and creatively added value providing the industry sector with an innovative, value-added concept.

- *Knowledge leadership*: development of sources of management information to enable first mover capability, and effective strategy formulation and implementation.

Illustration: Massarella Catering

In 1860, when the Italian Massarella family settled in South Yorkshire it set up what was to become one of the largest ice-cream manufacturers in Europe. This was based on knowledge leadership in that few people in Europe then knew how to produce and hold the ice-cream product. In the 1950s the business was sold to J. Lyons for a handsome sum of money which was re-invested in the creation of a new company Massarella Catering Group. Today, knowledge leadership for this firm is facilitated by computer packages, which Jeremy Massarella believes is the key to the expansion plans of his family's catering business. He is hoping to expand the company beyond its current management of about 116 restaurants and café units, located in department stores, at factory shop sites and in shopping centres. This illustration presents two businesses that started small, divided by a generation, and both using knowledge leadership as an entrepreneurial strategy.

- *Opportunity alertness*: continuous focus on emerging trends and opportunities to be captured and realised.

Illustration: Prêt à Manger

Prêt à Manger was started by two former property men, Julian Metcalfe and Sinclair Beecham. As office workers in the West End of London they had been dissatisfied when they could not find a quick tasty take-away lunch. Although not experienced in catering, they decided to remedy this. Prêt à Manger was the result. Its uncompromising commitment to high standards in respect of its freshly prepared food, service and surroundings has brought tremendous success. Since its opening as a single unit in 1986, the company has now expanded to around 40 outlets and a turnover of around £30 million. By any yardstick Prêt à Manger has been a tremendous success story. Metcalfe and Beecham are archetypal successful entrepreneurs who have built a multi-million pound business from their alertness to, and realisation of, an opportunity.

- *Relationship management*: maintenance of effective teams, networks, and flexible management structures.

Illustration: Life Restaurants

David Hinds, Tim Bacon and Jeremy Roberts turned a sketchy idea for a restaurant into a chain of four Mediterranean style café-bars within a year. Thus Via Vita was born. Although they knew that the idea had potential, they needed the financial backing of a large company to roll out Via Vita quickly. The trio formed Life Restaurants and approached Marston's, the brewer and pub operator, with a deal. The deal they struck with Marston's was to open 50 restaurants in five years and required each party to invest £100,000 start-up capital. On the strength of this, Life Restaurants raised £2.5 million to do four restaurants by April 1998. The Marston's clout proved useful in obtaining prime city-centre sites. Through relationship management in teams, networks and marketplace, in addition to dynamic management structures, Life Restaurants is achieving its entrepreneurial goals.

- *Timing of action*: acting within a limited window in which an opportunity can be optimised.

Illustration: Macdonald Hotels

Donald Macdonald formed Macdonald Hotels in 1990, taking advantage of a downturn in many businesses during the economic recession. The company began by purchasing two hotels in Scotland and then made further acquisitions, including a number from The Rank Organisation and De Vere Hotels. It also manages timeshare resorts in Spain, under contract for Barratt Developments, and UK hotels put into receivership by the Royal Bank of Scotland. In 1996 it owned 16 hotels and operated a further 53 under contract. Macdonald Hotels had a successful stock market flotation in 1996 that netted the three founder directors a paper profit of approximately £40 million, from an initial investment of £500,000. Acting within the limited window of opportunity of the recession, the company took advantages of a seemingly adverse business environment to establish and expand.

- *Vision and strategic orientation*: Formulation of ambitions, and strategies to realise them.

Illustration: Orange Balloon

Jerry Brand is sympathetic to the small businesspersons that, like him, sit in a carpeted sitting room and start their business from scratch. Brand has already opened two Orange Balloon restaurants but intends to have around 50 by the year 2000. He aims to take it nation-wide and eventually to the stockmarket, so who knows just how big the chain may become? Brand is into brands. The basis of the Orange Balloon concept's claim to success is that along with its modern design it will be offering quality food at decent prices and high-profile chef Brian Turner has been hired to make that happen. Turner has been given the option to buy a substantial stake in the business at the end of 1998. Brand's personal vision and ambitions are fuelling the development of Orange Balloon, accompanied by the embedding of strategies designed to ensure that they will be achieved.

Clearly, each of the above illustrations have been selected on the basis that they represent "best practice entrepreneurship", the typology of which has its origins in small firm creation. It is admitted that, to a certain degree, they present isolated incidents of a certain approach to business development and management. However, they do provide an indication of the ways in which such entrepreneurs, collectively, have the potential to add vitality to the hospitality industry through the introduction and application of innovative approaches to traditional activities.

Conclusions

This paper has reviewed what is currently understood about the effective management of small hospitality firms. From an analysis of industry-specific illustrations, it has emphasised that it is possible to identify positive outcomes of the process of entrepreneurship, which commences with the creation of a small firm. Specifically, it can be seen that new concepts and practices emerge which have the potential to revolutionise the hospitality industry sector and stimulate the competitive environment. Furthermore, many of the management challenges confronting small hospitality firms have the potential to be addressed through entrepreneurial practices.

Although more research is required, on the basis of available evidence, it seems that small firms will continue to play an important role in the development of the hospitality industry well into the next century.

References

Carson, D., Cromie, S., McGowan, P. and Hill, J. (1995), *Marketing and Entrepreneurship in SMEs: An Innovative Approach*, Prentice-Hall, London.
Church, I. and Lincoln, G. (1998), "Quality management", in Thomas, R. (Ed.), *The Management of Small Tourism and Hospitality Firms*, Cassell, London, pp. 138–55.
Deakins, D. (1996), *Entrepreneurs and Small Firms*, McGraw-Hill, London.
Department of Trade and Industry (DTI) (1996), *Statistical Bulletin: Small and Medium-Sized Enterprise (SME) Statistics for the UK, 1994*, DTI, Sheffield.
DTI (1997), *Statistical Bulletin: Small and Medium-Sized Enterprise (SME) Statistics for the United Kingdom, 1996*, DTI, Sheffield.
Friel, M. (1998), "Marketing", in Thomas, R. (Ed.), *The Management of Small Tourism and Hospitality Firms*, Cassell, London, pp. 117–37.
Goffee, R. and Scase, R. (1995), *Corporate Realities: The Dynamics of Large and Small Organisations*, Routledge, London.
Hughes, H. (1993), "The structural theory of business demand: a comment", *International Journal of Hospitality Management*, Vol. 12 No. 4, pp. 309–11.
Kirzner, I. (1980), "The primacy of entrepreneurial discovery", in Seldon, A. (Ed.), *Prime Mover of Progress: The Entrepreneur in Capitalism and Socialism*, Institute of Economic Affairs, London, pp. 101–16.
Litteljohn, D. (1993), "Western Europe", in Jones, P. and Pizam, A. (Eds), *The International Hospitality Industry*, Pitman Publishing, London, pp. 3–24.
McCrimmon, M. (1995), *Unleashing the Entrepreneur Within*, Pitman, London.
Margerison, J. (1998), "Business planning", in Thomas, R. (Ed.), *The Management of Small Tourism and Hospitality Firms*, Cassell, London, pp. 101–16.
Mogendorff, D. (1996), "The European hospitality industry", in Thomas, R. (Ed.), *The Hospitality Industry, Tourism and Europe: Perspectives on Policies*, Cassell, London, pp. 35–45.
Morrison, A. (1996), "Guesthouses and small hotels", in Jones, P. (Ed.), *Introduction to Hospitality Operations*, Cassell, London, pp. 73–85.
Morrison, A. (1998), "Small firm statistics: a hotel sector focus", *Service Industries Journal*, Vol. 18 No. 1, pp. 132–42.
Morrison, A., Rimmington, M. and Williams, C. (1998), *Entrepreneurship in the Hospitality, Tourism and Leisure Industries*, Butterworth-Heinemann, Oxford.
Mutch, A. (1998), "Using information technology", in Thomas, R. (Ed.), *The Management of Small Tourism and Hospitality Firms*, Cassell, London, pp. 92–206.
Peacock, M. (1993), "A question of size", *International Journal of Contemporary Hospitality Management*, Vol. 5 No. 4, pp. 29–32.
Pickering, J., Greenwood, J. and Hunt, D. (1971), *The Small Firm in the Hotel and Catering Industry (Committee of Inquiry on Small Firms: Research Report 14)*, HMSO, London.

Slattery, P. (1994), "The structural theory of business demand: a reply to Hughes", *International Journal of Hospitality Management*, Vol. 13 No. 2, pp. 173-6.

Storey, D.J. (1994), *Understanding the Small Business Sector*, Routledge, London.

Thomas, R. (1998a), "An introduction to the study of small tourism and hospitality firms", in Thomas, R. (Ed.), *The Management of Small Tourism and Hospitality Firms*, Cassell, London, pp. 1-16.

Thomas, R. (Ed.) (1998b), *The Management of Small Tourism and Hospitality Firms*, Cassell, London.

Thomas, R., Friel, M., Jameson, S. and Parsons, D. (1997), *The National Survey of Small Tourism and Hospitality Firms: Annual Report 1996-97*, Centre for the Study of Small Tourism and Hospitality Firms, Leeds Metropolitan University, Leeds.

Thomas, R., Church, I., Eaglen, A., Jameson, S., Lincoln, G. and Parsons, D. (1998), *The National Survey of Small Tourism and Hospitality Firms: Annual Report 1997-98*, Centre for the Study of Small Tourism and Hospitality Firms, Leeds Metropolitan University, Leeds.

Timmons, J. (1994), *New Venture Creation*, Irwin, Boston, MA.

Webster, M. (1998), "Strategies for growth", in Thomas, R. (Ed.), *The Management of Small Tourism and Hospitality Firms*, Cassell, London, pp. 207-18.

31
Economic Impact and Institutional Dynamics of Small Hotels in Tanzania
Amit Sharma

Small businesses are considered vital for economic development (Schumpeter, 1942). Still, the economic importance of hospitality small businesses such as hotels is seldom emphasized in developing countries. Mostly, this is because the appearance of these businesses as an organized industry in developing nations has been a relatively recent phenomenon. Furthermore, data on small businesses are usually hard to obtain, and statistics available in these countries are relatively unreliable. As a consequence, there is a gap in understanding the role of these businesses in economic development. Given that many developing countries, especially in Africa, are relying on hospitality and tourism industries for economic development and poverty alleviation, it becomes vital to understand small-business dynamics and relate them to local economic development.

The purpose of this recent study in Tanzania was to investigate the role of small hotels on local economic development and government policies that will maximize their economic potential. In response to the unavailability of national statistics, this study shows how firm-level financial and accounting data can be used in this methodology proposed by the system of national accounts (SNA; United Nations [UN], 1999). Due to inconsistencies in methodologies used in previous economic impact studies, this investigation also outlines a framework that can be used for future investigations and

Source: *Journal of Hospitality & Tourism Research,* 30(1) (2006): 76–94.

whose results can be used in the national statistical framework to strengthen sector statistics. Firm-level statistics of hospitality and tourism businesses in developing countries are not available. Therefore, this study is among the very few that is attempting to investigate economic impact using a production approach, requiring firm-level data.

Literature

Small Hotels' Economic Impact

Businesses operating in the hospitality and tourism industry are an essential component of basic consumer services (BCS; William, 1996). For the most part, BCS are still considered separate from mainstream economic development (Eadington & Redman, 1991). As a consequence, service sectors get limited attention from development economists. This is not unusual, because any government resource allocation decision toward an economic activity is based on the ability of that activity to contribute toward national economic development (Ruggles, 1999). Therefore, the hospitality and tourism industry must clearly demonstrate their economic contributions if they are to seek greater development resources. Even though more than 27 African nations have identified the hospitality and tourism business as a leading source of socioeconomic progress, it is still unclear how this sector will deliver the promise of economic development and under what government policies (Sharma & Christie, 2002).

In economic theory, Schumpeter (1942) emphasized the significant role that small businesses play in fueling a capitalistic and free-market economy. A recent study conducted by the World Bank (2004a), *Doing Business in 2004*, also emphasizes the role of small and locally owned businesses in the economic development of a nation, especially in developing countries. Other studies have identified small-business policies that are most effective for reducing regional economic disparities (Petrakos, 1996). Even though most economies are dominated by small businesses, researchers continue to identify the "glaring lack of understanding at both empirical and theoretical (microeconomic) level of the process by which human, financial, and technical capitalis accumulated, leading – or failing to lead – to small business creation" (Regnier, 1998). Much of the economic impact discussion in the hospitality literature has focused on larger and internationally owned properties in developing countries. Previous studies suggest that such hotels provide very little toward local economic development, as they tend to import a large amount of their inputs, including labor (Christie & Crompton, 2002; English, 1986). On the other hand, there seems to be a general consensus that small businesses tend to support local-factor markets and therefore have a higher capacity to contribute in economic development. However, there has been no systematic research to quantify their economic impact (Asia-Pacific Economic Cooperation, 2004).

Firm-level data on small hotels are practically unavailable, especially in developing countries. Furthermore, there is little consistency of methodologies in prior literature used to calculate the economic impact of hotel businesses. Most economic impact studies have either used regression-type models with macroindices or shown multiplier affects using aggregate data (Bélisle, 1983; Miller, 1985; Sugiyarto, Blake, & Sinclair, 2003; Zhou, Yanagida, Chakravorty, & Leung, 1997). Some studies have used input-output-type models, but there is no clarity of data sources and whether they included individual industry information at the disaggregate level (Thurlow & Wobst, 2003). Although these are valid methodologies, they require extensive data sets at both macrolevels and microlevels. For example, economic impact regression models require time-series data sets at the firm level. The requirements for input-output tables are even more elaborate, as they need data from multiple sectors at the firm and industry level. Although such methodologies are necessary in the medium to long term, some policy formulation challenges facing the developing countries are more immediate.

Consequently, the primary challenge that economic impact studies have faced has been the difficulty of obtaining reliable information. Growing needs for international statistics prompted the United Nations to approve tourism satellite account (TSA), a universally accepted framework for industry statistics. This framework now can be adopted by nations to ensure that international statistics are comparable and consistent with approved World Tourism Organization (WTO) and UN standards (WTO, 1999). However, the data required for developing TSA's core economic impact indices are enormous, because constructing input-output tables is an elaborate process that requires a combination of macroeconomic and microeconomic statistics. Although developing this framework is usually a national or a regional-level effort, the TSA provides general concepts for economic impact analyses that can be used in independent investigations. Economic impact assessment using TSA concepts of *gross value added*, *employment*, and *fixed capital formation* will ensure that analyses largely are consistent with internationally acceptable standards and, more important, are aiding in strengthening national and regional-level initiatives for developing the TSA. The value-added concept represents the total value of products and services created by these businesses after adjusting for operational inputs from total turnover (Ruggles, 1999).

Gross value added of a business is their contribution to the gross domestic product (GDP) of the nation. Essentially, by summing value-added estimates of all businesses in an industry, one could calculate the economic contribution of that industry to the national GDP. This contribution can be expressed as a percentage of a nation's total GDP and compared over time. An important by-product of the value-added calculations is the value of domestically used inputs, which can be expressed as a percentage of total gross output. This represents the proportion of *linkages* of businesses to other economic sectors of the economy. If hospitality businesses are buying most of their inputs from local markets, then the proportion of these linkages would be high. In general, it is expected that larger and internationally owned hospitality businesses would tend to have a lower linkage percentage, as they import most of their operational inputs (English, 1986). Employment and gross fixed capital formation indicators can be estimated using business financial information. These indicators also are presented as the proportion of total turnover, or their change is compared over time. Gross fixed capital formation is defined as the investment in fixed produced assets by these industries (WTO, 1999). At the firm level, it is an indicator of the firm's productive capacity.

As an alternative to input-output methodology, the UN (2000) proposes a more comprehensive method of estimating gross value added at the firm level – through the use of business income and expenditure statements. This approach provides the flexibility to use business financial statements to calculate gross value added, economic linkages, employment impact, and fixed capital formation. Currently, no investigation of the hospitality and tourism industries has attempted to use this methodology, even though it provides a more simplistic, disaggregate view of an industry's economic importance. Given that this method is used for reconciling national accounts and business financial statements, it can be useful especially in creating preliminary estimates for more elaborate and detailed economic impact models when existing cross-sectoral data are of low quality in industries such as hotels and restaurants (UN, 2000). As stated earlier, because small-business data are not widely available in a developing country, there is limited investigation of their dynamics. However, unless the role of these businesses in economic development is understood, governments will be unable to comprehensively link poverty-reduction objectives to hospitality and tourism industries.

The economic significance of small businesses, in general, has been attributed to being a function of their competitiveness, which is influenced by government policies (Fogel & Zapalska, 2001). Studies that evaluate small hotels suggest that profitability is sensitive to revenues, pricing policies, and levels of investments in fixed assets (Kaufman, Weaver, & Poynter, 1996; Poorani & Smith, 1995). Other factors influencing competitiveness are operators' previous experiences, marketing resources, and capital structure mix. Skills and educational levels of operators and employees also have received special attention in the literature (Romer, 1986, 1990). The high level of endogenous production in these businesses increases the relevance of *knowledge*, identified in earlier studies as an intangible asset. Often firm-level training efforts can reduce the gap of required knowledge and skill levels. Even though on-the-job training is prevalent largely in hotels, there is inconclusive evidence to suggest that such efforts are valuable (Worsfold & Griffith, 2003; Zhang, Cai, & Liu, 2002).

Also significant to hospitality organizations' performance are the influence of immediate and distant environments and various dimensions of these environmental forces (Olsen, West, & Tse, 1998). The concept of environment includes forces and factors external to the organization's boundaries. Given the important role of *entrepreneurship* in small-business development, prior research suggests that external environments can be hostile to these businesses in developing countries (Smallbone & Welter, 2001). For example, the scarcity of resources, informal networks, lack of capital, and overall pace of market reforms in these economies can constrain entrepreneurial activity. Fogel and Zapalska (2001) suggest macroeconomic policies and procedures as another dimension of the external environment important for small-business development. Evidence suggests that fixed capital formation in small businesses is a function of external financial resources, especially when free cash flows are not a stable source of internal funding (Gilchrist & Himmelberg, 1995; Kadapakkam, Kumar, & Riddick, 1998). Therefore, if financial markets are weak, it could affect the ability of small firms to form productive capital. In the context of these issues, evidence suggests that countries with minimum legal and institutional barriers are likely to have a better functioning and developed private sector that would allow opportunities and a stronger likelihood of business start-ups.

Case of Tanzania

Tanzania has identified hospitality and tourism as a primary sector of economic development and diversification. Recently, country officials successfully hosted an international investor forum and have attracted foreign direct investment (FDI) projects in the hotel industry. Yet, small businesses are being recognized as an important source of economic development in Tanzania. Economic estimates suggest that hospitality and tourism as a whole contributes between 5% and 8% (in value added) to the country's GDP (Multilateral Investment Guarantee Agency, 2002). The challenge with using such estimates for decision making is that individual industry contributions are not represented clearly. Although there are a few industry-specific estimates, their data source and representation are unclear. One such estimate suggests that hotels and restaurants contribute 2.69% as value added to Tanzania's economy using a social accounting matrix (SAM; an input-output-based model). But this study does not clarify the coverage of hotel industries (Thurlow & Wobst, 2003). This analysis does not provide the flexibility to evaluate small businesses separately unless those categories have been clearly defined in the underlying input-output tables. Furthermore, there is limited use of such broad estimates in conducting policy analysis.

In Tanzania, information on small businesses is available only as unofficial estimates and anecdotal references. The country recently committed to improving hospitality and tourism statistics; however, inclusion of small businesses in this process poses a significant challenge. Given the economic importance attributed to hospitality industries and, more recently, to small businesses, it is becoming increasingly crucial that the country formulates appropriate policies. This cannot happen without a better economic understanding of small businesses.

Research Objectives

The hotel industry in Tanzania has been unable to distinctly establish its economic relevance. Evidence suggests that small hotels have strong potential for contributing to economic development. However, there is a lack of understanding on how this process will take place in the context of government policies and competitiveness of these businesses. The difficulty of getting data from small businesses has contributed to limited research in this area. Therefore, this study attempts to begin a systematic investigation of these issues and address the following questions:

(a) What is the economic contribution of small hotels in Tanzania as measured by gross value added, employment impact, linkages to the economy, and gross fixed capital formation?
(b) What implications can be derived for industry policy, institutional arrangements, and firm-level statistics through economic impact estimates of small hotels?

Method

Research Design

Economic impact studies usually use existing data sets from the national accounts or national sector-level databases. Although some developing nations have hospitality and tourism industries classified in national accounts, for most others these statistics are aggregated in the services category. Most times, this aggregation limits the coverage of hospitality industries to larger scale operations. As a consequence, smaller hotels and restaurants are excluded from economic impact estimates. This certainly is true in many East African nations, especially Tanzania. Yet, it is likely that these businesses are important for local development. Given that there is no existing production- and firm-level statistics for these businesses, the task of estimating their economic impact becomes challenging. Such is a characteristic of this investigation when using traditional economic impact methodology (based on input-output modeling) will yield little or no success. Large-scale data-gathering exercises (of firm-level information) are at best a medium- to long-term strategy and may not provide timely assessment of small-business dynamics in these industries. As a consequence, firm-level data were collected from a selected but operationally representative sample of small hotels in Tanzania.

Three major concentrations of hotel developments in Tanzania are in the Dar-es-Salaam, Arusha, and Mwanza regions. Of these, the Arusha region has the maximum proportion of tourist traffic – this is the departure point for four of the top five tourist destinations in Tanzania, namely, Ngorongoro Crater, Serengeti National Park, Manyara National Park, and Mount Kilimanjaro. Mwanza has very little tourism activity, mostly limited to accessing the Serengeti from the west. Dar-es-Salaam is mostly a business center and provides access to Zanzibar and southern parts of the country. Clearly, Arusha is currently the most important focal point of Tanzania's tourism activity. Therefore, this study used the Arusha region due to its significance in the tourism sector. In addition, this region borders Kenya, thereby experiencing high regional tourism traffic and trading activity. There also is an international airport with direct daily flights from Europe. This region also has the most registered hotels (more than 25% of all hotels in Tanzania are in Arusha city) and those that can be classified as small properties.

The criterion used to define small hotels in this investigation was properties with 50 or fewer rooms, because the data on number of employees are not available in any government records. Therefore, it is not feasible to sample businesses by the number of employees, which has been the usual practice in previous studies. The average size of participating hotels was approximately 25 rooms. The average number of employees in properties surveyed was fewer than 20, which is the most common generic criterion for classifying small businesses in the United States. The total number of hotels registered in the Arusha region is 64, of which 53 properties were registered as having 50 or fewer rooms. Of these 53 small hotels, 20 properties were located, and their owners or managers agreed to participate in this survey; 8 refused to participate in this survey. For the other 25 properties, it was unclear whether some were in regular legal operation, and others could not be located either due to incorrect addresses or outdated registration records.

There are no firm-level statistics available in Tanzania for hotels. Only company registration information is available from the country's registrar of companies, and even that is of varying reliability. Data sets available from value-added and corporate tax filings are only representative of large hotels. Small hotels are not represented in these statistics (Multilateral Investment

Guarantee Agency, 2002). In addition to a complete absence of statistics, the government data that are available are mostly outdated. This paucity of data created challenges for conducting this research. It is also not unusual for development research to face the challenge of small sample sizes (Akker, 1999). Given sample size limitations, the value-added model selected for this investigation is the UN-proposed deterministic model, rather than an error model, which will further reduce the critical requirement of large sample sizes. As this model has been used extensively, its estimation errors have been corrected over time to make it a comprehensive representation of economic impact information (UN, 1993, 1999, 2000).

Questionnaire

The data collection questionnaire was based on the information required for completing the UN-recommended business financial statement value-added model, the international survey questionnaire of the World Bank that is currently being used to compile firm-level statistics in Africa and around the world, and Tanzania's Ministry of Natural Resources and Tourism's business survey (MNRT; UN, 2000; World Bank, 2004b). The Regional Program for Enterprise Development at the World Bank (RPED) has been conducting studies of small enterprises in developing countries (especially Africa), therefore this methodology was considered appropriate. This approach is also consistent with the survey process used by the Organization for Economic Cooperation and Development (OECD) for their economic impact assessment research (OECD, 2000). The RPED surveys in Tanzania did not include small hotels, and therefore no probability of likely overlap existed. All data collected are monetary (ratio), nonmonetary (ratio and interval), and nominal. No ordinal-type perception scales were used.

Data Collection

Due to the varying reliability of business information and a general apprehension on the part of business owners and managers to share proprietary or confidential data, use of mail survey for data collection likely would have resulted in relatively low response rates. To enhance data quality, this investigation collected primary data using face-to-face interviews conducted with owners and managers of hotels. Results from 18 interviews were analyzed. These 18 responses represent approximately 35% of the total registered hotels; however, the total number of legally operating properties is even lower. This is a significant representation of the small-hotel activity in the Arusha region.

Most interviews were conducted with either the owner of the business or a senior manager. In a few instances, when the manager was unable to provide information the interview was conducted with the owner. Also interviewed were the officials from MNRT, the East African Community (EAC), the National College of Tourism, four local commercial banks, and two private industry associations, including the apex Association of Tourism Industry Operators (ATIO). These interviews were conducted to gather secondary data and documentation on the institutional environment and policy framework for small businesses.

Meetings with the ATIO also facilitated networking with small businesses to ensure their participation and cooperation in the survey process. All interviews were conducted by the researcher to avoid any ambiguity in interpretations. To reduce the respondents' biases, the purpose of this study (independent research) and researcher's affiliation were clearly declared. Finally, the respondents were provided with a signed letter from the researcher (on official letterhead) ensuring complete confidentiality of respondents' identities.

Economic Impact Model

The economic impact of these businesses was evaluated using concepts of gross value added, employment, and fixed capital formation. These are generic economic impact assessment concepts that are widely accepted within the SNA and the TSA. The method used to calculate gross output and value added is also called the *production approach* (OECD, 2001; UN, 2000). The production approach relates to the maximum quantity that can be produced using a set of inputs; primary (X) includes labor and capital, and secondary (M) refers to all intermediate inputs, or inputs used for production that are purchased from other sectors of the economy. In the case of hotels, agricultural produce, for instance, will represent an intermediate input from the agricultural sector. Other examples of intermediate inputs in hotels will be cleaning supplies for rooms, guest supplies, utilities, and so on. The formulation contains a parameter, $A(t)$, of disembodied technical shifts that can result in an improved production process. It is termed *disembodied* because it affects all inputs proportionally. Essentially, the relationship between different inputs remains the same. Under these assumptions, the production function (Q) is represented as follows:

$$Q = H(A, X, M) = A(t) \times F(X, M),$$

where H and F are functional forms, A is the disembodied technical change, X represents primary inputs, and M represents secondary inputs.

Similarly, the value-added function could be stated as

$$G = G(A(t), X, P_M, P),$$

where G is a functional form, P_M is the price of intermediate inputs, and P is the price of primary inputs.

As a consequence, changes in value added will be affected by changes in prices of inputs or of any technical changes associated with production. In this investigation, technical changes only refer to the proportion of cost of sales for food, beverage, and room divisions. This is a generic formulation of value added and is derived from the SNA (UN, 1993).

To calculate these indicators, the survey questionnaire responses were organized into income statements using mean-performance and median-performance estimates of business revenues, operating costs, and investment and financing activities. If outliers and small sample sizes are likely to bias mean-performance measures, it is usually acceptable to use median-performances as estimates. Given the likelihood of outliers and the relatively small sample size of this study, median-performance estimates were used throughout the analysis. Income statement values were organized into the UN's (2000) national income accounting production approach to evaluate economic value added, economic linkages, employment, and gross fixed capital formation indicators.

The gross value added (G) and related indicators were calculated as follows:

$$G = \Sigma Q - A(t)(\Sigma X + \Sigma M),$$

where Q is the total turnover, $A(t)$ is the disembodied technical change (constant in this investigation), X is primary inputs, and M is the set of secondary inputs used for production. The relationship of technical change to all inputs is considered to be constant; any changes in technology will proportionally affect all inputs. The proportion of value added to total output was calculated as follows:

$$G\% = \frac{G}{\Sigma Q}$$

The proportion of linkages to the rest of the economy was calculated as follows:

$$XM_d\% = \frac{\Sigma XM_d}{\Sigma Q}$$

where XM_d represents locally sourced inputs (both primary and secondary). The proportions of leakages refer to the amount of primary and secondary inputs imported or bought from outside the country. These are represented as XM_m:

$$XM_m\% = \frac{\Sigma XM_m}{\Sigma Q}$$

The expenditure on gross fixed capital formation is based on last year's expenditure on high-use equipment: This includes equipment in the kitchen, guest rooms, front office, cleaning and laundry, vehicles, and computers for office use. The proportion of gross fixed capital formation is calculated as follows:

$$K_{t-1}\% = \frac{\Sigma K_{t-1}}{\Sigma Q_{t-1}}$$

Employment is calculated using the absolute number of employees, comparison of wage rates with regional average, and the total amount spent by businesses as cost of labor.

Results and Discussion

The majority of surveyed establishments were sole proprietorships (59%), 23% were partnerships, and 18% privately held limited companies. On average, the hotels in this study have been in operation for 9 years. They have domestic and regional clients of approximately 54%, whereas the balance of 46% was foreign travelers (including tourists). Average capacity of the surveyed hotel was 25 rooms. Peak-season occupancy (average) was 73%, although the low-season level could fall to 42%. The average room rate of these hotels is approximately $34 in U.S. currency. Restaurant and bar data suggest that the average food check is $3, and the average beverage check is $1. These rates are significantly lower (up to 400%) than those in larger hotels in the same region.

Gross Value Added

The value added (as a proportion of gross total output) is 47.4% for hotels. The leakage income from the region of approximately 5.8% represents purchases made from Kenya and Dubai. The linkage to other economic sectors of Tanzania was 46.8% from small hotels. These linkages represent retention of income in local communities. The figures are slightly lower than those investigated in an earlier study by English (1986), where the author found that in cases of high usage of locally produced intermediate products and services, hospitality and tourism activity could result in up to 85% retention of earnings. The value of linkages represents the inputs purchased from local markets that directly contribute to economic development per se. Lower linkages in this case are either likely due to low estimates of intermediate inputs, relatively higher prices, and/or high profit margins. In this study, the former is a more plausible scenario because most businesses that participated in this survey did not have (or were unwilling to share) official business statements. Therefore, one possibility is that they underestimated intermediate consumption, or that value added has improved in these businesses. Another reason is that increasingly, hotels are trying to provide international standards. But in doing so, they must buy inputs of appropriate qualities, which may not be available locally.

Yet, almost all (99%) purchases of food and beverage items were from within the country. The other items such as furniture, equipment, carpets, linen and uniforms, utensils, and electronic equipment, were purchased mostly locally. Although linkages to the economy appear to be higher than those expected in larger and internationally owned hotels, it is not clear how these purchases are distributed across the supply chain. There appeared to be no formal contractual arrangements between buyers and sellers in the domestic market. As a consequence, there remains a high level of uncertainty in pricing and supply of key inputs such as meats, vegetables, and so on. For instance, a food and beverage manager gave this example:

> When we need fish for a party of 100 pax [people], the suppliers don't have the appropriate type and quality. Even if this is available in the market, it would mean we pay a substantially higher price than usual. On the other hand, the supplier could be walking around with a bag full of fish and will have to reduce its price substantially to sell it before the day is out.

This exemplifies the usual situation in the supply chain, suggesting that even if inputs are being bought locally, significant inefficiencies could be reducing profit margins to suppliers and purchasers.

Table 1 shows the value-added contribution of small hotels to the country's GDP as approximately 2%. An earlier study estimated that hotel and restaurant industries as a whole contribute approximately 2.69% to Tanzania's GDP (Thurlow & Wobst, 2003). If it is assumed that hotels in Arusha contribute value added in exactly the same proportion as those in other parts of the country, then the value-added contribution of small hotels represents more than 64% toward regional GDP. With similar logic, and assuming that the government's estimates of the entire tourism industry's GDP contribution is approximately 6%, small hotels seem to contribute more than 31% of this value added. These figures suggest a relatively significant economic role of small hotels (see Figure 1).

Table 1: Value added, linkages, and leakages as percentage of gross output of small hotels in the Arusha region of Tanzania

Indicator	Hotels, (TZS millions)	% of Gross output
Gross output (basic prices)	11,836	
Intermediate consumption	6,229	52.62
Leakages	685	5.79
Linkages	5,544	46.84
Gross value added	5,608	47.38
Gross capital formation[a]	125	1.05
Per capita GDP 2002	6,113,362	
Tanzanian population 2002	34	
Arusha region population 2002	1	
Arusha GDP	322,290	
Contribution to regional GDP		1.74

Total GDP contribution of small hotels in Arusha = 1.74%
Earlier estimates of hotel and restaurant contribution to GDP = 2.69%
Share of small hotels toward total industries' contribution to GDP = 64.68%[b]
Share of hotels and restaurants toward total industries' contribution to GDP = 5.50%
Share of small hotels toward total GDP = 31.63%[c]

Note: TZS = Tanzanian shilling.
a. National average gross capital formation (% of GDP) was 17.4% in 2002 (World Bank, 2004b).
b. This is based on the assumption that Arusha's hotel and restaurant industries at large also contribute 2.69% to regional GDP.
c. This is based on the assumption that Arusha's tourism activity also contributes 5.5% to regional GDP.

To evaluate policies that could potentially affect competitiveness and economic contributions of these businesses, Table 2 presents a sensitivity analysis of how changes in key variables would affect small-business contribution to regional GDP. A 10% increase in number of establishments will result in a proportionate change (10%) in small hotels' GDP contribution.

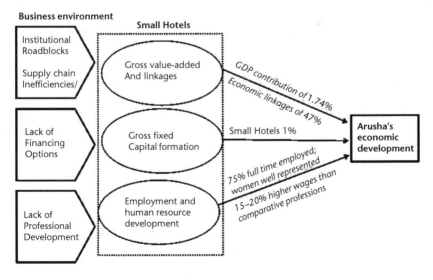

Figure 1: Economic impact of small hotels in Arusha

Table 2: Sensitivity analysis of impact on GDP contribution of small hotels, Arusha region in Tanzania

10% Change in variable	%[a] Change in GDP contribution
No. of establishments	10.0
Capacity	
Rooms (average size of hotel)	9.0
Seats	0.03
Demand, high-season occupancy	8.0
Demand, low-season occupancy	1.1
Demand, food and beverage occupancy	1.1
Room price for international travelers	8.0
Room price for domestic and regional travelers	1.1
Price for food	1.0
Price for beverages	0.25
Increased efficiency, rooms division	6.3
Increased efficiency, food division	1.4
Increased efficiency, beverage division	0.50
Increased salaries	1.7

a. Percentage of total GDP contribution of small hotels in Arusha.

As can be observed, the four variables that result in maximum increase in GDP contribution of these businesses are number of establishments, average size of hotels, room rates for international travelers, and efficiency in the rooms division.

Gross Capital Formation

Investment in productive assets in small hotels as a proportion of total output is about 1% (see Figure 1). This suggest a relatively low level of capital formation or essentially a lack of investments in *productive capital* in these businesses compared to more recent estimates of up to 13.5% in South Africa's hotel and restaurant industries (Christie & Crompton, 2002).

Findings from this study suggest that more than 66% of respondents have relatively new catering equipment that was purchased within the past 5 years. Most refrigerators and freezers are more than 5 years old. Although computer equipment is relatively new, the same cannot be said for vehicles and cleaning equipment. Even though the country does not produce this equipment indigenously, purchasing them locally would still add to the economic linkage chain. More important, lack of proper equipment may suggest the inability of these businesses to charge higher prices to their customers. This is because older equipment may be one of the reasons why these properties appear to be rundown and give a perception of lower or inferior quality of products and services. For example, a number of hotel managers suggested that because they do not have new and industrial laundry and cleaning equipment, it often breaks down. As a consequence, the hotel has to hire a commercial laundry service, which drives up their operating

Table 3: Sources of financing in small hotels in the Arusha region in Tanzania

	Working capital funding, %	New investment funding, %	Start-up finance, %
Internal funds/savings	95	90	66.82
Bank loans	5	6.50	1.86
Leases	0	0	0
Investment financing	0	0	0
Trade credit	0	0	4
Credit cards	0	0	0
Equity	0	0	3.18
Family and friends	0	3.50	10.86
Informal sources	0	0	0
Others	0	0	0

costs. If they fail to provide these services to the customer, the customer goes to the competition. Similarly, a lack of proper refrigeration leads to higher waste, in turn increasing the cost of materials purchased.

The major roadblock in increasing investments in fixed assets identified by these businesses was the lack of external financing. Table 3 presents the sources of financing for small hotels in Arusha. Although no formal estimates of cash flows were available in these organizations, profitability is generally low, and they are barely able to meet fixed costs. As a consequence, reliance on internally generated cash flows seems improbable to stimulate capital expenditure.

Employment and Related Factors

Full-time employees represented more than 75% of the total employed in these businesses, and only about one quarter of total employees are contracted on a seasonal basis (see Figure 1). There was a relatively high number of younger than 30-year-olds employed. Of the total, 80% of men and 90% of women were in this age group. As employees, women (56%) were represented marginally better than men; however, only 30% of the entrepreneurs were women. Of all employees, more than 70% had 9 years or less of schooling. All owners and managers had at least attended primary school, and more than 50% had university degrees or higher qualifications. However, only 10% of the respondents had any formal hospitality training. Evidence suggests that many of these businesses were not the primary source of income for the owners.

Although the wage structure appears to be competitive with other businesses (i.e., other nonagriculture professions such as secretarial-level jobs), the additional "service charge" or tips raises these wages by an estimated 15% to 20%. However, these increases were only seasonal, and during off-season the part-time employees would most likely be out of employment. The development of human resources through training and other activities seemed minimal. Almost all respondents (95%) agreed to have provided some form of on-the-job-training to their employees; few of the respondents (5%) seemed to have conducted any planned training sessions. Given that most owners and managers did not possess any formal hospitality training, the quality of on-the-job training efforts is questionable.

Contrary to previous evidence, results of this study provided evidence of year-round employment; a majority of those employed are younger than 35 years, and of these the larger proportion are women. There is further evidence that wages and skill transfer to those employed are also on a competitive level. However, it is not clear how the skill levels of these employees are being developed. Due to low to minimal investment in human resources, it is likely that these jobs are not providing adequate future career growth opportunities for employees.

Policy, Institutional Environment, and Industry Statistics

The entrepreneurial environment in general is not very conducive for small businesses, and this is especially so for women entrepreneurs. That is, in general it is not easy to start a business given the complex array of formalities. Furthermore, there are limited opportunities to get external funding, which implies that most entrepreneurs must depend on their internal sources of funds. These factors are creating operational and management challenges for hotel entrepreneurs that can be interpreted at the firm's operational level and at the industry level.

The results of the sensitivity analysis conducted on the economic impact model revealed certain implications for policy and institutional arrangements. At the operational level, there were clear indications that availability of capital for start-up finances, fixed capital investments, and working capital could enhance operational performance of small hotels (see Figure 1). Reduction in the complexity of business formation could stimulate entrepreneurial activity, especially for women wanting to set up and operate these businesses. There is also a need to enhance production capacities through increased capital investment. These can be achieved both via the provision of tax incentives for investments and the local availability of industrial equipment. Sensitivity analysis clearly revealed that increased international tourist traffic will boost value added by 8%. Therefore, the MNRT needs to review policies that would increase international tourist traffic so that small businesses are able to create critical demand levels essential for their profitability. Formalization of supply-chain networks and provision of start-up and investment capital for small supply-chain operators such as meat, fish, and vegetable vendors was also viewed to be a critical issue that will ensure these businesses are able to maximize on creating value added. Increased room rates was another variable that was found in the sensitivity analysis to boost value added, significantly. This can be facilitated if businesses have better quality products, services, and facilities. One potential intervention is to establish an institutional framework that would ensure that small hotels meet minimum standards of product quality and services, thereby guiding them to increase competitiveness. And finally, availability of training and education opportunities for employees and owners at the operational and management levels, and opportunities for professional development, would be a critical factor that will influence value added of this industry.

Even though the economic model in this investigation is a simple one, without the sophistication of an input-output-type analysis, it is able to provide indications that the policy and institutional framework for small hotels needs a thorough review. Results of this investigation have identified policy and institutional arrangements that appear to be critical for improving the competitiveness, and therefore the economic contribution, of small hotels in Tanzania.

Sector statistics definitely need to be improved. This study begins with no reliable firm-level data. The data availability for smaller businesses is nearly nonexistent, as even the basic company registration information is not available. If the government and researchers want a more accurate assessment of economic contributions, firm-level monetary and nonmonetary data are a prerequisite. Special consideration will need to be placed on sourcing data from small businesses. It is also essential that these statistics be improved within the recently proposed TSA framework, which is also currently being implemented in Tanzania.

There is a need to improve the reporting of business financial statements at the firm level. Unless small hotels properly prepare financial information, accuracy and reliability of these data sets will remain questionable. One big challenge of this investigation has been that most operators and owners are unaware of standard industry reporting criteria. Given such a situation, even if the government agencies were to improve the functionality of sourcing data, data accuracy will depend on the sophistication of data compilation and gathering techniques being used at the firm level.

Another issue is the data producer and provider relationship. Even though this issue is beyond the scope of this article, it is worth mentioning that unless the private sector begins to value the purpose and intentions of government's data needs, they will be reluctant to cooperate in such initiatives.

Conclusions and Implications

Results of this study show that small hotels may contribute up to 2% toward Tanzania's GDP. They also suggest that fixed capital formation in these hotels is low, as they have limited access to financing. These businesses are labor intensive and are likely paying competitive wages to their employees, but these employees lack training and technical expertise. Furthermore, the entrepreneurial environment for small-hotel operators is not conducive to maximizing the economic impact of these businesses, especially for businesses owned and managed by women entrepreneurs. This is likely affecting the quality of products and services that these properties offer to visiting tourists.

Small hotels have traditionally been neglected in mainstream policy analysis, especially in developing countries. This is largely due to the inability to demonstrate clearly how these businesses contribute to economic development. Although prior studies have created models to show the economic impact of tourism as a whole, industry-level disaggregate impact remains to be demonstrated clearly. The purpose of this article has been to investigate whether small hotels contribute to economic development in Tanzania and to assess institutional and policy dynamics within which these businesses operate. This investigation demonstrates a comprehensive and consistent framework to develop preliminary estimates of economic impact of small hotels in a developing-country situation. It also provides a framework to relate these impacts with institutional policies of the government so that these can be used for decision making by the government and private sector. The most significant contribution of this study is to present an alternative framework that can be used to develop baseline economic impact estimates for hospitality industries when practically *no reliable statistics* are available to develop elaborate input-output tables.

This article also raises the issue of assessing the economic significance of small businesses. Given that a great portion of international business activity in the hotel (and even restaurant) industry is largely in smaller properties, it is discouraging to see only a handful of studies that have paid attention to this phenomenon, let alone attempt to understand how these businesses can play a significant role in economic development.

Finally, this article raises the issue of data reliability and use of secondary data sets in assessing economic impact studies. Most economic impact studies in hospitality and tourism have used secondary data sets into input-output models. Although these models are powerful analytic tools, the underlying data sets are (at best) partial representation of economic activity. A medium- to long-term strategy will be to develop the TSA framework for estimating the economic significance of these industries. However, this process will not only take time but resource allocation and commitment. Meanwhile, baseline studies like these (using methodology consistent with the TSA) can fill the gap of our lack of awareness of small-hotel (and restaurant) dynamics in economic development, especially in developing nations.

Limitations

Although this article presents an alternative path to assess economic impact, it does so at the cost of using a limited sample size. The sample of companies interviewed in this study is limited to one region that was selected for the study. This was deemed necessary because small-hotel operators in this region are relatively more successful. Therefore, there was a higher probability of sourcing more reliable information from them than from small hotels operating in other parts of the country. This will bring an additional sample bias to this study, as it is most representative of high-performing small hotels. However, controlling for this bias would imply sourcing data from low-performing properties. This presents one of the challenges for future research, as in general it was found that small-hotel operators and managers are not accustomed to maintaining proper accounting and financial statements.

This study paves the way for future investigations that could improve estimates of economic impact from small hotels for the entire country, and even include other hospitality businesses such as restaurants and other eating and drinking places. Given the formative nature of this research, it is expected that even though generalization of this study's results will be a challenge, application of the proposed methodology and inductive reasoning of the research findings will contribute to the body of literature.

Author's Note

This study was funded by the Council on International Programs at Iowa State University during the summer of 2003.

References

Akker, J. V. D. (1999). Principles and methods of development research. In J. V. D. Akker, R. M. Branch, K. Gustafson, N. Nieveen, & T. Plomp (Eds.), *Design approaches and tools in education and training* (pp. 1–14). Boston: Kluwer Academic.

Asia-Pacific Economic Cooperation. (2004). *Development needs of small to medium sized tourism businesses*. Singapore: PPEC International Center for Sustainable Tourism.

Bélisle, F. J. (1983). Tourism and food production in the Caribbean. *Annals of Tourism Research, 10*(4), 497–513.

Christie, I., & Crompton, D. E. (2002). *Tourism in Africa, Africa region* (Working Paper Series No. 12). Washington, DC: World Bank Group.

Eadington, W. R., & Redman, M. (1991). Economics and tourism. *Annals of Tourism Research, 18*(1), 41–56.

English, E. P. (1986). *The great escape: An examination of north-south tourism*. Ottawa. Canada: North-South Institute.

Fogel, G., & Zapalska, A. (2001). A comparison of small and medium size enterprise development in central and eastern Europe. *Comparative Economic Studies, 43*(3), 35–68.

Gilchrist, S., & Himmelberg, C. P. (1995). Evidence on the role of cash flow for investment. *Journal of Monetary Economics, 36*(3), 541–572.

Kadapakkam, P. R., Kumar, P. C., & Riddick, L. A. (1998). The impact of cash flows and firm size on investment: The international evidence. *Journal of Banking & Finance, 22*(3), 293–320.

Kaufman, T. J., Weaver, P. W., & Poynter, J. (1996). Success attributes of B&B operators. *Cornell Hotel and Restaurant Administration Quarterly, 37*(4), 29–33.

Miller, L. G. (1985). Linking tourism and agriculture to create jobs and reduce migration in the Caribbean. In R. A. Pastor (Ed.), *Migration and development in the Caribbean* (pp. 348–370). London: Westview.

Multilateral Investment Guarantee Agency. (2002). *Tourism in Tanzania – Investment for growth and diversification*. Washington, DC: Author-World Bank.

Olsen, M. D., West, J. J., & Tse, E. C. Y. (1998). *Strategic management in the hospitality industry*. Hoboken, NJ: John Wiley.

Organization of Economic Cooperation and Development. (2000). *Workshop on business tendency surveys*. Retrieved January 10, 2004, from http://www.oecd.org/dataoecd/25/44/2671396.pdf

Organization of Economic Cooperation and Development. (2001). *Measuring productivity: OECD manual – Measurement of aggregate and industry level productivity growth*. Paris: Author.

Petrakos, G. (1996, March-April). Small enterprise development and regional policy. *Eastern European Economics*, pp. 31–64.

Poorani, A. A., & Smith, D. R. (1995). Financial characteristics of bed-and-breakfast inns. *Cornell Hotel and Restaurant Administration Quarterly, 36*(5), 57–63.

Regnier, P. (1998). Dynamics of small enterprise development: State versus market in the Asian newly industrializing economies. In P. Cook, C. H. Kirkpatrick, & F. Nixson (Eds.), *Privatization, enterprise development, and economic reform: Experiences of developing and transitional economies* (pp. 206–228). Northampton, MA: Edward Elgar.

Romer, P. M. (1986). Increasing returns and long-run growth. *Journal of Political Economy, 94*(5), 1002–1037.

Romer, P. M. (1990). Endogenous technological change. In E. Mansfield & E. Mansfield (Eds.), *The economics of technical change* (pp. 12–43). Aldershot, UK: Edward Elgar.

Ruggles, R. (1999). National income accounting and its relation to economic policy. In N. D. Ruggles & R. Ruggles (Eds.), *National accounting and economic policy: The United States and the UN systems* (pp. 3–38). Northampton, MA: Edward Elgar.

Schumpeter, J. A. (1942). *Can capitalism survive?* New York: Harper & Row.

Sharma, A., & Christie, I. (2002). *World Bank's tourism research in Africa: Private sector and finance division* (Working paper). Ames: Iowa State University.

Smallbone, D., & Welter, F. (2001). The distinctiveness of entrepreneurship in transition economies. *Small Business Economics, 16*(4), 249–262.

Sugiyarto, G., Blake, A., & Sinclair, M. T. (2003). Tourism and globalization impact in Indonesia. *Annals of Tourism Research, 30*(3), 683–701.

Thurlow, J., & Wobst, P. (2003). *Poverty-focused social accounting matrices for Tanzania*. Washington, DC: International Food Policy Research Institute, Trade and Macroeconomics Division.

United Nations. (1993). *System of national accounts*. Brussels/Luxembourg: Author.

United Nations. (1999). *Handbook of input-output table compilation and analysis*. New York: Author.

United Nations. (2000). *Links between business accounting and national accounting*. New York: Author.

William, C. C. (1996). Understanding the role of consumer services in local economic development: Some evidence from the Fens. *Environment and Planning A, 28*(3), 555–571.

World Bank. (2004a). *Doing business in 2004 – Understanding regulation*. Washington, DC: Author.

World Bank. (2004b). *Regional Program for Enterprise Development manual*. Retrieved March 21, 2004, from http://www1.worldbank.org/rped/index.asp

World Tourism Organization. (1999). *Tourism satellite accounts (TSA): The conceptual framework*. Madrid, Spain: Author.

Worsfold, D., & Griffith, C. J. (2003). A survey of food hygiene and safety training in the retail and catering industry. *Nutrition and Food Science, 33*(2), 68–79.

Zhang, L., Cai, L. A., & Liu, W. H. (2002). On-job training: A critical human resources challenge in China's hotel industry. *Journal of Human Resources in Hospitality and Tourism, 1*(3), 91–100.

Zhou, D., Yanagida, J. F., Chakravorty, U., & Leung, P. (1997). Estimating economic impacts from tourism. *Annals of Tourism Research, 24*(1), 76–89.

32

A Descriptive Examination of Corporate Governance in the Hospitality Industry

Basak Denizci Guillet and Anna S. Mattila

1. Introduction

The global economic downturn combined with massive corporate scandals highlights the importance of corporate governance. Hospitality companies are not immune to the current financial crisis and governance meltdown. In a report published by the HVS Global Hospitality Services, it is mentioned that shareholders increasingly demand accountability and transparency in daily operations, thus calling for significant transitions in different areas of corporate governance (Buqbil, 2007). For example, the Cheesecake Factory, Inc. had to make drastic changes in its corporate governance policies following sharp criticism from institutional investors (Nation's Restaurant News, 2008). These changes include a requirement that board terms served by its directors be reduced from 3 years to 1, and a requirement that directors be approved by a majority of shareholders. Corporate governance is the central issue with corporate scandals. Accordingly, the Sarbanes–Oxley act was signed into law in 2002 with the purpose of restoring public confidence in corporate governance in the wake of the infamous Enron case (Romano, 2005).

Source: *International Journal of Hospitality Management,* 29(4) (2010): 677–684.

Corporate governance refers to an amalgam of processes, customs, policies, laws, and institutions by which companies are directed, administrated and controlled (La Porta et al., 2000; Shleifer and Vishny, 1997). The most important stakeholders involved in the governance process are shareholders, the board of directors and executive management. Ultimate power is shared among these three parties. Shareholders have voting rights and an ownership claim to the company through share(s) of capital stock. Using their voting rights, shareholders elect a board of directors who jointly oversee the recruitment, supervision and general control of the executive management. The responsibility of the executive management is to manage the company in the best interest of the shareholders. The division of the power among shareholders, the board of directors, and executive management in each company depends on the defined rules of corporate governance. Gompers et al. (2003) discuss two extremes of the power sharing relationship, in which shareholders either have the power to replace the management easily or management sets strong limitations on the shareholders' ability to replace managers.

1.1. Contribution of the Study

Despite the topic's overall popularity in the mainstream management field, hospitality researchers have focused on a single dimension of corporate governance; namely the relationship between executive compensation and firm performance (Barber et al., 2006; Gu and Choi, 2004; Kim and Gu, 2005, Madanoglu and Karadag, 2008). In a recent study, Dahlstrom et al. (2009) investigated a new dimension of governance in the hotel industry in Norway. They discussed governance forms in the context of inter-firm contracting including independent hotels, voluntary hotel chains, franchises and vertically integrated hotel chains. Dahlstrom et al. concluded that hotel size, amenities, market size and distance from corporate headquarters influence governance. Apart from their study, research on alternative dimensions of corporate governance in the hospitality industry is scant. The objective of this descriptive research is, therefore, to explore the nature and extent of corporate governance practices in the U.S. hospitality industry. More specifically, we want to investigate the extent to which investors are protected from misconduct by executive management or from dangers from controlling shareholders that could result in poor firm performance. Controlling shareholders are investors who own more than 5% of the voting stock in their own right (Bureau of Licenses Pursuant to Rule-Making Authority, 2002). This research is highly relevant in today's corporate world, as hospitality companies are under tremendous amount of pressure to adopt strict governance principles and to prove to investors that their governance is in the shareholders' best interest.

2. Literature Review

From a theoretical perspective, corporate governance is linked to the agency theory. Agency relationships focus on the relationship and goal incongruence between managers and stockholders (Jensen, 1986; Jensen and Meckling, 1976). Managers are considered as shareholders' agents. There are potential conflicts of interest between the management and shareholders due to the delegation of decision-making authority from shareholders to managers. Shareholders cannot perfectly and costlessly monitor the actions of the managers, nor are they in a position to monitor and acquire the information available to or possesed by managers.

The purpose of corporate governance is to engender the successful operation of organizations (Keasey and Wright, 1993) and to minimize agency problem related costs. Corporate governance includes employing thorough contracts that specifically and in detail denote managements' duties and freedom as well as the profit sharing (Shleifer and Vishny, 1997). Previous studies on corporate governance and its relationship to firm performance are extensive in the finance literature (Baysinger and Butler, 1985; Bhagat and Black, 1998; Core et al., 1999; Hermalin and Weisbach, 1991; Morck et al., 1988; Yermack, 1996). However, the majority of these studies employ an event study method to measure the market's reaction following the announcement of a new corporate governance strategy. Coates (2000) draws attention to event study methodology's limitations in that it is not capable of assessing the effect of governance provisions.

Studies after 2000 focus on index-type studies where "presence of shareholder-disempowering corporate governance features" (Young, 2003, p. 4) and relationship between these features and firm performance are examined. Gompers et al. (2003) developed a governance index using 24 company-specific corporate provisions and argued that firms with strongest shareholder rights are more valuable. Bebchuk et al. (2009) and Brown and Caylor (2006) built on the index developed by Gompers et al. (2003) and created an entrenchment index and a summary governance measure based on 51 firm-specific provisions. Both of these studies support Gompers et al.'s (2003) findings. In addition to firm-specific provisions, Cremers and Nair (2005) provided evidence that internal and external governance are related to firm value.

To date, studies examining the relationship between corporate governance and firm performance fail to indicate causality. More specifically, it is not clear whether firms with good financial performance employ better corporate governance provisions, or whether firms with better corporate provisions have stronger financial performance (Lehn et al., 2007). Furthermore, there is no established theory to explain the ideal balance of power between the executive management and shareholders. There are two plausible scenarios.

Presumably, shareholders could allow for limitations to their rights, thus granting extensive power to management as long as the executive management operates the firm in the best interest of the shareholders. Alternatively, shareholders could maintain their rights and thus retain control over executives to ensure the proper management of their business. This would allow shareholders to replace or penalize the management in case of the executive management's misconduct.

3. Corporate Governance in the Hospitality Industry

According to Guillen (2000), different systems of governance are appropriate for different industries. In addition, he argues that governance structures should be developed in response to the varying needs of companies in each sector. We argue that governance of hospitality firms may be different from firms in other industries for several reasons. First, firms in the hospitality industry can be involved with real estate ownership as well as management. If property ownership is separated from management, there is a potential conflict of interest (Guilding, 2003). As Eyster (1988, p. 4) explains "As an agent, the operator pays, in the name of the owner, all operating expenses from the cash flow generated from the property, retains management fees and remits the remaining cash flow, if any, to the owner. The owner supplies the lodging property, including any land, building, furniture, fixtures, equipment, and working capital, and assumes full legal and financial responsibility for the project". This separation of management from real estate ownership can lead to agency related problems. Management tends to focus on long term success of the business with emphasis on customer relationships (Guilding et al., 2001) while owners tend to have a short-term focus with emphasis on payback and return (Beals, 1995). Owners might want to hold the power to ensure that management's focus is on achieving the desired return on equity within an acceptable time frame.

Second, the hospitality industry is characterized by a high level of capital intensity and relatively low level of operating inventories (DeFranco and Lattin, 2006). The real estate components (i.e., furniture, fixtures and equipment (FFE), land, buildings, facilities,) increase capital intensity for hospitality firms. High level of capital intensity is associated with high business risk and financial inflexibility due to limited alternate use and lower salvage value of facilities and equipment specific to the hospitality industry (Reich, 1994). Operating inventories refer to the items that must be available for the hotel to operate, or to offer the desired level of service (Barlow, 1997). Examples for operating inventory include food, beverage and guest supplies. Due to the nature of the products and services offered within the hospitality industry, operating inventories for hospitality firms are relatively low level compared to the manufacturing firms.

Third, "there are unique pressures on hospitality managers because of the high ratio of short- to long-run decisions" (Reich, 1994, p. 341). Reich's argument is related to capital intensity in that during short-run, production output in the hospitality industry can only be modified by changing variable inputs, such payroll and related expenses, and cost of sales as facilities and FFE cannot be easily altered. On the contrary, both fixed and variable inputs can be modified in the long run to increase production output.

Fourth, hospitality businesses are very sensitive to the changes in the economy and reliant on discretionary spending of their customers. Therefore, shareholders of hospitality businesses might demand increased power to monitor the management's activities. An alternative argument can be attributed to the dynamic and highly competitive environment that hospitality businesses operate in. As fast decision-making would be needed in this type of environment and management has the best insight and knowledge into the situation (Huse, 2007), authority and control could be transferred to management by the owners.

In the context of this study, the term "hospitality industry" refers to hotel, restaurant and casino firms. In line with Guillen's (2008) argument, even within the hospitality industry, hotels, restaurants and casinos are different enough that their governance practices may differ. Jones (1999, p. 432) explains the different characteristics of hotel and restaurant sector in terms of supply chain and cost structure: "Accommodation provision is largely an assembly operation (servicing of rooms) with most materials processing (laundering linen, etc.) being carried out by a supplier. Foodservice on the other hand can range from being largely an assembly operation (with meal items being largely prepared on site) to a full-blown production facility in which meals are processed from raw ingredients. There is also a significant difference in the relative cost structures of these two sectors with respect to such processed consumables-low in the accommodation sector (less than 10%), high in the foodservice sector (25–40%)". Of course, many hotels have restaurant outlets within their premises. Casino firms encompass hotel and restaurant components in addition to casino business and retail outlets. There are also differences among cash compensation of casino and hotel executives. A compensation survey conducted by Hospitality Valuation Services (HVS) International found that cash compensation of casino executives was nearly double compared to that of hotel executives with properties over six hundred rooms (Kefgen, 2004). The difference was attributed to the bigger size of casinos and the variety of businesses (casino, hotel, restaurant, retail) present within a casino.

Reich (1994) compares hotel, restaurant and manufacturing firms in terms of labor and capital intensity. He argues that both hotel and restaurant firms are considered to be highly labor intensive compared to manufacturing firms. He further states that restaurants are in general less capital intensive than hotel and manufacturing firms. Being highly capital and labor intensive at the same time, hotels are comparably very restricted in terms of finding turnaround options during an economic downturn. Turnaround options for manufacturing and restaurant firms are not as limited as hotels. For example, manufacturing firms can increase productivity through automation or change their product when they face with problems. Restaurant firms are also more flexible than hotels as they can change their concept or theme.

There are also observable differences in capital structures among hotel, restaurant and casino firms that can lead to differences in corporate governance provisions. Andrew et al. (2006) showed that for 1966–2002 period average leverage levels for hotel firms ranged between 49% and 65% while the range was between 44% and 54% for the restaurant firms. Tsai and Gu (2007) found that average leverage level for casino firms was 53% for 1999–2003 period. Corporate governance literature (Cremers and Nair, 2005; Novaes and Zingales, 1995; Stulz, 1988; Zwiebel, 1996) suggests that the governance mechanisms should be stronger for companies with low leverage and weaker for the firms with high leverage. They suggest that higher leverage reduces the probability of takeover even though these firms do not have many provisions to set back hostile bidders. In addition, high leverage encourages executives to perform better. Using the evidence provided by mainstream finance research as a guideline, given hotels and casinos tend to have higher leverage than restaurants, we can expect hotel and casino firms to have a higher level of managerial power, or in other words weaker shareholder rights in comparison to restaurant firms. For all of these reasons pointed out in this section, we feel that hospitality firms differ from other types of firms in their corporate governance structure, and that is why this study is conducted to explore corporate governance in hospitality companies.

4. Data and Methodology

The data for this study were collected from three resources: Standard and Poor's Compustat database, the Center for Research in Security Prices (CRSP), and RiskMetrics. The variables related to corporate governance were retrieved from RiskMetrics' database. At the time of data collection, RiskMetrics' database provided 8 years of data: 1990, 1993, 1995, 1998, 2000, 2002, 2004 and 2006. The sample period used in this study also corresponds with these 8 years. The balance sheet and income statement data were collected through Compustat, while stock price related data were retrieved from CRSP. The corporate governance dataset includes 211 observations of hospitality companies; 46, 126 and 39 represent the number of observations for hotels, restaurants and casinos, respectively. After the corporate governance data for hotels, restaurants and casinos were matched with the Compustat and

CRSP databases, the total number of observations varied between 145 and 179 depending on the variable retrieved. The hotel, restaurant and casino companies included in the study are presented in Appendix A.

RiskMetrics Group collects data on 28 unique corporate governance provisions from various resources including corporate bylaws and charters, proxy statements, annual reports, 10-K and 10-Q documents (Wharton Data Research Services, 2009). These provisions are divided into five categories (Gompers et al., 2003): (1) delay, (2) voting, (3) protection, (4) other, and (5) state. The delay category refers to four corporate provisions devised to set back hostile bidders. The voting category includes six provisions related to shareholders' voting rights in elections and/or charter/bylaw amendments. The protection category is composed of six corporate provisions that help executive management to be protected against job-related liability or provide compensation to the executive management in the event of a termination. The other category refers to six provisions that cannot be categorized in delay, voting and protection categories. The state category includes six state laws, some of which are similar to firm-level provisions included in other categories. Appendices B–F provide explanations of each provision under the five corporate governance categories. Gompers et al. (2003) developed a governance index ("G") with a possible range of 1–24 from 28 corporate governance provisions by adding one point for every provision that reduces shareholder rights and enhances managerial power. As an exception, authors added one point to the index if the firm is covered under the firm-level provision, the state law, or both. Consequently, the G index has a maximum value of 24 instead of 28.

The first part of the data analysis involves testing for differences in the G index and its five sub-categories for hotel, restaurant and casino firms. The second part of the analysis examines the relationship between the G index and firm performance by dividing the dataset into two groups as a proxy for the balance of power between shareholder and executives. This procedure is similar to Gompers et al.'s (2003) study which includes more than 5000 firms for a period of 4 years. G index value of 9 is used as cutoff value since both mean and median value of G index used in Gompers et al.'s (2003) study is 9. Firms with the G index value of less than 9 are placed in "firms with stronger shareholder rights", or in other words "firms with lower managerial power" portfolio. Firms with the G index value of more than 10 are placed in "firms with weaker shareholder rights", or in other words "firms with higher managerial power" portfolio.

The firm-related measures included in the study are market value, return on assets, return on equity, profit margin, capital expenditure per assets, Tobin's Q, and leverage. These measures have been used extensively in the hospitality and finance literature as performance related and control measures (Brigham and Daves, 2007; Kaplan and Zingales, 1997; Tsai and Gu, 2007,

Tobin, 1969). Return on assets, return on equity, profit margin and Tobin's Q represent firm performance measures while market value, capital expenditure per assets and leverage are control measures that might have an influence on corporate governance.

Firm-related measures are defined as follows:

$ROA_{i,t}$ = Return on assets for firm i at time t, calculated by dividing net earnings by book value of total assets.

$ROE_{i,t}$ = Return on equity for firm i at time t, calculated by dividing net earnings by book value of total common equity.

$PM_{i,t}$ = Profit margin for firm i at time t, calculated by dividing net earnings by total revenues.

Tobin's Qi,t = Proxy measure for Tobin's Q for firm i at time t is the book value of total assets, market value of common equity minus the sum of book value of common equity and deferred taxes, all divided by the book value of total assets.

$MV_{i,t}$ = Market value for firm i at time t, pre-calculated in Compustat database.

$CAPEX_{i,t}$ = Capital expenditure for firm i at time t, scaled by book value of total assets.

$LEV_{i,t}$ = Leverage for firm i at time t, calculated by dividing the book value of total liabilities by the book value of total assets.

5. Findings

5.1. Summary of Governance Index and Its Five Sub-components

Table 1 presents the descriptive statistics for the G index and its five sub-components, of delay, voting, protection, other, and state, by firm type. For the sample period, the mean G index value is the highest for hotel firms, followed by casino and restaurant firms respectively. As a reference, Gompers et al. (2003) named the portfolio of companies with G index value of less than 5 as a "democracy portfolio" and more than 14 as a "dictatorship portfolio". As shown in Table 1, hotel, restaurant and casino firms span the entire democracy–dictatorship continuum.

Hotel firms had the highest number of average delay provisions. The mean value of this provision for hotels is significantly different from restaurant and casino firms at 0.05 significance level.

Conversely, the mean values for protection and voting provisions are very similar across firm types. Both hotel and restaurant firms have significantly higher value for the "other" category of provisions compared

Table 1: Governance index and its five sub-components.

	Mean	Max	Min	H – R	H – C	R – C
G index						
Hotel	9.98	15	4			
Restaurant	8.90	14	4			
Casino	9.26	14	3			
Delay				*	*	
Hotel	3.17	4	0			
Restaurant	2.18	4	0			
Casino	2.49	4	0			
Protection						
Hotel	3.79	6	0			
Restaurant	3.62	6	2			
Casino	3.67	6	2			
Voting						
Hotel	0.52	3	0			
Restaurant	0.59	4	0			
Casino	0.64	3	0			
Other					*	*
Hotel	1.20	2	0			
Restaurant	1.05	3	0			
Casino	0.62	2	0			
State				*	*	
Hotel	1.09	3	0			
Restaurant	1.65	4	0			
Casino	2.03	4	1			

H – R represents mean difference between hotel and restaurant firms. H – C represents mean difference between hotel and casino firms. R – C represents mean difference between restaurant and casino firms.
*Represents significance levels of 0.05.

to casino firms. State provisions are the highest for restaurant firms followed by restaurant and hotel firms respectively. The difference in state provisions between hotels and restaurant and casino firms is significant.

5.2. Main Findings

The comparison of firm characteristics between hospitality firms with stronger shareholder rights and hospitality firms with weaker shareholder rights is presented in Table 2. The selected measures to represent the firm characteristics are market value, return on assets, return on equity, profit margin, capital expenditure per assets, Tobin's Q, and leverage. These t-test results between hospitality firms with stronger shareholder rights and hospitality firms with weaker shareholder rights are descriptive, but they provide some useful insight. Overall, it appears that firms with weaker shareholder rights tend be relatively larger in size (market value used as a proxy) with higher return on equity and leverage ratios, and lower capital expenditure per assets. There are no statistically significant differences observed for return on assets, profit margin, and Tobin's Q among the two groups of hospitality firms.

Table 2: The comparison of firm performance between hospitality firms with stronger shareholder rights and hospitality firms with weaker shareholder rights

	Mean		Sig. dif.
	FWSSR	FWWSR	
ROA	6.99	5.99	
Hotel	4.90	5.55	
Restaurant	8.28	7.65	
Casino	1.21	3.21	
ROE	5.97	14.50	*
Hotel	4.90	10.21	*
Restaurant	12.46	16.79	
Casino	3.63	6.89	
PM	5.63	7.27	
Hotel	4.45	8.31	
Restaurant	5.97	7.35	
Casino	4.56	5.84	
Tobin's Q	0.94	0.46	
Hotel	0.65	0.51	
Restaurant	0.51	0.46	
Casino	0.59	0.39	
MV	2,160.49	7,675.98	*
Hotel	1,349.67	7,177.88	*
Restaurant	1,903.29	9,986.33	*
Casino	3,958.72	4,269.10	
CAPEX	0.14	0.10	*
Hotel	0.11	0.06	
Restaurant	0.15	0.11	*
Casino	0.09	0.11	
LEV	47.14	58.06	*
Hotel	68.98	66.43	
Restaurant	40.92	46.57	
Casino	66.29	70.83	

FWSSR represents firms with stronger shareholder rights. FWWSR represents firms with weaker shareholder rights.
* Represents significant mean differences between firms with strong shareholder rights and firms with weaker shareholder rights at significance levels of 0.05.

In addition to the overall hospitality sample, Table 2 also gives summary statistics for the three industry segments. The t-test statistics indicate significant differences in size and return on equity between hotel firms with stronger shareholder rights and hotel firms with weaker shareholder rights. For restaurant firms, statistically significant differences between the two groups were found for size and capital expenditure per assets. Conversely, no statistically significant differences were observed for casinos across stronger and weaker shareholder rights.

An analysis of variance (ANOVA) with a post hoc Bonferroni test was conducted to examine whether there were any significant differences in firm-related variables among hotel, restaurant and casino firms with stronger shareholder rights and those with weaker shareholder rights. Statistically significant differences at $p < 0.05$ level exist among hospitality firms with stronger shareholder rights in return on assets, return on equity, capital expenditure per assets and firm size. The Bonferroni test revealed that restaurants have a significantly higher ROA and capital expenditure per assets than casinos and higher ROE than hotels. In addition, restaurant firms with stronger shareholder rights have significantly lower leverage ratios than hotels and casinos. There were statistically significant differences in ROA, capital expenditure per assets and leverage among hotel, restaurant and casino firms with weaker shareholder rights. Similar to restaurant firms with stronger shareholder rights, restaurants with weaker shareholder rights had a significantly higher ROA than casinos. The results from the Bonferroni test also indicated that hotels in this category have significantly lower capital expenditure per assets and significantly higher leverage ratios than restaurant and casino firms.

Fig. 1 shows the mean G index value for hotel, restaurant and casino firms throughout the sample period. The sample period includes 8 years, namely 1990, 1993, 1995, 1998, 2000, 2002, 2004 and 2006. The G index value is relatively stable at the industry level all through the observation period. With the exception of 1995, hotel firms have relatively high governance index values, followed by restaurant and casino firms, respectively. As firms with G index value of 10 and higher are defined as firms with weaker shareholder rights, it is interesting to note that hotel firms fall into this category more than restaurant and casino firms. During the sample period, there were some observable fluctuations in the governance index values of hotel and

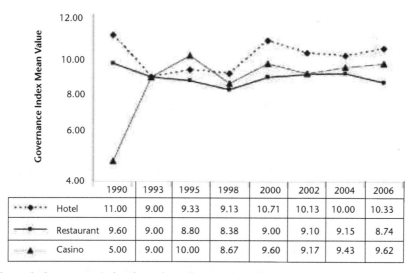

Figure 1: Governance index throughout the sample period

casino firms. Interestingly, the *G* index values of restaurant firms remain relatively stable over the years.

6. Discussions and Conclusion

The purpose of this exploratory study was to examine the degree of corporate governance in the hospitality industry and its three sub-sectors, hotels, restaurants and casinos. Corporate governance is a highly researched topic in mainstream financial management, yet research in this area in the hospitality literature is scant. To fill that gap, the results of this study contribute to our understanding of the relationship between governance and firm characteristics in the context of the hospitality industry. The study utilized the governance index and its five components to evaluate the degree of corporate governance in hospitality organizations over eight observation periods between 1990 and 2006.

Overall, the study findings indicate that the governance index for hospitality firms is relatively high, ranging from 8.90 to 9.98, thus indicating relatively weak shareholder rights. One possible explanation for this finding is the relatively high protection of hospitality executives from hostile takeovers and strong limitations on shareholders' ability to replace managers. Gompers et al. (2003) include firms with *G* index value of 5 or less in democracy portfolio and define them as firms with the strongest shareholder rights. Each provision in the *G* index (worth one point) represents restrictions in shareholder rights and therefore as the *G* index value increases, managerial power increases and shareholder rights decrease. Prior research shows that companies tend to use various governance mechanisms simultaneously to take advantage of their differential impacts (Bradach, 1997; Weitz and Jap, 1995; Brown et al., 2000). In terms of the sub-dimensions of the *G* index, hotel firms had significantly higher means for delay, protection and other category provisions. Delay provisions are related to tactics for delaying hostile bidders while protection provisions refer to executive protection. Other provisions include additional takeover defenses. Casino firms ranked highest for the voting and state sub-categories. Voting provisions are related to shareholders' rights in elections and state provisions refer to state takeover laws.

Further examining the firm characteristics, we found that firms with high corporate governance index value ($G \geq 10$) are larger firms with higher earnings per share, closing stock price, earnings per share, and return on equity, and lower capital expenditure per assets. This implies that hospitality firms with weaker shareholder rights tend to perform better compared to hospitality firms with stronger shareholder rights. In addition, larger size may play a role in decreasing the chances of being taken over, as the bidders need to secure more resources to acquire a larger firm (Cremers and Nair,

2005). Moreover, it is interesting to note that hospitality firms with weaker shareholder rights ($G \geq 10$) have significantly higher leverage ratios in comparison to those firms with stronger shareholder rights. One plausible explanation for this finding is management's eagerness to increase the debt levels in the firm's capital structure to take advantage of the interest tax shield and to show higher return on equity to the shareholders (Andrew et al., 2006). This explanation is supported by ROA and ROE ratios presented in Table 2. ROE is significantly higher for firms with weaker shareholder rights due to the effect of leverage. However, there are no significant differences in ROA between firms with weaker and stronger shareholder rights. Given that total assets equal to total liabilities and shareholders' equity and both ratios use net income as the numerator, ROE is higher than ROA for firms with higher leverage which are also the firms with weaker shareholder rights. In other words, as leverage increases, book value of equity falls. Although higher leverage can be useful to increase return on equity and to take advantage of interest tax shield, it also makes the company risky. Another alternative interpretation of this finding is related to the positive relationship between leverage and corporate governance (Jandik and Makhija, 2005). When the leverage increases, it is suggested that the managers will commit themselves to making improvements to create value due to the additional debt burden (Safieddine and Titman, 1999). Additionally, a higher leverage reduces the probability of takeover even though these firms have weaker shareholder rights.

In this study, capital expenditure per assets is included as a proxy for assessing the relationship of increased agency cost at firms with stronger shareholder rights and firm performance. Previous research suggests that production efficiency might decline for firms with takeover defenses and for firms covered by state takeover laws, which can be captured with a total factor productivity measure (Borokhovich et al., 1997; Bertrand and Mullainathan, 2000; Garvey and Hanka, 1999; Gompers et al., 2003). Our findings indicate that hospitality firms with higher G index value have higher levels of capital expenditure per assets. This finding is consistent with Gompers et al. (2003) in that capital expenditure increases subsequent to the adoption of new takeover defense mechanisms.

Today, shareholders are increasingly more aware of corporate governance issues. Shareholders of hotel, restaurant and casino firms and their financial advisers can use the findings of this study to better understand corporate governance provisions and their relationship to firm characteristics. Alternatively, hospitality practitioners and executives can compare their corporate governance measures with industry averages provided in this study. Such an exercise might help them to adjust their corporate governance policies. The literature on corporate governance is vast, but the message in the information is far from clear or complete for the hospitality industry. This study sheds some light on this area, but much more work remains to be done. For example, future studies can further examine the five sub-components of the *G* index. Each sub-component has important implications for the governance of the firm.

7. Limitations of the Study

There were some limitations with respect to the analysis and data that should be addressed. The hospitality companies included in the study are limited to the firms included in RiskMetrics Group database. Moreover, the sample period is limited to 8 years included in the same database. Due to data accessibility related issues, more traditionally used corporate governance mechanisms such as executive compensation, ownership concentration, and size, structure and composition of the board of directors were not included in study. In this respect, this study presents a partial perspective on corporate governance and focuses more on the power sharing relationship between shareholders and management. The findings of the study are descriptive in nature and do not indicate causality (Lehn et al., 2007) and hence should be interpreted with caution. Future research should investigate the main empirical relationships between governance and corporate performance for hotel, restaurant and casino firms using a regression approach. Regression analysis for all sub-sectors of the hospitality industry was not conducted in this study as data points did not permit for a time-series model. A richer understanding of the relationship between corporate governance and firm performance is a timely topic given the push for accountability and transparency in today's economic environment.

Appendix A

Sample of firms

Industry	Companies
Casino	Capstar Hotel Co.
	Ameristar Casino Inc.
	Boyd Gaming Corp.
	Circus Circus Enterprises Inc.
	Gaylord Entertainment
	Grand Casinos Inc.
	Harrah's Entertainment Inc.
	MGM Grand Inc.
	Mandalay Resort Group
	MGM Mirage
	Mirage Resorts Inc.
	Pinnacle Entertainment Inc.
	Station Casinos Inc.

Industry	Companies
Hotel	Cendant Corp. Choice Hotels International Inc. Extended Stay America Inc. Hilton Hotels Corp. La Quinta Corp. Marriott International Inc. Prime Hospitality Corp. Promus Hotel Corp. Starwood Hotels & Resorts Inc. Wyndham International Inc.
Restaurant	Applebee's International Inc. Brinker International Inc. CBRL Group Inc. Cheesecake Factory Inc. Cracker Barrel Old Country Store & Restaurant Darden Restaurant Inc. IHOP Corp. Landry's Restaurant Inc. Lone Star Steakhouse & Saloon Inc. Luby's Inc. McDonald's Corp. Morrison Restaurant Inc. Panera Bread Co. Papa John's International Inc. Rare Hospitality International Inc. Ruby Tuesday Inc. Ryan's Restaurant Group Inc. Sbarro Inc. Shoney's Inc. Showbiz Pizza Time Inc. Sizzler Restaurant International Inc. Sonic Corp. Starbucks Corp. Steak & Shake Co. Vicorp Restaurant Inc. Wendy's International Inc.

Appendix B

Corporate governance provisions: delay

Blank check	Preferred stock over which the board of directors has broad authority to determine voting, dividend, conversion, and other rights
Classified board	The directors are placed into different classes and serve overlapping terms so that an outsider who gains control of a corporation may have to wait a few years before being able to gain control of the board
Special meeting	Limitations to shareholders' ability to call a special meeting beyond that specified by state law
Written consent	The establishment of majority thresholds beyond the level of state law, the requirement of unanimous consent, or the elimination of the right to take action by written consent

Adapted from Gompers et al. (2003, pp. 145–150).

Appendix C

Corporate governance provisions: protection

Compensation plans	Provisions that allow management to cash out options or accelerate the payout of bonuses if there is a change in control
Contracts	Contracts between the company and executives indemni-fying the management from certain legal expenses and judg-ments resulting from lawsuits pertaining to their conduct
Golden parachutes	Cash and non-cash benefits (such as stock options) given to executives without shareholder approval in the event of a termination, resignation and demotion
Indemnification	This provision uses the bylaws, charter, or both to indemnify executives from legal expenses and judgments resulting from lawsuits pertaining related their conduct.
Liability	Charter amendments that limit executives' personal liability to the extent allowed by state law
Severance	Agreements that assure high-level executives of their positions or some compensation and are not contingent upon a change in control (unlike golden or silver parachutes)

Adapted from Gompers et al. (2003, pp. 145–150).

Appendix D

Corporate governance provisions: voting

Bylaws and charter amendment limitations	Limitations to shareholders' ability to amend the governing documents of the corporation
Cumulative voting[a]	This provision allows a shareholder to allocate his total votes (which are the product of the number of shares owned) in any manner desired
Secret ballot[a]	A voting method in which voters' choices are confidential and management usually agrees not to look at proxy cards
Supermajority	Charter provisions that establish voting requirements for mergers that are higher than the threshold requirements of state law, for example 66.7%, 75%, or 85%.
Unequal voting rights	Limit the voting rights of some shareholders and expand those of others

Adapted from Gompers et al. (2003, pp. 145–150).
[a] Cumulative voting and secret ballot are the only two provisions whose presence represents as an increase in shareholder rights, with an additional point to the governance index if the provision is absent.

Appendix E

Corporate governance provisions: other

Antigreenmail	Greenmail refers to a situation in which a large block of stock is being held by a shareholder. This forces the company to buy back its own stock at a premium. Antigreen-mail provisions prevent such arrangements unless the same repurchase offer is made to all shareholders or approved by a shareholder vote
Directors' duties	These provisions provide boards of directors with a legal basis to reject a takeover that would be to the benefit of shareholders
Fair price	Provisions that require a bidder to pay to all shareholders the highest price paid to any during a specified period of time before the commencement of a tender offer, and do not apply if the deal is approved by the board of directors or a supermajority of the target's shareholders. The goal of this provision is to make the acquisition more expensive to the bidder
Pension parachutes	These provisions prevent an acquirer from using surplus cash in the pension fund of the target to finance an acquisition

Poison pill	Provisions that allow a company any type of defensive maneuver such as stock issues, special distributions, spin-offs and management pay-outs in the event of a hostile takeover bid
Silver parachutes	These provisions are similar to golden parachutes, but differ in that a large number of a firm's employees are eligible for these benefits. Silver Parachutes do not protect the key decision makers in a merger

Adapted from Gompers et al. (2003, pp. 145–150).

Appendix F

Corporate governance provisions: state

Antigreenmail law	Five states have specific antigreenmail laws, and two other states have "recapture of profits" laws, which enable firms to recapture raiders' profits earned in the secondary market
Business combination law	These laws impose a moratorium on asset sales, mergers between a large shareholder and the firm, unless the transaction is approved by the board of directors
Cash-out law	These laws enable shareholders to sell their stakes to a "controlling" shareholder at a price based on the highest price of recently acquired shares
Directors' duties law	31 states have directors' duties laws allowing similar expansions of constituencies, but in Indiana and Pennsylvania the laws are explicit that the claims of shareholders should not be held above those of other stakeholders (Pinnell, 2000)
Fair price law	25 states had fair price laws in place in 1990, and two more states passed such laws in 1991. The laws work similarly to the firm-level provisions
Control share acquisition law	These laws require a majority of disinterested shareholders to vote on whether a newly qualifying large shareholder has voting rights. They were in place in 25 states by September 1990 and one additional state in 1991

Adapted from Gompers et al. (2003, pp. 145–150).

References

Andrew, W.P., Damiatio, J.W., Schmidgall, R.S., 2006. Financial Management for the Hospitality Industry. Pearson Education Inc., New Jersey, NJ.

Barber, N., Ghiselli, R., Deale, C., 2006. Assessing the relationship of CEO compensation and company financial performance in the restaurant segment of the industry. Journal of Food Service Business Research 9 (4), 65–82.

Barlow, G.L., 1997. Inventory: asset or liability? International Journal of Hospitality Management 16 (1), 11–22.

Baysinger, B.D., Butler, H.N., 1985. Corporate governance and the board of directors: performance effects of changes in board composition. Journal of Law, Economics, and Organization 1, 101–124.

Beals, P., 1995. The hotel management contract: lessons from the North American experience. In: Harris, P. (Ed.), Accounting and Finance for the International Hospitality Industry. Butterworth-Heinemann, London, pp. 278–294.

Bebchuk, L.A., Cohen, A., Ferrell, A., 2009. What matters in corporate governance? Review of Financial Studies 22 (2), 783–827.

Bertrand, M., Mullainathan, S., 2000. Enjoying the quiet life? Managerial behavior following anti-takeover legislation. Working Paper, Department of Economics, Massachusetts Institute of Technology. Retrieved on April 18, 2009 from http://law.usc.edu/academics/centers/cleo/assets/docs/mullainathan.pdf.

Bhagat, S., Black, B.S., 1998. The relationship between board composition and firm performance. In: Hopt, K., Roe, M., Wymeersch, E. (Eds.), Comparative Corporate

Governance: The State of the Art and Emerging Research. Clarendon Press/Oxford University Press, Oxford, UK/New York, NY.
Bradach, J.L., 1997. Using the plural form in the management of restaurant chains. Administrative Science Quarterly 42 (June), 276–303.
Brigham, E.F., Daves, P.R., 2007. Intermediate Financial Management, 9th ed. The Dryden Press, New York.
Borokhovich, K.A., Brunarski, K.R., Parrino, R., 1997. CEO contracting and antitakeover amendments. Journal of Finance 52, 1495–1518.
Brown, L.D., Caylor, M.L., 2006. Corporate governance and firm valuation. Journal of Accounting and Public Policy 25, 409–434.
Brown, J., Dev, C., Lee, D., 2000. Managing marketing channel opportunism: the efficacy of alternative governance mechanisms. Journal of Marketing 64 (2), 51–65.
Buqbil, I., 2007. Shareholders getting tough on hotel services industry corporate governance. Knight Ridder Tribune Business News, 1. Retrieved April 13, 2009, from ABI/INFORM Dateline database.
Calculation of Number of Controlling Shareholders, 2002. Administrative Rules Adopted by Bureau of Licenses Pursuant to Rule-Making Authority. Retrieved April 13, 2009 from http://www.portlandonline.com/auditor/index.cfm?print=1&c=27446&a=8862.
Coates, J., 2000. Takeover defenses in the shadow of the pill: a critique of the scientific evidence. Texas Law Review 79, 271–382.
Core, J.E., Holthausen, R.W., Larcker, D.F., 1999. Corporate governance, chief executive officer compensation, and firm performance. Journal of Financial Economics 51, 371–406.
Cremers, M., Nair, V., 2005. Governance mechanisms and equity prices. Journal of Finance 60, 2859–2894.
Dahlstrom, R., Haugland, S.A., Nygaard, A., Rokkan, A.I., 2009. Governance structures in the hospitality industry. Journal of Business Research 62, 841–847.
DeFranco, A.L., Lattin, T.W., 2006. Hospitality Financial Management. John Wiley & Sons, Inc., New York.
Eyster, J.J., 1988. The Negotiation and Administration of Hotel and Restaurant Management Contracts, 3rd edition. School of Hotel Administration, Cornell University, Ithaca.
Garvey, G.T., Hanka, G., 1999. Capital structure and corporate control: the effect of antitakeover statutes on firm leverage. Journal of Finance 54, 519–546.
Gompers, P.A., Ishii, J.L., Metrick, A., 2003. Corporate governance and equity prices. Quarterly Journal of Economics 118, 107–155.
Gu, Z., Choi, Y.H., 2004. CEO compensation in the casino industry. Journal of Hospitality and Tourism Research 28 (2), 143–155.
Guillen, M.F., 2000. Corporate governance and globalization. Is there convergence across countries? In: Cheng, J.L.C., Peterson, R.B. (Eds.), Advances in International Comparative Management, 13. JAI Press, Stamford, CT, pp. 175–204.
Guilding, C., 2003. Hotel owner/operator structures: implications for capital budgeting process. Management Accounting Research 14, 179–199.
Guilding, C., Kennedy, D., McManus, L., 2001. Extending the boundaries of customer accounting: applications in the hotel industry. Journal of Hospitality & Tourism Research 25 (2), 173–194.
Hermalin, B., Weisbach, M., 1991. The effects of board composition and direct incentives on firm performance. Financial Management 20, 101–112.
Huse, M., 2007. Boards, Governance and Value Creation: The Human Side of Corporate Governance. Cambridge University Press, Cambridge.
Jandik, T., Makhija, A.K., 2005. Debt, debt structure and corporate performance after unsuccessful takeovers: evidence from targets that remain independent. Journal of Corporate Finance 11 (5), 882–914.

Jensen, M.C, Meckling, W.H., 1976. Theory of the firm: managerial behavior, agency costs and ownership structure. Journal of Financial Economics 3, 305–360.

Jensen, M.C., 1986. Agency costs of free cash flow, corporate finance, and takeovers. American Economic Review 76, 323–329.

Jones, P., 1999. Operational issues and trends in the hospitality industry. International Journal of Hospitality Management 18, 427–442.

Kaplan, S.N., Zingales, L., 1997. Do investment-cash flow sensitivities provide useful measures of financing constraints? Quarterly Journal of Economics 112 (1), 169–215.

Keasey, K., Wright, M., 1993. Issues in corporate accountability and governance. Accounting and Business Research 91, 291–303.

Kefgen, K., May, 27, 2004. Casino executives still out-earn hotel colleagues as gap widens further. Retrieved September 4, 2009 from http://www.hvs.com/staticcontent/library/2004-0525-000.aspx.

Kim, H., Gu, Z., 2005. A preliminary examination of determinants of CEO cash compensation in the U.S. restaurant industry from an agency theory perspective. Journal of Hospitality and Tourism Research 29 (3), 341–355.

La Porta, R., Lopez-de-Silanes, F., Shleifer, A., Vishny, R.W., 2000. Investor protection and corporate governance. Journal of Financial Economics 58 (1–2), 3–27.

Lehn, K., Patro, S., Zhao, M., 2007. Governance indices and valuation: which causes which? Journal of Corporate Finance 13, 907–928.

Madanoglu, M., Karadag, E., 2008. Firm performance and CEO compensation: reflections from the U.S. restaurant industry. In: 2008 EABR&TLC Conference Proceedings, Rothenburg, Germany.

Morck, R., Shleifer, A., Vishny, R.W., 1988. Management ownership and market valuation: an empirical analysis. Journal of Financial Economics 20, 293–315.

Novaes, W., Zingales, L., 1995. Capital structure choice when managers are in control: entrenchment versus efficiency. NBER Working Paper 5384.

N.N., 2008. Cheesecake factory heeds critics, OKs board reforms. Nation's Restaurant News, 42(18), 140. Retrieved April 14, 2009, from ABI/INFORM Global database.

Overview of IRRC Governance Database in WRDS. Retrieved on April 9, 2009, from http://wrds.wharton.upenn.edu/support/docs/riskmetrics/riskmetrics_gset_overview.shtml.

Pinnell, Maria Carmen S., 2000. State Takeover Laws. Investor Responsibility Research Center Inc., Washington, DC.

Reich, A.Z., 1994. Applied economics of hospitality production: reducing costs and improving the quality of decisions through economic analysis. International Journal of Hospitality Management 12 (4), 337–352.

Romano, R., 2005. The Sarbanes–Oxley Act and the making of quack corporate governance. Yale Law Journal 114 (7), 1521–1611.

Safieddine, A., Titman, S., 1999. Leverage and corporate performance: evidence from unsuccessful takeovers. Journal of Finance 54 (2), 547–580.

Shleifer, A., Vishny, R.W., 1997. A survey of corporate governance. Journal of Finance 52, 737–783.

Stulz, R.M., 1988. Managerial control of voting rights: financing policies and the market for corporate control. Journal of Financial Economics 20, 25–54.

Tobin, J., 1969. A general equilibrium approach to monetary theory. Journal of Money, Credit, and Banking 1, 15–29.

Tsai, H., Gu, Z., 2007. Institutional ownership and firm performance: Empirical evidence from U.S. based publicly traded restaurant firms. Journal of Hospitality and Tourism Research 31 (1), 19–38.

Weitz, B.A., Jap, S.D., 1995. Relationship marketing and distribution channels. Journal of the Academy of Marketing Science 23 (Fall), 305–320.

Yermack, D., 1996. Higher market valuation for firms with a small board of directors. Journal of Financial Economics 60, 185–211.

Young, B., 2003. Corporate governance and firm performance: is there a relationship? Ivey Business Journal 1–5.

Zwiebel, J., 1996. Dynamic capital structure under managerial entrenchment. The American Economic Review 86, 1197–1215.

33

Going Green: Decisional Factors in Small Hospitality Operations

Nadia A. Tzschentke, David Kirk and Paul A. Lynch

1. Introduction

As a series of widely publicised environmental catastrophes signalled the globalisation of environmental concern, society had entered the last stage of a process that took humans "from fearing, to understanding, to using, to abusing, and now, to worrying about the physical and biological world around them" (Bowman, 1975, p. 94). Over a decade later, the Bruntdland Report (WCED, 1987) crystallised this concern by concluding that environmental protection should be accorded primary status in policy development. The formulation of an action plan for sustainable development followed in 1992 with Agenda 21. In 1996, Agenda 21 for the Travel and Tourism Industry drew attention to the need to develop tourism sustainably. As one of the largest industries and one that is reliant on the quality of the environment to ensure its survival, tourism plays a major role in environmental preservation. One of its integral components is the accommodation sector, which mainly consists of small, independent operations. Whilst their individual detrimental impact on the environment is limited, their collective one is significant. Yet, acknowledgement of this fact by the industry has only partially resulted in positive action. Within a Scottish context, noteworthy has been the work of the Tourism & Environment Forum, a private/public partnership aimed at encouraging sustainability in tourism, which resulted in the launch

Source: *International Journal of Hospitality Management,* 27(1) (2008): 126–133.

Table 1: Practices implemented by respondent businesses

Recycling glass, paper, cardboard, plastic, aluminium, cooking oil
Composting food and garden waste
Reusing leftover soaps/toiletries for personal or staff use, or use in public washrooms; reusing foil, paper, envelopes, menus
Using natural cleaning alternatives (e.g. lemon juice, vinegar, salt)
Fitting energy saving devices (e.g. dimmer/time switches, sensors, energy efficient lightbulbs); using energy efficient appliances
Supplying guests with small kettles, TV remote controls with rechargeable batteries
Monitoring consumption
Improving insulation
Installing water saving devices (e.g. flow regulators, waterless urinals)
Using economy wash cycle; towel/linen policy
Providing information on public transport, walks and cycle routes
Environmental policy; communicating policy to customers
Involving guests in waste segregation
Purchasing ethical and environmentally friendly products
Environmental training
Membership of environmental bodies/charities
Establishing a wildlife area in the garden; putting up bird/bat boxes

of the Green Tourism Business Scheme (GTBS) in 1998. A VisitScotland Quality Assurance Scheme, the GTBS is an environmental accreditation scheme tailored to tourism businesses. Participation is voluntary, with a fee charged depending on size. The number of measures implemented determines the level of award (Bronze, Silver, Gold). Over 500 businesses are now members in the UK (GTBS, 2007).

Limited academic interest has focused on small firms' decision-making and environmental response. Moreover, there has been a prevalence of normative literature, prescribing how decisions 'should' be made and why firms 'should' respond to environmental pressure. If positive action is to be encouraged it is crucial to understand the process by which it occurs and the factors that influence it. By investigating environmentally active firms, this paper offers an empirical understanding of how a sample of businesses actually 'did' go green. In the context of this study, going green refers to the adoption of environmental management practices, intended as practices aimed at minimising the detrimental impact on the environment, in terms of both resource depletion and pollution. See Table 1 for a list of measures implemented by respondent businesses.

2. Decisions and Decision-making Defined

Most simply a decision has been defined as "an act of choice between alternatives" (McGrew and Wilson, 1982, p. 4). A later elaboration viewed it as the point in an ongoing process of evaluating alternatives for meeting an objective at which the decision-maker selects the action most likely to attain that objective (Harrison, 1996, p. 46). It follows that decision-making is a dynamic process that occurs over a period of time and, as many argue, in a particular order. Within a managerial context, it has been defined as the organisation, prioritisation and sorting of information (Simons and Thompson, 1998, p. 7). Hence, its portrayal as a "rational, deliberate and purposeful process" (Tarter and Hoy, 1998, p. 212), though real-life decision-making rarely is logical or sequential. Rather it involves considerable backtracking and repetition. Several are the classifications of decisions found in the literature. Simon (1960) originally distinguished between non-programmed decisions, requiring unique solutions to their unique complexity, and programmed decisions, which are repetitive and routine. Ansoff (1969) later viewed them as a function of the organisational structure and distinguished between strategic, administrative and operating decisions, depending on their long versus short-term implications and the management level at which they are taken. In owner-managed firms this distinction vanishes, as the owner is the central decision-making unit. More recent classifications have kept the distinction between operational decisions, concerning day-to-day management, and strategic decisions, concerning organisational policy and direction (Dearlove, 1998).

Few studies have however considered small firms' perspectives and their distinctive features, namely: the fact that decision-making tends to rest with one or two owners; that direct involvement in the daily running of the business diminishes the need to formally collect information and that small businesses often face financial instability and greater risk exposure (Gore et al., 1992). A strong need for independence combined with lack of expertise often compounds the issue, preventing the adoption of a prescribed approach to growth and development (Ennis, 1999). The ensuing lack of structured, rational and long-term decision-making is reflected in simpler structures and strong evidence of personality-driven firms (Culkin and Smith, 2000). Further, owners' values play a key role, just as personal ethics act as the greatest determinant of ethical behaviour (Quinn, 1997). The strong degree of identification between owners and their business is in fact another characteristic feature of small businesses. This notion is emphasised by Greenbank (2000, p. 408) who recognises small firm decision-making as the product of a complex interaction between the owner-manager's individual, social and economic context. This leads to the argument that intuitive methods may represent the more appropriate and therefore 'rational' form of decision-making in small firms.

2.1. Environmental Concern and Behaviour

A prominent feature in public opinion surveys, environmental concern has been labelled as "an extra, affordable in a time of plenty, but disposable when hard times come" (Taylor, 1997, p. 113). Viewed as a general environmental attitude, concern was initially measured in relation to specific issues and correlated to socio-demographic and personality variables. Van Liere and Dunlap (1981) later disputed the uni-dimensional measurement of concern, with subsequent studies identifying a correlation between cognitive, attitudinal and behavioural variables using a multi-dimensional scale (Schlegelmilch et al., 1996). A gap nevertheless remains between concern and behaviour, as a high degree of environmental consciousness does not necessarily translate into pro-environmental behaviour. Studies aiming to prove the existence of this correlation followed various approaches. Ajzen's Theory of Planned Behaviour (1991) produced reliable estimates, with Hines et al. (1987) identifying, additionally, situational and personality factors, knowledge of issue and action strategies and locus of control. To date, Gustin and Weaver (1996) remains the only successful application of the theory within a hospitality context. Research following Schwartz's (1977) norm-activation theory found that individuals engaging in pro-environmental behaviour exhibited an eco-centric value orientation and a stronger moral obligation to protect the environment (Nordlund and Garvill, 2002). Studies investigating environmental behaviour from a motivational perspective, conversely, mainly evolved from De Young's (1986) and Vining and Ebreo's (1990) research, which established the importance of both intrinsic and extrinsic motivators.

2.2. Hospitality Businesses and the Environment

Interest in the environmental response of hospitality businesses has been scarce (Schaper and Carlsen, 2004) and mainly focused on the corporate sector, despite small concerns representing over 40% of the UK hotel and restaurant industry (DTI, 2005). Low levels of action were first exposed by Stabler and Goodall (1997), while Kirk's (1998) survey of Edinburgh hotels found that action primarily occurred where direct financial gains could be achieved. Similarly, Knowles' et al. (1999) and Donovan and McElligott's (2000) research on, respectively, London and Irish hotels revealed a shallow integration of environmental concerns into business values. Studies investigating small firms painted a similar picture, with action revolving around simple, low-cost measures, many "established priorities that do not necessarily involve owners in active and innovative environmental work" (Hobson and Essex, 2001, p. 141). Further, measures tended to be implemented ad hoc (Dewhurst and Thomas, 2003), rather than within a coherent environmental management strategy, though survey evidence indicates a move towards the formal integration of environmental responsibility, with 22% of the smallest businesses (0–9 employees) having an environmental policy in place (NetRegs, 2005). Small firms' limited awareness of their environmental footprint remains, however, a barrier (Vernon et al., 2003), not only in the UK tourism industry (Mensah, 2006). Moreover, research on European hotels found that inaction reflected a perceived lack of customer demand for environmental improvements, a reminder of the importance of raising both operators' and customers' awareness for action to occur (Bohdanowicz, 2005).

3. Methodology

Positivism has traditionally informed the line of research in a hospitality context (Lynch, 2005), contributing little to an understanding of small firms' environmental attitudes and behaviour. The adoption of an interpretivist stance in this study enabled the exploration of participants' personal worldview, outwith the parameters of predetermined analytical categories. Purposive criterion sampling (Patton, 1990) was used to identify independent, environmentally certified, serviced accommodation businesses. Independent ownership was a selection criterion because an investigation into decisional factors must take place with the decision-maker, i.e. the person responsible for making, not implementing, the decision, as may be the case in chain-owned operations. Explicit indication of environmental action (GTBS accreditation) was also a criterion, since a written environmental policy cannot be taken as the sole indicator of a business' environmental status; equally the lack of one does not imply the absence of involvement. The GTBS was the chosen sampling frame. Unlike other schemes, it counts a large number of smaller sized operations, primarily independent ones. Scotland was the area of study, as this is where the GTBS operated at the time of the research. Information from the GTBS website and the regional VisitScotland accommodation brochures was used to identify the sample. Following a telephone enquiry to confirm ownership status and obtain contact details, a sample of 48 businesses willing to participate was identified out of 96 which met the criteria. A letter detailing the nature of the study and requesting participation was sent to prospective informants. Subsequent to a follow-up telephone call to schedule interviews the sample figure fell to 39. Access and issue saturation determined the size of the final sample, which consisted of thirty lodging operations (see Tables 2 and 3). Geographically, the sample was spread across Scotland, though clusters occurred in the South West and North of the country, broadly matching the GTBS' distribution pattern, where the greatest concentration of members per area is in the Highlands, possibly because the scheme was first piloted there.

    A pilot study was conducted to ensure the validity of the research design. One-to-one, semi-structured interviews with the owner-manager (the decision-maker) were used to collect the data. To supplement the information obtained documentary evidence was also gathered. Interviews were transcribed

Table 2: Sample profile by establishment type

Type of establishment	No. of businesses
Small hotel	11
Guest house	7
Bed and breakfast	6
Hotel	5
Restaurant with rooms	1

Table 3: Sample profile by establishment size

No. of letting rooms	No. of businesses
5 or less	12
Between 6 and 10	10
Between 11 and 15	2
Between 16 and 20	3
Between 21 and 50	3

verbatim. Data were first analysed following Crabtree and Miller's (1992) template approach to coding, whereby a list of codes (template) representing the themes identified is developed, continually refined in the light of emerging data and used to guide the identification and interpretation of themes. Secondary analysis saw the use of cognitive mapping as a means of identifying the decisional factors leading to the adoption of environmental measures. The approach followed was that developed by Eden et al. (1983), based on Kelly's Personal Construct Theory (1955), whereby individuals' perception of an issue (constructs) are uncovered and portrayed in the form of cognitive maps. The software Decision Explorer was used as the analytical tool. The development of cognitive maps from interview transcripts poses an issue of validity; participants were therefore sent a copy of their interview transcript and corresponding map and asked to return it stating their dis/agreement. A 100% agreement rate was obtained out of a 66% response rate.

4. Findings

Firstly, businesses were found to have been environmentally active long before joining the GTBS. This indicated that participation in the GTBS was not a premise for action, but an incentive for further action. Also it meant that a distinction should be made between reasons for joining the scheme, and factors that influenced the adoption of environmental practices, which this paper now examines.

The 'path to greenness' varied as no individual or business is the same. Operators acting on cost grounds saw the introduction of environmental measures as a means of increasing operational efficiency. Operators acting in response to a growing environmental concern, conversely, viewed going green as a mere "evolution" to their way of thinking, thus a natural course of action. Lastly, a minority claimed to have always lived and operated sustainably in line with their environmental ethic. Respondents did not trace the adoption of environmental measures back to a particular point in time or a deciding moment, but identified factors that had influenced the process.

One key influence was the development of an environmental consciousness, to the extent that many directly associated it with their subsequent consideration of environmental practices. When probed, all respondents did in fact declare themselves environmentally concerned, though the extent of that claim varied. Indicatively, half of the sample viewed the environment as a "great concern", while the other simply regarded it as "a concern". Many took this as an opportunity to vent their frustration at the shameful waste of resources. Age was sometimes used to explain such reactions and greater levels of concern, as in this case:

> . . . if you had spoken to me when I was 19 I'd have had visions of Greenpeace and whale fighters!! I think it gradually creeps up on you. Now I even feel guilty for leaving the tap on while brushing my teeth!

Widely acknowledged was the role played by parental education:

> . . . paper! I used to think I was hard done by as a child 'cause I never got clean pieces of paper to draw on, it was always scrap and that had a big influence on me. I was always encouraged not to waste, it was sort of ingrained in me! So, now, I am very careful about resources . . .

Events such as having a family also proved influential. The most concrete example was that of a participant who, once a keen fisherman, had stopped fishing after becoming a father, as he felt unable to justify to his young daughter the act of killing a fish. Education and vocational background were other influences, together with personal experiences. For some, exposure to the values of countries with a more explicit environmental culture had been crucial in awakening a sense of responsibility and desire to contribute, just as the experience of living in less affluent societies had proved enlightening for this respondent:

> . . . I went to Morocco to work. They have nothing in the desert, it's very poor compared to us and yet they had so much, their eyes shone and that's because they treasured what they have. Since I came back I've been trying to live with the minimum I need . . .

Similarly, exposure to local environmental initiatives had raised the awareness of some respondents who now actively participated in green activities. Others simply attributed their concern to their interest and love of nature and country life, or to their vegetarian ethic, as this hotelier explained:

> . . . I am very aware of the environment, I've always been and I am vegetarian. I often wondered how I became one, my parents aren't, but these things came about because of beliefs. From a very early age I've been aware of the environment, I think there is definitely a connection there . . .

In one isolated case, a respondent referred to an eminent figure in the hospitality scene whom he greatly admired, as his source of inspiration. Surprisingly, only a few participants viewed customers as influential, as in this case:

> . . . I get irritated at the way some guests waste our electricity, they go out in the evening all the lights are left on, heating full on, windows open and nobody's there! So wherever we could we've put energy saving devices . . .

In another instance, a Scandinavian guest had insisted her towel did not need to be replaced daily; a request which had bemused the owner but was not acted upon. Media influence, in contrast, was widely acknowledged. Watching a documentary on animal cruelty had induced one respondent to only buy cruelty-free products, while a programme on slavery in coffee and cocoa plantations had prompted instant action in this young hotelier:

> . . . it really got to my conscience, so the next day I phoned the supplier and switched to fair-trade coffee and tea. Now the new menus are coming out with fair-trade information, it's in all the rooms so hopefully the message will spread . . .

Interestingly, when questioned on the perceived worth of their contribution most respondents contended that ". . . you have to think you are making a difference, no matter how small you are . . .", or as this owner argued:

> . . . it's very easy for people to feel totally pressurised and swamped especially on global issues because they feel the whole thing is out of your control, you are a tiny piece and your influence is negligible, so what's the point of making an effort? But no, I think it's like charity boxes, if everybody gave a penny then none of the charities would be short of money. Unfortunately it's hundreds of people out there who never even put one penny out and one or two people who put a fiver . . .

The exception were those who argued that no matter how much an individual contributed, responsibility for action lay with the big players, i.e. the government or the United States. Legislative pressure was rarely acknowledged. Location, on the contrary, was widely regarded as an influence, particularly by rural business owners, as stressed by this participant:

> . . . after all, our guests come here because they enjoy our pristine landscape, it all revolves around it, so it's extremely important to ensure we look after it.

5. The Green Journey

The fact that the adoption of an environmental profile had not been the fruit of a given decision at a particular point in time, nor represented a means to an end, is significant. With the exception of two medium-small hotels where measures had been introduced as part of a strategy to improve the overall performance of the business, action had in all other cases occurred in an evolutionary form under circumstances that, though particular to the individual and the business, shared elements of commonality, in terms of the contextual factors that influenced the process. Going green may thus be conceptualised as a journey, which saw the greening of business practice mirror the greening of the individual, with action originating, predominantly, in the domestic environment and gradually permeating through to business activities. Only where the owners did not live on site, as in the larger establishments, had the business acted as the vehicle for action. The clearer divide between the private and business domain in such cases is the distinctive feature here, and points to the idiosyncrasies of small, owner-managed operations where the family home fulfils a commercial purpose.

The absence of a deciding point explains the apparent lack of deliberation reported by participants and brings into question the relevance of much of the decision-making literature, which is more relevant to a decision made at a single point in time than to a series of events. According to conceptualisations found, strategic decisions are made by top management and influenced by their values; have major resource implications; are characterised by a high degree of risk and uncertainty and are accomplished through a rational thought process (Dearlove, 1998). Using this description, all decisions could technically be strategic, since the owner-manager is the single decision-making unit in the firm. Going green had also been a value-driven process, thereby fitting another criterion, but here is where similarities end. The implementation of measures did not have major resource implications, in that where a large capital outlay was required it matched the needs of the business, for example in terms of refurbishment or expansion. Accordingly, and because it happened gradually, it did not involve a high degree of risk. Lastly, the extent to which it occurred as a result of a rational thought process is debatable. Whilst the decision to use, for example, energy efficient lighting may have occurred following a rational evaluation of pros and cons, greening itself had not been the product of a rational and deliberate thought process, planned at the outset. Instead, it essentially reflected a personal lifestyle choice. The adoption of measures at a business level followed subsequently, their wider implementation often prompted by participation in the scheme, as, according to respondents, certification legitimised practices in the eyes of customers.

Central to the greening process had been the presence of an environmental consciousness, its development in turn influenced by factors that contributed to greening the individual and business practices. This is consistent with the notion that pro-environmental attitudes positively influence environmentally responsible behaviour (Hines et al., 1987). Also, stronger socio-environmental values have been attributed to small firm-owners (Ateljevic and Doorne, 2000). The tracing of action to an existing and/or rising concern is not surprising given the nature of the sample, which consisted of environmentally active businesses that had mostly acted out of their own initiative. Because no attempt was made to measure the extent of these claims in a statistically valid fashion, these reported levels of concern are only indicative, also owing to the potential for biases and over-claiming. Nevertheless, they provide interesting insights. Noteworthy is the apparent association between concern and action levels. Cross tabulation revealed that respondents claiming to be greatly environmentally concerned had also reached higher GTBS award levels (Silver & Gold), contrary to those claiming a slight concern, who mostly held a Bronze award. Though not a measure of concern, the award level is indicative of the level of action undertaken, since the number and range of measures implemented determine the level of accreditation reached. The question rises as to whether action levels represent a true measure of concern. In this respect, the data showed that the greater the concern claimed, the more ethically motivated respondents claimed to be with regards to their grounds for action. Conversely, the lower the level of concern claimed, the more financially oriented the motivation for action (see Fig. 1).

This suggests that though higher levels of concern may be manifested in greater levels of action (e.g. Silver and Gold award), one should steer clear of the assumption that the reverse is true, i.e. that greater levels of action imply higher levels of concern, as the underlying motivation for action (ethics, profit-maximising or both) becomes *the* determining factor. Further research could statistically validate this correlation, contributing to the understanding of environmental behaviour.

Noteworthy is also those influences predominantly related to the individual's personal life; an indication of the need to appreciate the complex set of circumstances surrounding owner-managers' personal sphere to under-

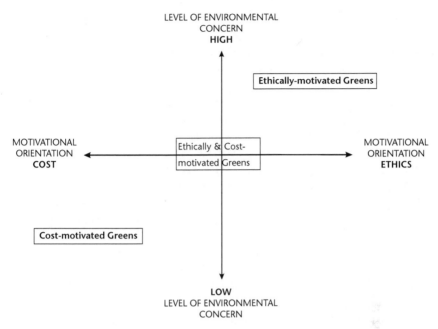

Figure 1: Level of concern and motivational orientation

stand their business behaviour, as echoed by Greenbank (2000) and Dewhurst and Thomas (2003). Formative had been the influence of upbringing, its effects still evident in some "ingrained habits". Many environmentally friendly activities were in fact none other than inherited thriftiness, thus explaining why some respondents took these activities for granted, in some cases not even regarding them as ecological, possibly because of a limited understanding of environment friendly action. Hence, there is scope for awareness-generating initiatives that can capitalise on the level of 'green' action already undertaken, often unknowingly, to recruit new members. Significant too is the fact that some participants attributed their environmental consciousness to their past occupation or vocational interest, despite circumstances being distinct for each respondent. This supports the notion that events are open to as many constructions as there are persons engaged in them (Kelly, 1955). The fact that justifications were a direct function of respondents' personal worldview also explains the diversity of influences, adding difficulty to, but simultaneously strengthening the case for, research into small business decision-making.

Also of interest is that rising levels of concern and engagement were attributed to age. Arguably, with maturity comes an increased sense of responsibility and awareness about the impact of one's actions. These changes are often compounded by value and priority shifts, which may engender greater interest in the environment. Only a few respondents openly acknowledged this influence, possibly because one may be less conscious of gradually occurring changes, or altogether not perceive them. Likewise, the responsibilities of parenthood had contributed to a renewed interest in environmental degradation and prompted behavioural changes. Perhaps less evidently green by some standards was the decision to "forgo fishing". Though not relating to a business situation this episode is indicative of the role personal circumstances play in decision-making. Similarly, the example of the young hotelier, whilst idiosyncratic of the respondent's temperament, further attests to the level of emotionality involved in decision-making where, in practice, rationality often succumbs to spontaneity. This contrasts with rational theory that purports the sequential consideration of alternatives in search of the highest payoff. In this case, switching to ethical products was a potentially risky decision, as public scepticism towards the quality of alternative products is still rife and their costs often higher. This behaviour also testifies to the owner's commitment to his stance, further illustrating the significance of personal values in decision-making. It thereby lends support to theories of decision-making that attribute a central role to intuition and emotion (Mellers et al., 1998).

Limited awareness amongst small business owners of their environmental footprint has consistently been identified as a barrier to change. This is where the study paints a rather encouraging picture, as most respondents seemingly felt strongly about the worth of their contribution, and valued it in the full realisation that its effect would be minimal in global terms. Though not a direct indication of greater awareness, the data goes some way to suggest that participants were conscious of their impact, and had acted upon that knowledge. Being aware and concerned is one thing; believing that one's actions bring positive change is another; one does not imply the other. A possible explanation as to why participants gave no indication of discounting their business' environmental footprint by virtue of its small size may be that they had a strong internal locus of control; in other words, they believed in making a difference. In the absence of a valid measurement of this trait, this remains a tentative suggestion, which further research may help validate. Similarly, it is interesting that only one respondent acknowledged the influence of another business as a driving force toward the adoption of an environmental profile. The spirit of independence that characterises many small business owners who may be unwilling to admit to following the example of other or larger establishments may be an explanation, as may be the absence of such role models. Locational aspects also emerged as influential in terms of fostering a conservation ethic. This was evident particularly amongst "amenity-seeking migrants" (Carlsen et al., 2001, p. 282) who exhibited a stronger inclination to preserve the environment, possibly a reflection of their original motivation to establish the business and ensuing recognition of the importance to preserve its major asset. Sensitivity to locational benefits has been recognised as a characteristic of tourism operators (Thomas, 2004).

Awareness of possible financial gain had also played a role in line with Bohdanowicz's (2005) findings. Recent efforts to promote environmental best practice have resulted in funding initiatives and partnerships agreements between the government and trade associations. Widespread promotion of the financial benefits associated with environmental improvements may thus have borne its fruits. That said, small business owners' awareness of energy efficiency funding schemes and support is limited (NetRegs, 2005). Coverage in the press and trade literature of the impact of environmental taxation may nevertheless have raised awareness, though legislative pressure was rarely acknowledged. Whether this indicates that proactiveness among small businesses-owners is confined to a minority is debatable, as arguably, all participating businesses were being proactive in addressing environmental pressure. In this respect, the study provides evidence that a number of hospitality operators are being environmentally responsible. Though the fact that only a minority had acted under legislative pressure raises doubts on the effectiveness of government policy, in comparison with other industries hospitality operators are also relatively unaffected by environmental legislation. The fact that those who mentioned it had all undertaken environmental improvements for cost-reasons, may also be interpreted as the product of resentment, since industry figures point to a 15% increase in energy bills following the introduction of the Climate Change Levy by the UK Government (HCIMA, 2003). On this basis, it can be speculated that businesses with a prevalent profit-maximising orientation may be more responsive to environmental taxation than businesses with dominant social values, whose acceptance of the 'polluter-pays-principle' might be greater. Further research may illuminate this aspect.

6. Conclusion and Implications

This paper reported on the factors that influenced a number of hospitality operators to adopt an environmental profile. The uniqueness and size of the sample limit the applicability of the findings, as does the purposeful selection of informants. These limitations should however be set against the contribution the study has made to the subject discipline. In uncovering the dynamics of the decision-making process, it addressed an under-explored area of research, both in terms of the issues explored (small firm decision-making and going green) and the context (hospitality). The fact that going green was not a decision taken at a single point in time, but can be seen as a journey reflecting a series of personal lifestyle choices has various implications. Firstly, it points to the role played by personal values in small firms' decision-making, thus pressing the case to understand how owner-managers view the world in order to make sense of how decisions are made. In this respect, the findings support the notion that personal ethics are a key determinant of business behaviour, especially with regards to ethical/environmental issues. Secondly, it attests to the importance of understanding the context in which decisions are made, as this in turn can help ground the investigation of the motives driving small business owners, not least in relation to environmental performance. Thirdly, it highlights some of the difficulties of formulating an intervention approach, given that going green was largely an intrinsically driven change, and its seed planted long before. Greening the values and behaviour of individuals who do not share a similar outlook as the participants in this study is an arduous task, and one that will take a long time, but one that should nevertheless be pursued. The difficulties become greater in the absence of a decision point or triggers. Whilst influences were identified, these had contributed to, rather than prompted, greening. Moreover, these had not acted in isolation but within the social and personal complexities of the owner-manager. Thus, scope for manipulation at this stage becomes limited. Nonetheless, the fact that personal values and beliefs were a powerful motivating force also means that if current barriers are removed, positive action is likely to follow. Finally, uncovering the dynamics of going green has provided a further insight into how owner-managed firms operate. In this sense, the gradual ad hoc implementation of measures outwith the parameters of a specific business strategy is consistent with the lack of formal planning and policy formulation so often encountered in small businesses. This same degree of informality is reflected in the traditionally low numbers of establishments addressing environmental issues through a formal environmental policy. In itself, this points to the importance of formulating initiatives in accordance with the needs of the target market in terms of its sectoral and size characteristics, whilst acknowledging the diversity of environmental motivators.

References

Ajzen, I., 1991. The theory of planned behaviour. Organizational Behaviour and the Human Decision Process 50, 179–211.
Ansoff, H., 1969. Business Strategy. Penguin, Harmondsworth.
Ateljevic, I., Doorne, S., 2000. Staying within the fence: lifestyle entrepreneurship in tourism. Journal of Sustainable Tourism 8 (5), 378–392.
Bohdanowicz, P., 2005. European hoteliers' environmental attitudes. Cornell Hotel and Restaurant Administration Quarterly 46 (2), 188–204.
Bowman, J., 1975. Cited in McCormick, J., 1995. Rio and beyond, In: McDonagh, P., Prothero, A. (Eds.), 1997. Green Management: A Reader, 1975, The Dryden Press, London, pp. 112–122.
Carlsen, J., Getz, D., Ali-Knight, J., 2001. The environmental attitudes and practices of family businesses in the rural tourism and hospitality sectors. Journal of Sustainable Tourism 9 (4), 281–297.
Crabtree, B., Miller, W., 1992. A template approach to text analysis: developing and using codebooks. In: Crabtree, B., Miller, W. (Eds.), Doing Qualitative Research. Sage, Newbury Park, CA, pp. 93–107.

Culkin, N., Smith, D., 2000. An emotional business: a guide to understanding the motivations of small business decision takers. Qualitative Market Research 8 (3), 145–157.
Dearlove, D., 1998. Key Management Decisions: Tools and Techniques of the Executive Decision Maker. Pitman, London.
Dewhurst, P., Thomas, R., 2003. Encouraging sustainable business practices in a non-regulatory environment: a case study of small tourism firms in a UK National Park. Journal of Sustainable Tourism 11 (5), 383–403.
De Young, R., 1986. Encouraging environmentally appropriate behavior: the role of intrinsic motivation. Journal of Environmental Systems 15 (4), 281–292.
Donovan, T., McElligott, B., 2000. Environmental management in the Irish hotel sector–policy and practice. In: Robinson, M., Swarbrooke, J., Evans, N., Long, P., Sharpley, R. (Eds.), Environmental Management and Pathways to Sustainable Tourism. The Centre for Travel and Tourism and Business Education, Sunderland, pp. 55–79.
DTI (Department of Trade and Industry), 2005. DTI News release: statistical press release. [Online] Available at: <http://www.sbs.gov.uk/SBS_Gov_files/researchandstats/SMEStats2004.pdf> (accessed 30 March 2006).
Eden, C., Jones, S., Sims, D., 1983. Messing About in Problems. Pergamon, Oxford.
Ennis, S., 1999. Growth and the small firm: using causal mapping to assess the decision-making process – a case study. Qualitative Market Research 2 (2), 147–160.
Gore, C., Murray, K., Richardson, B., 1992. Strategic Decision-Making. Cassell, London.
Greenbank, P., 2000. Training micro-business owner-manager: a challenge to current approaches. Journal of European Industrial Training 24 (7), 403–411.
GTBS (Green Tourism Business Scheme), 2007. The Green Tourism Business Scheme. [Online] Available at: <http://www.green-business.co.uk/AboutUs.asp> (accessed 15 December 2006).
Gustin, M., Weaver, P., 1996. Are hotels prepared for the environmental consumer? Hospitality Research Journal 20 (2), 1–14.
Harrison, E., 1996. A process perspective on strategic decision-making. Management Decision 34 (1), 46–53.
HCIMA (Hotel and Catering International Management Association), 2003. HCIMA News. Hospitality March, 4.
Hines, J., Hungerford, H., Tomera, A., 1987. Analysis and synthesis of research on responsible environmental behavior: a meta-analysis. Journal of Environmental Education 18 (2), 1–8.
Hobson, K., Essex, S., 2001. Sustainable tourism: a view form accommodation businesses. The Service Industries Journal 21 (4), 133–146.
Kelly, G., 1955. The Psychology of Personal Constructs. Routledge, London, pp. 1–2.
Kirk, D., 1998. Attitudes to environmental management held by a group of hotel managers in Edinburgh. International Journal of Hospitality Management 17 (1), 33–47.
Knowles, T., Macmillan, S., Palmer, J., Grabowski, P., Hashimoto, A., 1999. The development of environmental initiatives in tourism: responses from the London hotel sector. International Journal of Tourism Research 1, 255–265.
Lynch, P.A., 2005. Sociological impressionism in a hospitality context. Annals of Tourism Research 32 (3), 527–548.
McGrew, A., Wilson, M. (Eds.), 1982. Decision-Making: Approaches and Analysis. Manchester University Press, Manchester.
Mellers, B., Schwartz, A., Cooke, D., 1998. Judgment and decision-making. Annual Review of Psychology 49, 447–477.
Mensah, I., 2006. Environmental management practices among hotels in the Greater Accra region. International Journal of Hospitality Management 25 (3), 414–431.
NetRegs, 2005. SME-nvironment 2005:UK. [Online] Available at: <http://www.netregs.gov.uk/commondata/acrobat/2005_uk_summary_1197319.pdf> (accessed 15 December 2006).

Nordlund, A., Garvill, J., 2002. Value structures behind pro-environmental behavior. Environment and Behavior 34 (6), 740–756.
Patton, M., 1990. Qualitative Research and Evaluation Methods, second ed. Sage, Newbury Park, CA.
Quinn, J., 1997. Personal ethics and business ethics: the ethical attitude of owner/managers of small businesses. Journal of Business Ethics 16, 119–127.
Schaper, M., Carlsen, J., 2004. Overcoming the green gap: improving the environmental performance of small tourism firms in Western Australia. In: Thomas, R. (Ed.), Small Firms in Tourism: International Perspectives. Elsevier, London, pp. 197–214.
Schlegelmilch, B., Bohlen, G., Diamantopoulos, A., 1996. The link between green purchasing decisions and measures of environmental consciousness. European Journal of Marketing 30 (5), 35–55.
Schwartz, S., 1977. Normative influences on altruism. Advances in Experimental Social Psychology 10, 221–279.
Simon, H., 1960. The New Science of Management Decision. Harper & Row, New York.
Simons, R., Thompson, B., 1998. Strategic determinants: the context of managerial decision-making. Journal of Managerial Psychology 13 (1/2), 7–21.
Stabler, M., Goodall, B., 1997. Environmental awareness, action and performance in the Guernsey hospitality sector. Tourism Management 18 (1), 19–33.
Tarter, J., Hoy, W., 1998. Toward a contingency theory of decision-making. Journal of Educational Administration 36 (3), 212–228.
Taylor, B., 1997. Green in word. In: Jowell, R., Curtice, J., Park, A., Brook, L., Thomson, K., Bryson, C. (Eds.), British Social Attitudes: The 14th Report. Dartmouth, Aldershot, pp. 111–134.
Thomas, R. (Ed.), 2004. Small Firms in Tourism: International Perspectives. Elsevier, London.
Van Liere, K., Dunlap, R., 1981. Environmental concern: does it make a difference how it is measured? Environment and Behaviour 13, 651–676.
Vernon, J., Essex, S., Pinder, D., Curry, K., 2003. The greening of tourism micro-businesses: outcomes of focus groups investigations in South East Cornwall. Business Strategy and the Environment 12, 49–69.
Vining, J., Ebreo, A., 1990. What makes a recycler? A comparison of recyclers and non recyclers. Environmental and Behaviour 22 (1), 55–73.
WCED (World Commission on Environment and Development), 1987. Our Common Future. WCED, Oxford.

34

Customer Loyalty: The Future of Hospitality Marketing

Stowe Shoemaker and Robert C. Lewis

1. Introduction

For many years hospitality firms have believed that the goal of marketing is to create as many new customers as possible. While hoteliers believed it was important to satisfy the guests while they were on the property, the real goal was to continue to find new customers. This constant search for new customers is called conquest marketing. In the future, conquest marketing will not be sufficient, as most hotel-industry segments are mature and competition is strong. There is also too much parity among hospitality products in the same segment. For example, general managers from Sheraton in Asia were shown pictures of hotel rooms from their own chain and three competitors. Most managers could not identify the brand of one room – not even their own – although they were given a list of eight brands from which to choose (Bowen and Shoemaker, 1998).

Loyalty marketing has become a particularly poignant topic for research and practice in services over the last few years. In the face of overpopulated and hypercompetitive markets, service providers have shifted the emphasis in marketing strategies from customer acquisition to customer retention (loyalty) in many industries. In fact, in the airline industry, the cost of frequent flyer programs is often higher than advertising spending (about 3% of revenue for advertising and between 3 and 6% for frequent-flyers program, Asian Business, 1993). Frequent traveler programs are, of course, just one tactic to try to increase loyalty. Other tactics include service guarantees and complaint management programs (see Dwyer et al., 1987; Gronroos, 1994; Gummesson, 1987; Hu et al, 1998).

Reasons for starting a loyalty program are, of course, related to getting and keeping customers. According to Dick Dunn of Carlson Marketing (Dunn, 1997), a firm specializing in loyalty programs, reasons include the desire to:

- protect market share from competitors,
- steal high value customers from competitors,
- retain and grow high value customers,
- upgrade high value customer "look a-likes" (that is, reward non-high value customers who have similar characteristics as your best customers so they will become better customers),
- retain a "core group" of moderate value customers; and
- create "opportunity cost" for using a competitor.

Given the interest in customer loyalty, it is useful to understand more about this topic. The goal of this paper is to present such an understanding. We do this first by examining the economics of loyalty. We then define loyalty and explain the difference between frequency programs and loyalty programs. We also show why satisfaction does not equal loyalty. We then introduce the Loyalty Triangle©, which provides a framework for building customer loyalty. Each leg of the Loyalty Triangle© is then examined in-depth, including examples of how hotel companies use the Loyalty Triangle© to develop strategy. Next we present ways to measure the success of loyalty programs. Finally, we present future research issues.

2. The Economics of Loyalty

The figure used most frequently to quantify the value of customer loyalty is "lifetime value". As defined by Gordon (1988), the lifetime value of a customer is simply a projection of the customer's expenditures over their life of purchases with a company minus the cost of producing the product and serving and supporting each customer. The net profit of a customer over his or her lifetime is normally calculated in current dollars using net present value. To calculate the lifetime value one needs to estimate the retention rate, spending rate, costs, and the discount rate.

Lowder (1997) demonstrates the calculation of the lifetime net present value of a customer over a five-year purchase cycle. This appears in Table 1. The following assumptions are used in this calculation:

Table 1: Lifetime value calculation work sheet

		Year 1	Year 2	Year 3	Year 4	Year 5
Revenue						
A	Customers (same customers tracked one year to the next)	1000	400	180	90	50 (end of five years, only 50 of the initial 1000 are still customers)
B	Retention rate (% of those who return from one year to the next)	40% (400/1000)	45% (180/400)	50% (90/180)	55%	60%
C	Average yearly sale	(total sales/total customers) $150	$150	$150	$150	$150
D	Total revenue of customers from original group) A*C	$150,000	$60,000	$27,000	$13,500	$7500
Costs						
E	Cost percent or calculate any way that makes sense for your company	50%	50%	50%	50%	50%
F	Total costs (D*E)	$75,000	$30,000	$13,500	$6750	#3750
Profits						
G	Gross profit (D–F)	$75,000	$30,000	$13,500	$6750	$3750
H	Discount rate $D = (1 + i)n$	$1D$ $= (1 + 0.20)^0$	$1.2D$ $= (1 + 0.20)^1$	$1.44D$ $= (1 + 0.20)^2$	$1.73D$ $= (1 + 0.20)^3$	$2.07D$ $= (1 + 0.20)^4$
I	NVP Profit = profits/discount rate	$75,000	$25,000 ($30,000/1.2)	$9375 ($13,500/1.44)	$3902 ($6750/1.73)	($3750/2.07) = $1,812
J	Cumulative NPV (Y1 + Y2... + Y5)	$75,000	$100,000 ($75,000 + $25,000)	$109,375	$113,277	$115,088
K	Lifetime value (NPV)	$75	$100	$109.38	$113.28	$115.09

Lowder (1997).

- the customer spends $150 each year;
- a constant total of cost of 50% of sales;
- the discount rate is 20%;
- the original group consists of 1000 customers; and
- the retention rate for year two is 40% (400 of the initial 1000), for year three it is 45% (180/400), for year four it is 50%.

The reader will note that the lifetime value (row K) is calculated by dividing the cumulative net present value profit by the number in the original group. This is done because one cannot tell in advance which customers will stay through the whole purchasing period. If a customer only buys from the company just once, she/he is worth just $75. However, should the customer buy from the firm over a 5-year period, the current worth of the customer is $115.09. This suggests that if there is a service failure and it costs $80 to make the customer happy, the company should spend the money and make sure the customer is happy. The firm should not view the fix as a loss of $5, but should instead look at it as a profit of $35.09 ($115.09–$80).

To easily illustrate lifetime value, the numbers used in the calculations shown in Table 1 are very conservative. Actual revenue and costs from a hotel would show a much more impressive lifetime value. Research has shown that the costs associated with taking care of a loyal customer decline over time, while at the same time sales from loyal customers' increases (Reichheld and Sasser, 1990; Bowen and Shoemaker, 1998). In this example, costs and revenue were kept the same for illustrative purposes. Although it is not shown, the reader should verify that if the retention increases (defection rate decreases) an additional 50 customers each year (450 customers in year two, 230 customers in year three, 140 in year four, and 90 in year five), the net present lifetime value of the customer is $124.44. This is an increase of approximately 8%.

In a much-cited study, Reichheld and Sasser (1990) found that a 5% increase in customer retention resulted in a 25–125% increase in profits in nine service industry groups. This increase was due in part to lower sales and marketing costs, lower transaction costs, price premiums, referrals, and revenue growth.

Bowen and Shoemaker (1998) showed that the economics of customer loyalty apply to the luxury hotel segment. In a study of American Express platinum card members who took at least six overnight business trips per year where they stayed in luxury hotels (e.g., Ritz Carlton and Four Seasons), these authors found that loyal customers are less likely to ask about price when making a reservation. Loyal customers also claim they purchase other hotel services (e.g., laundry and restaurant meals) more frequently at hotels toward which they feel loyalty compared to purchases at hotels where there is little loyalty. Loyal customers are a great source of word-of-mouth advertising. Specifically, Bowen and Shoemaker (1998) found that loyal customers tell a median of 12 people about the hotel toward which they feel loyalty and that almost 20% claim that they would go out of their way to mention their favorite hotel when discussing hotels with friends or colleagues. They are also more likely to serve on an advisory panel to that particular hotel and they are more likely to tell management about a potential problem.

For instance, in the focus group phase of their research, Bowen and Shoemaker (1998) found one guest had spent $1000 to stay in a luxury suite only to find a dirty coffee cup in the kitchenette. When asked if he would tell management about this problem, he replied "Why bother, there are many places in New York City where I can spend $1000 for a hotel room". When asked if his response would be different if this occurred in a hotel toward which he felt loyalty, he replied "Of course. I realize mistakes can happen. I would tell management because I know something would be done to fix the problem".

3. Definition of Loyalty

Rob Smith (1998), president of the loyalty marketing firm Focal Point Marketing, claims that loyalty occurs when 'the customer feels so strongly that you can best meet his or her relevant needs that your competition is virtually excluded from the consideration set and the customer buys almost exclusively from you – referring to you as "their restaurant" or "their hotel". Bowen and Shoemaker (1998) claim that loyalty is the likelihood of a customer's returning to a hotel and that person's willingness to behave as a partner to the organization (e.g., spend more while on property, not serve on advisory panels, and tell management when problems occur).

Griffin (1995) argues that two factors are critical for loyalty to flourish. The first is an emotional attachment to the product or service that is high compared with that to potential alternatives. The second factor is repeat purchase. She further argues that there are four types of loyalty based on degree of repurchase and the degree of attachment.

A high level of attachment and high repeat visits characterizes premium loyalty. This is the type of loyalty for which firms should strive, as this loyalty is most resistant to competitors' offerings. In contrast, inertia loyalty is most susceptible to competitors' offerings. Inertia loyalty occurs when customers have high repeat purchase but no emotional attachment to the service provider. As will be discussed later, frequency programs create inertia loyalty. A properly designed loyalty program, however, can move customers from inertia loyalty to premium loyalty. Because customers in this segment already purchase the product frequently, they are an ideal group to move to the premium loyalty category.

Latent loyalty occurs when customers purchase the service infrequently, even though they feel a strong emotional attachment to the service. Situational factors rather than attitudinal influences determine repeat purchase. To increase the purchase behavior of members of this group, it is necessary to first determine why purchase frequency is low and then develop strategies to overcome these situational factors. The final category is no loyalty. Generally, loyalty programs do not impact these customers.

4. Frequency Programs versus Loyalty Programs

The differences between frequency and loyalty programs are shown in Table 2. As can be seen, the primary focus of frequency programs is to build repeat business, while for loyalty programs the focus is to build an emotional attachment to the brand. Smith (1998) states that "frequency occurs when customers give you a greater share of their transactions usually in exchange for accumulating miles, points, or other surrogate discounts". The problems with frequency programs are that the customer focuses on the rewards, not on product superiority or brand relevance. With many frequency programs, one reward is generally as good as another, thus creating a cost with no sustainable differentiable competitive advantage.

The differences between frequency and loyalty lead to different tactics. For frequency, the tactics involve free or discounted products, collateral product discounts (such as discounts on rental cars), and rewards such as points, miles, or both. (Hilton Honors provides guests with both points and miles.) For loyalty, the tactics involve customized recognition, emotional "trophy" rewards, and tailored offers or messages. An example of customized recognition is the guest profile form used by the Rancho Bernardo Inn (Rancho Bernardino, CA) to insure that when loyal guests arrive their favorite room will be stocked with their favorite beverages. As a point of perspective, Bowen

Table 2: Frequency versus loyalty

How it plays out	Traditional frequency	Real loyalty
Objectives	Build traffic, sales, and profits	Build sales, profits, and the brand
Strategy	Offer incentives for repeat transactions	Build personal brand relationships
Focus	A segment's behavior and profitability	An individual's emotional and rational needs and their value

Tactics	Segmented rewards:
	  Transaction status
	  Free/discounted product
	  Collateral product discounts
	  Rewards such as miles or points
	  Value-added upgrades and add-ons
	  Rewards "menu"
		Customer recognition
		  Individual value, tenure
		  Preferred access, service
		  "insider information"
		  Value-added upgrades and add-ons
		  Emotional "trophy" rewards
		  Tailored offers/messages

Measurement	Transactions Sales growth Cost structure	Individual lifetime value Attitudinal change Emotional responses

and Shoemaker (1998) found that 57.7% of the respondents in the American Express study referenced earlier would like the hotel to use prior information on them to customize their stay, yet only 24.3% of the hotels they stayed in did so. An example of emotional "trophy" awards is Hilton's policy of inviting its top guests to the Academy Awards.

Finally, an example of tailored offerings or messages is the policy of the Middlebury Inn (Middlebury, Vermont) to proactively call its regular guests and remind them to make a room reservation if they would like to visit during busy times. This is in contrast to the idea many hotels have where they only invite their regular guests to come during slow times under the assumption that in natural busy times there is no need to spend marketing dollars. Bowen and Shoemaker (1998) found that while 37.7% claimed they would like it if the hotel called them in advance to remind them to book during a busy time, only 3% of the hotels they stayed in did so.

5. Changes in Strategies for Creating Loyalty over Time

Fig. 1 from Dubé and Shoemaker (1999) shows how strategies to gain loyalty have changed over time. As can be seen, creating brand relationships is the ultimate goal of loyalty programs. Brand relationship is defined as "an exchange of *mutual value* between company and customer, which expands and deepens over time, adding value to one's products and strengthening one's brand" (Smith, 1998). The need for this brand relationship becomes important given the tenuous nature of loyalty based on frequency programs. For frequency programs to work, the customer must find them valuable. This value comes from exchanging points or airline miles for free airline tickets or

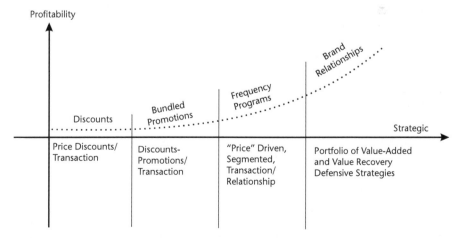

Figure 1: Defensive strategies to manage brand switching and loyalty

hotel rooms. However, once these points or airline miles are cashed in, the customer is suddenly vulnerable to competitors' offerings, because now she/he no longer has a vested interest in just one program.

For instance, a traveler may stay in only one hotel chain in order to earn enough hotel points for a free trip to an exotic resort. Once the traveler has earned the required hotel points and cashed them in, the account balance becomes zero. With a zero balance, the offerings of competitors may now be of interest, as there is no opportunity cost, in terms of lost points, in choosing one brand over another. In the situation just described, the loyalty is to the frequency program and not to the brand. This is obviously not a desirable situation; hence, the move away from frequency and the move toward brand relationship.

6. Why Have Frequency Programs at All?

The recommended move toward brand relationships poses the question, "Why have frequency programs at all?" One reason is that frequency programs identify a firm's best customers. Specifically, they provide an easy method for companies to track both customers' frequency and recency of visitation as well as customers' spending patterns. For individual properties, of course, this information can be collected without a frequency program. For companies with multiple locations, different ownership structures (i.e., corporate owned or franchised), and different methods of purchase (i.e., through central reservation system or by purchase at property level) frequency, recency and customers' spending patterns would be difficult to collect and collate in a timely and useful manner.

Customer information is important. As the manager of the frequency program for a major hotel company mentioned to one of the authors of this paper, "We are in the direct marketing business. The key to direct marketing is an accurate up-to-date database". As will be discussed later in this article, this information can also be used to track customers' preferences (i.e., they always stay in a room for non-smokers) and travel patterns. This later information, if combined with other information, can then be used as input in site selection models and for targeted communications, among other things.

A third reason for a frequency program is that firms can use the "value" of their customers as a negotiating point to gain financing for a new project, sign a management contract, or recruit new franchisees. This idea relates to the beliefs of some that the hotel business is really a real-estate business. Just like a real-estate business that relies on the right mix of tenants, the hotel business relies on the right mix of "heads-in beds". The database associated with frequency programs can enable a company to provide this right mix of customers and thus differentiate itself from competitors, who may also being trying to get a new property to carry "their flag". For the lender or builder of a hotel, the ability of a firm to provide the right mix of customers may be the feature that makes them choose one operator over another.

7. Loyalty versus Satisfaction

Customer loyalty is not the same as customer satisfaction. Customer satisfaction measures how well a customer's expectations are met by a given transaction, while customer loyalty measures how likely a customer is to repurchase and engage in partnership activities. Satisfaction is a necessary but not a sufficient condition for loyalty. In other words, we can have satisfaction without loyalty, but it is hard to have loyalty without satisfaction.

A study by Heskett et al., (1997) found that the link between customer satisfaction and customer loyalty was the weakest relationship in their service-profit-chain model. This model attempts to capture the influence on profit of operating strategy, service-delivery system, service concept, and target market. Proprietary research undertaken by Shoemaker in the casino industry also found a weak link between customer satisfaction and loyalty.

Some of the reasons for the failure of satisfaction to translate into loyalty are unrelated to either satisfaction or loyalty. Travelers may not be loyal to an individual property because they never return to the area where they were very satisfied with a specific property. Other guests may be satisfied with a hotel but their desire for novelty inhibits their loyalty to a specific property. Some guests remain price sensitive and always shop for the best deal; even though they were satisfied with a particular hotel, they will try another one if it makes a better offer. As a final consideration, some guests may not develop loyalty because they are never encouraged to become loyal customers. That is, the hotel never asks them to come back and does not collect the data necessary to develop a meaningful dialogue with the customer.

8. Creating Brand Relationships

Fig. 2 provides a framework for creating a brand relationship. The Loyalty Triangle© is an equal lateral triangle because of the belief that in order to create long-term loyalty, the service firm must execute all the functions described on each side of the triangle equally well.

On one side is the process, which is "how the service works". It involves all activities from both the guest's perspective and the service provider's perspective. For the guest, the process includes everything that happens from the time they begin buying the service (e.g., calling to make a reservation) to

304 The Hospitality Industry – Structures, Strategies and Markets

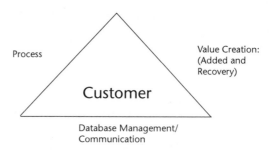

Figure 2: Loyalty triangle

the time that they leave the property (e.g., picking up their car from a valet). All interactions with employees are part of this service process. For the service company, the process includes the design of the service operations, the hiring and training of service personnel, and the collection of information to understand customers' needs, wants, and expectations.

A second side of the equilateral loyalty triangle is termed value creation. Value creation is subdivided into two components: value added and value recovery. Valued-added strategies increase the long-term value of the relationship with the service firm, offering greater benefits, on both current and future transactions, to repeat customers than to occasional customers (Dwyer et al., 1987; Gummesson, 1987; Gronroos, 1994). Providing the guest with an upgrade because she/he is a repeat customer or using knowledge of prior stays to customize the current stay are two examples of value added tactics. Value-recovery strategies, on the other hand, are primarily designed to rectify a lapse in service delivery occurring in specific transactions by providing amendments and compensations to alleviate the costs associated with failure (Fornell and Wernerfelt, 1987; Hart et al., 1990). It is the process that insures that the guest's needs are taken care of without further inconveniences. Providing loyal guests with a toll-free number to call if problems occur is an example of value recovery, as is a 100% guarantee.

The final leg of the loyalty triangle is communication. This leg of the triangle incorporates database marketing, newsletters, and general advertising. It involves all areas of how the service provider communicates with its customers.

Each leg of the Loyalty Triangle© is discussed in detail next.

8.1. The Process

As mentioned, the process is "how the service works". It involves all activities from both the guests' perspective and the service providers' perspective. Strategies geared around this leg of the Loyalty Triangle© are designed specifically to address the first three potential gaps set forth in the GAP Model of Service Quality (Zeithaml and Bitner, 1996). We do not discuss this model in-depth, as Lewis (1987) provides a thorough analysis of how this model can be used by hospitality firms. We do however provide a very brief review of Gaps 1–3. The goal for those wanting to create loyalty, of course, is to make sure that Gaps 1–3 do not exist.

Gap 1 refers to the discrepancy between what the company thinks customers' expectations are and what these expectations actually are. This gap may occur for any of the following reasons. One, there is an inadequate marketing research orientation. Companies do not ask their customers what their problems, wants, needs, or expectations are. Two, there is a lack of upward communication between management and customers and between contact employees and managers. Customers may communicate their wants and needs to employees in general conversation, but if there is no mechanism for these comments to get passed up "the chain of command", they will stay with the employee and be forgotten. And three, there is a lack of a relationship focus. In other words, management is more concerned on finding new guests and less concerned with building long-term relationships with their current customers.

Ways to close Gap 1 include informal research or "managing by walking around". This means spending time on the floor talking to guests and listening to what customers are telling each other and employees. Second, formal research, which involves putting together well-organized research agenda, that can be designed to ask very specific questions. Types of formal research methods include transactional surveys (e.g., survey measuring recent service experience); total market surveys (e.g., analysis of customers in the market, some of whom may have no experience with the hotel while others have lots of experience); service reviews; focus groups; and customer advisory panels.

Gap 2 occurs when the service provider fails to design service procedures to meet the expectations of guests. An example, from focus groups conducted by one of the authors with business travelers who spend at least six nights in a hotel during the year and pay at least $120 per night, concerns the checkout procedure. Not surprisingly, frequent business travelers claim they want to be able to checkout without having to wait in line at the front desk; hence, many hotels allow guests to leave without checking out if their invoice, which is put in their room, looks okay. Unfortunately for business travelers, these invoices do not show a zero balance, which guests' claim they need for their reimbursement. When asked why hotels do not zero-out the invoices before putting them in guests' rooms, hotel managers often claim that they cannot do it because of the belief that guests may make additional charges. From the operators' perspective, this is a rationale explanation. The guest who plans not to make any additional charges, however, is inconvenienced. This is an example of knowing what the guest wants, but not providing it because operational concerns take priority over guests' concerns.

Gap 2 also exists because of inadequate service leadership, which means "an operationally driven mentality". This mentality is present in the old phrase "This business would be a great business if only the guests didn't get in the way". A third reason for Gap 2 is a reward system that is counter to guests' needs. For instance, managers who are rewarded based on their meeting budget, will be less likely to go over budget to satisfy a guest than a manager who is rewarded based on overall guest satisfaction. A final reason for GAP 2 is a poor service design. A poor service design is one where the movement of guests and employees is restricted or otherwise inhibited. When one of the authors of this paper asked a food service waiter why it took so long to get served, the waiter replied, "We closed the kitchen close to this dining area to save costs, and now I have to walk all the way to the main kitchen, which is on the other side of the building".

To close Gap 2, management needs to be fully committed to customer service and loyalty. Employee rewards need to be designed so that the customer comes first. Organizations should also undertake a service blueprint. A service blueprint is defined as a picture or a map that visually displays the service by simultaneously depicting the process of the service delivery. It does this by breaking down the service into logical components and steps from both the employees' and the customers' perspective. (See Zeithaml and Bitner, 1996 for more on service blueprinting.)

Gap 3 is defined as the gap between the customer-driven service designs and standards and the service delivery. A gap here suggests that what was planned by management was not implemented by the staff. One of the main reasons for Gap 3 is the deficiency in management's human resource policies. These deficient policies usually occur because top management has failed to see the link between customer loyalty and employee satisfaction, and employee satisfaction and profits. Recent research by Reichheld (1996) found that service outlets (in this case, tire outlets, but the findings do occur across industries) with the highest customer retention also had the best employee retention. When looking at the fast food business, Reichheld (1996) found those restaurants with "low" employee turnover had profit margins more than 50% higher than stores with high employee turnover. This lack of understanding of an employee's impact on customer retention and profitability results in management's practice of hiring "warm bodies", as opposed to the right person for the job.

To close Gap 3, Zeithaml and Bitner (1996), among others (Reichheld, 1996, Heskett et al., 1997), argue that organizations must take a strategic approach to human resources. Rather than falling into the trap of hiring "warm bodies", it is necessary to develop a plan to ensure future employment needs are met. In order to have a customer oriented service delivery system, Zeithaml and Bitner (1996, pp. 313–328) argue that management must do the following:

1. *Hire the right people:* In order to hire the right people, it is helpful that the firm: (1) be the preferred employer, (2) compete for the best people, and (3) hire for service competencies and service inclination. Berry (1997) has stated that service work is 95% volunteer. What he means is that with 5% effort an employee can perform the necessary service task (i.e., check a guest into the hotel). The other 95% is the attitude the employee brings to the task.
2. *Provide needed support systems.* Components of this strategy include providing supportive technology and equipment, and developing service-oriented internal processes. For example, The Mirage hotel in Las Vegas, provides room service with its elevators (i.e., it does not need to share them with housekeeping) so they could deliver room service items hot and in a timely manner. It is usually easy to find out what employees need to do their jobs correctly; the best way is to just ask them.
3. *Develop people to deliver service quality.* Promoting teamwork, empowering employees, and training for technical and interactive skills are all ways to develop people to deliver service quality. In its first year of operation, The Mirage hotel invested over $3 million in employee development (Peters, 1995).
4. *Retain the best people.* In order to retain the best people, it is necessary to measure and reward strong service performers, treat employees as customers, and include employees in the company's vision. Employees are more likely to stay at a job if they feel they are treated fairly. At the Mirage, the employee dining room is as well decorated as the guests' dining room, and the food is of the highest quality. Treating employees like customers not only encourage employees to stay with the firm, it also effects the way they treat guests. As Bill Marriott says: "Take care of your employees and they'll take care of your customers (Cannie, 1991, p. 170)". Joan Cannie (1991) states that "customer relations mirror employee relations. The way you treat your employees is the way they will treat your customers". (p. 148.) For instance, if a company lets employees know what is happening, the employee is more likely to be able to help the customer with organization type questions. Similarly, if an employee knows that an organization is solidly behind them, she/he will not be afraid to do what it takes to help the guest.

The second leg of the triangle is discussed next.

8.2. Value-Added – Value-Recovery

Value-added and value-recovery strategies are designed specifically to enhance customer perceptions of the rewards and costs associated with present and future service transactions. Beyond the added value derived from increased reward or lower cost from specific transactions, value-added strategies permit customers to acquire additional rewards that accumulate for future transactions so long as they maintain their relationship with the brand. Most value-added strategy increases relationship rewards while relationship costs remain unaffected. Hotel customers, for example, can obtain additional privileges in present transaction, such as upgrades, expedited check-in, and guaranteed check-cashing privileges. Also available are cross promotions with complementary services such as airlines and car rental companies. These cross promotions can occur in either a current or future transaction and can be either free of charge or available at a minimal cost (Barlow, 1992).

In general, value-added and value-recovery strategies both affect the value of the buyer–provider exchange, but this influence is exerted in different ways. Value-added strategies increase the rewards associated with the current relationship, whereas value-recovery strategies reduce or eliminate the costs associated with service failure.

Consider the sources of value added or value recovery for current and future transactions in the hotel industry (see Table 3). Features are of six types: *financial* (e.g., saving money on future transactions, complete reimbursement if service failure, 10% discount at gift shop); *temporal* (e.g., saving time by priority check-in); *functional* (e.g., check cashing, web-site available); *experiential* (e.g., upgrades or turndown services); *emotional* (e.g., more recognition and/or more pleasurable service experience); and/or *social* (e.g., interpersonal link with a service provider) components of the customer/provider exchange. In fact, the companies Dubé and Shoemaker (1999) studied all had developed strategies that presented a relatively broad portfolio of these various sources of value. Most of them had created for each member in a value-added program a preference profile that allows the hotel to "customize" the stay for each guest, adding as much value as possible to each transaction as well as to the long-term relationship.

The combinations of value-added and value-recovery strategies, which are tied to current and future transactions, may very well be necessary to influence customer switching and loyalty decisions. Service guarantees, for example, are designed to reduce both the financial cost and the psychological uncertainty associated with a service failure.

Service providers have to be careful in choosing the appropriate features to include in shaping customers' perceptions of the value of their relationship with the brand, as well as the appropriate level on each feature. Research suggests that customers may be sensitive to the quality of these strategies (O'Brien and Jones, 1995; Dowling and Uncles, 1997). For instance, consider the cash value of the redemption reward. Members of one hotel company's frequency program can earn one free weekend room night with the redemption of 20,000 points. Since $1 equals 10 points, the redemption value costs $2000. This does not seem to be a great value, when examined closely.

Table 3: Features of value-added and value-recovery strategies in place in eight leading hotel companies

Benefits	Regular tier member	Middle tier member	Upper tier member
Financial rewards (value-added: current)	Either 1, 5, or 10 points per dollar spent with no bonus on base points earned	Bonus points earned on regular tier points; Bonus can be 10, 15 or 20%	Bonus points earned on regular tier points; Bonus can be 10, 25 or 30%
Financial rewards (value-added: future)	Either not available or can combine points with spouse	Either not available or can combine points with spouse	Either not available or can combine points with spouse
Financial rewards (value-added: future)	Either no upgrades available or automatic upgrade if room available	Either automatic upgrade if available or one confirmable upgrade every five qualifying stays	One confirmable upgrade every five qualifying stays + automatic upgrade available whenever paying minimum published room rate, based on availability; or automatic upgrade available whenever available
Financial rewards (value-added: future)	150 points for getting friend to join the program or no bonus threshold awards	Bonus points earned on regular tier points; Bonus can be 0, 10, 15 or 20% or 5000 bonus points after 7 paid VIP stays with calendar quarter	Bonus points earned on regular tier points; Bonus can be 0, 10, 25 or 30% or 5000 bonus points after 7 paid VIP stays with calendar quarter
Financial rewards (value-added: current)	500 points for government or commercial rate, 1000 points for others; get 20% when presenting rental agreement at check-in; or earn 25% bonus with car rental agreement; earn 250–500 points per Hertz rental; 100 points per car rental partner	500 points for government or commercial rate, 1000 points for others; get 20% when presenting rental agreement at check-in; or earn 25% bonus with car rental agreement; earn 500 points per Hertz rental	500 points for government or commercial rate, 1000 points for others; get 20% when presenting rental agreement at check-in; or earn 25% bonus with car rental agreement; earn 500 points per Hertz rental
Financial rewards (value-added: current)	Earn hotel points or airline miles; one chain lets you earn both hotel points and airline points; airline miles for stay instead of hotel points; some hotels can only hotel points	Earn hotel points or airline miles; one chain lets you earn both hotel points and airline points; airline miles for stay instead of hotel points; some hotels only hotel points	Earn hotel points or airline miles; one chain lets you earn both hotel points and airline points; airline miles for stay instead of hotel points; some hotels only hotel points
Financial rewards (value-added: future)	Affinity card where you earn hotel points for credit card spending; earn 2000 credit card points for: 150 hotel points, 330 hotel points, or 1000 hotel points	Affinity card where you earn hotel points for credit card spending; earn 2000 credit card points for: 150 hotel points, 330 hotel points, or 1000 hotel points	Affinity card where you earn hotel points for credit card spending; earn 2000 credit card points for: 150 hotel points, 330 hotel points, or 1000 hotel points

(Continued)

Table 3: (*Continued*)

Benefits	Regular tier member	Middle tier member	Upper tier member
Financial rewards (value-added: current)	No discount in gift shop	No discount in gift shop	10% discount in gift shop
Financial rewards (value-added: current and future)	Exchange points for free rooms: 8000 points = one free weekend night, 15,000 points = two free weekend nights; 20,000 points one night; 12,500 hotel points = 1 free night for mid-scale brand	Exchange points for free rooms: 8000 points = one free weekend night, 15,000 points = two free weekend nights; 20,000 points one night; 12,500 hotel points = 1 free night for mid-scale brand	Exchange points for free rooms: 8000 points = one free weekend night, 15,000 points = two free weekend nights; 20,000 points one night; 12,500 hotel points = 1 free night for mid-scale brand
Financial rewards (value-added: current and future)	Exchange hotel points for airline miles: Some, no change available; others 10,000 points = 2500 airline miles; 10,000 points = 5000 miles; some require minimum 9000 points per exchange	Exchange hotel points for airline miles: Some, no change available; others 10,000 points = 2500 airline miles; 10,000 points = 5000 miles; some require minimum 9000 points per exchange	Exchange hotel points for airline miles: Some, no change available; others 10,000 points = 2500 airline miles; 10,000 points = 5000 miles; some require minimum 9000 points per exchange
Functional/temporal (value-added)	Point statement sent every other month with activity; statement sent monthly; sent quarterly	Point statement sent every other month with activity; statement sent monthly; sent quarterly	Point statement sent every other month with activity; statement sent monthly; sent quarterly
Functional/temporal (value-added: current and future)	Some hotels offer members only reservation phone numbers at this level, while others have no members only reservation phone numbers at this level	Some hotels offer members only reservation phone numbers at this level, while others have no members only reservation phone numbers at this level	Some hotels offer members only reservation phone numbers at this level, while others have no members only reservation phone numbers at this level
Functional/temporal (value-added: current)	No turndown service; availability of service varies by owner of brand	No turndown service; availability of service varies by owner of brand	Turndown service normal at this level; availability of service varies by owner of brand
Functional/temporal (value-added: current)	No separate check-in; separate lines; Priority check-in; rooms assigned and room key waiting at check-in desk; zip-in, check-in;	No separate check-in; separate lines. Priority check-in; rooms assigned and room key waiting at check-in desk; zip-in, check-in;	No separate check-in; separate lines; Priority check-in; rooms assigned and room key waiting at check-in desk; zip-in, check-in;
Functional/temporal (value-added: current)	No check cashing for member at this level; Check cashing up to $250 per stay; no check cashing at all	Check cashing up to $250 per stay, up to $200 per day; no check cashing at all	Check cashing up to $500 per stay; up to $200 per day; no check cashing at all
Functional/temporal (value-added: future)	No web-site available; Web-site available where guests can redeem awards, change addresses, and conduct various transactions	No web-site available; Web-site available where guests can redeem awards, change addresses, and conduct various transactions	No web-site available; Web-site available where guests can redeem awards, change addresses, and conduct various transactions
Functional/temporal (value-added: current)	No direct billing through individual at this level; no direct billing at all	Direct billing through individual; no direct billing at all	Direct billing through individual; no direct billing at all

Benefits	Regular tier member	Middle tier member	Upper tier member
Functional/temporal (value-added: current)	Not available at all; not available at this level; 7 a.m. check-in; 9–5 check-in, check-out	Available at 10:00 a.m; 7 a.m. check-in; 9–5 check-in, check-out	Available at 10:00 a.m; 7 a.m. check-in; 9–5 check-in, check-out
Functional/temporal (value-added: future) Psychological/emotional (value-added: future)	No priority waiting list during busy times	No priority waiting list during busy times	Priority waiting list during busy times Attend the Academy Awards as guest of Hotel Company
Psychological/emotional (value-added: current and future)	Customer profiling so hotel knows your wants and needs	Customer profiling so hotel knows your wants and needs	Customer profiling so hotel knows your wants and needs
Psychological/emotional (value-added: future)	At least one hotel stay in past 12 months to be a member	Must have at least four qualifying stays during calendar year; Can pay to join this level or can be earned; 20 + nights; must stay 20 nights in 10 stays	Must have at least 15 qualifying stays or four stays and 30 nights; Invitation only; 60+nights; must stay 50 nights in 25 stays
Psychological/emotional (value-recovery: current and future)	Customer service centers that can help when problems occur that are not taken care of at hotel level; some hotels have international call centers; some call centers open 24 h	Customer service centers that can help when problems occur that are not taken care of at hotel level; some hotels have international call centers; some call centers open 24 h	Customer service centers that can help when problems occur that are not taken care of at hotel level; some hotels have international call centers; some call centers open 24 h
Psychological/emotional (value-recovery: current and future)	Perfect stay programs where all problems guaranteed to be resolved; if not send copy of folio and letter to specific address and get free guaranteed upgrade	Perfect stay programs where all problems guaranteed to be resolved; if not send copy of folio and letter to specific address and get free guaranteed upgrade	Perfect stay programs where all problems guaranteed to be resolved; if not send copy of folio and letter to specific address and get free guaranteed upgrade
Psychological/emotional (value-recovery: current)	100% satisfaction guarantee (note, hotel with this program does not offer any type of frequency program)	100% satisfaction guarantee (note, hotel with this program does not offer any type of frequency program)	100% satisfaction guarantee (note, hotel with this program does not offer any type of frequency program)

Dubé and Shoemaker (1999).

In the context of value-recovery strategy, research has shown that the magnitude of monetary compensation offered and the electiveness of the recovery (Goodwin and Ross, 1992; Webster and Sundaram, 1998) impact future loyalty and satisfaction. One hotel chain Dubé and Shoemaker (1999) talked with offers a 100% satisfaction guarantee. If anything goes wrong with the hotel stay, the stay is free. Another chain offers a free guaranteed upgrade certificate on the next stay for problems with the current stay.

Another parameter to set with caution pertains to the range of choice of these rewards and the degree of flexibility in their redemption format. For instance, many hotel chains allow customers to earn either airline miles or hotel points, which enables the guest to choose the reward that she wants. One chain allows for "double-dipping", which means the guest receives both miles and points. The aspirational value of the rewards for specific market segments also has to be assessed. That is, various benefits offered to elite members, for instance, systematic upgrade, beyond their monetary or functional value, may be highly sought due to the social image attached to them.

The perceived likelihood of achieving the rewards is another aspect that has to be set at the appropriate level. As one of the hotel frequency program managers mentioned in one of Dubé and Shoemaker's (1999) interview "If the goal, i.e., a free hotel room or a free airline flight, is unobtainable then the customer will find no value. That is why we have formed alliances with the airlines, credit card companies, and rental car companies. It is all about giving customers many chances to earn points or miles".

The program's ease of use is also critical to a strategy's ability to increase customers' perceptions of its relationship with a service provider. One of the problems with the AirMiles program was that initially customers were responsible for collecting and keeping track of their AirMiles. Many hotel firms now provide customers the ability to keep track of their points/miles via the Internet (Jones et al., 1991).

Finally, the immediacy with which the rewards or compensations are available is another parameter that may impact customers' perception of value. Some of the hotel companies Dubé and Shoemaker (1999) talked to have policies that allow guests to redeem their points anytime; others, however, impose blackout dates at some of the most desirable times.

The most important way in which service providers, and not just those in the hotel industry, attempt to make it more costly for customers to end the relationship is by differentiating the nature and magnitude of value being created at different membership tiers. In most companies, value-added strategies are differentiated in two to three tiers, corresponding to increasing amounts of purchase at qualifying condition service levels. By increasing the "added-value per unit of purchase" as one moves from one tier to the next, the provider is making it more costly for the guest, not only to switch to a competitor but also, to divide their share of purchases among various providers. For instance, as one moves up the tier level (e.g., from regular to middle to upper) the points earned for dollars spent increases. This can be seen in Table 3, which reveals that middle tier members can earn up to a 20% bonus on points while upper tier members can earn a 30% bonus.

As can be seen in Table 3, there is little evidence that either value-added or value-recovery strategies attempt to directly change consumers' perceptions of the rewards and costs associated with competition. Instead, the various providers attempt to differentiate their offering from the competitors' by multiple variations in the various features of their value-added and value-recovery strategies.

For instance, a hotel chain may offer 250 points toward a free stay if one rents a car with a particular rental car company and another hotel chain may offer 500 points for the same thing. One needs to be careful when comparing such programs because the rate at which one earns points can vary. While the business class chains (e.g., Sheraton, Hyatt, and Hilton) generally offer 10 points for each $1 spent, mid-scale properties (e.g., Holiday Inn and Best Western) generally offer fewer points.

There is still variability among programs. For instance, the bonus points one can earn as they move to higher tiers (such tiers are based upon stay frequency in a given time period) can range from 10 to 20% at the middle tier and 10 to 30% at the upper tier. Similarly, the availability of upgrades, shown by Bowen and Shoemaker (1998) to be very important to frequent business travelers who stay in luxury properties, can vary by program both within and between tiers. In the regular tier some chains allow no upgrades while others provide an automatic upgrade if a room is available. In the middle tier, there can be automatic upgrades depending upon availability or one can earn an upgrade every five qualifying stays.

Finally, program variability can also be seen in the way in which customers can earn points. As mentioned earlier, one hotel chain allows the customer to earn both hotel points and airline miles, while other chains make the customer choose one or the other. The redemption of points also varies. The cost of a free room varies between 8000 and 12,500 points and the conversion of affinity card points to hotel points also varies. For example, 2000 points earned on a credit card can be worth either 150, 330, or 1000 hotel points.

The third leg of the triangle is discussed next.

8.3. Database Management and Communication

Database management is critical to customer loyalty for it is the foundation of one-to-one marketing. A properly designed database enables firms to keep track of guests' preferences; enabling the service firm to provide customized services. For instance, consider the hotel guest that always wants a room that is designated for non-smokers. Also assume the guest always wants a room with a double bed and feather pillows. This information can easily be stored in a database so when the guest, or an administrative assistant, makes a hotel reservation, the guest will get the preferred room type. Bowen and Shoemaker (1998) found that such customization would increase loyalty. Specifically, they found the following:

- 57.7% of their sample claimed that they would be loyal to a hotel that uses information from prior stays to customize services. (Surprisingly, only 24.3% claimed that the hotels they stayed in most frequently provided this service.)
- 44.7% claimed they would be loyal to a hotel that allowed them to request a specific room.

- 41.1% of their respondents claimed they would be loyal to a hotel that expedited the registration process.
- 37.7% claimed they would be loyal to a hotel that called them and asked them if they would like to make a reservation if the hotel is going to be sold out at a time they normally visit the hotel.
- 38.3% claim they want to be recognized when they arrive.

All these activities can occur with a proper database. Ritz Carlton is probably the best example of chains that use databases to customize services. Other hotel companies, however, both independents and chains, are moving in similar directions. (To see how Ritz Carlton uses its database to customize services see Barsky, 1995). For Marriott Hotels,

> "... knowing their customers is their lifeblood. Through their computer system, the Marriott receptionist knows, as the customer checks in, whether he appreciates an iron in his room, whether she prefers a non-smoking room on the first floor, whether the bill will be customer-settled, sent to the firm, or charged to a monthly account, whether the customer is a member of the Diamond Club and entitled to an upgrade. This information is an important element in Marriott's strategy to stay ahead through customer knowledge (Cram, 1994, p. 123).

A database can also be used to estimate a customer's value. Examining how recently they last visited, how frequently they visit, and how much they spend per visit (monetary value) does this. This is referred to as *RFM* or *RFV* ($V =$ value) analysis; where R is recency, F is frequency, and M is monetary value. This information can then be used to classify customers into one of four cells. In addition, Magson (1998) explains that the strategic objectives for creating value information are as follows:

- understanding allowable marketing recruitment costs between different customers, and therefore helping to determine recruitment strategy;
- understanding the performance of different customer types over time and therefore forming communications strategy, i.e., allowable investment costs after recruitment;
- to be able to monitor effects of other elements of communications strategy, contact methods, etc.; and
- for business planning purposes to enable forecasting, trending, and understanding "what if" scenarios through generating predicted lifetime values, and therefore being able to estimate the added value of marketing activity for the benefit of an organization as a whole (p. 28).

One advantage of databases is that information from partners' databases (i.e., the partnership between a hotel company, a rental car company, and an airline) can be combined with the firm's current database to learn more about a customer's travel patterns. This information can then be used in site selection models and in targeted mailings.

When communicating with guests, it is critical that external communications do not over-promise what the service can deliver. Gap 4, occurs when external communications over-promise what the service can deliver. This gap is a result of (1) inadequate management of service promises; (2) promising unrealistic expectations and rewards in advertising and personal selling; (3) insufficient customer communication; and (4) inadequate horizontal communication, particularly among operations, marketing, and human resources. In other words, because customers are receiving the wrong message, they are forming the wrong expectations. Unfortunately, miscommunication can happen frequently when the team of employees involved in the development of the communication pieces is different than the team of employees who must execute the promises made through the communications. This leads to unhappy guests and a decrease in loyalty.

This ends the discussion of the Loyalty Triangle©. We now turn to measuring the success or failure of a loyalty program.

9. The Metrics of Loyalty

The key benchmark for any loyalty program is the incremental part; that is, what percentage of business would not be coming through the door if not affiliated with the loyalty program. Judd Goldfedder, president of the Customer Connection, a loyalty marketing firm specializing in restaurants, states that such as figure cannot be easily quantified.

> While we try to do all we can to objectively and accurately measure the sales generated by a frequent diner program, no analysis can provide absolute evidence that any program produces a definitive amount of incremental sales. Therefore, the best we can do is make some subjective assumptions, temper them with common sense and good business judgement, and reach a "comfort zone" regarding what portion of sales were generated as a direct result of the program versus guest patronage that would have occurred anyway (Goldfedder, 1998).

In interviews with managers of frequency programs at major hotel companies, Dubé and Shoemaker (1999) found that many measure the impact of their programs by performing different types of analyses. First, they make comparisons between members and non-members. To do this analysis, frequency program managers pull a sample from the entire universe of people who are staying at the hotel (or across a system of hotels) during a given time period. From this sample they examine the following pieces of information.

- Average folio revenue generated by program members relative to non-program members. This involves examining the total purchase behavior while they are on the property. As discussed earlier, Bowen and Shoemaker (1998) found that loyal guests spent more than non-loyal guests did.
- The differences in satisfaction scores between program members and non-members.
- The differences in willingness to return scores between program members and non-members.
- Average number of visits between program members and non-members.
- The "share of wallet" between program members and non-members. That is, the percentage of all hotel stays for both groups that goes towards the specific hotel or chain conducting the analysis.
- The contribution the program makes to overall occupancy at a particular property or throughout the system.
- The growth in program related occupancy to the growth in occupancy for the industry at large.

A second method to understand the impact of a program is to conduct research among the members who belong to the loyalty program and ask them if their purchase behavior would remain the same or if they would migrate to another company if the frequency program went away. One way to ask this question would be as follows:

> Please think about what a business hotel might offer you to develop a feeling of loyalty to that hotel. For each of the possible benefits listed below, please indicate the effect that benefit, if provided, would have on developing a feeling of loyalty to the hotel. Use a 1 to 7 scale where 1 means "would have no effect on loyalty" and 7 means "it would have great effect on loyalty".

Using this scale, Bowen and Shoemaker (1998) found that 27.8% of frequent business travelers who stay in luxury hotels when traveling for business rated the benefit "the hotel has a frequent-guest program that allows you to earn points toward free accommodations" a 7. A total of 49.2% rated the benefit a 6 or a 7. A second way to measure purchase behavior would be to use trade-off analysis techniques such as conjoint analysis (Dolan, 1990). One of the features would be the presence or absence of a frequency program.

A third method to understand the impact of a program is to examine the ROI both on a system basis and a property basis. Since most hotels pay a fee contributing to the program based on stay activity, it is necessary to examine whether the investment the hotels are making to the program are more than offset by the revenues generated by the users who are members of the program.

A fourth metric is what Goldfedder (1998) calls "they would have come anyway analysis". This method works by calculating the cost of the total program and the total revenue earned during the time the program is running. One then makes assumptions about the percentage of revenue that is generated by consumers who would have come anyway. The total costs of the program are then subtracted from the revenue generated by those who would have come anyway to determine the incremental revenues. An example of this type of analysis is shown in Table 4. In this example, even if people who would have come anyway generated 95% of the revenue, the program still would have been profitable. (Although the reader is correct in assuming that while the program was profitable it was not terribly successful, given the money spent to earn $8720. The program's success does look much better as more revenue is generated because of the program.)

A fifth method used to understand the financial impact of the program is to examine revenue lost because of a service failure that results in brand switching. In discussions with managers of loyalty programs at major hotel chains, Dubé and Shoemaker (1999) found that practically all the major hotel chains have customer service centers that handle customers' complaints about a particular property. Within certain constraints, the employees at these centers are authorized to resolve problems and offer compensation (e.g., extra award points or upgrade certificates) to guests who feel as if they have

Table 4: They would have come anyway analysis*

Assumptions regarding birthday card promotions:	
Redemption revenue from card-swipe frequent diner transactions	$1,329,150
Redemption revenue without using frequent diner card	65,258
Total revenue from promotion	$1,394,408
Total cost of the promotion	$61,000

Percent who would have come anyway	Sales anyway	Incremental amount less $61,000
5	$69,702(0.05*$1,394,408)	$1,263,688 ($1,394,408-$69,702-$61,000)
10	$139,441	$1,193,967
15	$209,161	$1,124,247
20	$278,882	$1,054,526
25	$348,602	$984,806
50	$697,204	$636,204
75	$1,045,806	$287,602
90	$1,254,967	$78,441
95	$1,324,688	$8720
100	$1,394,408	($61,000) ($1,394,408-$1,394,408-$61,000)

Goldfedder (1998).

been mistreated. The goal of such centers, of course, is to keep customers from switching to another brand. Not surprisingly, given the findings of Bowen and Shoemaker (1998), the majority of calls to the service centers are from program members. If one assumes that service failures occur equally to program members and non-members, one can estimate the revenue lost by non-members, who switch to another brand instead of calling the service center for compensation, by examining the number and type of complaints by members. One can refine this measurement by developing a classification of service failures that would cause a consumer to switch brands if the problem was not resolved sufficiently. Lost revenue could then be calculated as follows:

Total lost revenue = (Number of people who have complaint that would cause them to switch * potential revenue per guest) * percentage who would actually switch

A sixth and final method used to understand the financial impact of a program is to use an experimental design when conducting research. The most useful design would be a pre-test/post-test with a control group. With this type of design, a number of customers with similar behavior and demographic characteristics are randomly selected and divided into two groups. (The number depends upon such things as desired confidence interval and budget. See Churchill (1995) for more specifics on sample size characteristics.) The travel behavior of each group is then observed and recorded. One group then receives the treatment (i.e., a promotional offer), while the other group receives nothing. The travel behavior of both groups is then recorded. The difference in behavior between the groups can be attributed to the treatment effect. This type of design can be seen in Table 5.

This ends the discussion on customer loyalty. The next section examines future research issues.

Table 5: Basic form of pre-test post-test with control group

Classification number	Group type	Average number of visits last 3 months
01	Pre-test test group	5.3
02	Post-test test group	6.8
03	Pre-test control group (does not receive the treatment)	5.4
04	Post-test control group (does not receive the treatment)	5.6

Treatment effect = (Post-test test group − pre-test test group) − (post-test control group − pre-test control group)

$$= (02 - 01) - (04 - 03)$$
$$= (6.8 - 5.3) - (5.6 - 5.4)$$
$$= 1.3 \text{ increase in number of visits}$$

ROI = (No. of visits * average amount spent) − cost of the program.

10. Future Research Issues

In preparation for this article and an earlier article (Dubé and Shoemaker, 1999), Shoemaker asked each of the directors of the frequency programs at eight major hotel firms based in the U.S., what the issues were that kept them awake at night. The responses to this question, along with our own reading of the academic literature, provide the basis for this section.

One area for future research is to identify those features that can create value for both the guest and the firm that (1) do not raise the cost of the program; and (2) provide a competitive advantage. As discussed in this paper, those benefits can relate to any side of the loyalty triangle. The literature on the Process side of the loyalty triangle is well developed (see, e.g., Cannie, 1991; Barsky, 1995; Bhote, 1996; Zeithaml and Bitner, 1996). In contrast, literature on the Value Creation side and the Database/Communication side is relatively scarce in the hospitality field. Bowen and Shoemaker (1998) examined the benefits needed to create loyalty in the luxury segment. Similar studies need to be conducted for each of the lower tiers. Hoffman and Chung (1999) investigated hospitality recovery strategies for a hotel and restaurant in the southeast region of the United States. A similar study should be conducted with large hotel chains. The impact of communication also needs to be examined. For instance, what is the best way to communicate with the loyal customer (i.e., the internet, mailings) and the frequency of communication.

A second area for research is the need to develop better metrics to answer the question "would they have come anyway". While different metrics are presented in this article, firms are still searching for ways to measure the incremental business that results because of the program.

A third area for research is to investigate the usefulness of the loyalty triangle across different service businesses.

A fourth area is to investigate what creates customer loyalty across different cultures. Given that travel service firms operate internationally, the natural question is, "Should loyalty programs be tailored for specific geographic regions or will one program be sufficient for all cultures?"

A fifth area of research is to investigate the impact of partnerships on loyalty. Most hotel companies, rental car companies, and airlines have partnerships with each other. These partnerships do cost money. One question for a hotel firm would be "Is it necessary to be partners with all the airlines or would one or two suffice. What would be the impact on customer loyalty if the hotel firm dropped some of these partnerships?"

A final and fruitful area for research is to examine how loyalty creates an emotional attachment to the brand.

Researchers are urged to continue to study customer loyalty, which, we repeat, believe is the future of hospitality marketing. It is hoped that this paper provides a framework for understanding loyalty.

References

Asian Business, 1993. Extra life for airlines, pp. 44–66.
Barlow, R., 1992. Relationship marketing: the ultimate in customer services. Retail Control 29–37.
Barsky, J.D., 1995. World-Class Customer Satisfaction. Irwin, Burr Ridge, IL.
Berry, L., 1997. Speech at Frontiers in Service Marketing. Vanderbilt University, Tenn.
Bhote, K.R., 1996. Beyond Customer Satisfaction to Customer Loyalty: the Key to Greater Profitability. American Management Association, New York.
Bowen, J., Shoemaker, S., 1998. The antecedents and consequences of customer loyalty. Cornell Hotel Restaurant and Administration Quarterly 12–25.
Cannie, J.K., 1991. Keeping Customers for Life. American Management Association, New York.
Churchill, G.A., 1995. Marketing Research: Methodological Foundations, 6th Edition. The Dryden Press, Fort Worth.
Cram, T., 1994. The Power of Relationship Marketing: Keeping Customers for Life. Pitman Publishing, London.
Dolan, R.J., 1990. Conjoint Analysis: A Manager's Guide Case 9-590-059. Harvard Business School Publishing, Boston.
Dowling, G.R., Uncles, M., 1997. Do customer loyalty programs really work?. Sloan Management Review 38, 71–82.
Dubé, L., Shoemaker, S., 1999. Loyalty marketing and brand switching. In: Swartz, T. (Ed.), Handbook of Services Marketing and Management. Sage, Beverly Hills.
Dunn, D., 1997. Relationship marketing: a 35 minute primer. Frequency Marketing Strategies, Strategic Research Institute. Omni Chicago Hotel, Chicago.
Dwyer, F.R., Schurr, P.H., Oh, S., 1987. Developing buyer–seller relationships. Journal of Marketing 51, 11–27.
Fornell, C., Wernerfelt, B., 1987. Defensive marketing strategy by customer complaint management: a theoretical analysis. Journal of Marketing Research 24, 337–346.
Goldfedder J., 1998. Customer connection. Conversations with Shoemaker.
Goodwin, C., Ross, I., 1992. Consumer responses to service failures: influence of procedural and interactional fairness perceptions. Journal of Business Research 25, 149–163.
Gordon, I., 1988. Relationship Marketing. J Wiley, Canada.
Griffin, J., 1995. Customer Loyalty: How to Earn it and How to Keep it. Lexington Books, New York.
Gronroos, C., 1994. From marketing mix to relationship marketing: toward a paradigm shift in marketing. Management Decision 32 (2), 4–20.
Gummesson, E., 1987. The new marketing-developing long-term interactive relationship. Long Range Planning 20, 10–20.
Hart, C.W.L., Heskett, J.L., Sasser Jr, E., 1990. The profitable art of service recovery. Harvard Business Review 68, 148–156.
Heskett, J.L., Sasser Jr, E., Schlesinger, L.A., 1997. The Service Profit Chain. Free Press, New York.
Hoffman, D.K., Chung, B.G., 1999. Hospitality recovery strategies: customer preference versus firm use. Journal of Hospitality and Tourism Research 23 (1), 71–84.
Hu, M.Y., Toh, R.X., Strand, S., 1998. Frequent-flier programs: problems and pitfalls. Business Horizons 31, 52–57.
Jones, T., Schlesinger, L., Hallowell, R., 1991. AirMiles Canada. Case #9-694-008. Harvard Business School Publishing, Boston.
Lewis, R.C., 1987. The measurement of gaps in the quality of hotel services. International Journal of Hospitality Management 6 (2), 83–88.
Lowder, J., 1997. The relationship marketing report (May). Relationship Marketing Report, Occoquan, VA.

Magson, N., 1998. Database workshop: determining and measuring customer value. The Journal of Database Marketing 6 (1), 24–33.
O'Brien, L., Jones, C., 1995. Do rewards really create loyalty. Harvard Business Review 73, 75–82.
Peters, S., 1995. HR helps the mirage thrive in crowded Vegas. Personnel Journal 72–80.
Reichheld, F.F., 1996 (The Loyalty Effect) Harvard Business School Publishing, Boston.
Reichheld, F., Sasser Jr, W.E., 1990. Zero defections: quality comes to services. Harvard Business Review 68, 105–111.
Smith, R., 1998. Can you bribe your way to customer loyalty? Frequency marketing strategies. Strategic Research Institute, New York.
Webster, C., Sundaram, D.S., 1998. Service consumption criticality in failure recovery. Journal of Business Research 41, 153–159.
Zeithaml, V., Bitner, M.J., 1996. Services Marketing. McGraw-Hill, New York.

35

Tourism and Hospitality Marketing: Fantasy, Feeling and Fun

Alistair Williams

Introduction

Experiential marketing has become a cornerstone of many recent advances in areas such as retailing, branding and events marketing, however, marketing in the tourism and hospitality sectors does not appear to have explicitly engaged the theoretical issues involved. This raises the question what, if anything, does experiential marketing have to offer marketers in the disciplines of tourism and hospitality? In this paper, I will seek to introduce the experiential marketing debate and demonstrate how the questions raised by the concept are crucial to an understanding of marketing theory and research within the tourism and hospitality sectors.

Marketing and promotion is clearly essential for successful tourism and hospitality development, however, it is often overlooked or simplistic in nature (Hannam, 2004). Indeed, Morgan *et al.* (2002) argue that conventional tourism marketing tends to focus on confirming the intentions of tourists, rather than persuading them to consume differently. In addition the marketing of tourism and hospitality products has become increasingly complex, being associated not only with conveying an image of a place, but with attempting to sell an experience of a place through relating it to the lifestyle constructs of consumers. For many years we have discussed the characteristics of tourism

Source: *International Journal of Contemporary Hospitality Management*, 18(6) (2006): 482–495.

and hospitality products, which suggest that marketing within the sectors is different to many other industries, as purchase decisions are made on the basis of projected and perceived images, rather than prior experience. However, despite the amount of literature being written on these perceived differences, most marketing in the sector relies heavily on traditional marketing concepts, and it is often difficult to discriminate tourism and hospitality approaches to marketing from those advocated for other consumer products.

Tourism and hospitality has become a major economic activity as expectations with regard to the use of our leisure time have evolved, attributing greater meaning to our free time. The evolution of tourist behaviour encourages both change and the emergence of new meaning (Bouchet et al., 2004). This results in marketing having potentially a greater prominence in tourism and hospitality, than in other industries. Potential that is not always fully achieved (Morgan and Pritchard, 2002). The key reason for this failing is that in the main marketing for tourism and hospitality has been focussed not on the consumer, but on the destination or outlet, with marketing strategies being related to the products offered (Williams, 2000, 2002). As marketing within this sector has evolved however, the offer has become increasingly less important due to the enormous heterogeneity of consumer motivation and behaviour. The result is that firms and destinations within this sector need to redefine their strategies to reflect these changes.

Studying the behaviour of consumers has become increasingly complex, and it is fair to argue that tourism and hospitality by its very nature, should be in the vanguard of research into contemporary consumers (Williams, 2002). Tourism and hospitality offers a multitude of venues in which people can consume. Bars, restaurants, hotels, theme parks, casinos and cruise ships all operate as "Cathedrals of consumption" (Ritzer, 1999) offering increasingly complex consumption opportunities to increasingly complex consumers. Tourism and hospitality has developed into one of the most important global economic activities, due in part to a combination of a transformation of offers and increasingly postmodern demand. These changes mean that tourism and hospitality consumption has evolved to become more qualitative, more demanding, and more varied (Bouchet et al., 2004).

Anecdotal evidence delivered through media coverage, would suggest that contemporary consumers are self-indulgent, pleasure seeking individuals, easily dominated by marketers and advertisers, who act like sheep in the ways they mimic referent others. However, the reality is obviously much more complex than such a scenario suggests. Contemporary consumers are as likely to be driven by thrift as to they are to be hedonistic, they use consumption to make statements about themselves, they use consumption to create their identities and they develop a sense of belonging through consumption. For many people it is through consumption that relationships are formed, for example, colleagues enjoying a drink after work or children hosting their birthday parties at McDonalds, enabling them to define their circle of friends. Consumption also plays a part in finding fulfilment, developing creativity and expressing their individual abilities. Clearly such a complex phenomena cannot be easily understood.

Recent arguments have been sounded that aspects of contemporary tourism and hospitality consumption have reflected the phenomena of postmodernism. Whilst many believe postmodernism to be a meaningless intellectual fad, inaccessible to many involved in marketing within our sector, others agree that there are worthwhile insights to be gained from the debate on the post-modern condition and its consequences for tourism and hospitality consumption and marketing. I do not intend to discuss at length the use of post-modern discourse in tourism and hospitality marketing as I have exercised it in previous work (Williams, 2000, 2002). The term postmodernism refers to a break in thinking away from the modern, functional and rational, and during the last couple of decades it has spread across all domains of knowledge, including marketing. The key concepts of post-modern marketing are fragmentation, indeterminacy and distrust of universal discourse, but by eschewing modernism it introduces a radically new and different cultural movement which coalesces in a reconceptualisation of how we experience and explain our world. In terms of experiential marketing two aspects of the post-modern discourse are most relevant, hypereality and image.

Hypereality is one of the most discussed conditions of postmodernism, and refers to the argument that reality has collapsed and has become image, illusion, simulation and simulacra (copies for which no original exists). Hyperreality refers to a blurring of distinction between the real and the unreal in which the prefix "hyper" signifies more real than real. When the real is no longer a given but is reproduced by a simulated environment, it does not become unreal, but realer than real, to the extent it becomes what Baudrillard (1993, p. 23) refers to as "a hallucinatory resemblance of itself". In postmodernism, with the advent of hyperreality, simulations come to constitute reality itself. This scenario is exemplified throughout the tourism and hospitality industry. Baudrillard himself used the example of Disneyland, arguing it is more real than the USA itself. A point reinforced by Venturi (1995, p. 67) who suggested "Disneyland is nearer to what people want than what architects have ever given them. Disneyland is the symbolic American utopia". In postmodern society people have become fascinated by signs and as a result, they exist in a state where signs and images have become more important than what they stand for. The result is that today's consumers consume imagery and do not focus on what the images represent or mean. As Miller and Real (1998, p. 30) argue "we live in a world where the image or signifier of an event has replaced direct experience and knowledge of its referent or signified".

While it is accepted that there are problems with investigating tourism and hospitality marketing through a postmodern orientation, it clearly encompasses a broad range of consumer experiences. In addition it has the potential to reframe our thinking about marketing practice in an increasingly fragmented global marketplace. A better understanding of the underlying macro forces and micro behaviour, associated with postmodernism, can be leveraged by marketers to obtain competitive advantages in the increasingly dynamic, unpredictable, unstable and competitive tourism and hospitality environment.

Traditional marketing provided a valuable set of strategies, implementation tools and methodologies that tourism and hospitality firms could use in an earlier age. As Schmitt (1999, p. 55) argued "traditional marketing was developed in response to the industrial age, not the information, branding and communications revolution we are facing today". In a new age, with new consumers we need to shift away from a features-and-benefits approach, as advocated by traditional approaches to consumer experiences. We need to consider new concepts and approaches which capitalise on the opportunities offered by these new consumers. One such approach is experiential marketing; an approach which in contrast to the rational features-and-benefits view of consumers, takes a more postmodern orientation and views them as emotional beings, concerned with achieving pleasurable experiences.

Experiential Marketing of Tourism and Hospitality Products

The Transition to an Experience Economy

Experiential marketing is a growing trend worldwide, with enthusiasts reported in all sectors of the global economy, from consumer products such as Ford Motor Company (Kerwin, 2004) to health care providers such as the North Hawaii Community Hospital (Hill, 2003). As Schmitt (1999, p. 53) states "experiential marketing is everywhere". The question is what has caused this evolution in the world of marketing, and what are the implications for consumers of tourism and hospitality?

Experiential marketing was first introduced by Pine and Gilmore (1998) as part of their work on the experience economy, and further refined in many subsequent articles and books by the same authors. Pine and Gilmore (1999, p. 2) explained their view of experiential marketing in the following manner "when a person buys a service, he purchases a set of intangible activities carried out on his behalf. But when he buys an experience, he pays to spend time enjoying a series of memorable events that a company stages to engage him in a personal way". Experiential marketing is about taking the essence of a product and amplifying it into a set of tangible, physical, interactive experiences which reinforce the offer. Rather than seeing the offer in a traditional manner, through advertising media such as commercials, print or electronic messaging, consumers "feel" it by being part of it. As Gautier (2004, p. 8) argues "experiential marketing is a totally new way of thinking about marketing, if you think it's about simply tweaking around the edges, think again". Experiential marketing is not about one-off events, sponsorship, sampling or general field marketing. Experiential marketing describes marketing initiatives that give consumers in-depth, tangible experiences in order to provide them with sufficient information to make a purchase decision. It is widely argued that as the science of marketing evolves, experiential marketing will become the dominant marketing tool of the future (McNickel, 2004).

Experiential marketing has evolved as a response to a perceived transition from a service economy to one personified by the experiences we participate in. In such a perception experiences are as economically different from services as services are from goods. Pine and Gilmore (2004) explain that experiences have emerged as the next step, in what they refer to as the progression of economic value. If we accept such a position; that modern economies are seen as making a transition from the marketing of services to the marketing of experiences, all tourism and hospitality offers are acts of "theatre" that stage these experiences. The experience economy has been summarised by Petkus (2002) as follows:

- contemporary economies have evolved from the delivery of commodities to the delivery of goods, from goods to services and are presently evolving from services to experiences;
- as services became increasingly commodified, customer perceptions of competitive advantage diminish, as does satisfaction;
- the delivery of experiential market offerings involves engaging customers in a memorable way; and
- all actions of the organisation contribute to the performance of the experiential market offering.

A Move from Mass Media to Experiential Marketing

The huge growth in the field of experiential marketing appears to be the result of the effect of the numerous success stories cited in the media. As Kerwin (2004, p. 94) states "the beauty of a well designed experience is that while it doesn't reach nearly as many people as a TV spot, it can attract the very customers who are most likely to buy". The evidence seems to support this contention, for example, research undertaken by SRI, an international market research organisation, found that experiential marketing drove faster results than traditional methods, with consumers suggesting it led to quick positive purchase decisions. Amongst certain groups, younger consumers and females, the results were even more encouraging (Allen, 2005). The same research also demonstrated that experiential marketing made consumers more receptive to other forms of associated advertising, an important factor in an era of integrated marketing communication. Similar results were found by IMI International. Their research suggested that more than 55 per cent of consumers felt that the biggest single influence on propensity to consume was the ability to sample or interact with a product before purchase. In the UK, research undertaken by ID Live Brand Experience stated that as many as 85 per cent of consumers valued the opportunity to experience; touch, smell, taste or hear, products. Of those surveyed, 58 per cent confirmed that experiential marketing had encouraged them to make a purchase they were not previously planning to make. The importance of this development is not lost on marketing executives with more than 70 per cent of them recently stating that experiential marketing is the current "big theme" (Gautier, 2004). Pine and Gilmore (1999) the originators of much of the current thinking behind experiential marketing cite US Bureau of Labour statistics showing that consumer price indices, employment growth and growth in GDP have all increased at a faster rate for experiential offerings, than for commodities, goods or services. To summarise, the reason behind the continuing growth in demand for experiential marketing, is that it appears to work for both firms and customers. As Witthaus (2004, p. 10) states:

> . . . it achieves measurable results by offering innovative ways of communicating with customers in their own environment, leading to a better ROI. And it offers a memorable, engaging and exhilarating way of reaching customers.

Experiential marketing demonstrates that the media landscape has unalterably changed in recent years. In 1985, a commercial on peak-time television would have been expected to reach over 40 per cent of the population. A similar commercial today would be unlikely to reach more than 15 per cent of the population, and this figure is likely to continue falling (Gautier, 2004). Despite increased spend on traditional media many of the worlds top products and brands have suffered falling market share. There is a widespread belief that old models of advertising spend are no longer as effective as they were and alternatives have to be sought. As Pine and Gilmore (2004, p. 36) argue:

> . . . there seems to be three different reactions to the decreasing efficiency of advertising in reaching consumers. Some have denied it's happening, some have thrown money at the situation, and others have tried to forge a new direction, in the last category are those who've realised it's time to start staging marketing experiences.

Earlier we asked what were the implications of this re-orientation in marketing for the marketing of tourism and hospitality products? The answer would appear to be significant. As Frank Garahan, Rancho Las Palmas Resort General Manager, states "hospitality marketing is experiential, how do you explain the sensory excitement of being here? you can't get the ambiance from an advert" (Frasher, 2003, p. 3). It is clear that the fact that their product is almost always experiential puts tourism and hospitality marketers in a unique position to apply the principles of experiential marketing to their activities. The problem is that simply having an intrinsically, inherently experiential offering is very different from actively and deliberately marketing that offer in an experiential manner. To achieve this goal, frameworks through which tourism and hospitality marketers can strategically identify, enhance and deliver their offers have to be introduced.

The Four Dimensions of the Tourism and Hospitality Experience

Pine and Gilmore (1998) suggest that we think about experiences across two bi-polar constructs (Figure 1) customer participation (ranging from active to passive) and connection (ranging from absorption to immersion). For example, on the participation construct someone watching a film in a cinema would be passive, whilst someone dining in a restaurant, active. In a similar manner someone watching a tourism spectacle such as a parade from a hotel balcony, can absorb the event taking place beneath them, whilst someone on the street would be immersed in the sights, sounds and smells that surround them.

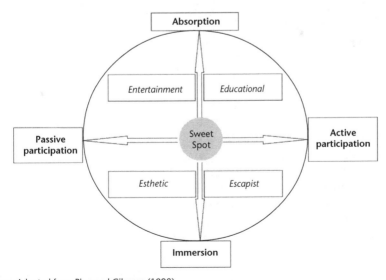

Source: Adapted from Pine and Gilmore (1998)

Figure 1: The four realms of experience

From their two bi-polar constructs Pine and Gilmore sorted experiences into four "Realms"; namely education, entertainment, escapist and esthetic. Those experiences we think of as entertainment; such as going to a show, usually involve customers participating in a passive manner where their connection with the activity is likely to involve absorption rather than immersion. The suggestion that in this Realm experiences are simply taken in may seem like an obvious application of much of the tourism experience. For tourism and hospitality marketers however, the key to this Realm may be to apply it more holistically, i.e. to incorporate entertainment into areas outside of the immediate experience.

Activities in the Educational Realm involve those where participants are more actively involved, but are still of an absorption nature, rather than immersion. In this Realm, participants acquire new skills or increase those they already have; such as ski instruction. Many tourism and hospitality offerings include educational dimensions; such as education programmes, informal lectures, guides or background information. If we consider the case of heritage sites, for example, Masberg and Silverman (1996) discuss aspects of personal experience at such sites, which includes education and learning. Cruise ships often employ well-known authorities to provide semi-formal lectures about their itiniries, and many resort destinations have recently sought to encourage guests to engage with local populations. Despite the success of many such initiatives the potential clearly exists for further increasing the "educational" element of many tourism and hospitality offers.

Escapist activities are those which involve both active participation and immersion in the activities environment, and are clearly a central feature of much of tourism and hospitality. Activities such as bungee jumping over gorges in New Zealand, for example, represent typical aspects of the Escapist Realm. In a similar manner participation in sporting activities whilst on holiday, such as water-sports or golfing, clearly represent escapist experiences. Membership of organisations such as the National Trust, or other volunteer organisations, also acts as a form of escapist experience, allowing participants to create new identities and realities for themselves.

When the element of activity is reduced to be more passive in nature, the event becomes esthetic. The participants are immersed in the activity, but have little effect on its environment, such as looking over the gorge in New Zealand, and simply admiring the view. The Esthetic Realm, according to Pine and Gilmore involves a more intense experience than the entertainment experience. Again it is easy to conclude that much tourism activity is of an esthetic nature, with tourists immersing themselves in the experience, but with little active participation in the experience.

In essence the Entertainment Realm involves sensing, the Educational Realm learning, the Escapist Realm doing, and the Esthetic Realm being there (Petkus, 2002). As the four Realms are not intended to be mutually exclusive, however, the richest experiences for consumers encompass aspects of all four Realms, producing a "sweet spot" where the Realms meet. The richness of an experience is a function of the degree to which all four realms are incorporated. Pine and Gilmore themselves extensively quote the example of Walt Disney World, as being one of the richest experiences available to consumers, due to the emphasis on employees, attention to the environment and attention to the backstage areas.

Strategies for Experientially Marketing Tourism and Hospitality

Pine and Gilmore originally suggested that there were five design principles in staging experiences, to which a sixth was later added.

Developing a cohesive theme for the experience is the first step, involving establishing a cohesive set of images and meanings for the experience. If we think about the many themed bars and restaurants in our industry, in particular those where the food often acts as a prop for what has become widely known as "entertainment", the brand name tells us exactly what to expect. Restaurant chains such as Hard Rock Café, Planet Hollywood or Rainforest Café have a well-defined theme which is achieved through consistency in operations, marketing communications, materials and employees. These businesses have taken the first step in experiential marketing. By contrast a poorly conceived theme gives consumers nothing to focus on with the result that consumers have no lasting memory of the experience. A bar chain such as Weatherspoons, for example, is driven by the paucity of the experience to compete solely on price.

Harmonizing impressions with positive cues refers to the creation of memorable sensory stimuli; what Pine and Gilmore refer to as the "takeaways" of the experience. In order to be successful these cues must be consistent with the theme and designed to fully support it. Schmitt and Simonson (1997) delineate the formation of impressions using the dimensions time, space, technology, authenticity, sophistication and scale. They argue that the strategic imperative is the balance of these dimensions that is desirable to the target market.

The time dimension refers to the various orientations of past, present and future, with different markets likely to be interested in different offerings or combinations of offerings. The space dimension can be used either to refer to geographical space, such as tourism regions, or physical space, such as indoor versus outdoor. The range of combinations such categories open up for tourism and hospitality marketers offers the opportunity for a huge number of innovative offerings. The technology dimension refers to natural versus man-made versus machine-made and again numerous opportunities exist for tourism and hospitality marketers to develop offerings that consider the various permutations possible. The authenticity dimension refers to original versus imitative representations, and again is manifest throughout tourism and hospitality. This dimension is inextricably linked to the discussion on postmodernism earlier in this paper, with its focus on the use of simulation and representation. Simulation is used throughout tourism and hospitality from the faux island of Labadee (in reality a promontory of Haiti) to which guests of Royal Caribbean cruise ships are transported, to the mock 1960s diners of the Rock Island restaurant chain. The level of sophistication refers to the "cultural" aspects of the experience, for example, the difference between the resort of San An in Ibiza and Martha's Vineyard. Finally, scale refers to the size and scope of the offering, represented by either physical space, the number of hotel rooms in a resort, for example, or temporal space, for example the length of a season.

Tourism and hospitality marketers need to identify the appropriate balances between and within these dimensions if they are to develop appropriate experiential marketing strategies. For example, the balance between uni-dimensional offerings or a more eclectic approach to the market.

Eliminating negative cues refers to the need for marketers to remove anything that diminishes, contradicts or distracts from the unity of the theme. The best example of which is Disney, where its "cast members" are always in character, whether acting out the role of Sleeping Beauty, or serving coffee in one of its many restaurants. An entire experience can be spoiled by a single inconsistent message, whose day at Disney would not be ruined by a miserable Mickey Mouse.

Mix in memorabilia refers to the fact that tourism and hospitality consumers have always bought or appropriated certain mementoes of their vacations and visits. Whether these be; post-cards, logo'd T shirts or baseball caps, ash-trays or bath towels. People spend billions of Euros on such mementoes, which often retail at well above the market value, because of the memory of the experiences that they refer to. It is worthwhile noting that people buy memorabilia from Airlines such as Virgin, but steadfastly refuse to purchase similar offerings from Ryanair or EasyJet, because of the different experiences on offer.

Engaging all five senses is important because the more sensory an experience, the more memorable it will be. Most tourism and hospitality offerings have a range of sensory elements, sounds, sights, smells, touch and taste. Pine and Gilmore (1998, p. 104) cite the example of the Rainforest Café:

> . . . the mist appeals serially to all five senses. It is first apparent as a sound, then you see the mist rising from the rocks and feel it cool against your skin. Finally, you smell its tropical essence, and you taste its freshness.

Soliciting feedback is the final strategic step and is critical if experiential marketing is to be effective. Whilst many tourism and hospitality businesses seek feedback through such mechanisms as guest questionnaires, experiential marketing requires more innovative and creative solutions.

Experiential Marketing in the Tourism and Hospitality Sectors

It is apparent from this paper that the clearest implications of experiential marketing for tourism and hospitality are in the design of marketing strategies, and some businesses and organisations have sought to introduce experiential marketing in this way. The earliest example of experiential marketing in our sector, and indeed the organisation that Pine and Gilmore suggest we should be copying, was Walt Disney Parks and Resorts. When Disneyland opened in 1955 it was a revolutionary entertainment concept. However, a key part of its success was the deal done with ABC to use the new media of television to market the enterprise. In return for assistance with funding, Walt Disney entered into a programming deal to produce a weekly TV series. Walt Disney visualised "Disneyland" the show and "Disneyland" the place as one and the same. The series featured a weekly rotation of shows with themes emanating from the different worlds in the park. As a result the show became a platform for Disney to update viewers on the construction of the park, its opening and continual expansions. The process is ongoing, for example, one of the most successful films in recent years, is based on a Disney attraction, Pirates of the Caribbean, and other attraction based films are currently in production. It is a key question as to why so few hospitality firms over the last 50 years, have sought to replicate such a winning marketing strategy?

Other early movers in experiential marketing in our sector tended to be those with readily defined products. An example of this type of organisation would be Guinness, with Guinness Storehouse, Ireland's premier visitor attraction. As Aine Friel Marketing Manager at Guinness Storehouse states "it is driving sales of Guinness around the world, we've created 2.5 million brand ambassadors who are talking about Guinness". At Guinness Storehouse the marketing experience includes many, but not all of the steps advocated by Pine and Gilmore, an education project, a cohesive theme, achievable memorabilia, the engagement of the senses and the soliciting of feedback. At Guinness Storehouse there is a postcard wall, on which people are encouraged to write and post feedback. The fact that all of it is left for others to peruse suggests a very brave venture. However, as Aine Friel suggests "when you watch peoples reaction to it, they don't feel like their being spun and there's a completely different respect for Guinness".

In the foodservice sector we can consider successful firms such as Starbucks, who have elevated the consumption of a routine commodity, coffee, to a memorable experience. As a result customers do not care how expensive their various concoctions are, they purchase the experience. As has been noted "in its attempt to deliver audiences a recreation of the Italian coffee shop experience, I think everyone will agree Starbucks has been widely successful". Commodities such as coffee are interchangeable and tangible, services such as coffee in a diner are intangible, but experiences such as a Starbucks latte grande with toppings, are memorable. As has been noted, "every café is a stage".

If we consider tourism marketing campaigns experiential marketing can be seen in for example the campaigns aimed at the Indian diaspora (Hannam, 2004) which seek to engage second and third generation Indians, living outside India, to rediscover their roots. This has been done through bringing the population together for a key experience, in this case the Pravasi Bharatiya Divas festival.

Despite its numerous benefits the internet has also caused many problems for the tourism and hospitality sectors, as Maitel (2002, p. 22) argues "the internet is the greatest force of commoditization known to man, both goods and services". Only those firms that develop customer valued web-based experiences will be successful in the era of e-commerce. The use of new technologies, such as satellite technology, CD/DVD, WIFI, and the web have aided the potential for experiential marketing and a number of initiatives are being developed utilising this technology. For some time tourism and hospitality organisations have marketed using web-technology, and this has become increasingly sophisticated with the development of real-time webcams (for example, at any time of the day you can see what is happening in the Bellagio Resort swimming pools). The use of technology to produce virtual visits is also increasing. Such sites as previsite or virtual tour use technology to give potential customers a 3D virtual visit to a wide range of tourist sites and hospitality offers. The use of electronic multi-media, is being increasingly investigated, in particular the use of integrated MP3/GPS systems, WIFI, CD/DVD, GPS systems in vehicles and the increased use of satellite technology. For example, in the Rhone-Alps the SITRA system is under development. This is a CRM system which collects information from organisations involved in tourism, such as hotels, restaurants, ski-resorts and tourism offices and dispenses it to a range of outlets including traditional media, but also PDA's, GPS systems, in-vehicle systems, mobiles and the web. Using the system tourists seeking information whilst on the move are constantly updated with the latest news. Project HOPPY uses similar technology to produce a multimedia mapping experience for tourists. The system generates audio and visual mapping for users using integrated GPS receivers and operating in a choice of languages and themes.

Technology in terms of virtual reality also assists marketers in our sector, as Allen (2005, p. 3) suggests:

. . . ask yourself which is more effective: a simple pop-up exhibit and promotional literature depicting the benefits of an ocean cruise, or to climb to the top of the bridge to take in the simulated view of the aqua-blue Caribbean waters.

A system known as TRYTON offers real and virtual sub-aqua experiences, using a computerised waterproof viewer that integrates the air tanks and facial mask allowing the user to breathe under water. The viewer diffuses multimedia productions – visual and audio contents – and creates moves and other effects simulating the actual dive. The viewer is connected to the internet through a computer terminal and can diffuse under water productions and information received from dive sites all over the world in real time.

Other simpler hospitality experiential marketing includes firms such as the MGM Grand Hotel & Casino who have reinvented the humble wake-up call to create a memorable experience by awakening guests with recorded voices of celebrities who have recently performed there. Another example would be the Raffles L'Ermitage Hotel which charges guests a 24 hour day rate not a room rate. Some of the best examples are those of spas, which are increasingly marketed as experiences. For example, the Thalassotherapy Centre of Carnac talks about its being "located 100 m away from the Ocean, protected by a peninsula, by a lagoon listed as a bird sanctuary". If we compare this to the fitness rooms and pools introduced as amenities in many hotels during the 1980s and 1990s, many of these offer little or no differentiation and are often considered a sink cost.

Whilst as we have seen there are examples of tourism and hospitality organisations using experiential marketing they are few in number and are often poorly executed or the concept is misunderstood. Many organisations suggest that they are using experiential marketing, when the reality is that they are simply repeating the mantra of traditional marketing strategies. The Ohio Travel and Tourism Division for example state that they are using experiential marketing to create a vibrant look and feel for their brand. However, the reality is that they are using traditional media; print, TV, the internet and radio, in a traditional manner; advertising and public relations, to promote their state. In a similar manner the Canadian Tourism Commission suggests that its new campaign is one of experiential marketing, arguing that potential travellers will not be given specific images of Canada, but will be inspired to "come, explore and reach their own conclusions". Again the reality is that this is not experiential marketing, as the media and approach are both from traditional marketing. As has been suggested when referring to the Canadian Tourism Commission marketing strategy "there is a big problem with the strategy, you can't create a positive experience if the experience hasn't been defined".

Conclusions

Experiential marketing is a relatively new orientation, which is gaining ground in western and other developed economies and which provides a contrast to traditional marketing. Whereas traditional marketing frameworks view consumers as rational decision-makers focussed on the functional features and benefits of products, experiential marketing views consumers as emotional beings, focussed on achieving pleasurable experiences. These experiences are achieved through "experience providers" (Schmitt, 1999) such as communications, visual and verbal identity, presence and media. As Schmitt (1999, p. 53) argues "the ultimate goal of experiential marketing is to create holistic experiences that integrate individual experiences into a holistic Gestalt". The difference between traditional and experiential marketing can be highlighted in a number of ways. Firstly, the focus is on customer experiences and lifestyles, which provide sensory, emotional, cognitive and relational values to the consumer. Secondly, there is a focus on creating synergies between meaning, perception, consumption and brand loyalty. Thirdly, it is argued that customers are not rational decision-makers, but rather driven by rationality and emotion. Finally, it is argued that experiential marketing requires a more diverse range of research methods in order to understand consumers. What are required, it is argued, are methods which are new and subjective and which look for difference and uniqueness rather than similarity and pattern (Williams, 2000).

Underpinning experiential marketing is the notion of a fourth economic stage of development. One which goes beyond our current pre-occupation with services marketing, to a stage where experiences are central to consumption activity. The identification of an experience economy points up the need for marketing to respond, which it has with experiential marketing. Tourism and hospitality marketing, too often grounded in positivistic assumptions, viewing consumption as an internalised state, has to begin to respond to alternative orientations. When rival tourism and hospitality offerings become more alike than different, in the concepts that dominate their design and operations they find their business commodified. They are then purchased on the basis of price. Experiential marketing helps firms to avoid the commodification trap. If firms are to be effective in the highly competitive tourism and hospitality industries, it is imperative that they understand contemporary markets and consumers. Referring back to the question with which I opened this paper, I would argue that experiential marketing offers tourism and hospitality marketers two things. Firstly, it offers a more meaningful insight into the ways in which consumers perceive or view tourism and hospitality's eclectic range of offers. Secondly, experiential marketing offers us the opportunity to consider a new approach to marketing; one with which to capitalise on the unique nature of tourism and hospitality products.

As Schmitt (1999, p. 53) argues "from now on, leading-edge companies, whether they sell to consumers or businesses, will find that the next competitive battlefield lies in staging experiences". The tourism and hospitality sectors cannot be seen to be immune to such fundamental changes in the orientation of marketing. Innovative experience design will become an increasingly important component of tourism and hospitality firms core capabilities. Those who go beyond service excellence and market experientially will lead the creation of value in the sector.

References

Allen, W. (2005), *Successful Meetings*, Vol. 54 No. 4, pp. 26–9.
Baudrillard, J. (1993), *The Transparency of Evil: Essays on Extreme Phenomena*, Verso, London.
Bouchet, P., Lburn, A. and Auvergne, S. (2004), "Sport tourism consumer experiences: a comprehensive model", *Journal of Sport Tourism*, Vol. 9 No. 2, pp. 27–140.
Frasher, S. (2003), "Palm springs area resorts court convention planners", *The Business Press*, 17 March, p. 10.
Gautier, A. (2004), "Why experiential marketing is the next big thing", *New Zealand Marketing Magazine*, p. 8, September.
Hannam, K. (2004), "Tourism & development II", *Progress in Development Studies*, Vol. 4 No. 3, pp. 256–63.
Hill, R. (2003), "Are you being served?", *Health Forum Journal*, September, pp. 12–16.
Kerwin, K. (2004), "When the factory is a theme park", *Business Week*, 3 May.
McNickel, D. (2004), "Hands on brands", May, available at: www.marketingmag.co.nz
Maitel, S. (2002), "Don't sell commodities sell experiences", *The New Corporate University Review*, May, available at: www.traininguniversity.com
Masberg, B.A. and Silverman, L.H. (1996), "Visitor experiences at heritage sites", *Journal of Travel Research*, Vol. 34 No. 4, pp. 20–31.
Miller, G. and Real, M. (1998), "Postmodernity and popular culture", in Berger, A.A. (Ed.), *The Post-Modern Presence*, Sage, London.
Morgan, N. and Pritchard, A. (2002), *Tourism, Promotion & Power: Creating Images, Creating Identities*, Wiley, Chichester.
Morgan, N., Pritchard, A. and Pride, R. (2002), *Destination Branding: Creating the Unique Destination Proposition*, Butterworth-Heinemann, Oxford.
Petkus, E. (2002), "Enhancing the application of experiential marketing in the arts", *International Journal of Non-profit and Voluntary Sector Marketing*, Vol. 9 No. 1, pp. 49–56.
Pine, B.J. and Gilmore, J.H. (1998), "Welcome to the experience economy", *Harvard Business Review*, July/August, pp. 97–105.
Pine, B.J. and Gilmore, J.H. (1999), *The Experience Economy*, Harvard Business School Press, Boston, MA.
Pine, B.J. and Gilmore, J.H. (2004), "Trade in ads for experience", *Advertising Age*, Vol. 75 No. 39, p. 36.
Ritzer, G. (1999), *Enchanting a Disenchanted World*, Sage, Thousand Oaks, CA.
Schmitt, B.H. (1999), "Experiential marketing", *Journal of Marketing Management*, Vol. 15, pp. 53–67.
Schmitt, B.H. and Simonson, A. (1997), *Marketing Aesthetics: The Strategic Management of Brands, Identity & Image*, The Free Press, New York, NY.

Venturi, R. (1995), "Distorted imagination", in Appignanesi, R. and Garrett, C. (Eds), *Postmodernism for Beginners*, Icon Books, Cambridge.

Williams, A.J. (2000), "Consuming hospitality: learning from postmodernism", in Lashley, C. and Morrison, A. (Eds), *In Search of Hospitality*, Butterworth-Heinemann, Oxford.

Williams, A.J. (2002), *Understanding the Hospitality Consumer*, Butterworth-Heinemann, Oxford.

Witthaus, M. (2004), "Does practice make perfect", *Precision Marketing*, 26 November, p. 27.

Further Reading

Gilmore, J.H. and Pine, J. (2002), "Differentiating hospitality operations via experiences", *Cornell Hotel and Restaurant Quarterly*, Vol. 43 No. 3, pp. 87–96.

Exploring Chinese Cultural Influences and Hospitality Marketing Relationships
David Gilbert and Jenny Tsao

The Taiwanese Hotel Industry and Rise in Competition

The devotion of the Taiwanese government to actively planning and promoting tourism began in 1956 and since then the number of hotels has increased continuously. Beginning in the 1960s, the Taiwanese hotel industry, especially the international tourist hotel category, has been invested in, built and developed until the saturation of the market especially in the capital, Taipei city. Throughout the 40 years of development, the numbers of international tourist hotels in Taipei alone has increased from three hotels in 1965 to 27 hotels in 1995 and the number of rooms has also risen from 736 to 10,257 (TNTO, 1996). The competition among the international tourist hotels in Taipei is anticipated to be even more aggressive in the future due to new developments, market structure changes and major business hotel competition as a result of the failure to choose alternative segments (nearly all the existing and planned international tourist class hotels in Taipei are positioned in the business segment). In addition, during the past few years, neither the sales nor the occupancy rate of the international hotels in Taipei have increased in line with national increases in tourism arrivals.

New Approaches to Marketing

Alternative marketing theories have emerged since the 1960s and specifically in recent service marketing literature new theories have emanated with diverse approaches to redefine the marketing concept. As such, relationship marketing (RM) has received increasing attention, (Kotler and Armstrong, 1996; Palmer, 1996; Grönroos, 1994a; Gilbert, 1996; Gummesson, 1994; Bennett, 1996). The traditional "marketing mix" and its 4Ps, which has dominated the marketing paradigm for decades is challenged by the RM writers as a production-oriented definition of marketing instead of a market-oriented, or customer-oriented approach (Grönroos, 1994b). This approach is an attempt to replace earlier notions of transaction marketing. In transaction marketing the focus is very short term and since there is not much more than the core product or, in some cases, the image of the firm, or its brand, which would keep the customer attached to the seller, customers are difficult to retain. This leads to the price becoming the determining factor as competition rises (Grönroos, 1994a).

On the other hand, relationship marketing embraces a function which has a longer term focus where its main philosophy is to build long-term relationships with customers. By maintaining a customer base and applying relationship marketing functions, the firm would create more value for its customers than the core product could provide alone. Within such circumstances, customers would tend to be less sensitive to a competitor's price attraction, which would generate more profit for the company. Grönroos (1994a) suggests that the emergence of RM represents a paradigm shift in marketing, away from a restricting focus on the clinical functions of the management of the marketing mix toward an emphasis on the development and management of diverse forms of customer relationships.

The long-term financial benefits RM could convey has been the impetus to the development of the theory and the growing awareness it is receiving. Basically, the ground of the economic benefits that RM delivers is based on the following notions:

- Acquiring customers is much more expensive than keeping them.
- The longer the relationship is maintained between the company and customer the more profitable the relationship is to the firm (Buttle, 1996).

The above also requires an understanding of the way quality and service depart from traditional orientations and play a part in retention strategies. RM therefore, encompasses a series of organisational and managerial strategies based on researching customers' personal needs to provide a more personal service or developing external partnerships to ensure third party support of company objectives. As part of this approach to retention, improving service and quality are as important as offering loyalty incentive schemes.

Cultural Approaches in Marketing Practice

In order to understand the contextual background of generating relationships with customers, the cultural variable should not be omitted. The approach to explain marketing and general business in an intercultural environment has been supported by writers such as Usunier (1993), Hall (1990), Hofstede (1984) and Adler (1991) emphasising that cultural differences have an important impact on the results of all aspects in business such as marketing, management, leadership, decision making, etc.

As the derivation of RM theory was from a Western viewpoint it could be argued that the prescriptions for RM in Western norms of behaviour may fail when transplanted to a market which is sustained by a different set of cultural variables. Western-based database marketing and incentive schemes may fail in cultures where buyer-seller relationships have to be understood in the broader context (Palmer, 1996). Meanwhile, "relationship" as interpreted and valued differently by each culture would also influence the process, quality and sustainability of relationship building.

In this study, the Chinese culture, which is heavily "relationally oriented", will be examined to analyse the practice of RM in a Chinese context. Therefore, some general background of culture, specifically the Chinese culture in a business context, will be presented. The Chinese-culture territory includes countries such as Taiwan, China, Hong Kong, Macau and Singapore. Although these countries may have distinct historical backgrounds, as they all belong to Chinese-dominated societies, similar cultural systems could apply to these so-called "Chinese Commonwealth" countries (Luo, 1997). Researchers in the study of Chinese cultural values find that although change is occurring, Chinese values have formed a clear and consistent system for generations (Yau, 1988; King, 1996).

Importance of Recognising Cultural Differences

Since culture is a difficult to define construct, "culture" could be generalised as:

> A shared pattern of being, thinking, and behaving; something learned from childhood through socialisation; something deeply rooted in tradition that permeates all aspects of any given society (Xing, 1995).

Within the context of RM, the exchange process between the parties is targeted at a long-term relationship where personal interaction is required. This causes both difficulties and opens up possibilities as it increases the role of human differences, similarities, antipathies, etc. In the terminology of Hofstede

(1984), different cultures imply different mental programming, which governs activities, motivation and values. This logic is also advocated by Adler (1991). To study RM related to Chinese culture the focal inclination we are pursuing is to study diverse relationship orientations.

No one who has had experience of Chinese society can fail to note that Chinese people are extremely sensitive to *mien-tsu* (face) and *jen-chin* (human obligation) in their interpersonal relationships. Similarly, a social phenomenon called *kuan-hsi* (personal relationship) cannot go unnoticed. These socialcultural concepts are key to the understanding of Chinese social culture as they are part of the essential "stock knowledge" of Chinese adults in their management of everyday life, including their business behaviour (King, 1991). Therefore, these socio-cultural concepts will be examined as an introduction to the characteristics of "relationship" as the Chinese way of dealing with business relationships.

Kuan-hsi (Personal Relationship)/Networking

Western marketing literature has increasingly seen the management of networks as an important aspect of strategic behaviour and the networking paradigm as a "means of understanding the totality of relationships amongst firms engaged in production, distribution, and the use of goods and services". In RM, networking is also considered as an important method of relationship building especially in buyer and seller relationships. Most of the networking literature is relatively recent and has been largely concerned with the Western business context. However, this is somewhat ironic because history suggests that networks, translated as *kuan-hsi*, have been the dominant form of transactional governance in Chinese society since long before the concept was taken up by Western theorists (Davies *et al.*, 1995). In business relations, *kuan-hsi* can be considered as drawing on connections or networks in order to secure personal or business favours. *Kuan-hsi* has been pervasive in the Chinese business world for the last few centuries and today it binds millions of Chinese firms into a social and business web. As Buttery and Leung. (1998) have indicated, the behaviour may involve the constant process of giving without obtaining a favour in return, as it is based upon building life-long relationships and trust between each party.

Knowing and practising *Kuan-hsi* is part of the learned behaviour of being Chinese. As a socio-cultural concept, it is deeply embedded in Confucian socio theory and has its own logic which forms and constitutes the socio structure of Chinese society. Although Confucian socio theory has a tendency to mould the Chinese into group-oriented and socially dependent beings, it must be emphatically argued that Confucianism does attach reasonable autonomy to the individual. According to a study done by Ichiro Numazaki

(1987, in Kao, 1991), "personal trust" is one of the key mechanisms on which *kuan-hsi* and partnerships are based. In recruiting people "personal trust" is the major criterion. In other words, this person must be either personally known by the boss or be introduced by a person whom the boss trusts. Analogously, when a firm or enterprise group seeks a partnership there will be no co-operation without intimate *kuan-hsi*. The co-operative inter-business relationship is primarily based on the personal trust between the two major bosses, if trust exists, the deal is very easy to accomplish (Kao, 1991).

Face *(mien-tsu)/(lien)*

In understanding Chinese interpersonal behaviour, the most significant factor is "face". Although this is a human universal behaviour, the Chinese have developed a sensitivity to it and used it as a reference point in behaviour in a much more sophisticated and developed way than in other cultural groups (Redding, 1982). This is a key component in the dynamics of *kuan-hsi*, as one must have a certain amount of prestige to cultivate and develop a viable network of *kuan-hsi* connections (Luo, 1997). Face can be further classified into the two dimensions of *lien* and *mien-tsu*. *Lien* is associated with personal behaviour and character whereas *mien-tsu* is something valuable that can be achieved. The amount of *mien-tsu* a person has is a function of social status. The Chinese interact with each other to protect, give, add, exchange or even borrow *mien-tsu*; it enters much more into everyday transactions as a form of social currency (Chen, 1995).

Similar to face, *jen-chin* (personal obligations) is also a form of social capital that can create leverage during interpersonal exchanges. In the cultivation and development of *kuan-hsi*, *jen-chin* plays an important role. Since *jen-chin* involves social exchange obligations, there is a need for people to keep equity in mind. When people fail to follow the rule of equity in exchange of *jen-chin*, they lose their face and this is not socially or morally appropriate. Thus, when people construct their *kuan-hsi* network, they are also weaving a web of *jen-chin* obligations. While they enjoy the benefits of connections of network, they also take on a reciprocal obligation which must be "repaid" in the future (Luo, 1997). For further explanation, the work of Pang *et al.* (1998) provides a fuller explanation of the history and culture of Chinese society.

Research Methodology

Since the research is interested in the conceptual particularities formed by cultural factors that Chinese hotel practitioners have developed toward the practice of RM and its relation to the Chinese culture, the whole study is therefore framed within the hotel sector of a Chinese-dominated country – Taiwan. Taiwan is a Chinese-dominated society which allows for an interesting sample to test the reality and applicability of RM in the hospitality service sector.

The research set out to study the perceptions of hotel marketing managers with a Chinese background, as well as some expatriate (Western background) managers from "Five Plum Blossoms" category hotels (upper-market) in Taipei. Qualitative data were collected on the "relational" factors in the practice of RM and more specifically, the Chinese culture variables that influence the implementation of RM.

Purposive sampling was chosen due to the need to arrange interviews during the high season of 1997 and the small number of hotels in the sample. Managers were approached for interview in 12 hotels. All had to fulfil the criteria of being sales or marketing managers or general managers with a marketing background. The response rate of the sample approached was 58.3 per cent. From the seven hotels participating, ten experienced managers provided hour-long, in-depth interviews, including seven of Chinese cultural background and three expatriate managers from Ireland, Belgium and Australia. A semi-structured interview was adopted for this research as the study required standard predetermined questions for each respondent. However, the semi-structured interview allows the interviewer to add supplementary questions to probe, or get a deeper insight into, the content and meaning of the answers given. Based on the literature, the research attempted to gain insight into the knowledge and application of RM in the hotel sector and how Chinese culture may affect RM practice in terms of its relational approach and mechanisms. Specifically the questions were developed to provide feedback on each individual's understanding of the applications and mechanisms of RM based on internal, lateral, supplier and customer relationships; the cultural orientations of Chinese/Western managers and their relational approach to business and also the perceptions of managers to Chinese methods of carrying out their business. Each interview lasted over one hour.

The size of the sample means that the results represent only an exploratory study but these should provide a basis for further research in the area.

Findings

All the managers were able to identify that customer retention and relationship building are allied to the concept of RM. When asked about background knowledge to RM, it seems that the managers have an understanding of what direct marketing, or one-to-one marketing generally encompasses but this is limited to practising, at the tactical level, the use of a customer database to promote food and beverage activities.

In the relationship with buyers, the hotels in Taiwan take a similar approach to that advocated by RM academics. Depending on the segment, repeat visits or the value of the customers, the hotels decide on whom to build a relationship and in what way to build it. As the most profitable customer segment for all the hotels interviewed is the business traveller, the hotels have devoted much effort to retaining this segment of customers, either through building a strong relationship with the intermediaries (such as secretaries of large corporations), or directly with the customers (through loyalty programmes, promotional activities and special gestures). The majority of hotels have a database list which is managed as part of the "Frequent Guest Programmes" to ensure incentives are appropriately calculated. The systems also collect personal details such as preferred room and restaurant, prices paid, length of stay, etc. The schemes are card-based and some of the listed benefits are shown in Table I.

One important prerequisite that constitutes a RM programme is a corporate culture which specifies a relationship framework. This is where service and quality are used in conjunction with loyalty schemes to build satisfaction and relationship loyalty so as to achieve relationship longevity and increased profitability. Six of the seven hotels reported their culture to be relation-oriented. By this they explained the emphasis is on a people-oriented approach which is to build relationships. According to the managers, they believe that customer retention is something natural, which is almost built in to the Chinese culture and need not to be emphasised. This explains the reason why managers have stressed the retention strategy as part of their "relational approach" to customers, but no formalised programme has been implemented. As part of improving the commitment of staff to customers, the Royal Hotel, Shangri La Hotel and Ambassador Hotel have attempted to ensure both work and private life spheres of employees are looked after.

Loyalty programmes have been a widely practised marketing tool in the Taiwanese hotels. Most of the chain hotels have claimed the success of their loyalty programmes mainly on the basis of the reasonably high returning rate of loyalty scheme members. As all the chain hotels interviewed have a loyalty scheme that is initiated by its head office, it has become a norm in the industry rather than a scheme which provides competitive advantage. One of the hotel managers said that the "necessity" of having such a programme is simply because every one else has done the same. Therefore, the high returning rate is only the result of the discount factor. Hence, the loyalty programme in the Taiwanese hotels, although widely practised, needs refinement to serve as an effective long-term relationship building tool.

The Taiwanese hotels do not have formalised internal marketing programmes. This mirrors the hotels' reluctance in empowering their employees and also a belief that customer retention is something natural and almost built into the Chinese culture. Therefore, the "smiling" and "act

Table 1: Some benefits

The Ambassador Hotel (independent hotel)	Grand Formosa Regent (management contract)
30 per cent discount for members	Club awards: Free stays based on points collected or bonus packs with redemption to vouchers to purchase dinner, drink, sauna etc.
Complimentary fruit basket, continental breakfast in the VIP lounge	Complimentary fruit basket, chocolates Priority waiting-list for reservations
Free access to happy hour in the VIP lounge twice each week	General manager's weekly cocktail party invitation Complimentary paper
Free access to swimming pool, health and business centre	Free late check-out facility to 3 o'clock
Free late check-out facility to 3 o'clock	Direct telephone numbers given for reservations, inquiries, club requests, etc.

by the book" service meets the hotel's standardised operation procedure (SOP) but may not enhance the employee's ability to satisfy the customers fully. This may be because the responsibility of implementing an internal marketing programme belongs to the human resource department and marketing have little input.

For the Taiwanese hotels, building relationships with the customers is thought of as a natural practice, which the managers perceive as the starting point of business and as a norm rather than a new marketing strategy. However, the evidence of this study indicates there is little integration of service, quality and loyalty schemes into an integrated approach to the creation of RM.

Relationship Marketing in Relation to Chinese Culture

The finding that there is evidence of a lateral relationship between the hotel and its competitors, government organisation and airlines indicates that the Taiwanese hotels have made efforts to maintain a beneficial relationship with different government bodies by use of relationship pricing and hospitality. As far as competitors are concerned, the relationship is harmonious but not close. As reported, it is hard to predict when you will need the assistance of your competitors on a small island with limited space and resources, therefore good relationships are important. The closest lateral relationships exist with the airlines. There have been some service partnership deals between the airlines and the hotels, for example a barter programme between Eva airways and the Ambassador hotel that shows the close connections between the industries. Therefore, the hotels are attempting to maintain long-term relationships with all stakeholder groups.

Using Trompenaars' (1997) dimensions (Universalism versus Particularism; Individualism versus Collectivism; Neutral versus Emotional;

Specific versus Diffuse and Achievement versus Ascription), of how human beings relate to other people, the following offers an exploratory examination of the business value orientation of the Chinese and the Western managers interviewed.

Universalism versus Particularism (Rules versus Relationships)

The overall findings showed that most of the managers prefer to follow a universalist approach to contracting, which is to conform to rules rather than to adopt a particularist stance. However, 42 per cent of the Chinese managers and, interestingly, one expatriate manager have identified special conditions in contracting with Chinese business partners. They pointed out that in dealing with Chinese business partners, a request for a legal contract is sometimes deemed to be evidence of bad faith and inappropriate as it carries no sense of commitment. It is the relationship from which all the obligations derive, not the piece of paper. The consensus of the expatriate managers was that they preferred a professional and "down to earth" business attitude while interacting with customers. This shows the universalist value of the Western managers which contrasts with the Chinese particularist approach of personal meandering before getting down to business.

The sample size is small but the findings support Ambler's (1995) observation that Chinese and Western managers approach new relationships from opposite ends. For Westerners, everything starts with a contract that they alter to fit different circumstances, whereas the Chinese depend on the long-term, valuable relationship and let the details be worked out, as long as the relationship remains stable and beneficial for both parties.

When asked about the manager's contact with their customers during the sales/marketing activity, all three expatriate managers preferred a professional "down to earth" business attitude. Moreover, the four managers who would approach customers first with personal meandering include both the independent and chain hotel managers. They emphasised that this approach is only applicable when contracting with the local Chinese customers, including their corporate clients, travel agencies, tour operators, suppliers, etc.

Collectivism versus Individualism (Group versus Individual)

Personal characteristics and achievements are how individualists define themselves, whereas in a collectivist society, people are group oriented and define themselves as members of communities with concern for the general welfare of the group (Adler, 1991). In a group-oriented society, the harmony, unity and loyalty to the group is emphasised. Nevertheless, individualists praise the achievements of a single individual.

In both questions to identify the collectivist or individualist tendency of the managers, the result showed that most Chinese and Western managers are collectivists representing the group orientation of these managers. This result has highlighted the literature suggesting that in a collectivist organisation such as most Chinese hotels belong to, the management needs to motivate the whole group of employees, not specific individuals as it may result in disharmony among the personnel.

In sum, there was no obvious difference among the Chinese and Western values as the majority of the managers are collectivists.

Of the total sample of managers, 80 per cent prefer to give positive regard to the employees as a group to motivate their employees, which indicates a collectivist value. On the other hand, 20 per cent of managers use both a collectivist and individualist approach. Replies to questions on whether managers would avoid showing favouritism and extol the whole group, or seek high performers in motivating employees, showed that 80 per cent of the managers would treat the whole group equally even "star" personnel.

On the other hand, the general manager of the Ambassador hotel stated: "There will be no improvements, if employees see no difference after devoting their efforts".

Neutral versus Emotional (Range of Feelings Expressed)

In the approach to establishing relationships with people, reason and emotion both play an important role. It is seen in some cultures that business is a human affair and expressing a whole gamut of emotions is considered appropriate. However, in a society where reason is deemed to be more adequate, interaction with business partners is neutral and objective. In this case the degree of visible "emotion" is what differs among cultures and the question of whether emotion should be exhibited in business relations is raised.

According to the research carried out by Trompenaars (1997), cultures such as the American tend to exhibit emotions, yet separate them from rational decision making. Conversely, Italians would exhibit emotions and not separate them from objective decisions. In contrast, another culture such as the Dutch have a tendency of not showing their emotions and separate rational issues. The results of this study demonstrated that both Chinese and Western managers are neutral in their contacts during their business encounters. In particular, the expatriate managers have shown a higher degree of neutral value by reporting they favour avoidance of physical contact and strong gestures during business interaction. This indicates the managers understand certain aspects of the culture and have overcome the problems found by Huyton and Sutton (1996) or Mwaura *et al.* (1998), where Western managers are seen as emotional, volatile and demanding, but with a high degree of skill and the ability to listen; and need to restrain themselves and indicate co-operation and humbleness rather than be too open and direct.

Diffuse versus Specific

When involved in a business relationship, a specific relationship is prescribed by a contract and a diffuse relationship by real personal contact. These two differences indicate how far a person would like to get involved in a business relationship. In some cultures, people are only willing to engage with others in specific areas of life and single levels of personality. On the other hand, diffuse cultures would devote multiple areas of life and at several levels of personality at the same time to a relationship.

The question regarding the manager's preference for a separate business agenda and private issues or the reverse has not revealed an obvious difference between the Chinese and Western managers. However, the question of giving precise or general instructions to employees has demonstrated that the Western managers are more specific as precise and detailed instructions are given to their employees.

Achievement versus Ascription

Achievement implies that a person is judged by his/her achievements on record, but ascription denotes the status procured by an individual's birth, kinship, sex, etc. In constituting a relationship with business partners from ascriptive cultures such as the Japanese, respect is paid with specific attention to the senior members of the company and care is taken over who negotiates.

During the interview process, the emphasis by managers on the way they see Chinese business partners, customers or employees confirmed that the business relationship in a Chinese society commences with building a "relationship". Therefore, the findings have confirmed that while Western influenced RM is not fully adopted, the Chinese place a great emphasis on the nature and quality of "relationship" in the business context.

In the attempt to distinguish the value orientations of Chinese and Western managers, the difference that existed was not obvious. In some respects, the Western managers are more rational and non-relational and the Chinese managers have shown a more emotional and relational tendency. However, the difference is vague. This result is not surprising if the rapid industrialisation of Taiwan is taken into account and the vast business information emerging from the Western countries. Moreover, the Chinese managers may have shown a more Westernised value system partly because they are working in hotels serving international markets. This may be a slow process as Kao *et al.* (1995)

have argued. Confucianism is essentially a system of substantive ethics which mitigates against individual economic acts on the basis of rational calculation.

Differences in Marketing Strategies to Chinese and Western Customers

The following are some reports from the managers of the differences in Chinese and Western customers and their different marketing strategies:

- During a business meeting, Chinese culture emphasises the degree of familiarity others have with you rather than focusing on the product during the initial contact as it is believed if the relationship is stable and trustworthy, the product quality can be further discussed and arranged. This can be contrasted to the western approach where once the purchase has been successful, the relationship will follow.
- Chinese customers are said to be more price sensitive than Western customers by the managers. The price concerns the Chinese buyers more than the quality of the product, whereas the Western consumers contemplate quality of products more and then evaluate it against the cost before purchasing. Therefore, to market to Chinese clients, the prices, the brand name and the prestigious status are the first concern. However, product features such as room size, security, proximity to shops, location, etc. will be the priority when marketing to Western customers.
- In the process of relationship building with customers the Chinese managers have had to adapt to different customers' expectations. They show a certain business flexibility in their approaches that may be different to that found in studies such as Mwaura *et al.* (1998).
- Chinese managers would more often use a third party who has appropriate connections or social status to reconcile business problems or acquire business advantages during business negotiations within the Chinese community.
- The basic approach of most Chinese managers in their marketing strategy is to establish *kuan-hsi* (relationship/networking) followed by business dealing, while the Western manager's technique would try to establish a closer relationship after business dealing in order to get more business in the future.

Conclusion

From the above findings, the emphasis of Chinese managers on Chinese personal relationships, including the use of *kuan-hsi, mien-tsu, jen-chin*, etc. when interacting with their business encounters is prevalent. This is also

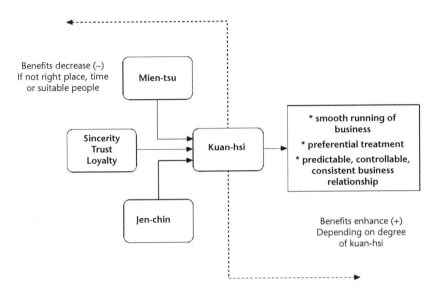

Figure 1: Representation of Chinese interpersonal relationships and their link to creating business advantages

confirmed by the three Western managers interviewed about their experience and observation in dealing with Chinese colleagues, business partners and customers. This finding correlates with the literature that *kuan-hsi, jen-chin* and face (*mien-tsu*) are the dominating characteristics in Chinese business relationships. It is the general consensus that once a good *kuan-hsi* has been established, a number of benefits will accrue. This finding allows for an understanding of how Chinese and Western business relationships can be developed by the use of cultural understanding as it offers practical guidelines to all parties. As such, Figure 1 is offered as a means of illustrating the influence of such relationships on the business world.

However, there are some negative aspects of *kuan-hsi* building from the managers' perspectives that are not mentioned in the literature. It is possible to argue from the findings of this study that if the *kuan-hsi* established is not of good "quality", based on sincerity, trust, etc., the intimate relationship may be manipulated as a means to request more service or value (as in the case of customers) than is appropriate. This may decrease the benefits of such relationship building for the hotels in the long run.

The managers also identified the importance of *jen-chin* and *mien-tsu* in building relationships with the various parties. Although doing favours is of less importance, in the building of *kuan-hsi*, it can be a very effective tool to initiate or enhance a relationship if required. If one can build *mien-tsu* for their encounters, it would be highly valued and appreciated. At the same time, the hotel managers would be able to tap into the customer's *kuan-hsi* and social resources if they consistently provide opportunities for their customers to "gain face", e.g. the customers may repay them by introducing them to other potential accounts.

Finally, this exploratory study has indicated the importance of understanding the cultural background of the customers marketed to. Hence, any study of the practice of RM needs to be informed of the cultural and personal relationships of those involved in the overall business relationships in order to comprehend fully the dynamics which may impact on RM delivery.

References and Further Reading

Adler, N. (1991), *International Dimensions of Organizational Behaviour*, PWS-Kent, Boston, MA.

Ambler, T. (1995), "Reflections in China: re-orienting images of marketing", *Marketing Management,* Vol. 4 No. 1, pp. 23–30.

Bennett, R. (1996), "Relationship formation and governance in consumer markets: analysis versus the behaviourist approach", *Journal of Marketing Management*, Vol. 12, pp. 417–36.

Buttery, E. and Leung, T. (1998), "The difference between Chinese and Western negotiations", *European Journal of Marketing,* Vol. 32 No. 3/4, pp. 374–89.

Buttle, F. (1996), *Relationship Marketing: Theory and Practice,* Paul Chapman, London.

Chen, M. (1995), *Asian Management Systems: Japanese and Korean Styles of Business,* Routledge, London.

Davies, H., Leung, T., Luk, S. and Wong, Y.H. (1995), "The benefits of *guanxi*: the value of relationships in developing the Chinese market", *Journal of Industrial Marketing Management*, Vol. 12, pp. 207–14.

Gilbert, D.C. (1996), "Relationship marketing and airline loyalty schemes", *Tourism Management*, Vol. 17 No. 8, pp. 575–82.

Grönroos, C. (1994a), "From marketing mix to relationship marketing: towards a paradigm shift in marketing", *Management Decision,* Vol. 32 No. 2, pp. 4–20.

Grönroos, C. (1994b), "*Quo vadis*, marketing? Toward a relationship marketing paradigm", *Journal of Marketing Management*, Vol. 10, pp. 347–60.

Grunert, S. and Scherhorn, G. (1990), "Consumer values in West Germany underlying dimensions and cross cultural comparison with North America", *Journal of Business Research*, Vol. 20, pp. 97–107.

Gummesson, E. (1994), "Service management: an evaluation and the future", *European Journal of Marketing*, Vol. 5 No. 1, pp. 77–96.

Hall, E.T. (1990), "The silent language in overseas business", *Harvard Business Review,* May–June, pp. 87–96.

Hofstede, G. (1984), *Culture's Consequences: International Difference in Work-related Values,* Sage Publications, London.

Huyton, J. and Sutton, J. (1996), "Employee perceptions of the hotel sector in the People's Republic of China", *International Journal of Contemporary Hospitality Management,* Vol. 8 No. 1, pp. 22–8.

Kao, C.S. (1991), "Personal trust in the large business in Taiwan: a traditional foundation for contemporary economic activities", in Hamilton, G. (Ed.), *Business Networks and Economic Development in East and South East Asia,* University of Hong Kong, Hong Kong, pp. 66–76.

Kao, H., Sinha, D. and Ng, S.-H. (1995), *Effective Organizations and Social Values,* Sage Publications, London.

King, Y.C. (1996), "*Kuan-hsi* and network building: a sociological interpretation", in Brown, R. (Ed.), *Chinese Business Enterprise: Critical Perspectives on Business and Management*, Vol. 2, Routledge, London, pp. 322-57.
Kotler, P. and Armstrong, G. (1996), *Principles of Marketing*, 7th ed., Prentice-Hall, Englewood Cliffs, NJ.
Luo, Y. (1997), "*Guanxi* and performance of foreign-invested enterprises in China: an empirical study", *Journal of International Business*, Vol. 37, pp. 51-69.
Mwaura, G., Sutton, J. and Roberts, D. (1998), "Corporate and national culture – an irreconcilable dilemma for the hospitality manager", *International Journal of Contemporary Hospitality Management*, Vol. 10 No. 6, pp. 212-20.
Palmer, A. (1996), "Relationship marketing: a universal paradigm or management fad?", *The Learning Organization*, Vol. 3 No. 3, pp. 18-25.
Pang, C., Roberts, D. and Sutton, J. (1998), "Doing business in China – the art of war", *International Journal of Contemporary Hospitality Management*, Vol. 10 No. 7, pp. 272-82.
Redding, S.G. (1982), "Cultural effects on the marketing process in Southeast Asia", *Journal of the Market Research Society*, Vol. 24 No. 2, pp. 98-114.
Terpstra, V. and Sarathy, R. (1994), *International Marketing*, Dryden Press, Orlando, FL.
TNTO (1996), *Taiwan National Trust Office Tourism Statistics Publication*, TNTO, Taipei.
Tourism Bureau, Ministry of Transportation and Communications (1997), *Annual Report on Tourism Statistics, Republic of China, 1996*, Tourism Bureau, Ministry of Transportation and Communications, May.
Trompenaars, F. (1997), *Riding the Waves of Culture: Understanding Cultural Diversity in Business*, Nicholas Brealey, London.
Usunier, J. (1993), *International Marketing: A Cultural Approach*, Prentice-Hall, Hemel Hempstead.
Xing, F. (1995), "The Chinese cultural system: implications for cross-cultural management", *SAM Advanced Management Journal*, Winter, pp. 14-20.
Yau, O. (1988), "Chinese cultural values: their dimensions and marketing implications", *European Journal of Marketing*, Vol. 22 No. 5, pp. 44-57.

37

E-Mail Marketing by International Hotel Chains: An Industry-Practices Update

Peter O'Connor

The prolific growth in the use of e-mail has been one of the most significant developments in business communication in the past quarter century. E-mail's widespread adoption has deeply affected both society and commerce, changing both how individuals interact with each other on a personal level and how businesses interact with customers. A 2004 study of U.K. organizations found that e-mail has become an integral part of how people work, with nearly all respondents using e-mail on a daily basis (Tassabehji and Vakola 2005). DuFrene et al. (2005, 66) maintained that e-mail has become an integral part of most companies' marketing strategy, as they use it to "notify prospects of promotions and services; acquire new customers; increase sales; and, most importantly, develop and nurture an ongoing dialogue and relationship with their customers." E-mail is thought to be widely used by hotel companies (Marinova, Murphy, and Massey 2002). For example, a survey of marketing professionals carried out by MarketingProfs.com revealed that e-mail marketing was being used by 84 percent of hotel respondents, considerably higher than the average for all sectors of 76 percent (Miller 2006).

From a commercial perspective, e-mail's popularity as a marketing communications tool can be attributed to the benefits that it brings. It is

Source: *Cornell Hospitality Quarterly,* 49(1) (2008): 42–52.

convenient; easy to use; and to a large extent highly effective as a method of interacting with, selling to, and converting the customer (Sipior, Ward, and Bonner 2004). Messages can be targeted selectively, and response rates compare favorably to alternative methods of customer communication, making e-mail effective from a cost–benefit perspective (Phelps et al. 2004). However e-mail's utility as a marketing communications medium is being severely limited by the continued growth of "spam" or "junk mail," terms commonly used to denote unsolicited bulk e-mail communications, usually of a commercial nature (Cheng 2004).

The U.S. Federal Trade Commission (FTC) defines a "commercial electronic mail message" as "any electronic mail message where the primary purpose is the commercial advertisement or promotion of a commercial product or service" (Clarke, Flaherty, and Zugelder 2005, 399). At what point, however, do commercial e-mails become spam? A useful definition is provided by France's Commission Nationale L' Informatique et des Libertés (1999, 7), which defined spam as "the bulk mailing, sometimes repeatedly, of unsolicited email messages, usually of a commercial nature, to individuals with whom the mailer has had no previous contact." This definition is supported by the U.S. Controlling the Assault of Non-Solicited Pornography and Marketing Act (CAN-SPAM) of 2003, which defined spam as "any commercial electronic mail that is addressed to a recipient with whom the initiator of the mail does not have an existing business or personal relationship, and is not sent at the request of, or with the express consent of, the recipient" (Rogers 2006, 228). Both definitions distinguish between mass mailed unsolicited commercial e-mails and those sent legitimately as part of marketing efforts by a company with whom the recipient has had prior dealings.

Spam has become an issue because, in contrast with more traditional methods of distributing information, sending additional e-mail is virtually free once appropriate systems are in place. From an economic perspective, the marginal cost of sending additional e-mails is low, and it costs practically the same to send one hundred thousand or even five hundred thousand e-mails as it does to send one thousand (Krishnamurthy 2001). E-mail addresses can be easily mined from the web or chat rooms, generated automatically by computer programs, or purchased cheaply online from other spammers (Hodges 2004). Coupled with the fact that e-mail has a relatively global reach, and that response is virtually instantaneous and highly measurable, this makes e-mail attractive as a marketing medium (Nettleton 2005). Its cost structure makes spamming commercially viable even when response rates are relatively low (Cerf 2005). As little as one response per one hundred thousand e-mails means that the spammer can make a profit (Fingerman 2004). As a result, spam levels continue to rise. Postini, an internet security firm, estimates that spam would comprise 91 percent of all traffic, or nearly 7 billion messages in November 2006 alone (Montague 2006). As a result, spam has become a problem for both individuals and businesses. More than three-quarters of e-mail users find spam unpleasant or annoying, while two-thirds are less trusting of e-mail as a result (InternetWeek.com 2004). There is also evidence that consumers are using e-mail less frequently and are shopping less (or not at all) on the web because of concerns about subsequently receiving spam (Sipior, Ward, and Bonner 2004; Gratton 2004). Most analysts agree the never-ending tide of spam is expected to continue to rise, even though most people's inboxes are already overwhelmed with messages offering links to triple-XXX porn sites; advertising for generic Viagra, home finance deals, or inkjet printer cartridges; solicitations for Nigerian get-rich-quick schemes; not-to-be missed stock tips; and offers to dramatically enhance various body parts (male or female, or both!) to name just a few (Perry 2004). Perhaps the greatest problem with spam is that people do respond to such messages, thereby risking becoming victims of fraud.

This onslaught has made it more difficult for legitimate businesses to use e-mail as a marketing communications tool as many consumers are now overwhelmed and frustrated by the sheer volume of irrelevant messages that they receive (Rainie and Fallws 2004). In response to consumers' concern about this issue, governments around the world have enacted legislation to try to address the issue. That was the reason for the CAN-SPAM Act in the United States, which established a federal framework for the regulation of commercial e-mail. Similarly, in the European Union, the issue has been addressed by both the 2000 Electronic Commerce Directive and the 2002 Personal Data & Protection of Privacy Directive, while Australia enacted its own Spam Act in 2003 (Cheng 2004). Legislation is currently pending in several other jurisdictions, including Singapore, Canada, and New Zealand (IDA Singapore 2004).

The CAN-SPAM Act 2003

Cheng (2004) provided a useful comparison and analysis of each of the pieces of legislation mentioned above, which naturally differ to take varying local philosophies into account (see also Baumer, Earp, and Poindexter 2004). However, as the online travel sector is most developed in the United States (PhoCusWright 2004), I decided to focus this article on analyzing compliance with the U.S. CAN-SPAM Act, which preempts any legislation by the individual states and also applies to any international company sending e-mail marketing messages to individuals within the United States (Swartz 2003).

According to Grimes (2004), the purpose of the CAN-SPAM Act is not to prohibit commercial e-mails, but to regulate the way in which the medium is used as a legitimate marketing tool. Thus, the act contains specific provisions with regard to message format and content that govern how e-mail should be used to communicate with customers (or potential customers). In effect, the act makes it legal to send unsolicited commercial e-mail as long as its source and nature are not disguised, resources were not misappropriated to send them, and consumers have a meaningful way to avoid receiving future mailings (Fingerman 2004). For the purposes of the act, commercial e-mails are defined as those whose primary purpose is the advertisement or promotion of a commercial product or service (including content on a website operated for commercial purposes). Its provisions apply to companies that use e-mail to solicit sales from both current and potential customers, irrespective of whether the e-mail is sent directly or through the use of a third-party e-mail marketing service. Thus, a company cannot sidestep the provisions of the act by hiring someone else to send e-mails on its behalf (Dixon 2005).

With regard to commercial e-mails, the law's specific requirements focus on the e-mail's subject line, the "from" line, physical contact details, and opt-out facilities, as follows (Lee 2005):

1. Subject lines must not be misleading and must include a clear and conspicuous indication that the e-mail is an advertisement (unless "prior affirmative consent" has been given by the recipient). In this way, recipients can know at a glance whether an e-mail is a marketing message and can delete the message without reading its content, thus saving time and minimizing inconvenience.
2. Messages must have a functioning and nonmisleading e-mail address in the "from" line of the header. This must serve as the reply-to address and, barring technical difficulties, must remain active for at least thirty days following transmission of the message.
3. The body of the message must contain a valid physical postal address.
4. The message must include easy-to-locate, clear, and explicit instructions explaining how to opt out of future mailings. Such opt-out requests must be honored within ten working days.

The act makes a distinction between commercial e-mail on the one hand and relationship or transactional e-mails on the other. Thus, the intended purpose behind contacting the recipient has become an important consideration in deciding whether the requirements of the act apply. Relationship or transactional messages are those for which the primary purpose is noncommercial ("FTC Issues Final CAN-SPAM Rules" 2005). For example, messages that facilitate completion of or confirm a transaction, deliver goods or services pursuant to a prior transaction, provide notices on warranties or recalls, provide notices regarding ongoing commercial relationships (such as subscription or service accounts), or provide employment or benefits information fit into this category (Dixon 2005). Such messages are not bound by the requirements that apply to commercial messages but are subject only to the requirement not to use fraudulent header information. It is unclear for how long a company can contact its former customers, but to be safe, if a company contacts its former customers with a new product or service, the firm should treat the transmission as a commercial message rather than a relationship or transactional one and fully comply with the act's requirements (Dixon 2005).

Although the act provides for both substantial criminal and civil penalties (damages of US$250 per message sent in violation, up to an aggregated maximum of US$6 million, as well as jail time of up to five years for specific infractions) and a variety of companies and individuals have already been prosecuted, the initial effects of the act seem to have been minimal (Deann-Rembert 2004). A January survey carried out by TMCnet (2004) found that 99 percent of a sample of commercial e-mails failed to comply with the guidelines. However this is not surprising as the act only came into effect on January 1, 2004, and thus companies would not have had adequate time to react. However, another study, conducted one year later, examined the practices of one hundred U.S.- based high-volume websites. Once again the researchers found a high degree of noncompliance with the provisions of the legislation. For example, nearly one-third of companies failed to include a valid postal address in their e-mail text, and a substantial number did not comply with the opt-out requirement. Even after unsubscribing, the researchers continued to receive e-mails from the surveyed sites or their partners in nearly 15 percent of cases (Spring 2005).

As I discussed earlier, companies' use (or misuse) of e-mail as a communications medium has become an important issue. Consumers have become concerned about how personal data are being used for commercial purposes, and unless these concerns are addressed, many consumers may refuse to provide online sites with the transactional data necessary for operations (Chen and Rea 2004). According to Hoffman, Noval, and Peralta (1999), "almost 95 percent of web users have declined to provide personal information to web sites at one time or another"; and a recent survey by the Trans-Atlantic Consumer Dialogue (TACD; 2003) – a consumer advocacy group – found that more than half of respondents were shopping online less or not at all because of concerns that submitting personal data would result in more spam. Harris Interactive found that more Americans are more concerned about the loss of personal privacy than they are about health care, crime, or taxes (Head and Yuan 2001), while a 2003 survey by Kandra and Brandt identified fears over misuse of personal data as being the biggest challenge facing online retailers.

In a 2003 study, I detailed the data collected by hotel companies about their customers (O'Connor 2003). Even when excluding the reservation function (where all users have to provide personal identifying data to successfully complete a booking), I found that more than 90 percent of hotel chains collected personal identification information, including e-mail addresses, as part of their normal website operations. Furthermore, as guests stay in a hotel property, such companies have the potential to collect further in-depth transactional data about both their preferences and actual behavior, which if combined with the aforementioned personal data could potentially be a valuable resource for marketing purposes. Although organizational and technical issues generally prevent such merging of databases from occurring at the moment (for example, see Piccoli et al. 2003), these barriers are gradually being overcome, and such scenarios are likely in the future. Given such access to extensive guest data, the question must be asked as to whether hotel companies behave ethically with their customer data resource. Do they currently use guests' personal data for e-mail marketing purposes, and do they pass these data on to third parties without the express permission of the guest?

Research Methodology

My objectives in this study were to establish the extent to which hotel companies use guest data to engage in online direct marketing practices and whether such marketing efforts comply with the U.S. CAN-SPAM Act of 2003. Furthermore, as sharing personal identification data with third parties without permission is a key concern for many consumers, secondary objectives included establishing whether the companies surveyed share personal data with third parties and, if so, to establish what effect these actions have on the level and type of e-mail communications received (Han and MacLaurin 2002).

The population for the study was defined as the direct-to-consumer websites of the top fifty worldwide hotel brands as identified in the July 2003 issue of *Hotels* magazine. As such, it included the full spectrum of hotel companies, from luxury to economy, with property locations throughout the world. I selected this group on the premise that the actions of these large companies should constitute industry best practices.

Visiting each company's website, I explored opportunities for the entry of personal data (this included joining their loyalty program, signing up for newsletters or other promotional activities, and entering competitions). Where such facilities were provided (in 88 percent of cases), I entered seed data (i.e., false but functioning postal and e-mail addresses) so that the company's subsequent actions on that specific account could be monitored. Four registrations were made on each site to compare company's compliance with opt-in and opt-out requests at the registration stage. So, to use Marriott as a hypothetical illustration, the e-mail addresses used would have been Marriott1@xxx.com, Marriott2@xxx.com, Marriott3@xxx.com, Marriott4@xxx.com, with xxx.com being the domain name especially created for the study. Actual use of these data was measured by subsequently monitoring the e-mail addresses to determine each company's actions for a one-year period. The resulting database of e-mails was analyzed to establish the purpose of each e-mail and to determine whether they conformed to the requirements of the legislation. At the end of the test period, I sent unsubscribe requests to all possible sender e-mail addresses to measure compliance with the requirement to honor opt-out requests within the prescribed ten working days.

Findings

A total of 397 e-mails were received on the set of e-mail addresses for which I opted in at registration over the twelve-month period (see Exhibit 1). Of these, 367 (or 92 percent) were internal messages originating from companies that were part of the study, and just 30 were unsolicited messages. The majority of the unsolicited e-mails (60 percent) were messages sent to e-mail addresses randomly created based on the unique domain name used and thus are outside the scope of the study, as they do not represent action on the part of the surveyed companies. However, a small number (3 percent of all messages received) were spam in the true sense of the word, representing unsolicited commercial solicitations from third parties, based on personal data provided by surveyed companies.

Types of promotional messages received. To measure compliance with legislative requirements, the database was split, and I analyzed only messages from the surveyed companies. Even though nearly 90 percent of the companies

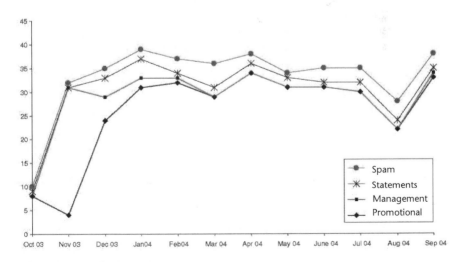

Exhibit 1: Pattern of e-mails received

Exhibit 2: Analysis of e-mail messages received

Type of message	Number	Percentage
Management messages	36	10
Statements	22	6
Promotional messages	309	84

collected personal data that could have been used for e-mail marketing purposes, I received messages only from twenty-four brands, or 55 percent of the population. On average, the hotel companies that did use e-mail as a customer communications medium sent 11.7 e-mails each over the test period. Two companies sent just a single e-mail, while one company filled the mailbox with 48 messages, or not quite one per week. Economy hotel companies sent significantly more e-mail messages than did midscale companies ($p = .036$) or upmarket companies ($p = .032$).

Based on each message's contents, I classified it into commercial or non-commercial. As can be seen from Exhibit 2, despite a fair number of messages related to managing interactions between the recipient and the hotel company (e.g., welcome messages, double opt-in e-mails, statements of account activity), the majority were promotional in nature and thus subject to the requirements of the CAN-SPAM Act of 2003.

Most of the commercial messages were periodic mass mailings incorporating special offers or discounts on a wide range of the chain's hotels. A smaller number were more specific, promoting a single property or a specific special offer. Newsletters that incorporated editorial material on developments within the company, as well as promotional material, were also common. I also received a small number of electronic greeting cards, invitations to participate in competitions, and e-mails promoting offers from partner companies. Irrespective of their content, all of these promotional messages should conform to the requirements the CAN-SPAM Act of 2003. A total of 281 e-mails were received by the opt-in to internal use of personal data accounts after the law's effective date on January 1, 2004. I assessed each of these on the following four criteria: the content of their subject lines, whether the "from" line included a valid and functioning e-mail address, whether the body of the message itself included a physical postal address, and whether the message contained a functioning opt-out facility. Findings are shown in Exhibit 3.

No e-mail message clearly identified itself as being an advertisement or commercial solicitation, as is required by the act. I find this surprising, but it reflects the grey area in the CAN-SPAM Act that allows companies to send unlabeled commercial messages if a "preexisting relationship" exists with the recipient. The exact definition of that "existing relationship" is subject to much debate and is scheduled to be the subject of a 2007 advisory paper that the FTC has yet to issue at this writing. Since I voluntarily signed up for mailings, the hotel chains could easily argue we had a relationship that would

Exhibit 3: Compliance with U.S. CAN-SPAM Act of 2003

Issue	Yes	Percentage
Subject lines advertising	0	0
Subject lines misleading	17	6
Functioning e-mail address	279	99
Valid postal address	175	62
Opt-out option	264	94
Opt-out option functional	263	94
Privacy statement	189	67

Note: CAN-SPAM Act = Controlling the Assault of Non-Solicited Pornography and Marketing Act.

exempt them from labeling their commercial e-mails, as long as they complied with the law's other requirements.

Assessing the subject line was obviously subjective, but in any case, the standard itself is vague (Fingerman 2004). Case law to date has focused on what a "reasonable" person would expect on examining the text. The rule of thumb used in this analysis was that the subject line should directly relate to the content of the message. Thus, any "creative" subject lines (e.g., "It's a May zing") fell, perhaps unjustly, into the "misleading" category during the analysis. Even with this broad interpretation, only 6 percent of messages were classified as misleading, indicating that hotel companies in general use meaningful and descriptive subject lines in their e-mail marketing messages.

The validity of the e-mail address shown on the "from" line was assessed by individually replying to each message. If the reply did not bounce (i.e., generate an error message stating user unknown or invalid domain name), the e-mail address was assumed to be valid. Only two replies bounced, and in both cases this was due to (presumably accidental) typographical errors in the e-mails originally received, as in both cases, the address on subsequent e-mails from the same company functioned correctly.

I noted the highest level of noncompliance in the requirement to include a valid physical mailing address. More than one-third (37 percent) of the messages received did not include a physical postal address and thus were in direct contravention of the CAN-SPAM Act, leaving their sender companies open to prosecution. Furthermore, more than one in twenty did not include an opt-out facility. For those that did have opt-out mechanisms, I found one company's opt-out facility to be nonoperational, generating an error message when clicked. All but two of the companies complied with the requirement to discontinue sending promotional e-mails when I so requested. The two exceptions had passed contact details on to partners without my permission. These partner companies had to be contacted separately for me to complete the opt-out process and stop the flow of e-mails.

Finally, although not part of the formal requirements of the CAN-SPAM Act, most analysts agree that promotional e-mails should include some reference or hyperlink to a privacy statement to reassure consumers as to how their personal contact details will be used. Scanning the content of each message for some reference or link to a privacy statement, I found such a link in more than two-thirds of cases.

The data were also analyzed to investigate potential differences in compliance based on the category of the hotel company. However, no significant differences in behavior could be identified among economy, midscale, and upmarket hotels, indicating a common set of behavior standards across international hotel chains as a whole.

Analysis

As Friel (2005) pointed out, businesses that use e-mail for commercial purposes cannot afford to ignore the CAN-SPAM Act. While initially only the more egregious violations will be prosecuted, the public outcry against spam will eventually lead to the enforcement net being widened. Every company that directly or indirectly uses e-mail needs to bring its activities into compliance with the regulations to avoid lawsuits or enforcement actions. Hotel companies, with their privileged access to in-depth personal data, need to be particularly vigilant to maintain the trust of their clientele.

The survey results reveal that just more than half of the hotel companies surveyed were using e-mail as a marketing communications tool during the period of the study. Such results were lower than I anticipated, particularly since a much larger percentage of companies collects personal data that could potentially be used for such purposes. A second, related finding was that, on average, economy hotels make more use of e-mail as a marketing and promotional tool than do either midscale or upmarket chains. This is also surprising as much published literature on the use of customer relationship management (CRM) in the hotel sector focuses on its use by upmarket rather than economy hotels (for example, see Murphy, Schegg, and Olaru forthcoming).

The study also revealed that hotel chains are for the most part complying with the requirements of the CAN-SPAM Act in their promotional e-mail communications. Apart from the highly debatable issue of whether their subject lines should be explicitly marked as advertisements, and the easily correctable issue of not including a valid physical address, most of the messages received during the course of the survey comply with legislative requirements. Few of the messages received had misleading subject lines, even when a strict interpretation of the definition of misleading was applied, and the reply-to addresses included in the headers of e-mails were valid in practically all cases. Most companies also seem to be aware of and concerned about personal privacy issues, as witnessed by the high number that specifically include links to privacy policies in their correspondence. Furthermore, there is little evidence of companies passing on e-mail address or other personal details to third parties for marketing purposes. In practically all cases, appropriate facilities were provided to unsubscribe, and my opt-out requests were on the most part honored, although not always as quickly as required by law.

The findings show that the behavior of hotel chains compares favorably with that of other sectors. For example, in the Spring (2005) study discussed earlier, nearly one-third of companies failed to include the required postal address in their messages, a figure similar to the percentage identified in this study. However, Spring also found that nearly 15 percent of survey participants failed to honor opt-out requests within the specified time periods, a finding that corresponds with the results of a different study by Miller (2004) of commercial e-mail marketing companies. In the case of hotel companies, the comparable figure is 4 percent, indicating a higher level of compliance with this requirement by hotel companies than by business in general. Overall, the survey reveals the hotel sector to be an example of good practice in terms of e-mail marketing, which may perhaps be a reflection of the need to build and maintain trust with the customer to be successful.

Hotel companies need to build on this position by reinforcing consumer perceptions that their personal data will not be misused. Statements detailing the company's policies regarding use of customer personal data (both internally and by third parties) should be posted prominently on websites and whenever users engage in a transaction or provide personal data to the company. E-mail communications should be reviewed to determine whether they comply with legislative requirements, and appropriate procedures should be put in place to ensure that all future communications are compliant. Perhaps the easiest ways to do this are to develop a standard template incorporating all the requirements of the CAN-SPAM Act or create a checklist that can be used to audit messages before they are sent. Procedures are also needed to ensure that opt-out requests are honored within the permitted time limit and that such addresses cannot be accidentally added back into the active database at a later date. Active management of this important data resource is essential. Hotels need to follow the lead of the major international chains detailed in this paper to continue to maintain the trust of their customers.

The study suffers from several limitations. First, surveying the entire population rather than using sampling methods means that the findings of the study cannot be generalized to the industry as a whole. However, as the objective was to benchmark the practices and compliance of the larger hotel chains to provide a baseline for subsequent studies, I deem this approach to be adequate. That said, future studies should consider using a broader sample of hotel companies and also include independent hotels to better develop a comprehensive picture of practices across the industry as a whole. Second, the number of messages received may in fact be understated. Poststudy discussion of the findings with marketing executives from several of the companies surveyed revealed that in some cases marketing campaigns are triggered by activity on the client's account (e.g., staying in a particular hotel property, or spending five nights in any combination of properties within the brand within a one-month period). Since the user accounts used for this survey were effectively dormant (that is, no stay activity was recorded over the test period for these accounts), such criteria would not be triggered and theoretically fewer e-mails would be received than if the account were active. That particular limitation, though, would only affect the subsidiary findings relating to number of e-mails received and would not affect the core objective of the study, which was to measure compliance with legislative requirements.

Several fruitful and topical areas for further development became apparent during the study. As discussed above, there would be advantages to repeating the study using a more representative sample of hotels to permit generalization of the results to the industry as a whole. Similarly, the finding regarding economy hotels making more use of e-mail marketing than higher classes of hotels warrants further investigation, as it seems to defy established beliefs. However, the research area with the most potential would be to examine consumers' reactions to the promotional e-mails they receive from hotel companies. While only just over half of hotel companies are currently using this technology, the remainder are actively collecting personal data, potentially with a view to carrying out campaigns in the future. Guidance as to what works – in terms of building brand awareness, encouraging bookings, and building the customer relationship – would clearly be welcome.

References

Baumer, D., J. Earp, and J. Poindexter. 2004. Internet privacy law: A comparison between the United States and the European Union. *Computers & Security* 23: 400–412.
Cerf, V. 2005. Spam, spim, and spit. *Communications of the ACM* 48 (4): 39–43.
Chen, K., and A. Rea. 2004. Protecting personal information online: A survey of user privacy concerns and control techniques. *Journal of Computer Information Systems* 44 (4): 85–92.
Cheng, T. 2004. Recent international attempts to can spam. *Computer Law & Security Report* 20 (6): 472–79.
Clarke, I., T. Flaherty, and M. Zugelder. 2005. The CAN-SPAM Act: New rules for sending commercial e-mail messages and implications for the sales force. *Industrial Marketing Management* 34: 399–405.
Commission Nationale L'Informatique et des Libertés. 1999. *Le Publipostage Electronique et la Protection Donnes Personnelles*. Vol. 14. Paris: Commission Nationale L'informatique et des Libertés.
Deann-Rembert, L. 2004. Will CAN-SPAM affect you? *Marketing Research* 16 (1): 8.
Dixon, J. H. 2005. Privacy laws and doing business online. *Intellectual Property & Technology Law Journal* 17 (2): 11–20.
DuFrene, D., B. Engelland, C. Lehman, and R. Pearson. 2005. Changes in consumer attitudes resulting from participation in a permission e-mail campaign. *Journal of Current Issues and Research in Advertising* 27 (1): 65–77.

Fingerman, D. 2004. Spam canned throughout the land? Summary of the CAN-SPAM Act. *Journal of Internet Law* 7 (8): 1, 11–17.

Friel, A. 2005. The spam spat: How will marketers be affected by the fight against spam? *Marketing Management* 13 (6): 48–50.

FTC issues final CAN-SPAM rules. 2005. *Information Management Journal*, March–April, p. 14.

Gratton, E. 2004. Dealing with unsolicited commercial emails: A global perspective. *Journal of Internet Law* 7 (12): 3–13.

Grimes, G. 2004. Issues with SPAM. *Computer Fraud & Security* 5:12–16.

Han, P., and A. MacLaurin. 2002. Do consumers really care about online privacy? *Marketing Management* 11 (1): 35–38.

Head, M., and Y. Yuan. 2001. Privacy protection in electronic commerce – A theoretical framework. *Human Systems Management* 20:149–60.

Hodges, J. 2004. Spam and junk mail – When will it ever end? *Tax Practice Management* 3 (1): 27–30, 47–48.

Hoffman, D., T. Noval, and M. Peralta. 1999. Building consumer trust online. *Communications of the ACM* 42 (4): 80–85.

IDA Singapore. 2004. *Proposed legislative framework for the control of e-mail spam*. Joint IDA-AGC Consultation Paper, March, Infocomm Development Authority, Singapore.

InternetWeek.com. 2004. Some people like spam according to a poll. Press Release, July 27. www.internetweek.com/breakingsNews/showArticle.jhtml?articleID=26100190 (accessed September 10, 2005).

Kandra, A., and A. Brandt. 2003. The great American privacy makeover. *PC World* 21 (11): 145–60.

Krishnamurthy, S. 2001. A comprehensive analysis of permission marketing. *Journal of Computer Mediated Communication* 6 (2): n.p.

Lee, Y. 2005. The CAN-Spam Act: A silver bullet solution? *Communications of the ACM* 48 (6): 131–32.

Marinova, A., J. Murphy, and B. Massey. 2002. Permission e-mail marketing as a means of targeted promotion. *Cornell Hotel and Restaurant Administration Quarterly* 43 (1): 61–69.

Miller, R. 2004. First can spam suit filed. www.internetnews.com/xSP/article.php/3322311 (accessed September 1, 2005).

Miller, S. 2006. An email marketing benchmark survey: Analysis and recommendations. www.marketingprofs.com/preview/?id=15&adref=1721 (accessed March 21, 2007).

Montague, B. 2006. Spam, spam, spam, spam . . . you've got mail. *Sunday Times*, November 19, p. A8.

Murphy, J., R. Schegg, and D. Olaru. Forthcoming. Quality clusters: Dimensions of email response by luxury hotels. *International Journal of Hospitality Management*.

Nettleton, E. 2005. Getting tough on spam? *Database Marketing & Customer Strategy Management* 12 (4): 357–61.

O'Connor, P. 2003. Privacy and the online hotel customer: An analysis of the use of fair information practices by international hotel companies. In *Proceedings of the ENTER Information and Communications Technology in Tourism Conference*, ed. A. Frew, M. Hitz, and P. O'Connor, 382–92. New York: Springer Computer Science.

Perry, M. 2004. Pre and post CAN SPAM: An in-depth comparison of unsolicited and deceptive versus unsolicited email. Paper presented at the DMEF 16th Annual Robert B. Clarke Direct/Interactive Marketing Educators' Conference, New Orleans, LA.

Phelps, J., R. Lewis, L. Mobilio, D. Perry, and N. Raman. 2004. Viral marketing or electronic word-of-mouth advertising: Examining consumer responses and motivations to pass-along email. *Journal of Advertising Research* 44 (4): 333–48.

PhoCusWright. 2004. *From property to screen: Managing online hotel & lodging distribution.* Sherman, CT: PhoCusWright.

Piccoli, G., P. O'Connor, C. Capaccioli, and R. Alvarez. 2003. Customer relationship management – A driver for change in the structure of the U.S. lodging industry. *Cornell Hotel and Restaurant Administration Quarterly* 44 (4): 61–73.

Rainie, L., and D. Fallws. 2004. The impact of CAN-SPAM legislation. Pew Internet Project Data Memo, March. www.pewinternet.org/pdfs/PIP_Data_Memo_on_Spam.pdf (accessed March 20, 2007).

Rogers, K. 2006. Viagra, viruses and virgins: A pan-American comparative analysis on the vanquishing of spam. *Computer Law & Security Report* 22:228–40.

Sipior, J., B. Ward, and P. Bonner. 2004. Should spam be on the menu? *Communications of the ACM* 47 (6): 59–63.

Spring, T. 2005. Spam law test. *PC World* 23 (1): 20–22.

Swartz, N. 2003. The international war on spam. *Information Management Journal* 37 (5): 18–24.

Tassabehji, R., and M. Vakola. 2005. Business email: The killer impact. *Communications of the ACM* 48 (11): 64–70.

TMCnet. 2004. Mx logic finds nearly 100 percent of SPAM not compliant with new CAN-SPAM law. www.tmcnet.com/usubmit/2004/Jan/1022594.htm (accessed September 2, 2005).

Trans-Atlantic Consumer Dialogue (TACD). 2003. Consumer attitudes regarding unsolicited commercial e-mail (SPAM). London: TACD.